Organized Crime

**Nelson-Hall Series in
Justice Administration**
Consulting editor: **Jon R. Waltz**
**Northwestern University
School of Law**

About the Author

Howard Abadinsky is Associate Director of the Criminal Justice
Program at Saint Xavier College/Chicago, and an Inspector for the Cook
County Sheriff; he was a parole officer in New York for 15 years. The author
of several books on organized crime, Abadinsky holds a Ph.D. in sociology
from New York University and is the founder of the International Association
for the Study of Organized Crime.

Organized Crime. Second Edition

Howard Abadinsky

Nelson-Hall
Chicago

To Donna, Alisa and Sandi.

PHOTOGRAPHS

Wedding scene from *The Godfather,* p. 2; Funeral of Angelo Genna, p. 8; Hells Angels, p. 24; Wall Street during the Panic of 1869, p. 43; Mulberry Bend Italians in New York, 1885, p. 54; Jacob Riis's photograph of the Short Tail Gang, about 1889, p. 68; Beer being poured into the Hudson River during Prohibition, p. 84; New York City corruption depicted by Thomas Nast, p. 94; St. Valentine's Day massacre, 1929, p. 129; Jeff Fort of the Blackstone Rangers before Senate Permanent Investigations Subcommittee, p. 153; Las Vegas, p. 171; Harvesting sap from poppies in Thailand, p. 194; Times Square, p. 215; Robert Kennedy and Jimmy Hoffa, p. 226; J. Edgar Hoover (with machine gun), p. 246; Al Capone (left) with his attorney, Michael Ahern, p. 253; Reinhard Heydrich (center), p. 282; William Bioff reading income tax fraud indictment, p. 296; *Scarface,* p. 310

LIBRARY OF CONGRESS CATALOGING IN PUBLICATION DATA

HV
6791
.A52
1985

Abadinsky, Howard, 1941–
   Organized crime.

   Bibliography: p.
   Includes index.
   1. Organized crime—United States—History.
2. Organized crime investigation—United States.
I. Title.
HV6791.A52   1985   364.1'06'073   85–8963
ISBN 0-8304-1126-7 (paper)
ISBN 0-8304-1165-8 (cloth)

Copyright © 1985 by Howard Abadinsky

All rights reserved. No part of this book may be reproduced in any form without permission in writing from the publishers, except by a reviewer who wishes to quote brief passages in connection with a review written for broadcast or for inclusion in a magazine or newspaper. For information address Nelson-Hall Inc., Publishers, 111 North Canal Street, Chicago, Illinois 60606.

Manufactured in the United States of America

10   9   8   7   6   5   4   3   2   1

The paper in this book is pH neutral (acid-free).

CANISIUS COLLEGE LIBRARY
BUFFALO. N. Y.

Contents

Preface   xi

Part One   Definition and Structure of Organized Crime   1

1 | **Defining Organized Crime**   2
    Attributes
    Author's Definition

2 | **Structure of Organized Crime, Model One: Italian-American
    Crime Families**   8
    Corporate/Bureaucratic Analogy
    Kinship and Patron-Client Networks
       Membership
       The Boss
       The Rules of Organized Crime

3 | **Structure of Organized Crime, Model Two: Outlaw
    Motorcycle Gangs**   24
    Structure
    Activities
    Place in Organized Crime

Figures
    2.1. An Organized-Crime Family
    2.2. Cities with Italian-American Crime Families
    2.3. Patron-Client Network of Italian-American Organized Crime
    3.1. Location of Bandidos Clubs
    3.2. Location of Hells Angels Clubs
    3.3. Location of Outlaws Clubs
    3.4. Location of Pagans Clubs
    3.5. National Organizational Structure, Outlaw Motorcycle Gangs
    3.6. Chapter Organizational Structure, Outlaw Motorcycle Gangs
    3.7. Formation during a Run of an Outlaw Motorcycle Gang
    3.8. Continuum of Organized-Crime Models

Feature Insets
    3.1. Rules and Regulations of Two Outlaw Motorcycle Gangs
    3.2. Profile of the Pagans

Part Two   Explaining Organized Crime   41

4 | Historical Antecedents of Organized Crime:
       The Robber Barons   43
    Astor
    Vanderbilt
    The Erie Ring
      Drew
      Fisk
      Gould
    Sage
    Stanford
    Rockefeller
    Morgan
    Kindred Spirits
    Conclusion

5 | Historical Antecedents of Organized Crime:
       Mafia, Comorra, and Onerate Società   54
    Mafia
      Mussolini and the Fascist Period: 1922–1945
      Postwar Trends
        Salvatore Giuliano
      The Nuovo Mafia
    Camorra
    Onerate Società
    American Cousins

6 | Theories of Organized Crime   68
    Anomie
    Differential Association
    Cultural Transmission
    Differential Opportunity
    Ethnic Succession

Part Three   History of Organized Crime   79

7 | Organized Crime: Patterns of Evolution   84
    Machine Politics
    Reform Politics
    Prohibition
    The End of Prohibition

8 | Organized Crime in New York   94
    Jewish Organized Crime in New York
      Arnold Rothstein
      Dutch Schultz

Lepke Buchalter
Meyer Lansky and Benjamin Siegel
Italian Organized Crime in New York
  The Castellammarese War
  The Luciano Family
  The Mineo Family
  The Reina Family
  The Profaci Family
  The Bonanno Family
Jewish-Italian Cooperation: Murder, Inc.

9 | **Organized Crime in Chicago**   **129**
Mont Tennes
Big Bill Thompson
Anton J. ("Tony") Cermak
From Colosimo to Torrio to Capone
"Scarface" Al Capone
  Prohibition
  Alderman's War in the Nineteenth Ward
  "When You Smell Gunpowder, You're in Cicero"
  War in Chicago
  Labor Racketeering
  Capone's Victory and His Downfall
  Capone in Perspective
Chicago Organized Crime after Capone
Enter Sam Giancana

10 | **Organized Crime after World War II**   **153**
Black Organized-Crime Groups
  Frank Matthews
  Charles Lucas
  Leroy ("Nicky") Barnes
  The Royal Family
  Jeff Fort and the El Rukns
Hispanic Organized-Crime Groups
  Mexican Groups
  Cuban and Colombian Groups
Japanese Organized-Crime Groups

Part Four   **The Business of Organized Crime**   **167**

11 | **Gambling and Loansharking**   **171**
Bookmaking
  Horse-race Wagering
    Wagers
  Sports Wagering
    Baseball
  Organized Crime Involvement in Bookmaking

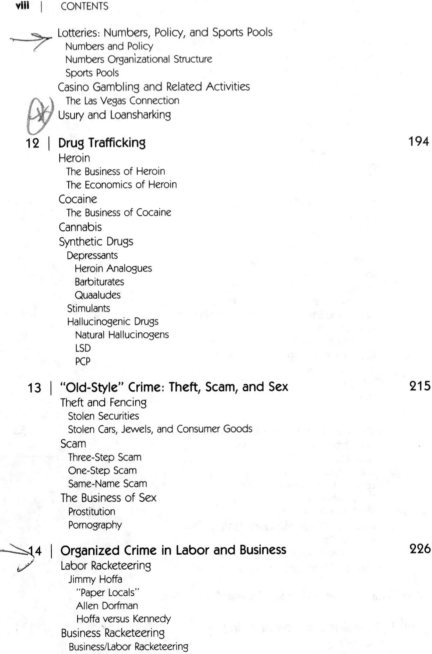

Lotteries: Numbers, Policy, and Sports Pools
Numbers and Policy
Numbers Organizational Structure
Sports Pools
Casino Gambling and Related Activities
The Las Vegas Connection
Usury and Loansharking

12 | Drug Trafficking   **194**
Heroin
The Business of Heroin
The Economics of Heroin
Cocaine
The Business of Cocaine
Cannabis
Synthetic Drugs
Depressants
Heroin Analogues
Barbiturates
Quaaludes
Stimulants
Hallucinogenic Drugs
Natural Hallucinogens
LSD
PCP

13 | "Old-Style" Crime: Theft, Scam, and Sex   **215**
Theft and Fencing
Stolen Securities
Stolen Cars, Jewels, and Consumer Goods
Scam
Three-Step Scam
One-Step Scam
Same-Name Scam
The Business of Sex
Prostitution
Pornography

14 | Organized Crime in Labor and Business   **226**
Labor Racketeering
Jimmy Hoffa
"Paper Locals"
Allen Dorfman
Hoffa versus Kennedy
Business Racketeering
Business/Labor Racketeering
Legitimate Business
"Laundering Dirty Money"

Figures
11.1. The Wagering Process
11.2. A Typical Sports Betting Line

11.3. A Sheet of Bets Seized in a Raid on a Policy Bank
12.1. Major Asian Opium Regions
12.2. Heroin Distribution Organization
12.3. Latin America
12.4. Major Cocaine-Smuggling Routes (Air, Land, Sea)
12.5. Typical Colombian Cocaine Organization
13.1. Conversion of Stolen Securities

Part Five   Laws and Law Enforcement   245

15 | Problems in Combatting Organized Crime:
      Complexity and Corruption   246

      Complexity
        Local Police
        Federal Law Enforcement
        Civil Liberties
      Corruption

16 | Federal Statutes and Their Enforcement   253
      The Internal Revenue Code
      The Controlled Substances Act
        Interdiction
        Buy and Bust
        Conspiracy
      The Hobbs Act
      RICO
        Problems with RICO
      The Consumer Credit Protection Act
      Conspiracy Laws
        Wheel Conspiracies
        Chain Conspiracies
        Enterprise Conspiracies

17 | Gathering Information about Organized Crime   282
      Intelligence
        Collecting Intelligence Data
        Processing Intelligence Data
        Problems of Intelligence
        The Law Enforcement Intelligence Unit (LEIU)
        Regional Information Sharing Systems (RISS)
        INTERPOL
      Wiretapping and Electronic Surveillance
        Regulation
        Costs
        Debate over the Issue
      Informants

18 | Organized Crime and Investigative Techniques 296
The Strike Force
The Investigative Grand Jury
Immunity
Types of Immunity
Transactional Immunity
Use Immunity
Penalties
Civil Contempt
Criminal Contempt
Other Consequences
When to Use Immunity
Witness Security Program
Administration
Problems with the Program

19 | Organized Crime: Policy Issues 310
Government Investigations
The Kefauver Crime Committee
The McClellan Committee
Joseph Valachi
The President's Commission on Law Enforcement
and Administration of Justice
The Media as Models for Organized Crime
Responding to Organized Crime: Policy Implications
Expanding Law-Enforcement Authority
Increasing Law-Enforcement Resources
Decriminalization
Latent Functions
Conclusion

Figures
16.1. Federal Penalties for Trafficking in Controlled Substances
16.2. Controlled Substances, Classified by Type and by
Federal Schedule Number

Tables
16.1. Net Worth Statement, John and Mary Roe
16.2. Internal Revenue Service Sanctions
16.3. Substances of Abuse

Feature Insets
16.1. *United States* v. *Frank Matthews*
18.1. Immunity Documents

References 325

Name Index 357

Subject Index 361

Preface

In 1964, fresh out of college, I was sworn in as a New York State parole officer. Soon afterwards, equipped with a badge and a .38, I was assigned to the waterfront section of South Brooklyn known as Redhook. As I struggled to become familiar with the neighborhood, I noticed that my presence on certain streets seemed to generate a great deal of curiosity (I am six feet one and in those days an athletic 200 pounds) and, at times, activity—windows opening and closing, people in the street suddenly melting away into doorways or shops. I discussed Redhook with some of my more experienced colleagues; some of the naiveté faded.

Redhook was dominated by a faction of one of New York City's five organized-crime families. Prior to my arrival, this faction had been involved in a conflict with the rest of the crime family, and Redhook was the scene of a great deal of violence. There was now a very tentative truce in effect and a six-feet-one-inch, 200-pound stranger who often wore sunglasses suddenly arrived. I became familiar with terms such as "wise-guy," and "made-guy," *capo* and *caporegime,* names such as "Crazy Joey," "Blast," "Carmine the Snake," "Punchy," and "Apples."

After fourteen years as a parole officer and supervisor, I left for Western Carolina University and an academic career. My interest in organized crime continued, and I began to teach a course on the subject. However, an adequate text, one that was accurate and realistic, was not available. That fact led to the first edition of this book.

I have been fortunate in knowing persons with a great deal of information about the inner workings of organized crime. This led to a study of the Gambino crime family (*The Mafia in America,* 1981) and the Genovese crime family (*The Criminal Elite,* 1983). These studies have been used in my lectures and courses on organized crime and the second edition of this book, which has been classroom-tested as a work-in-progress. I have attempted to write a book that is both interesting and informative. It has been designed to meet the needs of law-enforcement officers, college students, and general readers who want a comprehensive and accurate portrait of organized crime.

Part 1 discusses the problem of defining organized crime; it points to the relative strengths and weaknesses of various definitions and presents the author's working definition of organized crime. The chapter compares the bureaucratic/corporate analogy with the patron-client network view of organized crime. The structure of organized crime is viewed as a continuum ranging from the less formal Italian-American crime families to the highly structured outlaw motorcycle gangs. Much of this material did not appear in the first edition.

Part 2 provides a historical perspective to more recent organized criminal activity by reviewing the predatory proclivities of earlier "godfathers"—the industrial "pirates" and "robber barons." The relationships among immigration, ethnicity, and organized crime are explored, as are such cultural phenomena as Camorra and Mafia. The section reviews relevant sociological theory in order to provide an explanation for the existence of modern organized crime.

Part 3 begins by pointing out the problems inherent in presenting an accurate historical account of organized crime. Various historical inaccuracies are discussed as the reader is guided through a labyrinth of myth and misinformation that has been repeated so often that it has become part of the popular literature on organized crime. Using New York and Chicago as primary examples, the history of organized crime is examined as it developed from the political-vice cabals of the pre-Prohibition era to modern forms of sophisticated criminal organization. This section also looks at emerging organized criminal groups: black, Colombian, Cuban, and Mexican.

Part 4 examines each of the "business" activities of organized criminal groups: extortion, gambling, loansharking, drug trafficking, labor racketeering, business racketeering, theft and fencing, scam, pornography, and prostitution. This section discusses the "laundering of dirty money" and organized criminal involvement in legitimate business. It is an expanded version of the section in the first edition.

Part 5 looks at the problems of law enforcement and corruption. It reviews federal laws (e.g., Hobbs Act, RICO) and the techniques used to combat organized criminal activity. This is a greatly expanded version of the section in the first edition.

Part 6 provides insight into the policy issues that surround our response to organized crime and the alternatives that are available.

The major shortcoming of any attempt to present a comprehensive look at organized crime is the sources of information. There are four basic sources:

1. Persons who are or were involved in organized crime.
2. Law-enforcement agencies and government documents.
3. Journalistic (news media) reports.
4. Scholarly accounts based on one or more of these sources.

I have used all of the above, weighing and testing information from one source against information from other sources. I have attempted to maintain the highest scholastic standards, but, alas, there will be shortcomings—the subject matter is large and diverse; relevant and accurate data are quite limited. I've done my best and ask reader indulgence for the errors that may be encountered, all of which I hope are minor.

Persons interested in joining an organization devoted to research into organized crime should write to International Association for the Study of Organized Crime, Secretariat, Saint Xavier College, Chicago, Illinois, 60655.

I would like to express my thanks to Ron Warncke of Nelson Hall, and copy editor Carol Gorski.

Definition and Structure of Organized Crime

Part 1 is concerned with the basic nature of the phenomenon known as organized crime (OC). First, we will turn to the question of definition, which is problematic: organized crime is not a singular phenomenon; there are many variations. We will examine the definitions offered by law makers and law enforcers, and those from scholarly sources. We will detail the attributes of OC and provide the working definition used in the book.

Next we will examine two models of criminal organization as exemplified by: (a) Italian-American crime "families," and (b) outlaw motorcycle gangs. These alternate forms of organization help define the range of OC.

Defining
Organized Crime

Used by permission of the Museum of Modern Art/Film Stills Archive

Whether researching or investigating organized crime, one is faced with the problem of defining the phenomenon. Oddly enough, a great many works on organized crime avoid this problem, as if the obvious need not be defined. William Hogan points out: "The problem to date has been the use of broad, general labels such as 'Organized Crime' without clearly defining the term and setting parameters on what is and what is not organized crime" (1976: 21). Unfortunately, Hogan also fails to provide a definition. Paradoxically, the Organized Crime Control Act of 1970 does not define organized crime either.

The lack of an adequate definition is highlighted in a report by the Task Force on Organized Crime (1976) which noted the inadequacies of state efforts at defining OC. These range from the simple definition of the state of Mississippi—"Two or more persons conspiring together to commit crimes for profit on a continuing basis" (1976: 214)—to the more elaborate definition offered by the state of California (1976: 214):

Organized crime consists of two or more persons who, with continuity of purpose, engage in one or more of the following activities: (1) The supplying of illegal goods and services, i.e., vice, loansharking, etc.; (2) Predatory crime, i.e., theft, assault, etc.

Several distinct types of criminal activity fall within this definition of organized crime. The types may be grouped into five general categories:

1. Racketeering—Groups of individuals which organize more than one of the following types of criminal activities for their combined profit.
2. Vice-Operations—Individuals operating a continuing business of providing illegal goods or services such as narcotics, prostitution, loansharking, gambling, etc.
3. Theft/Fence Rings—Groups of individuals who engage in a particular kind of theft on a continuing basis, such as fraud and bunco schemes, fraudulent document passers, burglary rings, car thieves, truck hijackers, and associated individuals engaged in the business of purchasing stolen merchandise for resale and profit.
4. Gangs—Groups of individuals with common interests or background who band together and collectively engage in unlawful activity to enhance their group identity and influence, such as youth gangs, outlaw motorcycle gangs, and prison gangs.
5. Terrorists—Groups of individuals who combine to commit spectacular criminal acts, such as assassination and kidnapping of public figures to undermine public confidence in established government for political reasons or to avenge some grievance.

Criminologists, too, have their definitions. Donald R. Cressey (1969: 319) is concerned less with the criminal activities than with their perpetrators

3

and the relationships among them. His definition is of practical importance in law enforcement since it is used by the FBI:

An organized crime is any crime committed by a person occupying, in an established division of labor, a position designed for the commission of crime, providing that such division of labor also includes at least one position for a corrupter, one position for a corruptee, and one position for an enforcer.

Michael Maltz (1976) is also concerned more with organization than the actual criminal behavior. He points out a problem of semantics: we call a specific behavior or act organized crime, but when we refer to organized crime in the generic sense, we usually mean an entity, a group of people. In his "tentative" definition of organized crime (1975: 76) he is especially concerned with the dynamics of such groups—their means and ends:

A crime consists of a transaction proscribed by criminal law between offender(s) and victim(s). It is not necessary for the victim to be a complainant or to consider himself victimized for a crime to be committed. An organized crime is a crime in which there is more than one offender, and the offenders are and intend to remain associated with one another for the purpose of committing crimes. The *means* of executing the crime include violence, theft, corruption, economic power, deception, and victim collusion or participation. These are not mutually exclusive categories; any organized crime may employ a number of these means.

The objective of most organized crimes is power, either political or economic. These two types of objectives, too, are not mutually exclusive and may coexist in any organized crime.

There are a number of *manifestations* the objectives may take. When the objective is political power it may be of two types: overthrow of the existing order, or illegal use of the criminal process. When the objective is economic power, it may manifest itself in three different ways: through common crime (*mala in se*), through illegal business (*mala prohibita* or "vices"), or through legitimate business (white-collar crime).

This definition is quite broad—it fails to provide a basis for distinguishing between the James Gang (of "Wild West" fame) and the Capone organization (of Prohibition fame). While our predilections permit us to accept Al Capone as an "organized crime" figure, Jesse James does not seem to fit the conventional model. Perhaps, then, what is needed is a definition that includes Al Capone while excluding Jesse James.

The Federal Bureau of Alcohol, Tobacco, and Firearms (ATF) provides such a definition. It attempts to deal with means and ends, acts and actors:

"Organized crime" refers to those self-perpetuating, structured, and disciplined associations of individuals, or groups, combined together for the purpose of obtaining monetary or commercial gains or profits, wholly or in part by illegal means, while protecting their activities through a pattern of graft and corruption.

Organized crime groups possess certain characteristics which include but are not limited to the following:

1. Their illegal activities are conspiratorial;
2. In at least part of their activities, they commit or threaten to commit acts of violence or other acts which are likely to intimidate;
3. They conduct their activities in a methodical, systematic, or highly disciplined and secret fashion;
4. They insulate their leadership from direct involvement in illegal activities by their intricate organizational structure;
5. They attempt to gain influence in Government, politics, and commerce through corruption, graft, and legitimate means;
6. They have economic gain as their primary goal, not only from patently illegal enterprises such as drugs, gambling, and loan sharking, but also from such activities as laundering illegal money through and investment in legitimate business.

Attributes

Obviously, there is no generally accepted definition of OC. However, to set the parameters of this book, we will limit our discussion of OC to groups ongoing criminal activity and have a specified group of attributes. The list has been compiled mainly through observation and study of OC groups in an effort to identify shared traits. Such groups are:

1. Nonideological.
2. Hierarchical.
3. Limited or exclusive in membership.
4. Perpetuitous.
5. Organized through specialization or division of labor.
6. Monopolistic.
7. Governed by rules and regulations.

Let us examine each of these attributes.

Nonideological

An organized-crime group does not have political goals, nor is it motivated by ideological concerns. While political involvement is often part of the group's activities, the purpose is to gain protection or immunity for its illegal activities.

Hierarchical

An organized-crime group has three or more permanent positions of authority, each with authority over the next. The authority of a position does not depend on who happens to be occupying it at any given time.

Having Limited or Exclusive Membership

An organized-crime group has basic limitations on who is qualified to become a member. These may be based on ethnic background, kinship, race, criminal record, or similar considerations. In almost all cases, membership is limited to males. Those who meet the basic qualification(s) need a sponsor, usually a ranking member, and must also prove qualification for membership by their behavior—e.g., willingness to commit certain criminal acts, follow orders, or maintain secrets. There are often more persons who desire and qualify for membership than the OC group is willing to initiate. There may be an apprenticeship or a long period of probationary status prior to being admitted to full membership.

Perpetuitous

An organized-crime group constitutes an ongoing criminal conspiracy designed to persist through time, beyond the participation and life of the current membership. In other words, permanence is assumed by the members, and this provides an important basis for interesting qualified persons in becoming members, thus perpetuating the group's existence.

Organized through Specialization or Division of Labor

An organized-crime group will have certain functional positions filled by qualified members. Given the nature of an OC group, the position of *enforcer* is often crucial. This person carries out difficult assignments involving the use of violence, including murder. (Less difficult assignments involving violence can be carried out by any member.) The enforcer does not act independently but receives assignments, directly or indirectly, from the head of the OC group. Difficult executions will usually be assigned by the enforcer (who usually acts as an intermediary) to a member of the OC group who has this type of activity as a specialty, or to a nonmember "professional" employed by the enforcer. If the OC group is sophisticated enough, it may also have positions for a *fixer* and a *money mover*. The fixer arranges for the corrupting of law-enforcement efforts; the money mover is an expert at "laundering" illicitly gained money, disguising its origin through a string of transactions and investing it in legitimate enterprises.

In contrast to the patron-client networks of Italian-American crime Families is the bureaucratic organization of some outlaw motorcycle gangs. Their origins are quite different from those of Italian-American organized crime: they are not ethnic, they date from the years after World War II, and the groups are not based on blood ties or family loyalties.

Toward the end of the 1940s, many World War II combat veterans, particularly those residing in California, were seeking new outlets for pent-up feelings of hostility and alienation. They found some in the motorcycle and in association with others in motorcycle clubs. These clubs became a means of continued quasi-military comradery among the members. At the same time, the motorcycle became a symbol of freedom from accepted social responsibilities and restraints, and soon these new clubs or gangs became a threat to local communities.

Shortly after World War II, a group of California veterans formed a motorcycle club and called themselves the "Pissed Off Bastards of Bloomington" (POBOBs). By some accounts, the POBOBs were dedicated to mocking social values through acts of vandalism and general lawlessness. In 1946, following the arrest of a POBOB member for fighting in Hollister, California, a reported 750 motorcyclists descended on the town and demanded his release. When local authorities refused, the cyclists literally tore up the small community (a scene that was later depicted in the film *The Wild One*, starring Marlon Brando). After this incident, the POBOBs developed into a more disciplined group and became the first outlaw motorcycle gang to receive national notoriety as the Hells Angels.

The POBOBs' development was fairly typical. From the fun-loving and hell-raising clubs of the immediate post-World War II era, a number of motorcycle gangs have developed into self-perpetuating, structured, and disciplined organizations whose major source of income is from criminal activity. They have been particularly successful in exerting control over the methamphetamine market. George Wethern (with Vincent Colnett, 1978), a former ranking member of the Hells Angels motorcycle gang in Oakland, California, states that because of their reputation for violence and antiestablishment attitudes, the Hells Angels were perfect middlemen for drug dealers. The wholesalers sold to the Angels, who then acted as distributors for street-level operators. Using violence, they were able to restrict market entry and monopolize parts of California.

Not all outlaw motorcycle gangs are sophisticated criminal organizations. There are four that according to law-enforcement officials fit the definition of organized crime:

1. Bandidos   3. Outlaws
2. Hells Angels   4. Pagans

Figures 3.1, 3.2, 3.3, and 3.4 indicate where the chapters of these four organizations are located.

Structure

Consistent with their founders' background as military veterans, the Hells Angels, and the outlaw gangs that have copied them, exhibit a highly bureaucratic structure, as shown in fig. 3.5. The leader of the national group, the national president (who is always a man), has offices at or near the national headquarters, sometimes referred to as the "Mother Club." He is surrounded by a group of members who answer only to him and who serve as bodyguards and organizational enforcers. The national president can usually make final decisions over all club matters. The national vice-presidents have authority over regions to which they are assigned by the national president. A vice-president's duties include decision making on all problems that the local chapters are unable to solve. Any problems that involve the club as a whole will usually be sent up to the national headquarters. The national secretary-treasurer is responsible for the club's finances, makes revisions in the club bylaws, and records and maintains the minutes and other club records. The national enforcer answers directly to the national president and may act as the president's bodyguard as well as handling all special situations involving violations of club rules.

Each individual chapter, likewise, has a president, vice-president and secretary-treasurer, as well as an enforcer and a sergeant-at-arms (see fig. 3.6); all officers, and in fact all full members, are male. There is also the rather unique position of *road captain*. He fulfills the role of logistician and security chief for club-sponsored "runs" or motorcycle outings. The road captain maps out routes; arranges for refueling, food, and maintenance stops en route; and establishes strong points along the route to protect the main body from police harassment or rival gangs. The club limits membership, and each chapter has prospective members who spend from one month to one year on probationary status. During that time they must prove themselves worthy of membership by following orders and committing felony crimes— this helps to keep law-enforcement agents from infiltrating the organization. Probationers must be nominated by a member and receive a unanimous vote for acceptance into provisional status. They carry out all menial jobs at the clubhouse and for other members. When a man is admitted to membership, he is allowed to wear the club's "colors"—the proudest possession of any outlaw gang member. Colors refer both to the official emblem of the gang and a member's cutoff (sleeveless) denim or leather jacket, which has been embroidered with the club logo on the center rear of the jacket, the name of the club above the logo, and the chapter location underneath. Also sewed or pinned on the colors will be all other authorized patches, which are usually

Figure 3.1
Location of Bandidos Clubs

SOURCE: Permanent Subcommittee on Investigations, *Profile of Organized Crime: Mid-Atlantic Region* (Washington, D.C.: U.S. Government Printing Office, 1983).

Figure 3.2
Location of Hells Angels Clubs

SOURCE: Permanent Subcommittee on Investigations, *Profile of Organized Crime*.

Figure 3.3
Location of Outlaws Clubs

SOURCE: Permanent Subcommittee on Investigations, *Profile of Organized Crime: Mid-Atlantic Region* (Washington, D.C.: U.S. Government Printing Office, 1983).

Figure 3.4
Location of Pagans Clubs

SOURCE: Permanent Subcommittee on Investigations, *Profile of Organized Crime: Mid-Atlantic Region* (Washington, D.C.: U.S. Government Printing Office, 1983).

Figure 3.5
National Organization Structure, Outlaw Motorcycle Gangs

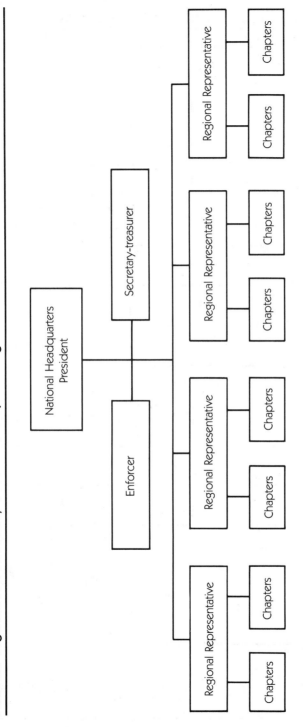

SOURCE: Permanent Subcommittee on Investigations, *Profile of Organized Crime: Mid-Atlantic Region* (Washington, D.C.: U.S. Government Printing Office, 1983).

Figure 3.6
Chapter Organizational Structure, Outlaw Motorcycle Gangs

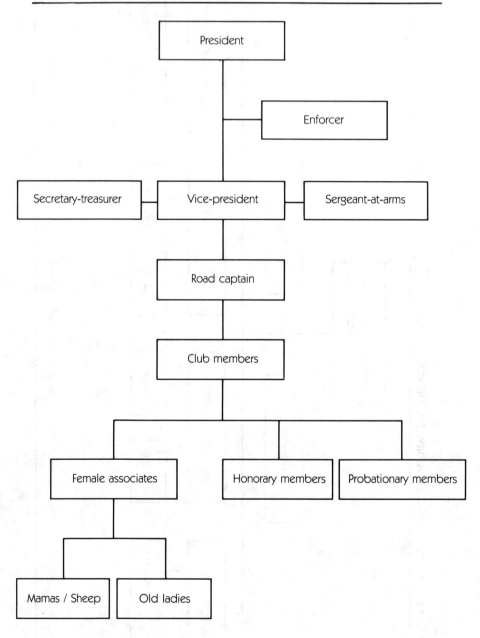

SOURCE: Permanent Subcommittee on Investigations, *Profile of Organized Crime: Mid-Atlantic Region* (Washington, D.C.: U.S. Government Printing Office, 1983).

Figure 3.7
Formation during a Run of an Outlaw Motorcycle Gang

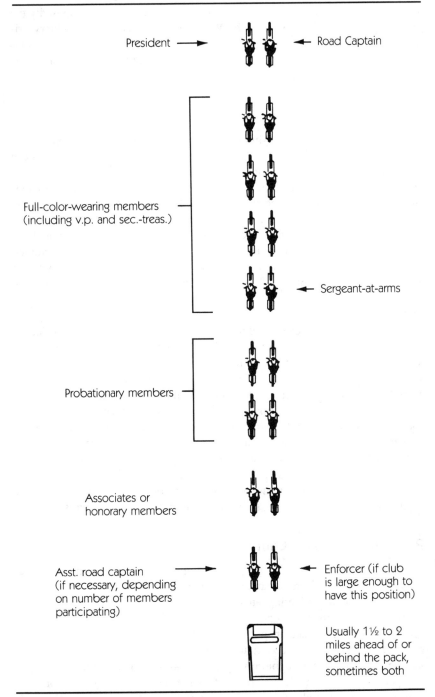

President ➔ ⬅ Road Captain

Full-color-wearing members
(including v.p. and sec.-treas.)

⬅ Sergeant-at-arms

Probationary members

Associates or
honorary members

Asst. road captain
(if necessary, depending
on number of members
participating) ➔ ⬅ Enforcer (if club
is large enough to
have this position)

Usually 1½ to 2
miles ahead of or
behind the pack,
sometimes both

quite offensive to conventional society—e.g., swastikas, 666 (supposedly the mark of Satan), F.T.W. ("Fuck the World"). Consistent with a military orientation, various offenses can result in the "pulling of patches." The clubs practice precision riding, and club "runs" are accomplished in military-style formation (see fig. 3.7).

Activities

Outlaw motorcycle gangs exhibit racist attitudes, and there are no known black males who hold membership in any white outlaw gang (there are a number of all-black outlaw motorcycle gangs). Women associated with the group are treated as nothing more than playthings—objects to be used, traded, and sold. *Old ladies* are the wives or steady girlfriends of club members. Sexual and other demands for their services can only be made by their husbands or boyfriends. *Mamas* or *sheep* belong to the gang at large and are expected to consent to the sexual whims of any club member. While women are not permitted to wear club colors, they may wear denim jackets with the inscription "Property of. . . ." (with the club's name embroidered on it). The women often carry the gang's weapons and engage in prostitution or drug trafficking.

Illegal income is derived from a number of criminal activities: trafficking in stolen motorcycles and motorcycle parts; prostitution, including supplying women for go-go bars and club-owned massage parlors; trafficking in automatic weapons and explosives. The most lucrative activity, however, is the manufacture and distribution of methamphetamines. Profits have been invested in mobile catering companies, bike-repair shops, wrecking yards, apartment houses, resort hotels, bars, tow companies, and even ice cream shops. Government officials report that the motorcycle gangs have accepted contracts for murder from Italian-American crime Family members and have been used as "muscle" to collect debts. The outlaw gangs have a reliable pipeline of members and chapters for the flow of illicit goods, and the members are highly mobile—they can find safety in many cities where chapters exist.

Place in Organized Crime

The outlaw motorcycle club/gang, like Italian-American organized crime, provides a *model* of organization for understanding OC. When analyzing, researching, or investigating an OC group (such as the emerging "Black Mafia" and Latin-American—Colombian, Cuban, and Mexican crime groups—to be discussed in part 3) it is important to identify their organizational structure on the continuum of organized crime models. In the following chapters we will explore why Italian-American OC "chose" its type of operating structure; this will lead to an examination of the history and culture of southern Italy, the development of *Mafia, Camorra* and *'Ndrangheta*. We will review the history and culture of black Americans and Hispanic

Americans in part 3 order to provide an explanation for their operating structures.

Feature Inset 3.1
Rules and Regulations of Two Outlaw Motorcycle Gangs

Pagans' Motorcycle Club Constitution

Club Organization

The Pagan motorcycle club is run by the Mother Club. The Mother Club has last and final say so on all club matters. Any violation of the constitution will be dealt with by the Mother Club.

Chapter Organization

Six (6) members needed to start a chapter. Four (4) officers, no new chapter may be started without approval of the Mother Club.

President

Runs chapter under the direction of the Mother club. Keeps chapter organized, makes sure chapter business is carried out and inspects all bikes before runs and makes President meetings.

Sergeant-at-Arms

Makes sure Presidents orders are carried out.

Vice-President

Takes over all Presidents duties when the President is not there.

Secretary-Treasurer

In charge of minutes of meetings and treasury. No members may change chapters without the Mother Club members permission in his area. All present chapter debts are paid and is approved by the president of the new chapter he wishes to change to. If a member has a snival, he must use chain of command, in other words, (1) His Chapter President, (2) Mother Club member in area, (3) President of Club.

Meetings

1. Chapters must have one organized meeting per week.
2. Chapters meetings are attended by members only.
3. Members must be of sound mind (straight) when attending meetings.
4. If a Mother Club member attends a meeting and a member is fouled-up, he will be fined by the Mother Club member.

5. Miss three (3) meetings in a row, and your out of the club.
6. Members must attend meeting to leave club and turn in his colors and everything that has the name "PAGAN'S" on it. (T-shirts, Wrist Bands, Mugs, Etc.)
7. If a member is thrown out of the club or quits without attending meeting, he loses his colors, motorcycle, and anything that says "PAGAN'S" on it, and probably an ass kicking.
8. When a member is traveling, he must attend meeting of the area he is traveling in.
9. If a vote is taken at a meeting and member is not there, his vote is void.
10. Members must have colors with him when attending meeting.

Bikes

1. All members must have a Harley Davidson 750-1200 CC.
2. If a member is not of sound mind or fouled-up to ride his motorcycle in the opinion of another member, his riding privilege may be pulled by said member until he has his head together.
3. All bikes must be on the road April 30th, or otherwise directed by the Mother Club.
4. All members must have a motorcycle license.

Mandatories

Two (2) mandatories, July 4th, and Labor Day. Mother Club may call additional mandatories if need be.

Funerals

1. If a member dies in a chapter, it is mandatory for all members in his chapter to attend funeral.
2. Chapter is in charge of taking care of all funeral arrangements, parties, police, procession, etc.

Parties

Pagan parties are Pagan parties only. Each chapter must throw (1) party or run per year.

Respect

1. Respect is to be shown to all Mother Club members, officer members, members personal property, Bike, Old Lady, House, Job, etc. In other words, if it's not yours, "Don't Mess With It."
2. No fighting among each other is allowed, any punches to be thrown will be done by the Sgt. Arms or a Mother Club Member.
3. No Stealing from members.
4. Respect your Colors.

Colors

1. President gets colors from Mother Club member in area when new member is voted in.
2. When a member leaves club, the president of his chapter turns over his colors to the Mother Club member in his area.
3. Respect your Colors, don't let anyone take them from you except the president of your chapter or a Mother Club member.
4. No colors are worn in a cage, except during funerals and loading or unloading a bike from a truck.
5. Nothing will be worn on the back of your jacket except your colors, Diamond, 13 patch.
6. No Hippie shit on the front.
7. Colors are to be put on cut off denim jackets only.
8. The only member who may keep his colors if he leaves the club is a Mother Club Member.

Old Ladies

1. Members are responsible for their old ladies.
2. Members may have more than one (1) Old Lady.
3. Members may not discuss club business with their Old Lady.
4. No Old Ladies allowed at meetings.
5. No property patch is worn on an old lady. So if you see a chick you better ask before you leap.

Prospects

1. Prospect must be at least 18 years old.
2. Prospect must be sponsored by one member who has known him at least one year.
3. Sponsor is responsible for prospect.
4. Prospect must have motorcycle.
5. Prospect must ride his bike to meeting at time of being voted into club.
6. Prospect can not do any drugs.
7. Prospects can not carry weapons at meetings and Pagan functions, unless otherwise directed by his President.
8. No stealing from Prospects.
9. Prospects must attend all meetings and club functions.
10. Prospects must do anything another member tells him to do, that a member has done or would be willing to do himself.
11. Prospect must be voted in by all members of the chapter and Three (3) Mother Club Member.
12. Prospects must pay for his colors before receiving them.
13. Prospects period is determined by Mother Club Member.
14. Pagan's M.C. is a motorcycle Club and a non-profit organization.

Hells Angels California Bylaws

1. All patches will be the same on the back, nothing will show on the back except the HELLS ANGELS patch. City patch is optional for each chapter. 1 patch and 1 membership card per member. Member may keep original patch if made into a banner. Prospects will wear California rocker on back and prospect patch left front where top of pocket is on a Levi jacket.
   FINE: $100 for breaking above by-law.
2. No hypes. No use of Heroin in any form. Anyone using a needle for any reason other than having a doctor use it on you will be considered a hype.
   FINE: Automatic kick-out from club.
3. No explosives of any kind will be thrown into the fire where there is one or more HELLS ANGELS in the area.
   FINE: Ass-whipping and/or subject to California President's decision.
4. Guns on CA runs will not be displayed after 6 PM. They will be fired from dawn till 6 PM in a predetermined area only. Rule does not apply to anyone with a gun in a shoulder holster or belt that is seen by another member if it is not being shot or displayed.
   FINE: $100 for breaking above by-law.
5. Brothers shall not fight with each other with weapons; when any HELLS ANGEL fights another HELLS ANGEL it is one on one; prospects same as members. If members are from different chapters, fine goes to CA Treasurer.
   FINE: $100 for breaking above by-law or possible loss of patch.
6. No narcotic burns. When making deals, persons get what they are promised or the deal is called off.
   FINE: Automatic kick-out from club.
7. All HELLS ANGELS fines will be paid within 30 days. Fines will be paid to that chapter's treasurer to be held for the next CA run.
8. One vote per chapter at CA officer's meetings. For CA 2 no votes instead of a majority to kill a new charter and if a charter goes below 6 they must freeze or disolve on the decision of CA Officers' Meeting.
9. If kicked out, must stay out 1 year then back to original charter. HELLS ANGEL tattoo will have an in-date and out-date when the member quits. If kicked out, HELLS ANGELS tattoo will be completely covered with a ½ X through the tattoo.
10. Runs are on the holidays; 3 mandatory runs are Memorial day, July 4th, and Labor Day.
11. No leave period except hospital, medical or jail.

Feature Inset 3.2
Profile of the Pagans

The Pagan outlaw motorcycle club was formed in 1959 in Prince Georges County, Maryland. The club eventually expanded its base by merging with other motorcycle clubs. With the increase in size, a form of governing structure was devised. The founding thirteen members became known as the Mother Club. The Mother Club convenes to set policies for the Pagan motorcycle club and to plan its business dealings.

Mother Club members can disband, restructure, or form new chapters in their respective regions without prior approval of the Mother Club. The members in the Mother Club have special status. They wear a black number *13* on their colors.

In 1980 the Pagan motorcycle club consisted of several hundred members in more than fifty chapters. Each chapter has a minimum of five members, while some have as many as fifty. A potential member goes through a trial period known as "prospectship." He (all are men) must know an active Pagan for at least one year. A period of prospectship follows, with the sponsoring Pagan taking full responsibility for what is called the "prospecting citizen." At the end of the prospectship, the chapter takes a vote which must be unanimous to admit the prospecting citizen. The Pagans can pick the "cream of the crop" because of the large number of prospective candidates.

To show their loyalty and sincerity, proposed members are required to commit crimes for the gang. This type of required behavior has made internal penetration of the Pagans virtually impossible for law-enforcement agencies.

Members of the Pagan hierarchy have flourished without going to jail by insulating themselves from actual crimes. In most cases, members of the hierarchy are insulated by so many people that it would be nearly impossible, under normal circumstances, to make a criminal case against them. Nonmember Pagan associates and lower-ranking members commit the actual crimes. It is estimated that for every member of the Pagans, there are three to four nonmember associates. Promotion within the club is usually the result of some expertise in income generation, physical enforcement, or political corruption—for example, owning a business that fronts for the club, operating a drug laboratory and controlling its chemists, being able to influence criminal-justice personnel. Demotions usually occur when a member becomes involved with the law and draws large amounts of attention to the club, fails to obey an order from superiors, becomes involved with injecting narcotics, or takes part in territorial or power disputes. The ultimate form of demotion is execution, which became a prevalent practice within the Pagans after Vernon "Satan" Marron became president in the 1970s. He is currently serving a thirty-year sentence for maiming and homicide.

Pagans are involved in the distribution of methamphetamines, cocaine, and PCP (angel dust). Competitors are usually subjected to intimidation. Several members of the Pagans have been convicted of drug trafficking and are serving federal prison sentences. The Pagans are well versed in corruption, and there have been occasions when police officers loyal to outlaw bikers have jeopardized their own positions to hinder their prosecution.

Because of the freewheeling image of the outlaw motorcycle gangs, teenage girls have been attracted to the Pagans. They are often gang-raped, which bikers refer to as "training," or pulling a train. They may be photographed for blackmail purposes or transported to other states to work as prostitutes or go-go dancers. One member of the Pagans is a nephew of John LaRocca, head of the Italian-American crime Family in southwestern Pennsylvania. Anthony LaRocca is considered quite dangerous and in 1980 was serving a federal sentence for drug trafficking and assault on a federal officer. A former ranking member of the Pagans testified before a Senate subcommittee (Permanent Subcommittee on Investigations 1983). Part of his account follows.

> I have orchestrated Pagan-related criminal activities such as prostitution, extortion, drug trafficking, gun trafficking, counterfeiting, and auto theft. Money generated by these operations went to me and my chapters. With the exception of narcotics operations, money generated was applied to the Pagan treasury and

bail fund. Money in the treasury was used for legal fees, the president's salary, parties, the support of clubhouses and Pagan women and various investments. The club supported the families of those members who were sent to prison—as long as they were in good standing with the club.

The secretary-treasurer of the mother club was responsible for handling the finances. We had a secretary-treasurer who was as astute as any CPA. He owned his own restaurant/bar in Baltimore. Money was laundered through his bar's accounts. Most accounts and assets were in the names of the secretary-treasurer and president.

Bail funds were maintained by the mother club and the chapters. This fund was separate from the main treasury. Much of the chapters' monthly dues went to build up the bail fund.

As a mother club member, I received more money than I knew what to do with. At one point in time, I owned three houses, two automobiles, and three motorcycles. Most of these assets were titled in the names of the Pagan women.

The single most moneymaking activity of the Pagans was the manufacture and distribution of drugs, specifically, methamphetamines—speed—and killer weed, or PCP.

Each mother club member could have his own meth operation. For example, I bought the chemicals, used to make meth, from my own source. I would have the chemicals made into meth and sell a supply to each of my chapter presidents. The chapter president would in turn sell the meth to his members and the members would sell to the public.

Each middleman received money first, before drugs were distributed. Our meth operations extended throughout Connecticut, New York, New Jersey, Pennsylvania, Virginia, Maryland, and Ohio.

SOURCE: Edited from Pennsylvania Crime Commission, *A Decade of Organized Crime: 1980 Report*. St. Davids, Pa.: Commonwealth of Pennsylvania, 1980.

Fig. 3.8
Continuum of Organized-Crime Models

Patron-client networks	Bureaucratic organization
Italian-American organized crime	Outlaw motorcycle gangs

---

[1] Information in this section is from the *Congressional Record*, reports of the Drug Enforcement Administration, and interviews with law enforcement officials.

Explaining Organized Crime

Organized crime is essentially a business enterprise that provides a career path, "in-service training," ongoing income and a reference group for those who find it attractive. For its successful practitioners, OC leads to a level of prosperity that might otherwise be unattainable.

This "business enterprise" is embedded in an American society that in many ways has promoted its continued existence. The unbridled greed of the "robber barons" of an earlier era provided examples of how wealth could be wrested from society with the right combination of brilliance and ruthlessness. Early capitalists often set a questionable example for those immigrants who followed them to these shores. Many of the great family fortunes of the early twentieth century had been made by a combination of means, fair and, often, quite foul, including the use of violence. These activities are highlighted in chapter 4.

Early twentieth-century America experienced the disappearance of the last of the western frontier, the traditional "land of opportunity" for the dispossessed and the adventuresome. Industrialization was growing at a rapid pace, and the newer immigrants found their opportunities in the urban environment of America's large cities. Here they lived in crowded enclaves under conditions that often encouraged the perpetuation of important aspects of the life-styles and family ties of the old country.

In the case of the Italians, whose organized-crime activities have been the most durable, these old country traditions played a critical role. They helped the future leaders of Italian-American OC adapt to their new environment and equipped them to take advantage of new opportunities for illicit gain. Chapter 5 provides a review of this background in a discussion of the Mafia, the Camorra, and the Honored Society of Southern Italy.

The propensity of the United States to legally proscribe a host of "goods and services" helped to create a climate of opportunity. History has taught us that the outlawing of something that is desired by a great number of people—alcohol, drugs, gambling, etc.—will not necessarily reduce either the desire or the supply. Instead, it raises the risk associated with purveying these goods and services, eliminating many suppliers and helping to promote a monopoly for those willing to take the risk. At the same time, scarcity raises prices, it becomes a seller's market, thus inflating the profit and increasing the attractiveness of the illicit enterprise. Prohibition, by outlawing a substance for which there was a widespread demand, created an unparalleled opportunity for illicit profit and spawned the type of activity we now refer to as OC.

The "American way of life" places undue stress on economic success, while its means of achievement are not readily available to large segments of our population. OC is seen as a response to this reality which, along with other sociological theories, is discussed in chapter 6 in an effort to explain the continued existence of OC.

chapter 4

Historical Antecedents of Organized Crime: The Robber Barons

Used by permission of Historical Pictures Service, Chicago

Organized crime in America has its roots in Prohibition (1920-33), but unethical American business enterprises provided fertile soil to support the growth of the phenomenon. Earlier generations of predatory Americans with English, Scottish, or German ancestry paved the way for later generations of Irish, Jewish, or Italian criminals who, in turn, are being emulated by criminals of Afro-American or Latin-American origin.

Astor

John Jacob Astor (1763-1848) arrived from Germany penniless and died the richest person in America. According to Gustavus Myers (1936), the Astor fortune was based on alcohol and fraud: drunken Indians were systematically cheated by agents of Astor's American Fur Company. When the Native Americans complained to the government, Astor agents resorted to violence. When the Indians retaliated, troops were sent in to quell the "Indian disorder." In addition to exploiting the Indians, Astor succeeded in forcing his employees in the western wilderness to buy from company-owned stores at exorbitant prices. By the time they returned east, most employees were in debt to Astor.

Astor was able to monopolize the fur trade and "was never prosecuted for the numerous violations of both penal and civil law invariably committed by his direction and for his benefit. With the millions that rolled in, he was able, not only to command the services of the foremost lawyers in warding off the penalties of law, but to have as his paid retainers some of the most noted and powerful politicians of the day" (Myers 1936: 103). The money gained through lawlessness and violence against Native Americans in the western fur trade was used for real estate speculation in New York. There, easily corrupted officials helped Astor become America's greatest "slumlord," extracting money from poor immigrants for the privilege of living in the vilest of tenement housing. These slums were the spawning ground for organized crime.

Vanderbilt

Cornelius Vanderbilt (1794-1877) came from a small farming family in Staten Island (now part of New York City). He parlayed profits from a ferryboat venture into shipping and shipbuilding. At age forty-seven he was a rich man. The government of Nicaragua had given his Accessory Transit Company a monopoly over transportation across the isthmus connecting the two great oceans. In 1853, while Vanderbilt was on a European vacation, two members of the board of directors, in accord with business practices of the day, usurped control of Accessory Transit. Vanderbilt retaliated by setting up a competing line and cutting prices until the two directors, C.K. Garrison and Charles Morgan, capitulated. In 1855, Garrison and Morgan financed an insurrection in Nicaragua where Accessory Transit had its charter. The revolutionary forces, led by an American adventurer, achieved a great victory; in early 1856 the Vanderbilt charter was cancelled, and the property of Accessory Transit was confiscated. Vanderbilt responded that same summer by persuading the governments of Honduras, San Salvador, and Costa Rica to form an alliance against Nicaragua. Then, on Vanderbilt's orders, two American adventurers led an invasion of Nicaragua. By the end of the year the invasion force was progressing quite well; however, the Nicaraguans counterattacked. Vanderbilt thwarted the offensive by having the State Department send in the United States Marines. They succeeded in deposing the revolutionary government, and the Vanderbilt charter was restored (Andrews 1941). Even Mario Puzzo's Godfather of fiction fame did not use "muscle" on this scale.

Like many other businessmen, Vanderbilt was a "war-profiteer." During the Civil War he acted as an agent for the Union Army, securing unfit and rotting vessels for the transportation of federal troops, at exorbitant prices. However, his primary interest was civilian transportation, and he moved from shipping to the railroads. Striving for monopoly, he controlled the Hudson River and Harlem lines and forced the competing New York Central to sell out. In 1866 he sought to complete his transportation stranglehold by taking over the Erie Railroad line, which was a direct competitor. However, he was ambushed by three of America's greatest pirate capitalists (Gould, Drew, Fisk) who, collectively, were referred to as the "Erie Ring."

The Erie Ring

The Erie Ring secretly authorized the issuance of 10 million new shares of Erie stock as Vanderbilt was busy buying up shares to gain control of the line. The more Vanderbilt's agents purchased, the more stock was issued by the ring, which declared their actions in accord with "freedom of the *press*." In 1868, an obliging New York Supreme Court judge (part of the infamous "Tweed Ring") issued an injunction against further issues of Erie stock and ordered the ring to return to the treasury one-fourth of what they had issued. This drove up the price of Erie stock, but it did not stop the Erie Ring. They had their "own" judge issue a counterinjunction, and chaos and riots swept Wall Street. Trading in Erie stock was suspended by the stock exchange. Vanderbilt lost between $5 and $7 million, and he had "his" judge issue contempt-of-court arrest warrants for the members of the ring.

The Erie Ring withdrew all of its combined funds from New York banks, took all its securities and documents from safes, and crossed the Hudson to Jersey City with their printing press. They arrived just ahead of pursuing sheriff's deputies and set up headquarters in Taylor's Castle hotel, dubbed "Fort Taylor." In Jersey City they were guarded by railroad police and cooperative Jersey City police officers. Cannons were mounted on piers to thwart any invasion from the New York side, and the ring counterattacked by reducing fares to Buffalo, undercutting the hard-pressed Vanderbilt line. Vanderbilt ordered a band of New York toughs into New Jersey, and the members of the ring fled to New York. The field of battle shifted to the state capital.

In Albany, the ring spread $1 million worth of "goodwill" in an effort to legalize their theft of the Erie from Vanderbilt. Vanderbilt joined the fray but soon grew tired of trying to sate the seemingly insatiable appetites of state legislators; the ring achieved a legislative victory. Vanderbilt sued for peace. In return for $4.5 million, he relinquished all his interest in the Erie, and the arrest warrants were quashed (Josephson 1962).

Drew

The oldest member of the Erie Ring, Daniel Drew, was born in Carmel, New York, in 1807. An illiterate, he began his business career as a cattle drover, buying cattle on credit from New York farmers and driving them to market for sale. He often failed to settle his debts and was forced to move operations to Ohio. Drew perfected the technique that resulted in the term *watered stock*. His cattle were kept thirsty by a liberal diet of salt and very little water. Before arrival at the drover's market, the cattle were allowed to quench their thirst and increase their poundage accordingly. With money thus earned, he purchased a tavern and also became a moneylender, a steamship owner, and a stockbroker. Drew gained notoriety by his comments on the advent of the Civil War: "Along with ordinary happenings, we fellows on Wall Street now have in addition the fortunes of war to speculate about, and that always makes great doings on the stock exchange. It's good fishing in troubled waters" (O'Connor 1962: 51).

Drew became treasurer and, according to W.A. Swanberg (1959: 24), virtual dictator of the Erie Railroad. He would issue stock for new steel rails and other vital equipment and divert the money for his own speculative investments. As a result, the Erie's "schedules were fictional, its rolling stock ruinous, its iron rails so worn and chipped as to invite derailment." Drew was an ardent churchgoer who was responsible for the founding of Drew Theological Seminary in New Jersey, now part of Drew University. A typical Drew enterprise involved the Erie, which ran from Jersey City to Lake Erie. In 1866, the line was in financial trouble and borrowed $3.5 million from Drew. As collateral, he received 28,000 shares of unissued stock and $3 million in convertible bonds. The securities had been entrusted to him only as collateral; they were not to be sold. Drew converted the bonds into 30,000 more shares of stock and began selling short (speculating that the price of the stock would go down). To ensure that this would happen, Drew dumped all 58,000 shares on the market and realized a profit of almost $3 million. (This at a time when most workingmen earned less than $25 a week and New

York State legislators were paid $300 a year.) While Vanderbilt died leaving an estate valued at $90 million and a university named in his honor, Drew was a pauper when he died in 1879 (Swanberg 1959).

Fisk

James Fisk, Jr., (1835-72) was the youngest member of the Erie Ring, born in Vermont to a family of English ancestry. He left home at age fifteen to join the circus, returning a few years later to join his father as an itinerant peddler. His success at this trade led to a job as salesman for Jordan Marsh & Company of Boston. During the Civil War he acted as an agent for Marsh to the Union Army, lobbying congressmen and generals with lavish entertainment and liberal spending. This led to lucrative contracts for Marsh and advancement for the young Fisk. While the young men of the Union Army were dying in battle by the thousands, Fisk was operating an enormous smuggling operation to get southern cotton to the northern mills of Jordan Marsh—a fortune was made. At the end of the war, Marsh presented Fisk with a handsome bonus of $65,000.

Fisk took his Civil War profits and used them to swindle buyers of Confederate bonds in England—after the fall of Richmond, he sold short to Englishmen who did not know that the Confederacy had collapsed. He went on to become a stockbroker and associate of Daniel Drew and Jay Gould. Fisk was thirty-seven when he was murdered by the lover of his mistress. He left an estate valued at only $1 million, although his wife was reputed to be worth about $2 million. She died in 1912, a poor woman living on $50 a month from some rental property (Swanberg 1959).

Gould

Jay Gould (1836-92), the third member of the Erie Ring, was the son of a poor farmer in Delaware County, New York. At age sixteen, while working as a clerk for a village storekeeper, Gould discovered that his employer had negotiated to buy a piece of property for $2,000. Gould secured a loan of $2,500 from his father, purchased the land, and sold it to his employer for $4,000. Taking advantage of positions of trust was to become the basis for Gould's early financial success. By age twenty he had accumulated $5,000, which he used to enter the leather market in New York.

Gould was befriended by a wealthy businessman who, impressed with his ability, gave him $120,000 to found a large tannery in Pennsylvania. The company did well, but no profits were being received by the owner in New York—Gould was diverting the funds for his own speculative investments. When the owner traveled to Pennsylvania, he found the books in disarray and feared for his investment. He offered to sell the company to Gould for only $60,000. Gould found another backer, paid off the original owner, and continued to divert funds for his own use, until the new backer attempted physically to take back the property. Using thugs and idle workers, Gould resisted the effort; officers of the law finally ousted him (Josephson 1962).

With funds purloined from the tannery, Gould entered the railroad business, buying first mortgage bonds of the Rutland and Washington Railroad. For ten cents on the dollar he was able to gain controlling interest of this small, bankrupt line. Gould hired men of managerial ability, had them improve the railroad, and consolidated it with other small lines whose stock he had also purchased. By complex stock manipulations, he was able to drive up the price of his holdings. With profits from bond speculation, Gould purchased a controlling interest in the Cleveland and Pittsburgh Railroad, whose stock he manipulated to an all-time-high price. He then sold the line to the Pennsylvania Railroad Company. The next great enterprise involved him as part of the Erie Ring in its battle with Cornelius Vanderbilt (Myers 1936).

In 1869, Gould was speculating in gold; he owned about $7 million worth, and it would be to his advantage if the price were to go up. This required assurances that the federal government would not release any of its $100 million in gold reserves as it periodically did in the interest of trade and commerce. Gould attempted to influence President Grant through a financial relationship with Grant's brother-in-law. Gould also had stories planted in the newspapers indicating that the government was going to refrain from releasing any gold reserves. These activities, in addition to his own feverish buying of gold, caused a "bull market," and the price of gold skyrocketed. Gould discovered, however, that his efforts to influence President Grant had failed and a release of gold reserves was imminent. Secretly, he began to sell even as the price of gold was increasing. Suddenly, news of the federal decision became public and on September 24, 1869, "Black Friday," the price of gold plummeted. Half of Wall Street was ruined; major investment houses went bankrupt—Gould made a profit of $11 million and narrowly escaped being lynched by an angry mob (Swanberg 1959).

When Gould died in 1892 he left an estate valued at $70 million (Josephson 1962). On January 3, 1884, the *New York Times* reported that the jewelry collection of the late daughter-in-law of "the railroad magnate Jay Gould" would be auctioned at Christie's on April 11. The widow of the youngest son of Jay Gould had a jewelry collection insured for more than $100 million, in addition to an art collection of 120 works by Van Gogh, Renoir, Manet, Degas, Goya, and others. The bulk of the estate was to go to the Gould Foundation to promote French-American friendship (Reif 1984: 21).

Sage

Russell Sage was born in 1816 in Oneida County, New York. He worked in his brother's grocery store as a clerk and in 1839 became a partner in a wholesale grocery establishment. In 1851 he engaged in the first of his major swindles, and the resulting legal action reached the United States Supreme Court (*Wheeler* v. *Sage*). For seven years Sage held the offices of alderman of the city of Troy and treasurer of Rensselaer County in New York. As such, using rather involved chicanery, he succeeded in having the city of Troy sell its Troy and Schenectady Railroad, which had been constructed at great public expense. Sage, through intermediaries, bought the line for $200,000—$50,000 down and fourteen years to pay. He then arranged for the sale of the line to the New York Central Railroad for $1 million.

In 1853 Sage was elected to Congress, and during his stay enormous grants of land and financial subsidies were given to railroad corporations. When he left Congress, Sage was a major bondholder of the La Crosse and Milwaukee Railroad, which had received land grants from the state of Wisconsin worth more than $17 million—which cost the line about $1 million in bribes. Sage eventually gained control of the line and swindled stockholders and creditors. The line was driven into bankruptcy and turned over to the major bondholders, who were Sage front men. It was renamed and (on paper) reorganized, and the whole scam was repeated. The overplundered line was unsafe and inefficient; its owner was a multimillionaire.

With funds from his railroad successes, Sage became one of America's great usurers, charging as much as 2 percent per day to hard-pressed businessmen. At his death, $50 million in personal property was inherited by his widow (Myers 1936). In 1907 she established the Russell Sage Foundation "for the improvement of social and living conditions in the United States." Through the efforts of the foundation, small-loan acts were passed to protect workers from the usurious practice known as "salary lending."

Stanford

The railroading tradition was not reserved for the eastern United States. But in the West there was none of the cutthroat competition that pervaded the East. In California, Leland Stanford, governor and United States senator and, according to Gustavus Myers (1936: 250), "one of the arch-bribers and thieves of the time," formed the Pacific Association with three colleagues. Without any background in railroading, they set up the Central Pacific Railroad Company in 1861 and raised $200,000 for the construction of a railroad line that was estimated to cost $25 million. The $200,000, however, was not for construction costs; it was to help cover the cost of "legislative activity." Cash and enormous quantities of stocks and bonds (whose only expense was the cost of printing) resulted in a grant from Congress of 9 million acres of land and $24 million in government bonds to finance the Central Pacific Railroad. The line would run from the Pacific to as far as it could reach in a race east with the Union Pacific racing west—the lines linked up in 1869. For every mile of track, the lines received a subsidy from the government. This did not satisfy Stanford and his associates. The trio (Stanford, Mark Hopkins, and Collis Huntington) intimidated local governments into providing millions of dollars by threatening to have the line by-pass their communities. San Francisco, for example, provided $550,000 (Myers 1936; Josephson 1962). Stanford University is part of this legacy.

Rockefeller

John D. Rockefeller (1839-1937) was born in Richford, New York, the son of a vendor of quack medicines. A studious, hardworking youngster, at age sixteen he secured a job as a bookkeeper for a produce merchant. He saved meager earnings to become a successful broker, buying and selling grain and produce. During the Civil War, he made a fortune selling grain to the military while avoiding conscription. In 1862, he invested in a technique to extract kerosene from crude oil and in 1865 sold his share in the produce business to devote all his time and money to oil. His remarkable success in the oil business was aided by the Vanderbilt-owned railroad, which shipped the Rockefeller oil at a discount—a portion of the shipping costs was rebated, "kicked back," allowing Rockefeller to undercut his competitors.

In 1870, Rockefeller and Henry Flagler incorporated the Standard Oil Company, and the next year they conspired to control the entire oil industry in the United States. First, they obtained the Pennsylvania charter of a defunct corporation that had been authorized to engage in a plethora of business activities—the South Improvement Company (SIC). Then, in collusion with railroad officials, shipping rates were doubled for competing oil companies, but the increase for SIC was rebated. By 1872, Rockefeller was intimidating rival oil companies into selling out to SIC. An "oil war" resulted, as independent oil dealers fought the SIC by refusing to sell their oil to the Rockefeller-controlled refineries. The oil boycott hurt railroads, which rebelled, and the Pennsylvania legislature revoked the SIC charter (Lloyd 1963).

The great monopolist struck again, this time conspiring with refinery owners to gain control over the setting of railroad oil-shipping rates. The owners of the fifteen strongest oil firms in the United States swore an oath of secrecy and became part of the Standard Oil conspiracy. In league with the railroads, they controlled the delivery of oil, forcing competitors to sell out to Standard or pay exorbitant shipping costs that would render them noncompetitive. Those who were stubborn enough to resist were harassed with price wars and, if that didn't work, dynamite. By 1876, Standard Oil controlled 80 percent of the oil production in the United States.

In 1877, a great oil boom threatened to break the Standard Oil monopoly. Rockefeller fought the new independents by refusing them use of the railroads, pipelines, and storage facilities. The independents organized and fought back, financing the construction of the Tidewater Pipe Line to break the Rockefeller control over railroad rates. They attacked Standard Oil in the courts, and

Flagler and Rockefeller were indicted in Pennsylvania for conspiracy in restraint of trade.

Undaunted, Rockefeller built a rival pipeline, slashed prices, attacked Tidewater credit in the money market, and had "his" judges enjoin the issuance of Tidewater bonds. In the finest tradition of direct action, Standard Oil operatives plugged up Tidewater pipelines. Tidewater capitulated and was bought out by the National Transit Company, which was owned by Standard Oil (Lloyd 1963).

Although John D. Rockefeller died in 1937, his legacy lives on in the form of the University of Chicago, Rockefeller University, and the Rockefeller Foundation. His progeny have served as governors of New York, Arkansas, and West Virginia and as vice-president of the United States.

Morgan

J. Pierpont Morgan (1837-1913) was born in Connecticut and educated in Germany. His father was a wealthy banker, and by virtue of the family fortune Morgan was able to escape conscription during the Civil War. As did many of his ilk, Morgan became a war profiteer, financing the sale of defective carbines to the Union Army. In 1869, he engaged Gould and Fisk in a battle over a railroad line that had been constructed with public funds. The contest over the Albany and Susquehanna's stock moved into the courts as each side accused the other of fraud. The ensuing battle threw the railroad into chaos, and it had to be shut down. Unfortunately for Gould and Fisk, the court fight took place in upstate New York, not in the Tammany courts of New York City. As a result, the Morgan-influenced judges handed him control of the line. Morgan continued to feed at the public trough, and his banking firm (Drexel, Morgan and Co.) earned $5 million for acting as brokers in the sale of government bonds that Myers (1936: 560) argues the government "could have disposed of . . . without intermediaries."

In 1889, Morgan convened a secret meeting of the major banking houses in order to form a cartel—a monopoly to corner federal gold reserves. The cartel began buying up government gold reserves by redeeming bonds for gold coin. By 1895, they had $120 million in gold hoarded away in bank vaults. Morgan, through an emissary, offered to release the gold in negotiations with President Grover Cleveland. The only thing he wanted in return was exclusive rights to a government bond issue of over $62 million. Cleveland agreed, and the cartel sold the bonds for a net profit of $18 million—money that otherwise would have gone to the government.

By his control over banking and, thus, sources of credit, Morgan wielded more power than Andrew Carnegie or John D. Rockefeller. By merely threatening to withhold credit, he could destroy companies or coerce them into submission. As a result, Morgan controlled railroads and steel production: about half the nation's railroad mileage and, as a result of his great "Steel

CANISIUS COLLEGE LIBRARY
BUFFALO. N. Y.

Trust" (United States Steel), 75 to 100 percent of the market for finished steel. When Morgan died while vacationing in Rome in 1913, he left an estate valued in excess of $131 million. In addition, his son, Pierpont, Jr., inherited an empire valued at about $2.5 billion (Myers 1936; Josephson 1962).

Kindred Spirits

This sampling of "godfathers" from an earlier era is far from complete. For example, we could have included the DuPonts, who made vast fortunes during the Civil War and who arranged for the formation of a cartel of gunpowder manufacturers, the "Powder Trust." After the Civil War, the cartel drove competition out of business by cutthroat pricing, bribery, and sabotage— competing companies disappeared in mysterious explosions (Zilg 1974). We could have given "dishonorable mention" to Andrew Carnegie, who gained control over a more efficient steel competitor by sending to railroads through-out the country a libelous circular warning that his competitor's product was unsafe. This lie enabled Carnegie to buy out his rival at bargain prices (Wall, 1970). Carnegie steelworkers put in twelve-hour days, seven days a week, "and Carnegie went on giving to libraries and wondering why so few adults made use of his magnificent gifts" (1970: 579).

We could have provided details about James Jerome Hill of the Great Northern Railroad and Edward H. Harriman of the Union Pacific, and their battle to monopolize the rails, a battle that began in the stock exchange, moved to the courts, and finally was fought through melees and killings by thugs from both sides (Holbrook 1953). Harriman later joined with Hill and Pierpont Morgan to form a combine (Northern Securities Company) to monopolize the railroads, but the trust was ordered dissolved by the United States Supreme Court in 1904. Edward's son, Averell Harriman, was elected governor of New York in 1954. He was defeated in a bid for reelection by Nelson Rockefeller, grandson of John D.

We could have mentioned Henry Ford, a notorious anti-Semite, whose credo was: "There is something sacred about big business. Anything which is economically right is morally right" (Sinclair 1962: 369). In that spirit, Ford hired ex-pugilist Harry Bennett, who employed a small army of gangsters to beat and terrorize Ford workers.

We could have moved our historical review to the West, where cattle barons and land grabbers were not above using any means at their disposal to achieve their ends, as evidenced by the sensational escapades of the "Lincoln County War" (1876-78) in New Mexico and the "Johnson County War" (1891-92) in Wyoming. William H. Bonney, born Henry McCarty, better known as "Billy the Kid," began his murderous career in the Lincoln County War.

Conclusion

What does all this add up to; what are we to conclude? First, we must understand that the United States, as the Eisenhower commission[1] pointed out, is quite a violent country. Important features of the development of America have hinged on violence, both figurative (e.g., "financial piracy") and literal (e.g., the use of gunmen, thugs, private police, law-enforcement agents, the National Guard, and the military to further *private* ends). With the western frontier closed, with the wealth of the "robber barons" now institutionalized and their progeny firmly in control of the economy, there has been little opportunity for the poor but ambitious adventurers of our urban frontiers. These later immigrants, Irish, Jewish, Italian, have sought to innovate, not on the grand scale of the Vanderbilts, the Rockefellers, and the Morgans, but in a manner more consistent with available opportunity.

Among the financial pirates of an earlier era we can see the strength of the so-called Protestant ethic (Weber 1958), distorted out of its theological origins and twisted into a savage temporal credo. In latter-day pirates, our contemporary gangsters, can be seen the remnants of a primitive culture that gave strength to the now-dominant group in organized crime, the Italians.

---

[1]National Advisory Commission on Causes and Prevention of Violence, 1969.

Historical Antecedents of Organized Crime:
Mafia, Comorra, and Onerate Società

Used by permission of Historical Pictures Service, Chicago

Most Italians who came to the United States did so during the years 1875–1920. Ninety percent of them were from the poorest part of their country, the *mezzogiorno,* southern Italy.

These poor immigrants encountered an economy shaped by the Morgans and Vanderbilts, in which powerless people had little opportunity. They faced enormous economic hardship exacerbated by ethnic prejudice.

Like earlier generations, some Italian immigrants sought success by bending and breaking both moral and legal codes. Being relative latecomers, they could not imitate the scions of earlier generations who had already, by "hook or crook," secured a place in society. Instead, a small number of these immigrants adapted their southern Italian culture to the American experience. In order to understand the type of organized crime that resulted, we have to understand the phenomena of *Mafia, Camorra,* and *Onerate Società.*

The island of Sicily in the Mediterranean Sea is separated from mainland Italy by the Strait of Messina and a unique history and culture. Until 1860, Sicily was ruled by a series of foreign conquerors: Byzantine, Arab, Norman, Spanish. The history of Sicily (and the rest of southern Italy) is one of political, social, and economic repression: a succession of foreign rulers culminating in a revolution in 1860 that eventually united Italy. For the people of Sicily, however, little changed. Instead of foreign repression, the *contadini* ("peasants") were repressed by Italians from the north.

This southern Italian experience dates back more than a thousand years, and it led to the development of a culture that stressed the variables necessary for survival in a hostile environment. Neither government nor church was to be trusted. The only basis of loyalty was the *famiglia, sangu de me sangu* ("blood of my blood"). Richard Gambino (1974: 3) describes the family of southern Italy:

> The *famiglia* was composed of all of one's blood relatives, including those relatives Americans would consider very distant cousins, aunts and uncles, an extended clan whose genealogy was traced through paternity. The clan was supplemented through an important custom known as *comparatico* or *comparaggio* (godparenthood), through which carefully selected outsiders became to an important (but incomplete) extent members of the family.

Gambino (1974:4) notes that the family patriarch, *capo di famiglia,* arbitrated all ambiguous situations, and the family was organized hierarchically: "One had absolute responsibilities to family superiors and absolute rights to be demanded from subordinates in the hierarchy." Luigi Barzini (1977: 36) describes the dynamic qualities of the southern Italian family:

> The family, first source of power, had to be made prosperous, respected, and feared with antlike tenacity; it was enlarged (like dynasties of old) by suitable

marriages, strengthened by alliances with families of equal status, by negotiated submission to more powerful ones, or by establishing its domination over weaker ones.

The southern Italian (from Sicily, the city of Naples, or the province of Calabria) developed an ideal of manliness, *omertà,* which included non-cooperation with authorities, self-control in the face of adversity, and the *vendetta*—any offense or slight to *famiglia* had to be avenged, no matter what the consequences or how long it took. Out of this history and culture developed the famous "secret societies" of southern Italy.

Mafia

Norman Lewis (1964: 25) states:

> The word Mafia probably derives from the identical word in Arabic and means "place of refuge." As such, it no doubt recalls the predicament of the relatively civilized Saracens after the conquest of Sicily by the Normans in the eleventh century. The Arabs had introduced small holdings and scientific irrigation. Their rule by comparison with anything the island had known before (or has known since) was mild and beneficent. Had they remained, there is no reason why the prosperity and civilization of Sicily should not have equaled that of Spain, but the Normans dislodged them and plunged the country back into the polar night of feudalism. Most of the Arab small holders became serfs on the reconstituted estates. Some escaped to "the Mafia."

James Inciardi (1975: 112-13) states:

> . . . explanations of *Mafia* come from Sicilian historical and literary works that link its root and meaning to elements prevailing within Sicilian culture. *Mafia* is seemingly Sicilian-Arabic descending from the etyma *hafa:* to preserve, protect and act as guardian; from *mo'hafi:* friend or companion; from *mo'hafah:* to defend; and from *mo'hafiat:* preservation, safety, power, integrity, strength, and a state that designates the remedy of damage and ill. . . *mo'hafiat* became *mafiat* by elision, and *mafia* by apocope, . . . *mafia* as a dialect term common in pre-1860 Palermo. . . expressed "beauty and excellence," united with notions of "superiority" and "bravery"; in reference to *man* it also meant: "the consciousness of being a man," "assurance of the mind," "boldness" but never "defiance," and "arrogance" but never "haughtiness." Thus, both Arabic-Sicilian references and common Palermitani usage contributed to *Mafia*'s meanings: protection against the arrogance of the powerful, remedy to any damage, sturdiness of body, strength and serenity of spirit, and the best and most exquisite part of life.

Thus, *mafia* is a state of mind, a way of life—not a secret criminal organization. Barzini (1965: 253) separates *mafia* from Mafia as an illegal secret organization. The former (*mafia*) is shared by all Sicilians, the honest and the criminal: "they must aid each other, side with their friends and fight the common enemies even when the friends are wrong and the enemies are right; each must defend his dignity at all costs and never allow the smallest slight to go unavenged; they must keep secrets and beware of official authorities and laws." Barzini points out that the two (Mafia and *mafia*) are closely related, that Mafia could not flourish without *mafia*.

Eric Hobsbawm (1976: 92) notes that *mafia* represents a general attitude toward the state:

> A *mafioso* did not invoke State or law in his private quarrels, but made himself respected and safe by winning a reputation for toughness and courage, and settled his differences by fighting. He recognized no obligation except those of the code of honor or *omertà* (manliness), whose chief article forbade giving information to the public authorities.

Gaia Servadio (1976) notes that up until unification in 1860, the large estates of Sicily were under the ownership of absentee landlords. Unwilling or unable to manage their land, the absentee landlord rented his estates to a *gabelloto*, a manager who had already gained the reputation of *uomo inteso*— "a strong man." The *gabelloto* ruled over the estate with brute force. He was assisted by *famiglia* and *amici* ("friends") and *campieri:* armed, mounted guards. The *campieri* were hired because they were *uomini di rispettu*, "men of respect," meaning that they were quick to use violence and people were in fear of them. The *gabelloto* was a patron to his peasants. He controlled their access to farming land, and he acted as a mediator between official power and government and the peasantry, a position he maintained by the exercise of force. In league with the landlords, he fought land reform and revolution.

The inability of foreign rulers, and subsequent to 1860 the northern Italian government, to impose "law and order" on Sicily resulted in the development of *Compagnie d'Armi* ("Companies at Arms"). These locally recruited men soon became part of the unofficial power network (which included *gabelloti* and *campieri*), extorting money and making alliances with the very bandits they were organized to defeat. The *Compagnie d'Armi* were particularly important in overseeing criminal activity in eastern Sicily, where the phenomenon of Mafia did not emerge (Servadio 1976).

While its roots are clearly discernible during colonial periods, Mafia is the result of unification and democracy. Hobsbawm (1976: 92) notes:

> In lawless communities power is rarely scattered among an anarchy of competing units, but clusters round local strong points. Its typical form is patronage, its typical holder the private magnate or boss with his body of retainers and dependents and the network of "influence" which surrounds him and causes men to put themselves under his protection.

Thus, the center of Mafia is the *padrino* or *capo mafioso,* around whom other *mafiosi* gather to form a *cosca.* Henner Hess (1973) notes that Mafia is neither an organization nor a secret society—it is a *method. Mafiosi* come together in some type of instinctive solidarity to form a *cosca,* a small, cliquelike association, to support one another in the pursuit of their aims. Anton Blok (1974) states that one becomes a member of a *cosca* gradually and not through any type of formal initiation. The *cosca* is devoid of any rigid organization; it is simply *gli amici degli amici*—"friends of friends." The "members" are simply *gli uomini qualificati* ("qualified men"). Hess (1973) notes that the *mafioso* succeeds because he commands a *partito,* a network of relationships whereby he is able to act as an intermediary providing services, which include votes and violence for the holders of institutionalized power. All he requests in return is immunity to carry out his activities. Hobsbawm (1976) points out that some standardized rituals developed in the 1870s, and once initiated into the *cosca* the *mafioso* became a *compadre,* a practice based on the custom of *comparatico* (fictional kinship or godparenthood). The remnants of pre-unification power in western Sicily, *gabelloti, campieri, Compagnie d'Armi* and, in some instances, clergymen, form the *cosche* (plural of *cosca*). Each village has its own *cosca,* larger ones have two, and collectively they are Mafia.

Barzini (1965) delineates four levels of organization that constitute Mafia. The first, the family, constitutes the nucleus. Some families, he notes, have belonged to the *società deqli amici* for generations, each *padrino* bequeathing the family to his eldest son. The second level consists of a group of several families who come together to form a *cosca* in which one family and its *padrino* is recognized as supreme. The *cosca* establishes working relationships with other *cosche,* respecting territories and boundaries. The third level is achieved when *cosche* join in an alliance called *consorteria* in which one cosca is recognized as supreme and its leader is the leader of the *consorteria— capo di tutti capi,* the boss of bosses. "This happens spontaneously . . . when the *cosche* realize that one of them is more powerful, has more men, more friends, more money, more high-ranking protectors. . . . All the *consorterie* in Sicily . . . form the *onerata società,*" and a form of solidarity unites all mafiosi: "they know they owe all possible support to any *amico deqli amici* who needs it . . . even if they have never heard of him, provided he is introduced by a mutual amico" (1965: 272).

Servadio (1976: 17) points out that a constitutional state and elected parliament that accompanied union with Italy provided a crucial step in the rise to power of the Mafia—"Sicily's special kind of middle class." Because of its ability to control elections, the Mafia has been courted by the political powers in Rome. Lewis (1964: 41) reports that "the Mafia had become the only electoral force that counted in Sicily and the government was realistic in the acceptance of the fact." The situation remained unchanged until the rise of Benito Mussolini and the Fascist government.

Mussolini and the Fascist Period: 1922-1945

The rise to power of Mussolini in the 1920s had important implications for the Mafia (and Italian-American organized crime). Jack Reece (1973: 266) notes that "during the years immediately after 1922, the Mafia supported Fascism more or less freely. When they were not encumbered with too notorious a prison record or sunk in absolute illiteracy, individual *mafiosi* openly joined the local party organization and at times attained leading positions in it." Reece points out that "alliance with Fascism appeared not only to be the best guarantee of preserving their property, advantages, and prestige, but it also provided a timely opportunity for the acquisition of social and political respectability" (1973: 266) The impact of the Mafia can be seen by comparing the elections of 1922, when no Fascist was elected to Parliament from Sicily, to the elections of 1924, when thirty-eight Fascists were elected out of fifty-seven from Sicily (Servadio 1976).

Mussolini visited Sicily in 1924 and was introduced to Don Ciccio Cuccia,[1] a *capomafioso* who was also a local mayor. Don Ciccio accompanied *Il Duce* on a tour and, after seeing the large number of police officers guarding him, is alleged to have said, "You're with me, so there's nothing to worry about."[2] A totalitarian regime does not tolerate pockets of authority that are not under its control—Mussolini moved to destroy the Mafia. Elections were abolished in 1925, depriving the Mafia of its major instrument of alliance with government and the basis for its immunity from criminal justice. Mussolini invested Prefect Cesare Mori of Lombardy, a career police officer, with emergency police powers and sent him after the Mafia.

Mori assembled a small army of agents and set about the task of purging the island of *mafiosi*. Servadio (1976: 74) states:

> Under the jurisdiction of Prefect Mori, repression became savage. Many mafiosi were sent to prison, killed or tortured, but also many left-wingers were called "mafiosi" for the occasion, and were disposed of. . . . In many cases the landowners provided Mori with information against the mafiosi they had so far employed, who had been their means to safeguard their interests against the peasantry. This was logical because they saw that the regime would provide a better and cheaper substitute.

Mori swooped down on villages and arrested hundreds of persons. He arrested Don Ciccio and other important *capomafiosi*. The *gabelloto* were required to be free of any police record, and in 1928 Mori declared that the Mafia had been destroyed. However, the reality was otherwise, and the Mafia began to reassert itself by 1941. When questioned by Allied officials at the end of World War II, Mori stated: "I drove the mafia underground all right. I had unlimited police powers and a couple of battalions of Blackshirts. But how can you stamp out what is in people's blood?" (Sciascia 1963: 6).

The campaign against the Mafia succeeded in driving out of Sicily some very important *mafiosi*. They traveled to the United States at an opportune time, during the Prohibition era. The impact of these men on organized crime in America will be discussed in the next chapter. Back in Sicily, the Mafia awaited "liberation," which came in the form of the Allied landing in 1943.

Postwar Trends

The end of the war resulted in a Mafia renaissance. There was a brief flirtation with Separatism, seceding from the mainland in favor of affiliation with the United States. That idea was discarded when the government announced Sicilian autonomy in 1946. In return, the most important *capomafioso*, Calogero Vizzini (Don Calò), pledged support for the Christian Democratic Party. Don Calò had been imprisoned by Mussolini but was now a *gabelloto*. Lewis (1964: 43) notes, however, that one powerful *capomafioso*, Don Vanni Sacco of Camporeale, refused to join with the Christian Democrats: "It took lunch with the Archbishop . . . before Don Vanni would agree to change his politics." Church officials and landowners joined with the Mafia in a campaign to defeat the "leftists"—Communists, socialists, and trade unionists. As part of their campaign, the Mafia struck a deal with the noted bandit leader Salvatore Giuliano.

Salvatore Giuliano[3]. Salvatore Giuliano, known as Turiddu or Turi, was conceived in New York where his father lived for 18 years, but was born in the poverty-stricken Sicilian village of Montelepre (about 15 miles from Palermo) in 1922. In 1943 he was caught by two *carabinieri* (federal police) with black-market flour. Although the police were often employed as escorts by large-scale black-marketeers, small-time operators were usually dealt with harshly. Giuliano resisted, shot one officer to death and was wounded by the other. He subsequently liberated a number of inmates from the Monreale jail and they fled to the mountains to begin lives as bandits.

Giuliano's exploits were reported widely in the press and he was viewed by many as a Sicilian Robin Hood. He robbed from the wealthy, and criminals who preyed on the poor were apprehended and executed by his band. Giuliano distributed much of his loot among needy peasants and was, in turn, protected by them. He was also protected by the important *cosche* of Monreale and Partinico. Thus, while other bandits fell to the police, Giuliano and his men often slept in their own houses in Montelepre.

Between 1943 and 1946 the Mafia helped to organize the Sicilian Separatist Movement, and Giuliano was commissioned as a colonel in the struggle to free Sicily from the Mainland. Although separatist forces in the eastern end of the island fared badly against the Italian military, in the western mountains Giuliano succeeded in attacking police stations and other government installations. When the Italian government announced autonomy for Sicily, important *capomafiosi* abandoned the separatist movement—"Colonel Giuliano" was, once again, nothing but a bandit.

While the rebellion had been short-lived, its spirit lingered with peasants and bandits who attacked the feudal estates, seizing supplies and land which had been under the protection of the Mafia. At the behest of Don Calò, Giuliano agreed to support the Christian Democrats in the area under his control and to eliminate rival bandit groups who were endangering the Mafia-protected estates. In return, the Mafia offered to use its considerable influence to secure a pardon for Giuliano and his men. Bandit after bandit was betrayed and fell victim to Mafia assassins or Giuliano's men. In 1947 the threat to the Mafia came from leftist political parties, particularly the Communist Party. In the regional elections which took place on April 20, 1947, the Christian Democrats, despite the active support of the church and the Mafia, were defeated. The Mafia ordered Giuliano into action: on May Day, May 1, 1947, his men attacked a Communist rally, killing eleven and wounding fifty others. With the help of Giuliano and the combined strength of the church and Mafia, the Christian Democrats routed the opposition in the elections of 1948.

The Sicilian Robin Hood was of no further use to the Mafia, and Giuliano soon realized that he had been abandoned. He turned on the Mafia and its allies, even threatening the life of Don Calò. While Giuliano continued to roam the mountains, he could not freely enter the towns which were under control of the Mafia. With the help of the Mafia, members of his band were captured or killed by the authorities. In 1949, a force of 400 police officers and soldiers entered the hills of northwestern Sicily to pursue the bandit chieftain. The end came on July 5, 1950—Giuliano was apparently shot to death by his best friend who had made a deal with the Mafia.

The Nuovo Mafia

Don Calò died of natural causes in 1954; this illiterate son of a poor farmer left an estate worth several million dollars (Pantaleone 1966: 80). He also appears to have been the last of the old-style *capomafioso,* characterized by modesty in both speech and dress: "The old Mafia chief was a rural animal, holding sway over the countryside, dressed in shirt-sleeves and baggy pants: a multi-millionaire who chose to look like a peasant" (Servadio 1974: 21). The "New Mafia" is centered in Palermo and its urban environs. The "new" *mafioso* is not bound by the traditions of the rural *cosca*. He dresses like a successful businessman, sometimes a bit flashy, like the American gangster whose pattern he seems to have adapted—cross fertilization, perhaps, as the result of the influence of deported American gangsters.

The level of competition and violence has intensified with the proliferation of Mafia "gangs," at least 20 in Palermo and about 200 throughout Sicily (Hoffman 1983). The "New Mafia" has killed government officials: the regional president of Sicily; the provincial secretary of the Christian Democratic Party; the deputy police chief of Palermo; a judge; two police investigators; and General Dalla Chiesa and his thirty-two-year-old bride of six weeks. A retired rural *mafioso* is quoted: "Never would that (old) Mafia have cruelly and uselessly murdered the wife of General Dalla Chiesa. Even more, never would that Mafia have attacked and killed the general. Offenses against symbols of authority were foreign to the methods of a Mafia that, considering itself an authority and surrogate for the state, wanted to preserve and respect certain values" (Kamm 1982/a: E3). In a more traditional vein, the New Mafia assassinated the regional chairman of the Communist Party.

The New Mafia has moved its activities north, often working in cooperation with criminal organizations from other parts of Italy. In one of the more sensational scandals of modern Italy, the Mafia assisted Michele Sindona, a Sicilian businessman who served as a confidant and financial advisor to the Vatican, in a scheme to sell millions of dollars in stolen and counterfeit securities. (See, for example, DiFonzo 1983; Hammer 1982; Pileggi 1980.) The major innovation of the New Mafia, however, appears to be the level of involvement in international narcotics trafficking. In 1984, the disclosures of one Sicilian *mafioso*, Tommaso Buscetta, who was on the losing side of a Mafia "war," led to the arrest of dozens of Sicilians in Italy and the United States. They were tied to an international network that smuggled heroin into the United States.

The New Mafia has also lost the support of important elements of Italian society. In 1982, Cardinal Salvatore Pappalardo of Palermo issued a public condemnation of the Mafia. Sicily's bishops, "reversing decades of church indifference toward and even tolerance of the local dons," issued a document that decried "the black stain of the Mafia, which pretends to resolve problems of justice and honor in the most vulgar and criminal way, while it infiltrates the building industry and the markets with up-to-date gangster methods" (Withers 1982: 5). In November, 1982, Pope John Paul II issued an attack on the Mafia while on a visit to the island of Sicily. The Christian Democratic Party also took a stance against the Mafia, a move that cost the party heavily at the polls in Sicily. Furio Colombo (1983: 21) notes that "the Christian Democrats were punished in the south because they were moving against organized crime, abandoning convenient but questionable alliances." Instead, support went to the party identified with the Fascists: "That party was rewarded, at least in part, because so many 'godfathers' in the south gave the signal. They wanted revenge on the Christian Democrats . . ."

Camorra

While the Mafia was holding forth in Sicily, the Camorra was developing in Naples. Unlike the Mafia, however, the Camorra was a criminal society from the very beginning.

The term *Camorra* comes from the Castillian *kamora,* meaning "contestation," and was imported into Naples during the years of Spanish domination (Serao 1911a: 722). The forebears of the Neapolitan Camorra were the Spanish brigands of the Sierras known as the *gamuri.* Ernest Serao reports (1911a: 723):

Not a passer-by nor a vehicle escaped their watchful eye and their fierce claws, so that traveling or going from one place to another on business was impossible for any one without sharing with the ferocious watchers of the Sierras either the money he had with him or the profits of the business that had taken him on his journey.

The Camorra developed in the Spanish prisons during Bourbon rule of the Two Sicilies, early in the nineteenth century. The members of this criminal society eventually moved their control of the prisons into Naples proper. Eric Hobsbawm notes that they were "rather tightly, centrally and hierarchically organized" (1959: 55). John McConaughy reports (1931: 244):

> The Camorra in Naples was organized as openly and carefully as a public school system, or an efficient political machine in one of our own cities. Naples was divided into twelve districts, and each of these into a number of sub-districts. Although burglary and other remunerative felonies were not neglected, extortion was the principal industry; and the assassination of an inconvenient person could be purchased by any one with the price. In the case of a friend in need, a murder could be arranged without any cost—a simple gesture of affection.

One English diplomat in Naples (quoted in Hibbert 1966: 181-82) during the 1860s observed:

> There was no class, high or low, that had not its representatives among the members of the Society which was a vast organized association for the extortion of blackmail in every conceivable shape and form. Officials, officers of the King's Household, the police and others were affiliated with the most desperate of the criminal classes in carrying out the depredations, and none was too high or too low to escape them. If a petition was to be presented to the Sovereign or to a Minister it had to be paid for; at every gate of the town *Camorristi* were stationed to exact a toll on each cart or donkey load brought to market by the peasants; and on getting into a hackney *carrosel* in the street, I have seen one of the band run up and get his fee from the driver. No one thought of refusing to pay, for the consequences of a refusal were too well known, anyone rash enough to demur being apt to be found soon after mysteriously stabbed by some unknown individual, whom the police were careful never to discover.

Ianni states that after 1830 "they were more efficiently organized than the police, and set up a parallel system of law in the typical southern Italian style" (1972: 22). When Garibaldi became active in the Two Sicilies, the Bourbon king actually turned police power over to the Camorra, and those in jail were set free. The Camorra constituted not only the de facto but also the legally constituted police power in Naples (McConaughy 1931: 245). The Camorra welcomed Garibaldi, and after his success their power increased. Gambino states that the Camorra was at the peak of its power from 1880 until 1900 (1974: 292). "If they so decided, there would not be, in some regions, a single vote cast for a candidate for the Chamber of Deputies who was opposed to their man" (Gambino 1974: 246).

In contrast with the Mafia, the Camorra was highly organized and disciplined. Serao provides a look at the organizational structure (1911a: 724):

> There is a *capo'ntrine*—a sectional head—and a *capo in testa,* or head-in-chief of the Camorra, a kind of president of the confederation of all the twelve sections into which Naples is divided and which are presided over by the *capi'ntrini.*

The society had its own judicial structure (Serao 1911a: 725-26). The Cammorista was obliged to avenge all wrongs and slights he might have suffered,

> . . . to avenge the offense with one's own hands, if possible, after having first laid the complaint before the natural judges or the Camorra Tribunal. Whoever transgresses this all-important rule loses his right to have recourse to the Social Tribunal, which must decide as to the punishment.
>
> The Tribunal is manyfold and there is a high and low judicature. The meetings of the judges may take place anywhere; either in the towns to condemn Camorrists who are free, or in the prisons to judge imprisoned associates. . . .
>
> The low judicature Tribunal is composed of three members, presided over by the Camorrist of highest rank among them, and deals with cases implying only a small penalty.
>
> The high judicature Tribunal is constituted of twelve high-rank Camorrists only, presided over by a *capo in testa,* and it deals with cases implying an attempt against the safety of the Society, the betrayal of the secrets of the association, denunciations, habitual theft from the social funds, etc., all punishable by death, and it appoints the executioner or executioners.

The lowest or entry level of the Camorra is the *picciutto,* which requires an act of daring often simply a bloody deed, including "very dreadful crimes committed against very peaceful and quiet people . . ." (Serao 1911b: 781). The *picciutto*

> . . . has no share in the social dividend. If he wishes to live on other people's money, he must do the best he can by stealing, cheating, or swindling whom he can, giving, however, to his superiors of the Camorra proper *shruffo* or proportionate percentage.
>
> Only the regular Camorrist participates in the social dividends. In the prisons, when there are *picciuotti* and Cammorists, the former must make the beds and wait upon the latter, collect the dues from the non-associates and give them to the *cuntaiuola,* treasurer, who will pass the amount to his superiors. The *cuntaiuolo* must produce every Saturday a balance-sheet giving an account of all the dues collected during the week. As before said, the *picciuotti* do not receive anything as "right of Camorra," but their superiors usually let them have something in view of their assiduous and diligent attentions, and this optional profit is called the *sgarro.* Thus the imprisoned Camorrists often send out to their families handsome sums of money. These families enjoy just the same the "right of Camorra" *(shruffo),* and the wives and children of the Camorrist receive every week from the *cuntaiuola* of the gang to which he belonged the sum of money which would have been due to him had he been at liberty (Serao 1911b: 781).

Below the *picciuotti* are specialized associates of the Camorra such as the *basista*—a person who can plan burglaries because of his access to the homes of wealthy persons. The Camorra also has its own authorized fences, usually dealers in second-hand goods, who arrange for the auction of stolen articles (Serao 1911b: 780).

> Out of the proceeds of the sale so much is due to the *basista*, so much to the Camorrist who had knowledge of the burglary and patronized it, so much to the sectional chief of the society, and, when the burglary is a very important one, a small offering—"a flower," as it is called—is sent to the Supreme Head of the Camorra; the remainder, which is usually a meager thing, is divided among the material executors of the deed.

Gambino argues that there were actually "two Camorras"; that as noted above, the Camorra was quite stratified. The "low" Camorra did the actual physical work, while the "high" Camorra gave the orders and acted as patrons, intermediaries between institutionalized power and the "lower" Camorra. The men of the "high" Camorra, he states, were often lawyers, doctors, college professors, members of Parliament, and cabinet ministers (1974: 246).

Ianni states that the Camorra did not survive Mussolini, since, like the Mafia, it required weak governmental control (1972: 7). In 1931, Mc-Conaughy wrote that the Camorra welcomed the Fascists as they had Garibaldi; after that, there was not a Camorra: "They are all Fascists, and everything they do is legal" (1931: 248). While there are still criminals operating in Naples identified as being the Camorra, Ianni states that they have no direct links to the Camorra of an earlier era (1970: 7).

P.A. Allum (1973: 62) refers to Camorra (he uses *camorra*) as a system of racketeering. He reports that

> since 1945 a series of gangs and gangsters, variously called locally *camorristi* or *magliari*, have been operating rackets, mainly in tobacco, petrol and "exemptions" of one kind and another. Moreover, the fruit, vegetable, cattle and milk trades in the Nolan and Vesuvian areas have largely been in the hands of racketeers. The tie-up with politics is simple: the racketeer supplies the politicians with the vote (often today the preference vote) in return for protection for his various activities.

Postwar Naples has been plagued with violence attributed to the *Nuova Camorra Organizzata*, the "New Camorra." The leader of one of the important Camorra groups, Don Raffaele Cutola (born in 1941), has reportedly been running his "Family" operations for more than a dozen years while serving a twenty-four-year sentence for murder. His expansionist activities brought him into conflict with other New Camorra organizations—in 1980 and 1981 there were 380 murders attributed to the "Camorra War." In one 1984 incident, fifteen men with hunting rifles jumped from a private bus outside a church in a Naples suburb and killed eight members of a rival Camorra group (*New*

York Times, August 24, 1984: 5). Consistent with its historical origins, Cutola's group does most of its recruiting in jails. Naples has always had a reputation as a major center for smuggling, and the New Camorra is involved in the smuggling of narcotics (in cooperation with the Mafia), cigarettes, and other consumer goods, as well as extortion (Schmetzer 1982; Kamm 1982c).

Onerate Società

A third part of southern Italy, Calabria, was the home of the Onerate Società ("Honored Society") or *'Ndrangheta* ("Brotherhood"), another cousin of the Mafia. Actually several bands that grew out of government repression, the Honored Society gained popular support because of its political stance against the central government. Richard Gambino (1974: 289) states:

> In 1861 the new Italian government sent troops to police Calabria. The old economic order had collapsed under the strains of national unification, and the numbers of gangs had increased. Because of the government's deliberate policy of favoring the North over the South of Italy in its programs of economic development, and because of its ignorant and arrogant insensitivity to the customs of the South, the Calabrians soon grew to hate the new government in the North. They naturally turned to the gangs. . . .

These bands mixed political insurrection with banditry and were supported and romanticized by the repressed peasants. Eric Hobsbawm notes (1969: 56), however, that The Brotherhood had no positive program; its sense of social justice was basically *destructive:*

> In such circumstances to assert power, any power, is itself a triumph. Killing and torture is the most primitive and personal assertion of ultimate power, and the weaker the rebel feels himself to be at bottom, the greater we may suppose, the temptation to assert it.

Just as we continue to have reports coming out of Italy referring to Mafia and Camorra, there are still gangs in Calabria referred to as *'Ndrangheta.* As in Sicily (New Mafia) and Naples (New Camorra), we can assume that this is a "New Brotherhood" devoid of historical ties to the older organizations.

American Cousins

As we would expect, the patron-client networks (*partito*) of the Sicilian Mafia are quite similar to the structure of Italian-American organized crime. The Mafia also comprises elements of the more bureaucratic Camorra—e.g., hierarchical organization, formal initiation rites. The unique form of organization that resulted from adapting a southern Italian culture to American criminality provides a partial explanation for the domination of OC by Italian-

American criminals. Indeed, there has never been an important Italian-American OC figure whose heritage was not that of southern Italy.

However, domination does not explain duration—why does Italian-American OC persist more than six decades after the major Italian immigration into the United States ceased? Some theorizing is in order.

---

[1]The appellation *Don* is an honorific title used in Sicily to refer to clergymen, government officials, and important *mafiosi*. It derives from the Latin *dominus*, "lord."

[2]Cesare Mori (1933: 69) noted that *rispetto* required "a concrete recognition of the prerogative of immunity belonging to the *mafioso*, not only in his person, but also everything that he had to do with or that he was pleased to take under his protection. In fine, evildoers had to leave the *mafioso* severely alone, and all the persons or things to which, explicitly or implicitly, he had given a guarantee of security."

[3]Information on Giuliano is from a number of sources including Lewis (1964) and Servadio (1976).

chapter 6

Theories of
Organized Crime

Used by permission of the Museum of the City of New York

Sociologists have offered a number of theories to explain crime and criminal behavior. Several of these theories provide some insight into the development and continued existence of organized crime in America.

Anomie

In 1938, Robert K. Merton set forth a social and cultural explanation for deviant behavior in which organized crime is conceived of as a normal response to pressures exerted on certain persons by the social structure. Merton points to an American preoccupation with economic success—*pathological materialism*. It is the goal that is emphasized, not the means, which are, at best, only a secondary consideration: "There may develop a disproportionate, at times, a virtually exclusive stress upon the value of specific goals, involving relatively slight concern with the institutionally appropriate modes of attaining these goals" (1938: 673).

This being the case, the only factors limiting goal achievement are technical, not moral or legal, considerations. According to Merton, "emphasis on the goals of monetary success and material prosperity leads to dominant concern with technological and social instruments designed to produce the desired result, inasmuch as institutional controls become of secondary importance. In such a situation, innovation flourishes as the *range of means* employed is broadened" (1938: 673).

Thus, in American society, "the pressure of prestige-bearing success tends to eliminate the effective social constraint over means employed to this end. 'The-end-justifies-the-means' doctrine becomes a guiding tenet for action when the cultural structure unduly exalts the end and the social organization unduly limits possible recourse to approved means" (Merton 1938: 681).

In this chapter we have already reviewed the activities of earlier "godfathers" who exemplified the spirit that Merton refers to as *innovation*. The names of these men now adorn universities, foundations, and museums. Taking advantage of every (legitimate and illegitimate) opportunity, these men became the embodiment of the great American success story. However, economic opportunity is not equally distributed, and the immigrants who followed these men to America found many avenues from "rags to riches" already closed.

Anomie results when numbers of people are confronted by the contradiction between goals and means and "become estranged from a society that promises them in principle what they are deprived in reality" (Merton 1964: 218). Despite numerous success stories "we know in this same society that proclaims the right, and even the duty, of lofty aspirations for all, men do not have equal access to the opportunity structure" (1964: 218). Yet, those with ready access to success (e.g., born with a "silver spoon") *and* those who are at a distinct disadvantage are constantly exposed to the rewards of "fame and fortune" by the mass media. For some, anomie is the result, and Merton states that there are five modes of individual adaptation to this phenomenon: conformity, ritualism, rebellion, retreatism, and *innovation.* We are concerned only with the last adaptation, since it includes organized criminal activity.

Ian Taylor and his colleagues, British sociologists, summarize the anomic condition in the United States (1973: 97): "The 'American Dream' urges all citizens to succeed whilst distributing the opportunity to succeed unequally: the result of this social and moral climate, inevitably, is innovation by the citizenry—the adoption of illegitimate means to pursue and obtain success." However, "routine," pedestrian criminal acts do not lead to any significant level of economic success. Innovation, then, is the adoption of *sophisticated,* e.g., well-planned, skilled, organized, criminality. A question remains: Why do some persons suffering from anomie turn to criminal innovation, while others do not? Edwin Sutherland, the "father" of American criminology, provides an answer: *differential association.*

Differential Association

According to Sutherland (1973), the principal part of learning criminal behavior occurs within intimate personal groups. What is learned depends on the intensity, frequency, and duration of the association. The actor learns the techniques of committing crime, the drives, attitudes, and rationalizations that add up to a favorable precondition to criminal behavior. Thus the balance between noncriminal and criminal behavior is tipped in favor of the latter.

Sutherland presents the nine basics of differential association:

1. Criminal behavior is learned.
2. Criminal behavior is learned in interaction with other persons in a process of communication.
3. The principal part of the learning of criminal behavior occurs within intimate groups (e.g., family, gangs).
4. When criminal behavior is learned, the learning includes *(a)* the techniques of committing the crime, which are sometimes very complicated, *(b)* the specific direction of motives, drives, rationalizations, and attitudes.
5. The specific direction of motives and drives is learned from definitions of legal codes as favorable and unfavorable. Sutherland notes that in America, attitudes toward rules are usually mixed, and this results in culture conflict with respect to the legal codes.
6. A person becomes delinquent/criminal because of an excess of definitions favorable to violation of law over definitions unfavorable to violation of law.

7. Differential association may vary in frequency, duration, priority, and intensity.
8. The process of learning criminal behavior by association with criminal patterns involves all the mechanisms that are involved in any other learning.
9. Though criminal behavior is an expression of general needs and values, it is not explained by those general needs and values, since noncriminal behavior is an expression of the same needs and values.

Socioeconomic conditions relegate persons to an environment wherein they experience a *sense of strain*—anomie—as well as differential association. In the environment that has traditionally spawned organized crime, this "strain" is intense. Conditions of severe deprivation, with extremely limited access to ladders of legitimate success, are coupled with readily available success models that are innovative, e.g., racketeers. Thus, participation in organized crime requires anomie and differential association. However, learning the techniques of sophisticated criminality also requires the proper environment—ecological niches where this education is available.

Cultural Transmission

Clifford R. Shaw and Henry D. McKay, sociologists at the University of Chicago, used that city as a "laboratory" for their study of patterns of criminality during the 1920s and 1930s. They found that certain clearly identifiable neighborhoods maintained a high level of criminality over many decades—despite changes in ethnic composition. Thus, although one ethnic group replaced another, the rate of criminality remained constant. What was it about the environment of these neighborhoods that made them criminogenic?

Shaw and McKay (1972: 73) note that such neighborhoods are characterized by attitudes and values that are conducive to delinquency and crime, particularly organized crime:

> . . . the presence of a large number of adult criminals in certain areas means that children there are in contact with crime as a career and with the criminal way of life, symbolized by organized crime. In this type of organization can be seen the delegation of authority, the division of labor, the specialization of function, and all the other characteristics common to well-organized business institutions wherever found.

Furthermore:

> The heavy concentration of delinquency in certain areas means that boys living in these areas are in contact not only with individuals who engage in proscribed activity but also with groups which sanction such behavior and exert pressure upon their members to conform to group standards (Shaw and McKay 1972: 174).

The attitudes and values, as well as the techniques, of organized criminality are transmitted culturally:

> . . . delinquent boys in these areas have contact not only with other delinquents who are their contemporaries but also with older offenders, who in turn had contact with delinquents preceding them, and so on back to the earliest history of the neighborhood. This contact means that the traditions of delinquency can be and are transmitted down through successive generations of boys, in much the same way that language and other social forms are transmitted (Shaw and McKay 1972: 174).

Gerald D. Suttles (1968: 3) studied one of these neighborhoods, the Addams area,[1] "one of the oldest slums in Chicago," during the mid-1960s. In this area is found the University of Illinois at Chicago and the "Little Italy" of Taylor Street, an important ecological niche for organized crime. This Near West Side neighborhood was a stronghold of Al Capone and the spawning ground for many important figures in organized crime (called "The Outfit"). It is in the notorious First Ward, a political entity dominated by Italian politicians and reputed to be controlled by the Outfit.

Suttles emphasizes the clannishness of the neighborhood, where people will not make complaints to the police. There are a number of adult social-athletic clubs (SACs), which have storefront headquarters and whose members include persons who belong to the Outfit. The younger Italian males form street groups, and

> each street group tends to see the adult SAC's as essentially an older more perfect version of itself. What may be just as important, however, is their equally strong sense of history. Locally, many of the members in the street groups can trace their group's genealogy back through the Taylor Dukes, 40 gang, Genna Brothers, and the Capone Mob . . . they see themselves in a direct line of succession to groups reputed to be associated with the "Outfit" . . . (Suttles 1968: 110-11).

Walter Miller (1958: 6) studied adolescent gang behavior and concluded that it is "the product of a distinctive cultural system which may be termed 'lower class.' " It emphasizes such items of behavior as "toughness" and "smartness" (gaining money by use of one's wits), and the movie gangster is often a role model. Donald Goddard (1974: 36) reports that the Brooklyn gangster Joseph ("Crazy Joey") Gallo at age sixteen "would stand on a corner like George Raft, endlessly flipping a half-dollar and talking to himself without moving his lips." Raft apparently patterned himself after the gangster Benjamin ("Bugsy") Siegel.

Miller (1958: 14) points out some of the qualities of the adolescent street-corner group that correlate well with the prerequisites for organized crime: "The activity patterns of the group require a high level of intra-group solidarity; individual members must possess a good capacity for subordinating individual desires to general group interests as well as the capacity for intimate and persisting interaction." Status is achieved by "toughness" and "smartness," which add up to one's reputation—"rep"—while the routine patterns of these groups include law-violating behavior.

In his classic study of Chicago street gangs originally published in 1927, Frederic Thrasher (1968: 270) notes: "Experience in a gang of the predatory type usually develops in the boy an attitude of indifference to law and order—one of the basic traits of the finished gangster." He points out (1968: 273): "If the younger undirected gangs and clubs of the gang type, which serve as training schools for delinquency, do not succeed in turning out the finished criminal, they often develop a type of personality which may well foreshadow the gangster and the gunman." Thrasher observed that in the Chicago of that era (Prohibition), there was no hard-and-fast dividing line between gangs of boys, youths, and adult criminal organizations (1968: 281): "They merge into each other by imperceptible gradations. . . ."

Differential Opportunity

Richard A. Cloward and Lloyd E. Ohlin (1960: 107), in agreement with Merton, note that American preoccupation with economic success, coupled with socioeconomic stratification, relegates many persons to an environment wherein they experience anomie:

> . . . many lower-class male adolescents experience extreme deprivation born of the certainty that their position in the economic structure is relatively fixed and immutable—a desperation made all the more poignant by their exposure to a cultural ideology in which failure to orient oneself upward is regarded as a moral defect and failure to become mobile as proof of it.

Conditions of severe deprivation with extremely limited access to ladders of legitimate success result in collective adaptations in the form of delinquent subcultures. Cloward and Ohlin distinguish three types:

1. Retreatist subculture: activities in which drug usage is the primary focus
2. Conflict subculture: gang activities devoted to violence and destructive acting out as a way of gaining status
3. Criminal/rackets subculture: gang activity devoted to utilitarian criminal pursuits

The last of these adaptations begins to approximate organized crime.

Cloward and Ohlin turn from *anomie* (Merton) to the *cultural transmission* (Shaw and McKay) of a criminal tradition by way of *differential association* (Sutherland). They conclude that illegitimate means of success, like legitimate means, are not equally distributed throughout society (1960: 145): "Having decided that he 'can't make it legitimately,' he cannot simply choose from an array of illegitimate means, all equally available to him." In other words, access to criminal ladders of success are no more freely available than are noncriminal alternatives (1960: 148):

> Only those neighborhoods in which crime flourishes as a stable, indigenous institution are fertile learning environments for the young. Because these environments afford integration of different age-levels of offender, selected young people are exposed to "differential association" through which tutelage is provided and criminal values and skills are acquired. To be prepared for the role may not, however, ensure that the individual will ever discharge it. One important limitation is that more youngsters are recruited into these patterns of differential association than the adult criminal structure can possibly absorb. Since there is a surplus of contenders for these elite positions, criteria and mechanisms of selection must be evolved. Hence a certain proportion of those who aspire may not be permitted to engage in the behavior for which they have prepared themselves.

Nicholas Gage (1971: 113) points out that *The Mafia Is Not an Equal Opportunity Employer:* "No door is more firmly locked to blacks than the one that leads to the halls of power in organized crime." He states that Irish, Jewish, and Italian mobsters have tended to recruit and promote from within their own ethnic groups, while cooperating with one another. Organized crime is no less stratified than the wider "legitimate" society, and the dominant groups in both have always been white. This leads us to the question of "ethnic succession" in organized crime.

Ethnic Succession

Daniel Bell (1964: 115) refers to crime as an American way of life: "A Queer Ladder of Social Mobility." He points out (1964: 116): "The jungle quality of the American business community, particularly at the turn of the century, was reflected in the mode of 'business' practiced by the coarse gangster elements, most of them from new immigrant families, who were 'getting ahead' just as Horatio Alger had urged." Francis Ianni (1974: 13–14) notes that this "queer ladder" had organized crime as the first few rungs:

> The Irish came first, and early in this century they dominated crime as well as big-city political machinations. As they came to control the political machinery of large cities they won wealth, power and respectability through subsequent control of construction, trucking, public utilities and the waterfront. By the 1920s and the period of prohibition and speculation in the money markets and real estate, the Irish were succeeded in organized crime by the Jews, and Arnold Rothstein, Lepke Buchalter and Gurrah Shapiro dominated gambling and labor racketeering for over a decade. The Jews quickly moved into the world of business and the professions as more legitimate avenues to economic and social mobility. The Italians came next. . . .

Ianni refers to this as "ethnic succession," and he maintains that it is continuing (1974: 14): ". . . the Italians are leaving or are being pushed out of organized crime [and] they are being replaced by the next wave of migrants to the city: blacks and Puerto Ricans." While the development may not have been obvious to Ianni when he was researching and writing in the early 1970s, today we would have to add other Hispanic groups—Mexicans, Cubans, Colombians. Before examining the Ianni "ethnic succession" thesis, we need to determine why Italians have been dominant for so long in organized crime.

While the sons of Jewish immigrant families played a vital role in organized crime, by the third generation the Jews moved out, and organized crime was dominated by the Italians. Jackson Toby (1958: 548) provides an explanation by comparing the cultural differences between the Jewish and southern Italian immigrant:

> Jews and Italians came to the United States in large numbers at about the same time—the turn of the century—and both settled in urban areas. There was, however, a very different attitude toward intellectual accomplishment in the two cultures. Jews from Eastern Europe regarded religious study as the most important activity for an adult male. The rabbi enjoyed great prestige because he was a scholar, a teacher, a logician. He advised the community on the application of the Written and Oral Law. Life in America gave a secular emphasis to the Jewish reverence for learning. Material success is a more important motive than salvation for American youngsters, Jewish as well as Christian, and secular education is better training for business and professional careers than Talmudic exegesis. Nevertheless, intellectual achievement continued to be valued by Jews—and to have measurable effects. Second-generation Jewish students did homework diligently, got high grades, went to college in disproportionate numbers, and scored high on intelligence tests. Two thousand years of preparation lay behind them.
>
> Immigrants from Southern Italy, on the other hand, tended to regard formal education either as a frill or as a source of dangerous ideas from which the minds of the young should be protected. They remembered Sicily, where a child who attended school regularly was a rarity. There, youngsters were needed not [sic] only to help on the farm. Equally important was the fact that hard-working peasants could not understand why their children should learn classical Italian (which they would not speak at home) or geography (when they would not travel in their lifetime more than a few miles from their birthplace). Sicilian parents suspected that education was an attempt on the part of Roman officials to subvert the authority of the family. In the United States, many South Italian immigrants maintained the same attitudes. They resented compulsory school attendance laws and prodded their children to go to work and become economic assets as soon as possible. They encouraged neglect of schoolwork and even truancy. They did not realize that education has more importance in an urban-industrial society than in a semi-feudal one. With supportive motivation from home lacking, the second-generation Italian boys did not make the effort of Jewish contemporaries. Their teachers tried to stuff the curriculum into their heads in vain. Their lack of interest was reflected not only in low marks, retardation, truancy, and early school leaving;

it even resulted in poor scores on intelligence tests. They accepted their parents' conception of the school as worthless and thereby lost their best opportunity for social ascent.

While the pool of available candidates for membership in organized crime dwindled in the Irish and Jewish communities, it remained adequate enough in the Italian community.

Peter Lupsha (1981: 22) questions the "ethnic succession" thesis. He argues that, despite Ianni's (1972: 1974) limited findings, Italian organized-crime figures who have gained economic status are not leaving organized crime and, in many instances, their progeny are following them into the "business." He states that entry into OC is not based on blocked aspirations, i.e., *anomie,* but "is a rational choice, rooted in one perverse aspect of our values: namely, that only 'suckers' work, and that in our society, one is at liberty to take 'suckers' and seek easy money. . . ." As for blacks and Hispanics replacing Italians in OC, Lupsha argues that black and Hispanic groups have only succeeded in controlling crime markets that Italian-American groups have discarded because of poor risk-to-profit ratios.

However, ianni (1972: 193) reports a different outcome in his study of one Italian crime Family, which he calls the "Lupollos": in the fourth generation "only four out of twenty-seven males are involved in the family business organization. The rest are doctors, lawyers, college teachers, or run their own businesses." Ianni argues that ethnic succession continues (1974: 12): "We shall witness over the next decade the systematic development of what is now a scattered and loosely organized pattern of emerging black control in organized crime into the Black Mafia." Gus Tyler (1975: 178) does not find Ianni convincing: Ianni's evidence "consists of a pimp with a stable of seven hookers, a dope pusher, a fence who dabbles in loan sharking and gambling, a con man who gets phony insurance policies for gypsy cabs, and a numbers racketeer, etc." Tyler points out that, although these activities are "organized," they are not in a class with white organized crime either qualitatively or quantitatively. Indeed, early in his (1974) book Ianni reports that the brother and partner of the aforementioned "dope pusher," actually a large-scale dealer in Paterson, New Jersey, was found sans his genitals—a "message" from the "White Mafia."

The Kerner Commission (National Advisory Commission on Civil Disorders 1968: 279) stated that timing had a negative impact on blacks: "The Negro migrant, unlike the immigrant, found little opportunity in the city; he had arrived too late, and the unskilled labor he had to offer was no longer needed." Reform groups were beginning to attack the urban political machines that had aided immigrant mobility, so that when the blacks arrived, "the machines were no longer so powerful or so well-equipped to provide jobs and other favors." They also could not provide political protection for ambitious black criminals. If there is a road to ethnic succession, it is *paved with drugs*.

Ianni (1974: 143) has noted that the one sector of organized-crime activity that seems to offer some possibility for black and Hispanic innovators to expand beyond the confines of the ghetto is drug trafficking: "Narcotics and drug traffic have the same pattern of relationship which surrounded alcohol and bootlegging during the prohibition era." David Durk, a New York City police officer and former partner of Frank Serpico, states that if anything positive can be said for the drug business, it is that it has become an *equal opportunity employer* (Durk and Silverman 1976).

In recent years not only blacks but also Hispanics of various nationalities have taken up organized crime. And OC groups based in Japan have followed their honest compatriots into the "export" business, establishing outposts of their operations in various parts of the western United States. These developments will be described in more detail in part 3.

There are two other developments that could affect ethnic succession in organized crime. The first is the smuggling of illegal aliens, in this case Sicilians by Italian-American crime Families. These aliens often serve in the pizza parlors and Italian restaurants that proliferate in the New York metropolitan area. While working for substandard wages, these Sicilians stand available as "muscle" when the occasion arises. Paul Meskil (1973: 252–53) states that these Sicilians are reminiscent of earlier immigrants from that island with their *mafia* ways. He quotes a United States Department of Justice official who refers to them as "animals on a leash." When crime boss Carmine Galente was slain in 1979, two of the men dining with him, reputedly members of his Family serving as bodyguards, had come to the United States several years earlier from the Sicilian town of Castellammare del Golfo.[2]

A second development, contrary to Ianni's observations, is the continued entry of Italian-Americans into organized crime. In New York, this is highlighted by the rise of a gang of young Italians in the Pleasant Avenue section of Harlem, a syndicate stronghold, dubbed the "Purple Gang," apparently after the murderous Detroit (Jewish) mob of Prohibition days. In addition to their other activities, especially drug trafficking, Mark Schorr (1979: 44) reports that the Purple Gang is being used as "muscle" and as executioners for the syndicate. They have allegedly been responsible for many gangland murders, and their reputation for violence has apparently made them quite useful: "No one wanted to mess with them. Informants began to grow forgetful when they remembered the man who informed on the Purple Gang and was found with fourteen stab wounds and two bullets in his body—or another suspected informant who lost his head, literally, by the Grand Central Parkway." In his study of some members of the Purple Gang, Lupsha (1983) found that they tended to be born between 1946 and 1951, third-generation Italian-Americans who are related by blood and marriage. While they come from the Pleasant Avenue neighborhood, most reside in the Bronx or suburban Westchester County: "They are now, like so many New York suburbanite businessmen, commuters to the old neighborhood for work, money, and visiting rather than residents" (1983: 76).

---

[1]So-named for Jane Addams (1860-1935), a social worker who founded Hull House with Ellen Gates Starr in 1889. Addams was a leader of the women's suffrage movement and a pacifist. She shared the 1931 Nobel Peace Prize.

[2]The two men, Baldasarre ("Baldo") Amato (born 1952) and his cousin Cesare Bonventre (born 1951), were believed to have been involved in the murder of Galente. In 1984, the two were named as key figures in the "Pizza Connection" smuggling conspiracy, which imported 1,650 pounds of heroin into the United States. (A pizza parlor in the small Illinois town of Oregon was a central communications point for the smuggling ring.) On April 16, 1984, the body of Bonventre, reputedly a *caporegime* in the Bonanno Family, was found stuffed into two barrels in a Garfield, New Jersey, warehouse ("Drug Ring Suspect Surrenders. . . ." 1984. See also Dionne 1984c).

History of
Organized Crime

The task of presenting an accurate history of organized crime in the United States is insurmountable. This is not for lack of material, for it is abundant. But quantity cannot replace quality, and the latter is the problem. Alan Block (1978) notes that there is a reliance on unsubstantiated accounts of informers or the ideological preconceptions of law enforcement agencies. John Galliher and James Cain (1974: 69) point to the lack of scholarly material relating to organized crime, with the dominant literature being journalistic and tending toward sensationalism, or else government documents: "There are two troublesome aspects to this reliance on such sources, one empirical, the other political. In arriving at conclusions and statements of fact, the journalist or political investigator is not bound by the canons of scientific investigation as is the social scientist." They note the journalist's need to produce exciting copy even at the expense of "careful accumulation and sifting of information characteristic of scientific investigation."

Some anecdotal examples: According to eastern newspapers during the 1870s, Palisades, Nevada, was the toughest town west of Chicago. Passengers travelling west on the Central Pacific Railroad, upon alighting in Palisades, found street brawls, gunfights, bank robberies, and shootouts between Indians and soldiers. The press demanded that something be done. However, Palisades never even elected a sheriff—it didn't need one. The brawls and shootouts were staged; local Indians and army troops were in on the joke—the eastern press was not (Wallace et al. 1983). In 1981 it was revealed that a reporter for the *Washington Post* had fabricated a story about an eight-year-old heroin addict she called Jimmy. The story had won the reporter a Pulitzer Prize (which was revoked after the fabrication was revealed). In 1968 newspaper headlines reported that a strike on Chicago's Belt Line Railroad had resulted in 10,000 employees being laid off at the 324 industrial plants served by the line. The information, which came from the Chicago Association of Commerce, was a lie. A simple telephone check by the *Wall Street Journal* revealed that fewer than 100 employees had been laid off as a result of the strike (Rottenberg 1983).

Dwight Smith (1975: 85) points to an American preoccupation with conspiracy, from the "Bavarian Illuminati" of 1798 to the "Red Scare" of 1919. One of the conditions required for an "alien conspiracy" theory is a set of "facts" or assumptions that can be constructed into evidence supporting a conspiratorial explanation. Such "facts" often make fascinating reading; they sell newspapers, books, and magazines; and, Smith argues, they provided the Federal Bureau of Narcotics with an explanation for failure: "The notion of total suppression of illegal narcotics use through importation control was a self-proclaimed mission, and it had not been attained. How better to explain failure (and, incidentally, to prepare the ground for increased future budgets) than to argue that, dedicated though it might be, the bureau was hard pressed to overcome an alien, organized, conspiratorial force which, with evil intent and conspiratorial methods, had forced its way on an innocent public?"

In one week in 1977, major news stories appeared in the *New York Times* (Franks 1977) and *New York Magazine* (Meskil 1977) revealing that Carmine Galente, a sixty-seven-year-old mob leader, was emerging as the new *capo di tutti capi*, "boss of bosses." Paul Meskil, an investigative reporter, stated that law-enforcement officials thought Galente's immediate goal was to bring all five New York crime Families under his direct control; according to these officials, he would succeed: "Soon, federal agents predict, Carmine Galente's peers on the Mafia Commission, will elect him boss of all bosses" (1977: 28). Lucinda Franks, a *New York Times* reporter, stated: "Officials say that Mr. Galente is moving to merge the five New York crime families under his own leadership and aims to become a national chieftain who would try to restore the Mafia to a position of power it has not held in at least 20 years" (1977: 34). Jerry Capeci (1978: 28), writing in *New York Magazine*, reported the *real* "godfather" to be Frank ("Funzi") Tieri, a seventy-four-year-old Brooklyn mob leader. He noted that Carmine ("Lilo") Galente was being proclaimed boss of all bosses as "the result of a well-planned 'leak' by the Drug Enforcement Administration of a 'confidential' report by its Unified Intelligence Division." Capeci added: "It now turns out that the report was based on quite old information and was leaked in self-interest by the drug agency." In any event, on July 12, 1979, while he was dining in a Brooklyn restaurant, three gunmen put an end to the would-be *capo di tutti capi*. Anthony Villano, an FBI agent for twenty-three years who specialized in organized crime, states that the bureau regularly "leaked" false reports to the press in order to stir up dissension among organized-crime figures. This is made possible by use of the journalistic convention known as "sources." David Shaw (1984: 57) argues: " 'Sources,' under the protective cloak of anonymity, are permitted to use the press for personal and political purposes—to grind axes, advance ambitions, attack rivals and mislead the public."

Peter Reuter and Jonathan Rubinstein (1978: 57) state:

> The difficulty the government had in obtaining accurate information on the reserves of energy-producing companies in the wake of the 1973 oil boycott should serve as a sober reminder of how difficult it is to collect accurate information even from legitimate organizations operating in a highly regulated environment. The challenges are immeasurably greater in collecting information about people who are consciously involved in illegal activities.

They report on a United States Department of Justice effort to determine the amount of illegal gambling revenues; the department frequently asserts that organized crime derives its major income from that source. After noting the totally unscientific basis for the estimate, Reuter and Rubinstein conclude: "In truth, we suspect that the real failing of the estimate was that no one really cared precisely how it was developed, but only that it produce a large number. The assumption that the details of the calculations would not be subjected to any scrutiny led to a cavalier use of the available data. Also, the estimate had no possible consequences; it was produced for rhetorical purposes and has served these purposes well" (1978: 62).

In 1974, a book by Martin Gosch and Richard Hammer purported to be *The Last Testament of Lucky Luciano* dictated by Luciano himself during the final months of his life. The book's introduction explains that in 1961 Luciano made a decision to provide the details of his life as a crime boss to Martin Gosch. According to the introduction, the syndicate, acting on orders from Meyer Lansky, vetoed a movie that Gosch was producing titled *The Lucky Luciano Story*. Luciano, who was living in exile in Italy, was to be technical advisor, and now he was angry. However, according to Gosch, who died of a heart attack before publication, Luciano extracted a promise that his autobiography not be published earlier than ten years after his death; he died in 1962. The book earned more than $1 million before it was even published, and paperback rights were auctioned for an additional $800,000 (Gage 1974: 1).

On December 17, 1974, in a front-page article, Nicholas Gage of the *New York Times* questioned the authenticity of the book by pointing to numerous errors of fact: "It is widely known that Mr. Gosch met on a number of occasions with Mr. Luciano on the aborted film project, and presumably the gangster recounted some of his experiences during these meetings. But contradictions and inaccuracies in the book raise questions to the claim that Mr. Luciano told his whole life to Mr. Gosch and that everything in the book attributed to Mr. Luciano actually came from him."

In 1981, Grossett and Dunlop published the story of a *Mafia Kingpin,* the autobiography of Sonny Gibson. Sonny claimed to have been an enforcer for the Chicago Outfit, but that is the least of his claims: he was sent to Sicily to be trained by the Mafia; executed twenty-four persons; ran 150 different corporations; threw nine prison guards over the wall. He appeared on national television, *Today, Tomorrow,* where he was taken seriously. Perhaps his interviewers were hoping for a private discussion of his wildest claim: sex with ten thousand different women.

The problem inherent in presenting an accurate history of organized crime is highlighted by a 1931 incident. On September 10, 1931, Salvatore Maranzano, the self-appointed boss of bosses, was killed by gunmen dispatched by Meyer Lansky and Benjamin ("Bugsy") Siegel at the request of Luciano—a historic event in interethnic cooperation. Donald Cressey (1969: 44) reports "On that day and the two days immediately following, some forty Italian-Sicilian gang leaders across the country lost their lives in battle." Fred Cook (1972: 107–108) refers to this episode as the "Purge of the Greasers" and states: "Within a few short hours, the old-time crime bosses who had been born and reared in Sicily and were mostly illiterate—the 'Mustache Petes' or 'the greasers,' as they were sometimes called—were liquidated by the new breed of Americanized, business-oriented gangsters of the Luciano-Costello-Adonis school." Cook adds: "Beginning on September 11th and lasting through the next day, some thirty to forty executions were performed across the nation. . . ." A special publication of *New York Magazine* (Plate 1972: 45) adds to the story: "During the bloodbath nearly 40 of the Old Guard were executed in various *ingenious ways*" (emphasis added). As late as 1978 this episode was being reported as *historical fact*—"the 'Night of the Sicilian Vespers,' so named because Luciano had not only engineered the slaughter of Salvatore Maranzano for the night of September 10, 1931, but had gone ahead and wiped out 40 of the 'Mustache Petes' across the country." This last quotation is from Jerry Capeci (1978: 26), the journalist for *New York Magazine* who would not be "duped" by the Drug Enforcement Administration.

Alan Block (1978: 460) surveyed newspapers in eight major cities, beginning with issues two weeks prior to Maranzano's murder and ending two weeks after, looking for any stories of gangland murders that could be connected, even remotely, with the Maranzano case. He reports: "While I found various accounts of the Maranzano murder, I could locate only three other murders that might have been connected." As he notes, three murders do not constitute a nationwide purge.

The remainder of this chapter contains a history of organized crime that represents a summary of the best available literature on the topic. When the literature conflicts, the divergence of opinion will be noted. Otherwise, the material will be presented as "history," although we have already seen the weaknesses inherent in much that passes for the history of organized crime. *Caveat emptor.*

Organized Crime:
Patterns of
Evolution

Used by permission of Historical Pictures Service, Chicago

Gus Tyler (1962: 89) notes that organized crime in America "is the product of an evolutionary process extending more than a century." He points out that the roots of organized crime can be found in such cities as New York and Chicago decades before Prohibition. Our historical analysis will focus on these two cities, since only in the cases of New York and Chicago do we find information sufficient for such a study (Albini 1971: 177).

Machine Politics

In both cities we see a similar pattern. The saloon keeper, gambling-house operator, and politician were often the same person. The saloon was a center of neighborhood activity, an important social base for political activity, and saloon keepers became political powers in both cities. Larry Englemann (1979: 4) points out:

> . . . part of the appeal of the saloon was due to the social services it provided. In saloons files of newspapers in several languages were available along with cigars, mail boxes for regular patrons, free pencils, paper, and mail services to those wishing to send letters, and information on employment. Saloons provided a warm fire in the winter, public toilets, bowling alleys, billiard tables, music, singing, dancing, constant conversation, charity and charge accounts, quiet corners for students, and special rooms for weddings, union meetings, or celebrations. No other institution provided such a variety of necessary services to the public.

The saloon keeper was in a position to deliver the votes of the district (New York) or ward (Chicago), often with the help of the street gangs that proliferated in the ghetto areas. The politicians employed the gangs for such legitimate purposes as distributing campaign literature, hanging posters, canvassing for votes; they were also used as "repeaters" who voted early and often, and as sluggers who attacked rival campaign workers and intimidated voters. The "ward heeler," however, was usually a popular figure who in the days before social-welfare programs provided important services to loyal constituents—jobs, food, assistance with public agencies, including the police and the courts. All that he asked in return were votes and a free hand to become wealthy in politics. To the impoverished and powerless ghetto dweller, this was a small price to pay for services that would otherwise not be available.

Robert Merton (1967: 128) states:

> The political machine does not regard the electorate as an amorphous, undifferentiated mass of voters. With keen sociological intuition, the machine recognizes

that the voter is a person living in a specific neighborhood, with specific personal problems and personal wants. Public issues are abstract and remote; private problems are extremely concrete and immediate. It is not through the generalized appeal to large public concerns that the machine operates, but through the direct quasi-feudal relationships between local representatives of the machine and voters in their neighborhood.

The very personal nature of the machine is highlighted by one day in the life of George Washington Plunkitt, a Tammany district leader at the turn of the century who died a wealthy man in 1924 at the age of eighty-two (Riordon 1963: 91–93):

2 A.M. Aroused from sleep by ringing of his doorbell; went to the door and found a bartender, who asked him to go to the police station and bail out a saloon keeper who had been arrested for violating the excise law. Furnished bail and returned to bed at three o'clock.

6 A.M. Awakened by fire engines passing his house. Hastened to the scene of the fire, according to the custom of the Tammany district leaders, to give assistance to the fire sufferers, if needed. Met several of his election district captains who are always under orders to look out for fires, which are considered great vote-getters. Found several tenants who had been burned out, took them to a hotel, supplied them with clothes, fed them, and arranged temporary quarters for them until they could rent and furnish new quarters.

8:30 A.M. Went to the police court to look after his constituents. Found six "drunks." Secured the discharge of four by a timely word with the judge, and paid the fines of two.

9 A.M. Appeared in the Municipal District Court. Directed one of his district captains to act as counsel for a widow against whom dispossess proceedings had been instituted and obtained an extension of time. Paid the rent of a poor family about to be dispossessed and gave them a dollar for food.

11 A.M. At home again. Found four men waiting for him. One had been discharged by the . . . for neglect of duty, and wanted the district leader to fix things. Another wanted a job . . . The third sought a place on the Subway and the fourth . . . was looking for work . . . The district leader spent nearly three hours fixing things for the four men, and succeeded in each case.

3 P.M. Attended the funeral of an Italian . . . Hurried back to make his appearance at the funeral of a Hebrew constituent . . . and later attended the Hebrew confirmation ceremonies in the synagogue.

7 P.M. Went to the district headquarters and presided over a meeting of election district captains. . . .

8 P.M. Went to a church fair. . . .

9 P.M. At the clubhouse again. . . . Listened to the complaints of a dozen pushcart peddlers who said they were persecuted by the police and assured them he would go to Police Headquarters. . . .

10:30 P.M. Attended a Hebrew wedding. . . . Had previously sent a handsome wedding present to the bride.

12 P.M. In bed.

If this were not enough to tie the immigrant to the political machine, rampant nativism often precluded any other alternative. The president of the

National Association of Manufacturers referred to an "unrestricted invasion of our national household by foreign hordes, many of whom have brought and kept inferior moral and political conceptions, ideals and habits" (Grant and Davison 1930: 5). From the Carnegie Institution came a condemnation of the American policy of admitting "cheaper" stocks: "We must expect the ever-broadening appreciation of the value of hereditary quality to support henceforth the policy of limited and selected immigration" (Grant and Davison 1930: 53); while the president of the American Museum of Natural History warned *native* Americans "of the threat to American institutions by the influx of alien elements of population with alien ideas and ideals in the principles of self-government." In an attack on machine politics he pointed to "what is going on in our large cities in which the original American element has entirely lost control and the alien or foreign-born element is in absolute power. . . ." (Grant and Davison 1930: 208).

Harold Gosnell highlights the interdependence of machine politics and gangsters. He notes that the immunity that gangsters receive is dependent on the money and votes they deliver (1977: 42; originally published in 1937):

> Not only are the contributions from the underworld interests an important item in the campaign funds of the dominant party, but the services of the underworld personnel are also significant. When word is passed down from gangster chiefs, all proprietors of gambling houses and speak-easies, all burglars, pick-pockets, pimps, fences, and their like, are whipped into line. In themselves they constitute a large block of votes, and they frequently augment their value to the machine by corrupt election practices.

In return for "delivering the vote," the ward/district boss was rewarded with patronage and recognized as lord of his area in a system that resembled feudalism. He appointed, directly or indirectly, police officials in his area; thus he was in a position to protect vice activity (gambling, prostitution, liquor-law violations) which he "licensed." M. R. Werner (1928: 293–94) reports about New York:

> In each district of the City saloon keepers, owners of houses of prostitution, grocers who wanted to obstruct sidewalks, builders who wanted to violate the building regulations of the City, paid tribute at election time to the district leaders, who turned the money over to the general campaign fund of Tammany Hall. The organization collected not only from those who wished to violate laws, but also from those who wished to live peacefully without having the windows of their shops smashed by the district leader's gang, or without being unnecessarily molested by the police.

Reform Politics

In New York and Chicago we see a pattern of corruption-reform-corruption-reform, often interspersed with investigations and widely reported hearings. It is important to recognize the political motivation, and a not insignificant degree of hypocrisy, behind many of these exposés. In New York, investigations were often initiated by upstate, rural, Protestant Republicans against downstate (New York City), urban, Catholic, and Jewish Democrats. The Republicans were able to dominate many state legislatures by gerrymandering districts in a most outrageous manner—a practice eventually declared unconstitutional by the United States Supreme Court in the 1962 landmark "one-man, one-vote" decision (*Baker* v. *Carr*). The threat of investigation and public disclosure was used to secure the support of city politicians for legislation favored by more rural interests. Corruption was real and often rampant, but many of the efforts purporting to deal with it were just as corrupt, morally if not legally.

This is exemplified by legislation passed as a result of the efforts of New York governor Charles Evans Hughes—it banned betting on horses and book-making. In 1909, the law was vigorously enforced during the metropolitan racing season, that is, when horses ran in the New York City area. In Saratoga, a Republican stronghold just north of Albany, gambling continued unabated; the racetrack was big business and an important tourist attraction (Katcher 1959). Historically, in New York and Illinois, the urban masses had to place their bets illegally with a bookmaker, while their more affluent brethren enjoyed the "sport of kings" in the sunshine of the great outdoors, at the racetrack where they could bet legally.

Even so-called reform mayors showed not an inconsiderable amount of hypocrisy. New York's Mayor Fiorello La Guardia ("The Little Flower") moved vigorously against gangster Frank Costello, a Democratic stalwart, but did not bother racketeers in East Harlem where his Republican protege, congressman Vito Marcantonio, held sway. In Brooklyn, Joe Adonis (born Giuseppe Doto) was equally untouchable until 1937, when he switched his support to La Guardia's opponent. The Little Flower had the police drive him out of New York, and Adonis stayed in New Jersey until 1945, the year La Guardia's term ended (Repetto 1978). Enoch J. ("Nucky") Johnson, the racketeer overlord of Atlantic City, New Jersey, was a Republican stalwart. As such, he avoided prosecution until Democrat Franklin Roosevelt became president, at which time Johnson was convicted and imprisoned for income-tax evasion. (Treasury agents counted the number of towels sent to the laundry from local brothels. They were thus able to determine the number of customers and hence Johnson's estimated income (Repetto 1978). The tax weapon was used freely against Roosevelt's political enemies such as Johnson, Tom Pendergast of Kansas City, James Michael Curley of Boston, and Huey Long of Louisiana. Friendly politicians such as Frank Hague of Jersey City and Chicago's Edward J. Kelly escaped criminal sanctions.

It must be noted that New York and Chicago were not just isolated cases. In New Orleans, for example, Thomas C. Anderson was the saloon-keeper political boss of the Fourth Ward. He was a two-term member of the state legislature and the proprietor of several bordellos. Herbert Asbury (1936) reports that when Prohibition arrived, instead of investing in bootlegging and speakeasies, Anderson went into the oil business, prospered, and was eventually bought out by Standard Oil. In Kansas City, Missouri, James Pendergast began his political career as a saloon keeper. He became a dominant power in the First Ward, and his ability to "deliver the votes" enabled him to provide police protection to organized gambling. The police acted on his behalf, forcing independent operators to join a gambling combine or get out of the business. Lyle Dorsett (1968) reports that between 1900 and 1902, Pendergast named 123 of the 173 policemen on the Kansas City force. The Pendergast machine, under brother Tom, received the support of the gang bosses, and they in return secured police protection. James Henry ("Blackie") Audett, a professional armed robber, reports that he received protection while living and working in Kansas City from John Lazia, a gangster and part of the Pendergast organization. In return, Audett looked up vacant lots (1954: 120):

> I looked them up, precinct by precinct, and turned them lists in to Mr. Pendergast—that's Tom Pendergast, the man who used to run Kansas City back in them days. When we got a precinct all surveyed out, we would give addresses to them vacant lots. Then we would take the addresses and assign them to people we could depend on—prostitutes, thieves, floaters, anybody we could get on the voting registration books. On election days we just hauled these people to the right places and they went in and voted—in the right places.

Prohibition

Prohibition changed the relationship among the politicians, vice operators, and gang leaders. Before 1920, the ward boss acted as a patron for the vice entrepreneurs and the gangs. He protected them from law enforcement, and they assisted him with financial and electoral support. The (usually Irish) ward boss was at the top of an unofficial structure that below him included Jewish and Italian vice operators and gang leaders—the latter were clearly at the bottom. Prohibition, however, unleashed an unsurpassed level of criminal violence, and violence is the specialty of the gangs. Physical protection from rival organizations was suddenly more important than protection from law enforcement. Andy Logan (1970) notes that Prohibition turned gangs into empires. The *New York Times* ("Schultz Product of the Dry Law Era," January 22, 1933: 23) noted the transition made by Arthur Flegenheimer, better known as "Dutch Schultz." In 1919 he was a street thug sentenced to imprisonment for unlawful entry; by 1933, he was "a wealthy man with widespread interests." Schultz had become the "beer baron" of the Bronx, owner of speakeasies, a bail-bond business, and an architectural firm. At the beginning of Prohibition, Schultz worked for Otto Gass, who went from the trucking business into the beer business. In 1928, Schultz became a partner with Joe Noe when they became owners of a Bronx speakeasy. They soon bought trucks and garages and became major beer distributors, aided by a vicious crew of gunmen including John T. Nolan ("Legs Diamond"), the Weinberg brothers, Bo and George, and the Coll brothers, Vincent ("Mad Dog") and Peter. Next they began to expand into the territory of rival beer businesses. In the case of Joe Rock, the Schultz gang kidnapped him, beat him severely, hung him by his thumbs, and eventually blinded him—a message that was not lost on other recalcitrant beer distributors.

Herbert Packer (1968: 263) reminds us that people do not necessarily respond to new criminal prohibitions by acquiescence. He points out that resistance can be fatal to the new norm, and moreover, when this happens, "the effect is not confined to the immediate proscription but makes itself felt in the attitude that people take toward legal proscriptions in general." Thus, primary resistance or opposition to a new law such as Prohibition can result, secondarily, in disregard for laws in general: *negative contagion*. Andrew Sinclair (1962: 282) notes what occurred during Prohibition: "A general tolerance of the bootlegger and a disrespect for federal law were translated into a widespread contempt for the processes and duties of democracy."

The Eighteenth Amendment to the Constitution was ratified by the thirty-sixth state, Nebraska, on January 16, 1919. Subsequently, it was ratified by an additional ten states. According to its own terms, the Eighteenth Amendment became effective on January 16, 1920:

> *Section 1.* After one year from the ratification of this article the manufacture, sale, or transportation of intoxicating liquors within, the importation thereof into, or the exportation thereof from the United States and all territory subject to the jurisdiction thereof for beverage purposes is hereby prohibited.
>
> *Section 2.* The Congress and the several States shall have concurrent power to enforce this article by appropriate legislation.
>
> *Section 3.* This article shall be inoperative unless it shall have been ratified as an amendment to the Constitution by the legislatures of the several states, as provided in the Constitution, within seven years from the date of the submission hereof to the States by Congress [December 18, 1917].

Ten months after ratification, over a veto by President Woodrow Wilson, Congress passed the National Prohibition Act, usually referred to as the Volstead Act after its sponsor, Congressman Andrew Volstead of Minnesota. The Volstead Act strengthened the language of the amendment and provided for federal enforcement; the Prohibition Bureau, an arm of the Treasury Department, was created. The bureau soon became notorious for employing agents on the basis of political patronage, persons who were untrained and often unfit. In addition to being inept and corrupt, they ran up a record of being killed (by 1923 thirty had been murdered) and for killing hundreds of civilians, often innocent women and children. The bureau was viewed as a training school for bootleggers because agents frequently left the service to join their wealthy adversaries. The Treasury Department was headed by Secretary Andrew Mellon, a man who had millions invested in the liquor trade before Prohibition and was not interested in enforcing the new laws (Sinclair 1962).

In the ninety days preceding the date when the Eighteenth Amendment became effective, $500,000 of bonded whiskey was stolen from government warehouses, and afterwards it continued to disappear (Sinclair 1962). Thomas Coffey (1975) reports that less than one hour after Prohibition went into effect, six armed men robbed $100,000 worth of whiskey from two Chicago boxcars (1975). He notes that in February of 1920, a case of whiskey purchased in Montreal for ten dollars could easily be sold in New York City for eighty dollars. In fact, the Canadians began making so much money from American Prohibition that provinces with similar laws soon repealed them (Sinclair 1962).

William Chambliss (1973: 10) states that Prohibition was accomplished by the political efforts of an economically declining segment of the American middle class: "By effort and some good luck this class was able to impose its will on the majority of the population through rather dramatic changes in the law." Sinclair (1962: 163) states: "In fact, national prohibition was a measure passed by village America against urban America." We could add: much of Protestant America against Catholic (and, to a lesser extent, Jewish) America. "Thousands of Protestant churches held thanksgiving prayer meetings. To many of the people who attended, prohibition represented the triumph of America's towns and rural districts over the sinful cities" (Coffey 1975: 7).

While America had organized crime before Prohibition, it "was intimately associated with shabby local politics and corrupt police forces"; there was not organized-crime activity "in the syndicate style" (King 1969: 23). The "Great Experiment" provided a catalyst of opportunity that caused organized crime, especially violent forms, to blossom into an important force in American society.

Prohibition acted as a catalyst for the mobilization of criminal elements in an unprecedented manner. Pre-Prohibition crime, insofar as it was organized, centered around corrupt political machines, vice entrepreneurs, and, at the bottom, gangs. Prohibition unleashed an unparalleled level of competitive criminal violence and changed the order—the gang leaders emerged on top.

Prohibition also encouraged cooperation between gang leaders from various regions. A number of meetings between important OC figures have been documented (Nelli 1976: 212):

> Meetings were held for a number of reasons—to settle disputes, choose successors for slain or deposed leaders, divide local or regional markets, or discuss production, supply, and distribution problems. Some gatherings consisted of Italian criminals and limited their discussions to problems of interest to them. Others involved only Jews or Irish or some other ethnic group; still others were formed of members of a variety of ethnic syndicates.

One of the more important meetings took place in Atlantic City on May 13–16, 1929, and was hosted by Knucky Johnson, criminal boss of that New Jersey city. The New York delegates included Luciano, Costello, Lansky, Schultz, and Torrio; Chicago luminaries included Capone, Guzik, Nitti, McErlane, and Saltis; from Philadelphia, Max ("Boo Boo") Hoff, Sam Lazar, and Charles Schwartz. This conference, among other items, is reported to have dealt with the excessive violence of the Capone organization. It was on the way back from this meeting that Capone stopped off in Philadelphia to be arrested (Nelli 1976; Kobler 1971).

The End of Prohibition

With the repeal of Prohibition and the onset of the Depression, the financial base of organized crime narrowed considerably.[1] Many "players" dropped out; some went into legitimate enterprises or employment; others drifted into conventional criminal activity. Bootlegging required trucks, drivers, maintenance personnel, garages and warehouses, bookkeepers and lawyers—skills and assets that could be converted to noncriminal endeavors. For those who remained in the "business," reorganization was necessary.

Burton Turkus (with Feder, 1951: 99) reports that in 1934 the major leaders of OC in the East gathered at a New York hotel with Johnny Torrio presiding, and they came to an understanding:

> Each boss remained czar in his own territory, his rackets unmolested, his local authority uncontested. In murder, no one—local or imported—could be killed in his territory without his approval. He would have the right to do the job himself or permit an outsider to come in—but only at his invitation. In fact, no lawlessness, on an organized scale could take place in his domain without his sanction and entire consent, unless he was overruled by the board of governors. . . .
>
> Each mob leader now had behind him not just his own hoods, but a powerful amalgamation of all hoods. Every gang chieftain was guaranteed against being interfered with in his own area—and against being killed by a rival mobster.

Furthermore, Turkus states (1951: 99):

> The Brooklyn stoolpigeons told us a second meeting was called in Kansas City, to hear from the Western executives. The Capone crowd from Chicago and the Kansas City mob liked the idea. Reports came from Cleveland and Detroit that the Mayfield Gang and the Purple Mob wanted in. Boston and Miami, New Orleans and Baltimore, St. Paul and St. Louis—all flocked to the confederacy of crime, until it was nationwide.

Hank Messick (1967: 141-42) reports:

> The country was divided into territories. Wars ended between regional groups, between religious groups, between national groups. Meyer Lansky was assigned Florida and the Caribbean. His partner, Bugsy Siegel, got the Far West, including

Nevada. The Eastern Syndicate came into being along the Atlantic coast, and assignments were made according to racket as well as geography. . . .

Broadly speaking, the Cleveland Syndicate (Sam Tucker, Moe Dalitz, Ben Rothkopf) obtained the Middle West—outside of Illinois, of course, where the successor of Al Capone held sway.

These rules remained "in force" until the end of World War II.

---

[1]Prohibition ended with the repeal of the Eighteenth Amendment on December 5, 1933.

chapter 8

Organized Crime in New York

Used by permission of UPI/Bettmann Newsphotos

In 1790, a group of white men decked out in feathers and bucks' tails sat cross-legged in wigwams pitched along the Hudson River. They were there at the request of President George Washington to "smoke the peace pipe" with a delegation of Creek Indians. The white men were members of the Society of Saint Tammany; the Creek Indians had been attacking American settlements in Georgia and Florida. For several days the Creek delegation was treated to banquets, concerts, theater, and the wonders of Tammany's New York. The result was a peace treaty that was transmitted to President Washington. Beginning as a fraternal and patriotic society in 1789, Tammany soon emerged as a full-fledged political organization whose leader, Martin Van Buren, was elected the eighth president of the United States in 1836 (Connable and Silberfarb 1967). It became synonymous with the Democratic Party of New York City.

Tammany established a system of district leaders and precinct captains in each Assembly district and by 1838 had a reputation for dispensing favors and social services from funds extorted from vice operators and 6 percent kickbacks from all city employees. The tie-in between criminals and politicians was now firmly established.

During the late 1840s and early 1850s, large numbers of immigrants fled the famine in Ireland for New York. Despite nativist and anti-Catholic sentiment in the Tammany society, the Irish rose quickly to leadership positions there. By the turn of the century, the Irish clearly dominated "The Hall." (The Irish immigrant spoke English and was at home in a saloon, and his willingness to engage in fisticuffs made him a "natural" for the politics of that period.)

From the mid-1800s until World War II, old-style gangs were an important feature of the Tammany-criminal tie-in. By the 1920s, when they were disappearing, the *New York Times* (September 9, 1923) could wax nostalgic about the "old breed" of gang with its twisted sense of valor, as compared with the current (1923) gang style with "the calculation and efficiency of an industrial tool for breaking strikes or wrecking factories" ("New Gang Methods Replace Those of Eastman's Days," Section 9: 3). The *Times* was referring to the demise of the Shirt Tails, Dead Rabbits, Plug Uglies, Bowery Boys, Hudson Dusters, Cherry Hill Gang, Gophers, Five Pointers, and Whyos. The last gang used printed price lists for mayhem commissions, e.g., punching, $2, leg or arm broken, $19, murder, $100 and up (Asbury 1928). Before he left for Chicago, Al Capone was a member of the Five Points Gang, as was Lucky Luciano. These gangs were used by the politicians as "repeaters" and "sluggers," a situation that led the notorious, apelike gang leader Monk Eastman (born Edward Osterman) to utter: "Say, I cut some ice in this town. Why, I make half the big politicians" ("New Gang Methods. . ."). Andy Logan notes that gangs such as the Whyos were so useful on election day that the politicians made natural alliances with them (1970: 56): "To keep gang members in funds between elections, the politicians found jobs for them in the off-season months." They worked as lookouts, steerers, and bouncers—resident thugs for the gambling houses and brothels.

In contrast, on November 8, 1909, when the gangs were at their height, the *New York Times* decried their use for "hired mayhem" and murder, and pointed to their election-day "specialties" as particularly sinister (White 1908). Herbert Asbury (1928) noted that early in the twentieth century several gangs operated with protection from Tammany, and they controlled various city neighborhoods.

One of the more infamous was the Five Points Gang which had 1,500 members and was led by Paul Kelly (born Paolo Vaccarelli), an ex-pugilist. Kelly eventually left the mayhem of lower Manhattan for Harlem, where he founded the Harlem Branch of the Paul Kelly Association. He became a labor organizer and, with the help of some of his Five Pointers, a vice-president of the International Longshoremen's Association. One of the highlights of New York gang history is the feud between Kelly and his Italian Five Points Gang and the Jewish gang led by Monk Eastman over a small piece of Manhattan real estate that each claimed as its "turf." When their political patrons insisted that they cease the bloodshed, Kelly and Eastman fought it out in a fracas that lasted two hours and ended in a draw.

Eastman was eventually imprisoned, and after his release he served with distinction in the First World War. During that time his gang faded, but Eastman received a full pardon from Gov. Alfred E. Smith for his outstanding military service. Eastman was shot to death by an old crony after a petty quarrel that followed a Christmas Eve drinking bout. The friend, a federal Prohibition agent, received a three-to-ten-year sentence by claiming self-defense—he thought the unarmed Monk was reaching for a gun (Lee 1963).

During this same period, from the mid-nineteenth century through World War I, gang activity and political activity were well coordinated. In Manhattan, organized criminal activities were presided over by a three-man board: a representative of Tammany Hall, a police member, and Frank Farrell, the bookmaking czar who represented gambling interests. Logan (1970) points out that during the years prior to the First World War, the New York City Police Department was more or less a branch of Tammany; indeed, to secure a job as a policeman, a fee of $250 to Tammany was required, and promotions were handled in the same manner. The police not only tended to be corrupt but were also brutal toward the poor and helpless, as the story of Alexander ("Clubber") Williams highlights. This vicious and corrupt officer, who rose to the high rank of inspector, told his recruits: "Boys, there's more justice in the end of this nightstick than there is in all the courts in the land" (Logan 1970: 106). For $15,000 he effected a transfer to the midtown Manhattan area where lucrative graft was available from gambling establishments and brothels, and Williams informed a newspaper reporter: "I've had nothin' but chuck steak for a long time, and now I am going to get a little of the tenderloin" (Connable and Goldfarb 1967: 215), as this Manhattan section soon became known. Williams was eventually dismissed from the force by New York City Police Commissioner Theodore Roosevelt (Logan 1970).

Leo Katcher (1959) points out that at this time, prior to the First World War, gangsters were merely errand boys for the politicians and the gamblers; they were at the bottom of the heap. The gamblers were under the politicians, who were "kings." Gambling in Manhattan was "licensed" by Tammany state senator Timothy Sullivan with the support of Police Chief "Big Bill" Devery. When Devery's post was abolished by the state legislature, Sullivan notified the city Democratic leader, "Boss" Richard Croker of Tammany Hall, that unless Devery was reappointed to head the police, "ten thousand gamblers in the Sullivan-Devery syndicate would make no further campaign contributions to Tammany" (Connable and Silberfarb 1967: 224). Devery was reappointed to head the police department. When a Tammany alderman, Paddy Divver, opposed brothels in his district, Sullivan organized a primary election fight against him. With Tom Foley as his candidate, Sullivan sent in the Kelly and Eastman gangs to beat and intimidate Divver voters; Foley won by a margin of three-to-one (Connable and Silberfarb, 1967).

In addition to the likes of Monk Eastman and Paul Kelly, Sullivan used Charles Becker, a New York City police lieutenant in charge of Special (Vice) Squad No. 1, to "muscle" uncooperative gamblers. Sullivan eventually became insane, was committed, escaped, and died on some railroad tracks in Westchester County, New York, in 1912. In 1911, while Sullivan was ill, Lieutenant Becker moved to take over. This move was thwarted on July 5, 1912, the day Herman ("Beansy") Rosenthal was murdered. Rosenthal was a well-known gambler and an associate of Sullivan. When his gambling establishment was raided by the ambitious Becker, Rosenthal went to the newspapers and implicated Becker as his gambling partner; he claimed the raid was a double-cross. This brazen violation of the "code of silence" resulted in the inevitable—Rosenthal's murder. The four gunmen, Harry ("Gyp the Blood") Horowitz, Louis ("Lefty Louie") Rosenberg, Jacob ("Whitey Lewis") Seidenshner, and Frank ("Dago Frank") Cirofici, were convicted and electrocuted ("Conviction of Becker" 1913). Becker was convicted of ordering the murder and became the only American policeman ever to be put to death by the state. (Logan concludes that Becker was framed.)

Charles Murphy, a former saloon keeper, became Tammany boss in 1902, replacing Richard Croker. He remained in the position until his death twenty-two years later. Murphy changed Tammany operations: open gambling and prostitution were ended; total immunity for gangsters was withdrawn. He also moved to cut down the power of the police who, like Charles Becker, had occasionally challenged the politicians (Katcher 1959). Murphy "concluded that the use of the police as major graft collectors was an antiquated concept"

(Logan 1970: 340). Modern organization was needed—a conduit between the politicians and the gamblers, who would be organized into a dues-paying trade association as were the brothel owners. Organized crime began to evolve; Jewish OC in general and Arnold Rothstein in particular were major agents of change.

Jewish Organized Crime in New York

At the turn of the century, the Irish still comprised the dominant force in Tammany Hall. But in the "outside work"—organizing gamblers and brothels at one remove from "The Hall"—Jews began to gain a niche. They helped not only to rationalize illicit activities but to provide a conduit between local crime personnel and the politicians who were so interested in their activities. Among these Jewish OC operatives, Arnold Rothstein was most important, as organizer and innovator.

Arnold Rothstein

The spectre of Arnold Rothstein looms so large over organized crime in New York that it would not be much of an exaggeration to call him its "Godfather." Jenna Weissman Joselit (1983: 143–44) states:

> Rothstein transformed criminal activity from a haphazard, often spontaneous endeavor into one whose hallmarks—specialized expertise, administrative hierarchy, and organizational procedure—correspond to the classic sociological model of a bureaucracy. Thus, Rothstein's illegal business had a definite administrative structure based on specific skills; competence and not ethnic pedigree determined one's rank and, of course, one's position, in his outfit.
>
> . . . Rothstein's office, . . . in the middle of the midtown business district, employed a staff comparable with that of any large (and legitimate) commercial firm, replete with secretaries, bookkeepers, and legal counsel. . . . A decision to enter some new illegal venture tended to be based not on personal motives of revenge or power but on strictly commercial considerations: the amount of profit to be made and the length of time it would take to make it. Finally, by investing the money he earned through illegal channels into legal enterprises such as real estate and the theater, Rothstein made it difficult to ascertain where the illegal enterprise left off and the legitimate one began.

"A.R.," or "The Brain," as Damon Runyon called him, was born in New York in 1882 and served as the inspiration for Meyer Wolfsheim in F. Scott Fitzgerald's *The Great Gatsby* and for Nathan Detroit in the musical *Guys and Dolls*. His father, an Orthodox Jew born of immigrant parents, was a respected and successful businessman. Arnold Rothstein was also respected and quite successful, but his "business" comprised gambling, bootlegging, drug smuggling, labor racketeering, etc. (Katcher 1959).

The young Rothstein worked in poolrooms and became a "shark," an expert billiard player.[1] The money he earned was used for usurious loans, and Monk Eastman was employed as a collector. Rothstein would later employ Waxey Gordon (born Irving Wexler), the Diamond brothers, "Legs" and Eddie, and other important hoodlums of the day. Rothstein began running dice games and became a bookmaker and the owner of a gambling house. He was associated with "Big Tim" Sullivan, which afforded him political police protection. He became the "bookmaker's bookmaker" in 1914, handling "layoff" bets from other bookmakers. He contracted a crew of thugs for unions, using a gang led by Jacob ("Little Augie") Orgen, who employed, among other prominent hoodlums, Louis ("Lepke") Buchalter and Jacob ("Gurrah") Shapiro. Eventually, Rothstein went into the bail-bond business, insurance, and real estate (Katcher 1959).

Rothstein also fenced stolen bonds and securities, and when Prohibition arrived he organized the importation of liquor from England and Canada. At the same time, he had diamonds and drugs, heroin and cocaine, smuggled in on his whiskey ships, and Rothstein established an international drug-smuggling network. His buyers overseas shipped the drugs into the United States, where they were distributed to organizations in several states: to Torrio and Capone in Chicago; Harry Stromberg ("Nig Rosen") in Philadelphia; Charles ("King") Solomon in Boston; and to Luciano and Buchalter in New York.

His power was enormous, as this pre-Prohibition incident illustrates. Rothstein, who had never been convicted of a crime, was overseeing one of his floating dice game operations when a police raid was announced. Incredulous that in 1919 the police would raid one of *his* games, and fearing a ruse by robbers, Rothstein opened fire, wounding several policemen. The actual evidence against Rothstein was not very strong, but the case was pursued by Inspector Dominick Henry, an honest police officer working for anti-Tammany Mayor John F. Hylan. The grand jury reviewed the evidence but failed to indict Rothstein—they indicted Inspector Henry instead for perjury. Needless to say, (even honest) policemen became rather reluctant to tangle with A. R. (Katcher 1959).

Rothstein continued to play the role of a broker or "middleman," not only between the politicians and the gamblers but between two of New York's political-crime factions. One faction was headed by James J. Hines, a Tammany renegade with ties to Ownie ("Killer") Madden, Dutch Schultz, Bill Dwyer, Vannie Higgens and Larry Fay—important non-Italian gangsters. The other faction was headed by Albert C. Marinelli, a port warden and Tammany stalwart with ties to mainly Italian gangsters: Joe ("The Boss") Masseria, Lucky Luciano, Frankie Yale, Frank Costello, and Albert Anastasia (Katcher 1959). Alfred Connable and Edward Silberfarb (1967) report that during Prohibition, nearly half of the Tammany Democratic clubs were controlled by gangsters. Rothstein was tied to both factions and did favors for both sides—pistol permits, bail bonds, fencing of stolen merchandise, financing illegal operations, etc. (Katcher 1959). Rothstein is perhaps best remembered by the general public for his alleged involvement in the "Black Sox Scandal," the fixing of the 1919 World Series.

On Sunday night, November 4, 1928, Arnold Rothstein was found staggering in the service entrance of the Park Central Hotel, where he resided; he had been shot once in the abdomen with a small-caliber gun. Rothstein died without naming the person who shot him, and the murder was never solved. It has been attributed to Rothstein's refusal to pay a gambling debt in excess of $300,000—he maintained that the card game was rigged ("Gamblers Hunted in Rothstein Attack" 1928). After his death, federal officials opened many of his safes and files. Papers found in his apartment linked Rothstein to what Charles H. Tuttle, the United States attorney, called "the largest drug ring in the United States" ("Unger Indicted in Drug Conspiracy" 1928: 1; see also "$4,000,000 Narcotics Seized Here, Traced to Rothstein Ring" 1928). Tuttle, in 1930, became the Republican candidate for governor of New York. He lost to Franklin Delano Roosevelt primarily because of the issue of Prohibition (Sinclair 1962). Rothstein left a public estate appraised at $1,757,572; his hidden assets, of course, are not known (S. Smith 1963).

Dutch Schultz

By the time of Prohibition, most important gangsters were Jewish and Italian, though there were Irish criminals involved in bootlegging and related activities (for example, Bill Dwyer). Arthur Flegenheimer, better known as Dutch Schultz, was the "Beer Baron" of the Bronx, and his territory extended well into Manhattan. While Prohibition was in full swing, important gangsters did not pay attention to the numbers (illegal lottery), often referring to it as "nigger pool." With Prohibition on the way out, Schultz began searching for new areas of profit. His attorney, Dixie Davis, also represented some numbers operators, and he engineered Schultz's takeover of the business in Harlem from independent black, Hispanic, and some white numbers bankers. Schultz was able to offer political and physical protection as well as financing—several operators had had a run of costly bad luck. Eventually, the operators were reduced to being employees of the Schultz organization (Sann 1971). Schultz also moved into labor racketeering, and on January 31, 1934, the *New York Times* reported an alliance between officials of the restaurant workers union and the Schultz organization—employees and employers paid for "protection" ("Gang Linked to Union Charged at Trial").

In 1931, the Coll brothers, Schultz gunmen, rebelled and began killing off the Dutchman's drivers and payoff men: the "band of killers would wake the Schultz employees in their homes at the dead of night and kill them in their own bedrooms" (Berger 1935: 17). In a five-month period in 1931, seven Schultz men were murdered ("Schultz Aid Slain; 7th in Five Months" 1931). Schultz responded by placing a $50,000 contract on Coll and began to return the gunplay ("Woman, 2 Men, Slain as Gang Raids Home in Coll Feud" 1932: 1). It was during this feud that Vincent Coll received his nickname, "Mad Dog." His men opened fire at a leader of the Schultz organization, Joe Rao, who was standing in the street near a group of playing children. Rao escaped injury, but a five-year-old child was killed, and four other children lay on the ground wounded. Coll was arrested as one of the shooters, but his attorney, Samuel J. Leibowitz, who later became a New York State supreme court judge, disclosed that the witness to the shooting had a criminal record and a history of providing false testimony. Coll went free (O'Connor 1958).

Another important Prohibition figure would soon play a role in the Schultz-Coll feud. Owen ("Ownie the Killer") Madden was born in England and began his career in crime as the head of the Gophers, a notorious and widely feared gang that controlled the area of Manhattan appropriately named "Hell's Kitchen." In 1915, Madden was sentenced to Sing Sing Prison for ordering the murder of one of his rivals. In 1923 he was paroled and became a partner with George Jean ("Big Frenchy") de Mange, a bootlegger and speakeasy owner who saw the need for the services that Madden and his Hell's Kitchen stalwarts could provide (O'Connor 1958). Madden became a millionaire during Prohibition, and he continued his operations until 1932, when he was arrested for parole violation and returned to prison. A year later he was paroled again and retired to Hot Springs, Arkansas. There he married and lived out his days in comfort. On April 24, 1965, the front page of the *New York Times* reported that Madden, an "ex-gangster" who had given big contributions to charity, had died of chronic emphysema.

In need of money to help finance his campaign against Shultz, Coll kidnapped de Mange and demanded ransom from Madden, who turned over $35,000 for "Big Frenchy's" return. Coll then tried to extort some money from Madden by threatening to kidnap him. The outraged Madden joined forces with Schultz in an all-out war against Coll. They divided the city into zones and dispatched their gunmen to find the "Mad Dog." In the interim, Madden fled to Florida, while Schultz barricaded himself in a bordello surrounded by bodyguards. In the end, one of Coll's bodyguards "fingered" him for Schultz. On January 8, 1932, Coll stepped into a drugstore phone booth and made a call. As he was busy on the telephone his bodyguard discretely left, and two men entered; one carried a Thompson submachine ("tommy") gun. They ordered the customers to remain calm, and several bursts of machine-gun fire entered the phone booth; Coll was almost cut in half by the barrage (O'Connor 1958).

With Coll out of the way, Schultz began to expand into midtown Manhattan until he ran into the area controlled by Irving Wexler, better known as Waxey Gordon. In 1933, warfare finally broke out as Schultz gunmen made an unsuccessful attempt on Gordon's life ("2 Women Wounded as Gang Opens Fire in Upper Broadway" 1933).

Gordon was another Prohibition success story. In 1933, the *New York Times* cited him as an outstanding example of "what the golden opportunities of the prohibition era could do for a man without scruples and anxious to get ahead" ("Gordon Made by Dry Era" 1933: 6). Born in 1889 in New York's teeming Lower East Side, the son of poor tenement dwellers, Gordon took to the streets. On October 5, 1905, he was arrested for practicing his trade, picking pockets, and sent to the Elmira Reformatory. He was later sent to Sing Sing Prison for robbery, and in 1916 he was released ("Gordon Says He Got Up to $300 a Week" 1933). Gordon married the daughter of a rabbi, but his future looked bleak—then came Prohibition.

Gordon teamed up with Max Greenberg, hijacker and member of the notorious St. Louis gang known as "Egan's Rats." The two were financed by Arnold Rothstein, and they soon had a fleet of rum ships riding the seas and making them rich. Despite Greenberg's murder, Gordon was able to control the beer business in New Jersey (with the help of Abner "Longie" Zwillman) and much of New York City. To avoid legal problems, Gordon ceased importing liquor from abroad and began to invest in breweries. He took advantage of a loophole in the Volstead Act that allowed for the manufacture of beer with less than 0.5 percent alcohol, "near beer." However, brewing near beer requires first manufacturing the real thing and afterwards removing its alcoholic content. The potential for profit is obvious, and Gordon produced thousands of gallons of beer each year (Joselit 1983).

As befitting a multimillionaire, Gordon lived in a castle, complete with a moat, in southern New Jersey. He owned extensive property in New Jersey and Philadelphia, as well as nightclubs and gambling casinos. However, he paid an average of only $33 a year in income taxes from 1928 to 1930 (Schnepper 1978). A second apparent mistake was his feud with Meyer Lansky, who reputedly fed information to the Internal Revenue Service about the source of Gordon's enormous income (Hammer 1975). In 1931, apparently worried about federal efforts to prosecute gangsters for tax violations, Gordon paid $35,000 in federal taxes. It was too little, too late. Elmer Irey, the head of the Treasury Department's Special Intelligence Unit, and the man who "got" Capone, began to work on Gordon. Thomas E. Dewey had been appointed interim United States attorney for the Southern District of New York. Based on Irey's investigation, on November 20, 1933, Gordon was brought to trial; Dewey personally prosecuted the case.

Among other items that Dewey was able to prove was that Gordon had spent $36,000 to install a bar in his $6,000-a-year apartment; this was during the Depression (Schnepper 1978). It took the jury only fifty-one minutes to find Gordon guilty, and on December 1, 1933, he was sentenced to ten years' imprisonment ("Waxey Gordon Guilty; Gets 10 Years, Is Fined $80,000 for Tax Evasion" 1933). After Gordon's release from federal custody, Prohibition was over, and he looked for other areas of profit. During the war he was convicted for black-market operations (Hammer 1975), and following the war he was active in heroin trafficking. In 1952, he was one of twenty-three persons indicted in a nationwide case. On December 13, 1951, he was sentenced in a New York State court for narcotics violations. Under New York's "Baume's Law," as a fourth-felony offender Gordon was sentenced to a term of twenty-five years to life. On April 10, 1952, a federal detainer brought him to Alcatraz to await trial on the federal drug charges. On June 24, 1952, while at Alcatraz, Gordon became ill and died in the prison hospital ("Waxey Gordon Dies in Alcatraz at 63" 1952).

With Coll and Wexler out of the way, Schultz began to experience a new problem—the Internal Revenue Service. He went into "hiding"—at least law-enforcement officers could not find him. Paul Sann (1971) reports that for eighteen months Schultz was actually in Harlem watching over his business interests. On November 29, 1934, the front page of the *New York Times* reported: "Dutch Schultz Surrenders." He subsequently succeeded in obtaining a change of venue based on his New York City notoriety. His case was moved to Syracuse, New York, where a mistrial ("hung jury") resulted. The trial was next moved to a small upstate community, Malone, New York. Schultz travelled to Malone in advance of his trial, bought candy and flowers for the children he visited in the hospital, held a grand ball to which he invited the entire town, and generally endeared himself to the good people of Malone. Schultz was acquitted, a verdict that led the presiding judge, Frederick Bryant, to admonish:

> Your verdict is one that shakes the confidence of law-abiding people. You will go home with the satisfaction—if it is a satisfaction—that you have rendered a blow against law enforcement and given aid and encouragement to the people who flout the law. In all probability, they will commend you. I cannot [R.N. Smith 1982: 166].

Schultz could not safely return to New York City. The federal government had several counts of the original indictment held in abeyance and, to avoid possible double-jeopardy problems, also had Schultz indicted for a series of misdemeanors. In addition, New York State had a warrant outstanding for income-tax evasion; Schultz reportedly owed the state $36,937.18 in back taxes. It was understood that if Schultz could be arrested in New York City, the authorities would be able to institute a prohibitive bail and thus keep him in custody. Schultz travelled to New Jersey and surrendered to the federal charges. Bail was set at an amount that enabled him to remain at liberty (Sann, 1971). The *New York Times* reported that Schultz could not return to New York City because of Mayor La Guardia's threat to have him arrested if he showed up in New York ("Schultz Succumbs to Bullet Wounds without Naming Slayers" 1935). La Guardia often made outrageous public pronouncements—poor civil liberties, great politics. The Dutchman set up headquarters in a Newark tavern. Now he faced threats from two sources: Thomas E. Dewey and Lucky Luciano.

In 1935, Thomas E. Dewey, a former Republican United States attorney, was appointed special prosecutor by Gov. Herbert Lehman, a Democrat. Dewey went after Schultz, threatening to convene a special grand jury to investigate the Dutchman's activities. Luciano and his colleagues expected Schultz to be convicted and imprisoned. They were planning to move in on his numbers and restaurant rackets, and Schultz's "victory at Malone" was to them a serious setback. Schultz, for his part, became even more unpredictable, murdering his top aide, Bo Weinberg, whom he (correctly) suspected of dealing with Luciano. The Dutchman was also threatening to kill Dewey, an idea that had been rejected by the other leading gangsters in New York—they were fearful of the "heat" that would result (R.N. Smith 1982).

On the evening of October 25, 1935, Dutch Schultz entered the Palace Chop House and Tavern in Newark, where he had established his headquarters "in exile." With him were his bodyguards Bernard ("Lulu") Rosenkrantz and Abe Landau, as well as Otto ("Abbadabba") Berman, the financial wizard of the Schultz organization. Schultz left the group and entered the men's room; two men suddenly entered the tavern—one was Charles ("Charlie the Bug") Workman, a top professional killer, and the second is believed to have been Emanual ("Mendy") Weiss. The pair opened fire with handguns and a shotgun, and the Schultz men were mortally wounded. Workman entered the men's room and shot the Dutchman, who died about twenty hours later. Less than two hours after the Newark attack, a top Schultz aide, Martin Krompier, was shot and seriously wounded in a Manhattan barbershop. The *New York Times* reported that Krompier's shooting was connected to the takeover of loan-sharking operations in Schultz's territory by Luciano, Lepke Buchalter, and Gurrah Shapiro ("Usury Racket Stirred Gang War" 1935).

Workman was tried for the Schultz murder six years later, and during his trial he suddenly entered a guilty plea. The thirty-four-year-old "Bug" received a life sentence. He was paroled in 1964 and permitted to return to New York under parole supervision. He worked in the garment center for several years until age and illness overcame him and he was placed in a Long Island nursing home. Weiss was electrocuted in 1944 for an unrelated murder.

Lepke Buchalter

The man who "vetoed" the murder of Dewey (Turkus and Feder 1951) was Lepke Buchalter; he probably lived to regret that decision. Lepke (an affectionate expression in Yiddish) was born in New York on February 12, 1897; his father died when Lepke was thirteen, and his destitute mother sent him to live with his older sister. Lepke was arrested and imprisoned for burglary several times. After his release from Sing Sing Prison in 1922, he teamed up with Gurrah Shapiro, and the two began working for "Little Augie" Orgen as labor-industrial racketeers. Shapiro subsequently killed Orgen (Turkus and Feder 1951), and Lepke and Gurrah revolutionized industrial racketeering (Berger 1944: 30): "Instead of using his sluggers and gunmen to terrorize labor unions during strike periods, Lepke worked them directly into the unions. By threat and by violence they controlled one local after another." Meyer Berger (1944: 30) points out that manufacturers who hired Lepke to deal with the unions "soon found themselves wriggling helplessly in the grip of Lepke's smooth but deadly organization. He moved in on them, as he had on the unions."

Until 1940, Lepke was the head of an organization that extorted wealth from the garment, leather, fur, baking, and trucking industries in New York City. Burton Turkus (with Feder, 1951) estimates his income at between $5 million and $10 million annually—this was during the Depression. Berger (1940: 30) notes: "All through the Prohibition era, when other mobsters were splashing headily in alcoholic wealth and getting their names in headlines with a series of competitive killings that strewed urban and suburban landscapes with untidy corpses, Lepke went his quiet way."

Alan Block (1975) presents a slightly different picture of Buchalter's operations. He notes that while Lepke and Gurrah had their share of successes, they also experienced dramatic setbacks. In 1932, for example, Buchalter and Shapiro were invited into the fur industry, where the Protective Fur Dressers Corporation was attempting to put an end to the cutthroat competition that was hurting the business owners. Buchalter and Shapiro were notified when dealers, dressers, or manufacturers were not "cooperating." Bombings, assaults, acid, and arson were the responses. However, the duo had a great deal of difficulty dealing with the fur union, and this led to their sudden exit from the fur industry. On April 24, 1933, Buchalter and Shapiro had their thugs stage an attack on the headquarters of the fur workers' union, where a membership meeting was taking place. Although heavily armed, the gangsters met fierce resistance and were driven out into the street by the irate workers. There they were joined by other workers as news of the attack spread throughout the fur district. A number of men were killed, and several gangsters were severely beaten; seven gangsters were convicted of felonious assault, and this ended Buchalter's activities in the fur industry.

Special prosecutor Thomas E. Dewey began to move against Buchalter and Shapiro, and by 1937, Lepke was forced into hiding, leaving Mendy Weiss in charge. In an effort to remove all possible witnesses, Buchalter ordered a murder rampage; the number of persons killed at his direction is estimated between sixty and eighty (Berger 1940). Turkus reports that the murder binge backfired; the terror of the killings turned loyal Lepke men into terrified informers seeking police protection (1951). Lepke surrendered on August 1, 1937, according to a prearranged plan, to columnist Walter Winchell and F.B.I. director J. Edgar Hoover. There was a $50,000 reward for Buchalter, and reportedly pressure on organized crime had grown as efforts to capture Lepke intensified. Berger (1940) reports that when one of his gunmen killed the wrong person, an innocent music publisher, there was a great public outcry and demand for Buchalter's apprehension. Turkus (1951) states that Buchalter had been misled into believing that a deal had been arranged with the authorities, that he would only have to stand trial for federal (drug) and not state (murder) charges. On January 2, 1940, Buchalter was convicted in federal court of antitrust and narcotic law violations and sentenced to fourteen years. (Alan Block, 1975, reports that Buchalter's involvement in narcotics was limited to declaring himself in for half of the profits of a lucrative narcotics-smuggling business—simple extortion.)

To Buchalter's dismay, he was subsequently turned over to New York authorities and prosecuted by Dewey for extortion, for which he received a sentence of thirty years to life. Then in 1941, he was prosecuted by Turkus, an assistant district attorney in Brooklyn, for murder along with Mendy Weiss and Louis Capone (no relative of Al's). The three were convicted and, after a protracted legal battle, electrocuted on March 4, 1944. Buchalter has the dubious distinction of being the only major organized-crime-figure to be executed by the state.

Meyer Lansky and Benjamin Siegel

Meyer Lansky was born Maier Suchowljansky in either 1902 or 1904 in Grodno, Byelorussia (now one of the fifteen republics of the Soviet Union, bordering on Lithuania, Latvia, Poland, and the Ukraine), and was brought to the United States by his parents along with his brother (Jacob) and a sister in 1911. He attended Public School 34 on the Lower East Side where he completed the eighth grade and left school, at age seventeen, for a job as a tool and die maker (McFadden 1983). His first recorded arrest was on October 24, 1918. Up until that time, the various popular sources report, Meyer was an honest and hardworking craftsman. On that date he was arrested for assaulting Lucky Luciano with a crowbar. According to Hank Messick (1973), Lansky was returning home from work, tools in his hand, when he came upon Luciano beating a woman in an alley, as the young (age twelve) Ben Siegel feebly attempted to stop him; Meyer and his crowbar succeeded. They were all arrested, and Lansky was fined two dollars for disorderly conduct. The judge is reported to have stated to Siegel and Lansky: "You boys have bugs in your heads," and Messick notes that Siegel not only kept the nickname, but lived up to it.

Benjamin Siegel was born on February 28, 1906, and raised in the Williamburg section of Brooklyn with four sisters and a brother, Maurice, who became a respected Beverly Hills physician. Ben grew into a handsome and powerfully built young man who was quick to violence (Jennings 1967). The diminutive Lansky (five feet, four inches, 135 pounds), with his friend Ben Siegel, is reported to have organized floating dice games to supplement his legitimate income. As they grew successful, the duo surrounded themselves with *shtarkers* (Yiddish for "tough guys"), men such as Phil ("Little Farvel") Kovolick, described as a "hulking brute" (Nash 1975: 195). Their gambling operations attracted the attention of Italian crime boss Joe Masseria, whose men tried to "muscle in." The altercation that ensued resulted in Lansky and Siegel's arrest and conviction for disorderly conduct and two-dollar fines. At this point, apparently admiring the feistiness of these Jews, Luciano intervened—he was working for Masseria—and reconciled the differences between the Jewish and Italian gangsters (Messick 1973). Throughout his career, Luciano was apparently able to act as an intermediary between Jewish and Italian gangsters, a position that enabled him to gain important stature in organized crime.

In 1921, Lansky became an automobile mechanic. His reputation and mechanical ability soon led to servicing and "souping up" stolen vehicles for use by bootleggers. Hauling whiskey, however, was a very risky business, and the "Bug and Meyer Gang" was soon providing the *shtarkers* necessary to ensure these valuable shipments. By the end of Prohibition, Lansky and Siegel were major powers in organized crime.

In 1936 or 1937, Siegel left New York for the West Coast. Turkus (1951) reports that he was sent by eastern gang leaders who were interested in exploiting opportunities in California. Turkus also states that syndicate units in Cleveland, Chicago, and New York sent men to join the Siegel organization on the West Coast, one of them being the notorious Mickey Cohen. Cohen, in his (1975) autobiography, confirms that he was sent to California by Lou Rothkopf of the Cleveland syndicate: "When I was told to come out here and that Benny was out here, I actually wasn't told that I was *fully* under Benny's arm" (1975: 35). Dean Jennings (1967), in his biography of Siegel, asserts that Ben went to California, not at the behest of organized crime bosses, but for personal reasons—he was partial to the glamour that it offered and a French actress who left New York for Hollywood. Mickey Cohen (1975: 41) reports that Jack Dragna, Italian crime Family boss, was not running things well: "The organization had to pour money on to help Dragna at all times. So Benny came out here to get things moving good."

Siegel "got things moving good." His thugs forced bookmakers in California and Arizona to subscribe to the syndicate-backed Trans-America Wire Service (which reported racing results from throughout the country). In California he gained control of the union that represented movie extras and extorted money from the movie industry. He was the (hidden) owner of the California Metals Company in Los Angeles, which handled salvage metals during the Second World War. Although he established himself in a host of rackets, Siegel is best remembered for his activities in Las Vegas. With financial backing from eastern gang leaders, Siegel built the first of the grand-style Las Vegas gambling casino hotels, the Flamingo. However, his activities apparently took on a streak of independence that alienated him from Lansky and the other gang leaders in the East. At midnight, June 20, 1947, Siegel was hit by a "fusillade of bullets fired through the living room of a Beverly Hills house [home of Virginia Hill] where he was staying" ("Siegel, Gangster, Is Slain on Coast" 1947: 1).

During the 1930s, Lansky was able to arrange with the Cuban dictator Fulgencio Batista for the syndicate to control gambling in Havana. This domination was not broken until Fidel Castro booted both Batista and the syndicate out of Cuba. Lansky moved his gambling interests into the Bahamas and Haiti. He became known as the premier "money mover" for organized crime, "washing" illegitimate funds and investing them in legitimate enterprises.

During World War II he registered for the draft but was never called. In 1953, he served a brief jail term for running a gambling operation at the Arrowhead Inn in Saratoga Springs, New York. Afterwards, he moved to Florida and concentrated on investments in the southern part of that state. His operations were so lucrative that he is reputed to have kept a former bootlegger associate in Switzerland as his full-time money manager (McFadden 1983).[2] In 1970, fearing an indictment for income-tax evasion, Lansky fled to Israel, where he touched off a twenty-six-month legal fight. Claiming citizenship as a Jew under Israel's "Law of Return," Lansky sought permission to settle in the Holy Land. The United States pressured for his return. Lansky claimed that his efforts before the 1948 War of Independence resulted in badly needed munitions being smuggled out of East Coast ports to Palestine. The United States pressed its claim: Lansky was a dangerous criminal. The case went to Israel's highest court, which ruled that he was not entitled to citizenship because his past made him a "danger to public safety" (McFadden 1983: 21).

When he returned to Miami, Lansky was arrested and posted a cash bail of $250,000. He was ultimately cleared of, or ruled too ill to stand trial on, all the tax evasion, conspiracy, and Las Vegas "skimming" charges against him. He spent his last years in seclusion in a Miami Beach condominium with his second wife. His first marriage, in 1929, had ended in divorce in 1946. The couple had two sons and a daughter. In 1948, Lansky married his second wife, a manicurist at a Manhattan hotel. Lansky died of cancer on January 15, 1983 (McFadden 1983).

Italian Organized Crime in New York

Between 1891 and 1920, 4 million Italians entered America, with the overwhelming majority coming from southern Italy. They were poor and uneducated (Gallo 1981: 33); "It has been estimated that the average Italian immigrant who arrived in New York in 1910 had a total of $17 in his possession." Italian immigrants "found work in the city's construction crews, laboring as ditch diggers, hod carriers, and stone cutters. As long as they had strong arms, it did not matter if they could not speak English or operate a complex machine" (Gallo 1981: 44). They experienced nativist prejudice and discrimination from employers, organized labor (Gallo 1981), and public officials. Arthur Train (1912: 83), a former assistant district attorney, wrote in 1912 that

> the Italians from the extreme south of the peninsula have fewer of these [American characteristics than the northern Italian], and are apt to be ignorant, lazy, destitute, and superstitious. A considerable percentage, especially of those from the cities, are criminal.

Ironically, in 1912 gambling and prostitution in Manhattan were well organized under the able leadership of Tammany Hall; the southern Italian was not part of this Irish-Jewish cabal.

The Mafia is mentioned in a *New York Times* article on October 21, 1888, quoting New York City police inspector Thomas Byrnes, who stated that he had discovered the murderer of one Antonio Flaccomio to be "an Italian fruit dealer and a member of a *secret society* to which Flaccomio also belonged." Inspector Byrnes went on to report that the *secret society* was known as the Mafia, and the persons involved in the killings were fugitives from Sicily: "There are two principal headquarters of this society in this country—one is in this city and the other in New Orleans—so that members of the society who commit a serious crime in this city find refuge among friends in the South and vice versa" ("By Order of the Mafia" 1888: 8; emphasis added). David Chandler (1975) agrees that this was a Mafia killing, although it appears that Flaccomio was actually killed because of an altercation over a card game. According to follow-up stories in the *New York Times,* no evidence was presented linking either the deceased or the accused to the Mafia.

Whether or not New York had a Mafia is subject to one's definition of the phenomenon. However, without any doubt, New York did have *La Mano Nero,* the Black Hand, and it also is the subject of a great deal of controversy. Francis Ianni states (1972: 52): "The Black Hand activities were the work of individual extortionists or small gangs, and there is no evidence which suggests that there was any higher level of organization or any tie with the *Mafie* in Sicily, or the Camorra in Naples." Thomas Pitkin and Francesco Cordasco (1977) present a different version. They state that leaders of a prominent Black Hand group—Ignazio Saietta ("Lupo the Wolf"; *lupo* means "wolf" in Italian) and Giuseppe Morello—maintained affiliations with Mafia chiefs back in Sicily. When Morello was arrested in 1909 by agents of the United States Secret Service (he and Saietta were also counterfeiters), correspondence was found linking him to Don Vito Ferro, the prominent Sicilian *capomafioso*. It is believed that Ferro spent some time in the United States at the turn of the century.

Arthur Train (1922: 290) points out that the Camorra and Mafia were never transferred to the United States. Indeed, he argues that many immigrants who were involved with these groups in Italy became quite honest and respectable in the United States: "The number of south Italians who now occupy positions of respectability in New York and who have criminal records on the other side would astound even their compatriots." Train points out, however, that there were Mafia and Camorra gangs in New York and each was headed by a *capo:* "Each *capo maestra* works for himself with his own handful of followers who may or may not enjoy his confidence, and each gang has its own territory held sacred by the others" (1922: 287). Train points out that these gangs rarely attempted blackmail or terrorized anyone but Italians. Occasionally an important *capomafioso* from Sicily arrived and local "friends" had to "get busy for a month or so, raising money for the boys at home and knowing they will reap their reward if they ever go back" (1922: 288). The most popular method of collecting the money was to hold a banquet that all "friends" were required to attend: "No one cares to be conspicuous by reason of his absence and the hero returns to Italy with a large-sized draft on Naples or Palermo" (1922: 301).

In 1895, Giuseppe (Joseph) Petrosino, a New York City police officer, was put in charge of a special squad of Italian detectives and assigned the task of investigating "Italian crime," in particular Black Hand extortion. The latter flourished in Italian ghettos until Prohibition began to offer greater criminal opportunities. Italian families with varying amounts of wealth would receive a crude letter "signed" with a skull or black-inked hand. The letter "requested" money with dire threats offered as an alternative. These threats, often bombings, were sometimes carried out. Petrosino and his squad were quite successful in their work. Petrosino was eventually sent to Italy to check judicial records for lists of criminals about to be released or recently released from Italian prisons so that these men could be picked up on arrival in the United States and returned to Italy. Petrosino left New York on February 9, 1909; on March 12, 1909, he was shot down on a street in Palermo. No one ever apprehended the murderer(s) (Petacco 1974).

By early 1900 there were about 500,000 (mostly southern) Italians in New York City, living in the most deprived social and economic circumstances. The Italian immigration "made fortunes for speculators and landlords, but it also transformed the neighborhood into a kind of human antheap in which suffering, crime, ignorance and filth were the dominant elements" (Petacco 1974: 16). The Italian immigrant provided the cheap labor vital to the expanding capitalism of that era. Robert Merton (1967: 127) states that "functional deficiencies of the official structure generate an alternative (unofficial) structure to fulfill existing needs somewhat more effectively." Randall Collins (1975: 463) adds that "where legitimate careers are blocked and resources are available for careers in crime, individuals would be expected to move in that direction." Thus, Collins notes, the prominence of Italians in organized crime "is related to the coincidence of several historical factors:

the arrival of large numbers of European immigrants from peasant backgrounds who demanded cultural services that the dominant Anglo-Protestant society made illegal; the availability of a patrimonial form of military organization that could be applied to protecting such services; and the relatively late arrival of the Italians in comparison with other ethnic groups (e.g., the Irish) who had acquired control of legitimate channels of political and related economic mobility." Luigi Barzini (1965: 273) adds: "In order to beat rival organizations, criminals of Sicilian descent reproduced the kind of illegal groups they had belonged to in the old country and employed the same rules to make them invincible." Richard Gambino (1974: 304) concludes that, although southern Italian characteristics do not dispose people toward crime, "where the mode of life has been impressed onto organized crime it has made it difficult to combat effectively the criminal activity." He argues that Italian criminals "totally corrupted and perverted traditional codes of la famiglia and vendetta" (1974: 297).

Humbert Nelli (1976: 136) reports that there were Mafia gangs in every American city that had a sizable Sicilian population, "feeding off the common laborer's honest toil and claiming to serve as a means of easing adjustment to American society." Eric Hobsbawm (1969: 686) states that the Mafia "was imported by Sicilian immigrants, who reproduced it in the cities in which they settled, as a ritual brotherhood consisting of loosely linked but otherwise independent and uncoordinated 'families' organized hierarchically." Nelli points out that Mafia organizations "served important social as well as financial functions. The group produced a sense of belonging and of security in numbers. This function was achieved at least in part through the use of initiation ceremonies, passwords and rituals, and rules of conduct with which members must abide" (1976: 138). One of Ianni's (1972: 57) informants describes a Mafia gang operating in Brooklyn in 1928:

> . . . all the old Sicilian "moustaches" used to get together in the backroom of the club—it was a *fratellanze* [brotherhood] and they used to call it the *Unione Siciliana*. They spent a lot of time talking about the old country, drinking wine and playing cards. But these were tough guys too, and they were alky cookers [bootleggers] and pretty much ran things in the neighborhood. They had all of the businesses locked up and they got a piece of everything that was sold.

James Inciardi (1975: 115) describes the *Unione Siciliana:*

> *L'Unione siciliana* emerged in late nineteenth-century New York as a lawful fraternal society designed to advance the interests of Sicilian immigrants. The *Unione* provided its members with life insurance and additional social benefits, and was energetic in the eradication of crime within Sicilian-American communities. . . . Additional branches of *L'Unione siciliana* were chartered wherever new colonies of Sicilians expanded. . . .
> The respectability and benevolence of the *Unione* declined as Prohibition approached. First in New York and later in distant city branches, cadres of gangsters

began to infiltrate and pervert the association. *L'Unione siciliana* acquired a dual character: it was open and involved in good works among needy Sicilians, yet it was hidden and malevolent, dealing in theft, murder and vice. With an expanding criminal front, leaders of this "society" became natural catalysts for any racketeers seeking to widen their influence and profit potentials. *L'Unione* membership included old and clannish *Mafia* types who stressed maintenance of the cultural traditions of the Sicilian *Società onorata*. To these were added the younger Americanized factions that were anxious to increase their operations through cooperative agreements with a greater variety of criminal groups, even with those not of their blood. The *Unione* of the 1920s became the object of power struggles, with both orientations contending at local, regional, and national levels for the more advantageous posts. This struggle terminated in 1931 in the Castellammarese war.

The Castellammarese War

In 1930, there were two major factions in Italian organized crime in New York, one headed by Giuseppe ("Joe the Boss") Masseria, and the other by Salvatore Maranzano. Prohibition had enabled the Mafia gangs to break out of the bounds of the "Little Italy" and operate in the wider society. The struggle for domination of Italian-American organized crime in New York became known as the Castellammarese War because many of the Maranzano group came from the small Sicilian coastal town known as Castellammare del Golfo. The Maranzano group consisted mainly of Sicilians, especially the "moustaches," many of whom had fled from Mussolini's prosecution of *mafiosi*. The Masseria group consisted of both Sicilian and non-Sicilian elements: e.g., Lucky Luciano (a Sicilian), Vito Genovese (a Neapolitan), and Frank Costello (born Francesco Castiglia in Lauropoli, Calabria). They were allied with non-Italians such as Meyer Lansky and Benny Siegel. As the war turned against Masseria, five of his leading men—Luciano, Genovese, Ciro Terranova, Frank Livorsi, and Joseph ("Stretch") Stracci—went over to the Maranzano camp, and they failed to notify Joe the Boss. On April 15, 1931, Masseria drove his steel-armored sedan, a massive car with plate glass an inch thick in all of its windows, to a garage near the Nuova Villa Tammaro at 2715 West Fifteenth Street in the Coney Island section of Brooklyn. He then walked to the restaurant for a meal with Luciano and several of his trusted lieutenants. It was Masseria's last meal ("Racket Chief Slain by Gangster Gunfire" 1931). The Castellammarese War was over.

Maranzano irritated many of his followers, particularly the more Americanized Italian gangsters. Joseph Bonanno, who was born in Castellammare del Golfo, was a staunch ally of Maranzano. However, he points out in his autobiography (1983: 137-38):

> Maranzano was old-world Sicilian in temperament and style. But he didn't live in Sicily anymore. In New York he was advisor not only to Sicilians but to American-Italians. Maranzano represented a style that often clashed with that of

the Americanized men who surrounded him after the war. It was difficult, for example, for Maranzano even to communicate effectively with many of these men, for they only understood American street cant.

On September 10, 1931, four men carrying pistols entered a suite at 230 Park Avenue, the Grand Central Building in New York City. "One of them ordered the seven men and Miss Frances Samuels, a secretary, to line up against the wall. The others stalked into the private office of Salvatore Maranzano. There was a sound of voices raised in angry dispute; blows, struggling, and finally pistol shots, and the four men dashed out of the suite." Maranzano was found with "his body riddled with bullets and punctured with knife wounds" ("Gang Kills Suspect in Alien Smuggling" 1931: 1). The killers are believed to have been Jews (whom Maranzano and his bodyguards would not recognize) sent by Meyer Lansky and Benny Siegel at the behest of Luciano. The killers flashed badges, and apparently Maranzano and his bodyguards believed them to be federal agents who had visited him before. They attempted to kill him silently with knives, and when he fought back, they shot him to death.

In the aftermath of the Castellammarese War, five Italian-American crime Families emerged. They continue to maintain distinct identities.

The Luciano Family

Luciano was born in Lercara Friddi, a sulphur-mining area in western Sicily, in 1897. He arrived in New York with his parents, Antonio and Rosalia Lucania, early in 1907, and the family settled on Manhattan's Lower East Side. Nelli (1976) reports that, although Luciano's conduct in school was satisfactory, his academic record was poor and made worse by chronic truancy. He left school when he reached the age of fourteen and secured employment as a shipping boy in a hat factory. He became a member of the Five Points Gang, a drug user and pusher, and on June 26, 1916, at age eighteen, was found guilty of possessing narcotics and sent to a reformatory for six months (Nelli 1976).

With the advent of Prohibition, Luciano emerged as a leader in the Masseria Family. With the death of Masseria and Maranzano in 1931, Luciano became the most important Italian organized-crime figure in New York, a status he continued to enjoy until 1935. In that year, investigators for Thomas E. Dewey discovered an extensive prostitution network which, although independent at one time, had been taken over by Luciano henchmen headed by David ("Little Davie") Betillo. In a single raid, Dewey's investigators arrested prostitutes, madams, and "bookers" (pimps). They were pressured and cajoled into testifying against Luciano, who protested that he had no knowledge of or involvement in Betillo's activities. Dewey charged that Betillo had acted on behalf of Luciano to "organize" two hundred bordellos and three thousand prostitutes into a $12 million-a-year business. On June 7, 1936, Luciano was found guilty of sixty-one counts of compulsory prostitution and sentenced to a term of thirty to sixty years in prison (R.N. Smith 1982).

Luciano languished in Clinton State Prison at Dannemora while war raged in Europe and the Pacific. By May 1942, German submarines operating in American coastal waters had sunk 272 U.S. ships. It was suspected that information on American shipping was being leaked to the Germans by people working in eastern ports. It was also suspected, incorrectly, that German submarines were being supplied by American fishing boats. The spectre of sabotage was raised when the luxury liner *Normandie,* which had been refitted as a naval vessel, rolled over in flames while harbored in the Hudson River.

With the help of Frank Hogan, Dewey's successor as Manhattan district attorney, naval intelligence officials met with Joseph ("Socks") Lanza, the vicious criminal "czar" of the Fulton Fish Market, who was under indictment for conspiracy and extortion. Lanza agreed to help, but noted that his influence was limited; he suggested the man to see was Lucky Luciano. Luciano was transferred to Great Meadow Prison, which is closer to New York City, and there he met with naval intelligence officers.

Through Meyer Lansky the word went out. According to Rodney Campbell (1977), in addition to ordering port workers and fishermen to "keep alert," crime figures helped to place intelligence operatives in key areas by supplying them with union cards and securing positions for them on the waterfront, on fishing boats, and in waterfront bars, restaurants, and hotels. They also provided another important service. At the request of naval officials they prevented strikes and other forms of labor unrest that could interrupt wartime shipping. While Campbell provides documentation of Luciano's domestic role during the war, his data on Luciano's role in the invasion of Sicily are tenuous. Campbell states that Luciano had word sent to Sicilian *capo-mafiosi* to assist the Allied landing. However, *mafiosi* did not need encouragement from Luciano—their desire to rid the island of Mussolini's iron hand was incentive enough. R.N. Smith presents a more modest claim (1982: 572): "Sicilians expelled by Mussolini proved willing to help devise maps of possible landing sites. The island coastline and the contour of land off the coast were assessed with the help of underworld informants."

In 1945, then-governor Thomas E. Dewey received a petition for executive clemency on behalf of Luciano, citing his efforts during the war. On January 3, 1946, the governor announced that Luciano would be released from prison and deported to Italy. Luciano left the United States on February 9, 1946. He died of a heart attack while in Italian exile in 1962.

With Luciano in prison and then deported to Italy, the Family was headed by Frank Costello. Christened Francesco Castiglia, Costello was born on January 26, 1891, in Calabria. Like several other Italian criminals, he affected an Irish surname, something that was certainly no hindrance in New York, where the Irish dominated Tammany and Tammany dominated the city. In _costello_

1915 he served a ten-month sentence for carrying a concealed weapon. By 1923, he was a successful bootlegger working for Bill Dwyer, an ex-longshoreman turned rumrunner, who brought liquor from Canada across the Great Lakes in armored speedboats (Talese 1965: 67–68). Costello moved into gambling and eventually became a successful (and legitimate) real estate dealer.

Known as "King of the Slots," Costello operated an extensive network of the "one-armed bandits" in New York City until Mayor Fiorello La Guardia went on a highly publicized campaign to rid the city of "that bum." Many sources report that Costello was then invited to bring his slot machines to New Orleans by the political boss of Louisiana, United States Senator Huey P. Long. Costello moved into New Orleans and placed Philip ("Dandy Phil") Kastel in charge. The "Kingfish's" biographer, T. Harry Williams (1969), questions Long's connection to Costello. Costello had informed a federal grand jury that Long had invited him into New Orleans to set up a thousand slot machines for a fee of thirty dollars per machine. However, Williams argues that such a setup would require police protection in a city that in 1935 was controlled by Semmes Walmsley, a bitter enemy of the Kingfish.

Costello was noted for his political influence. In one widely reported incident in 1943, a telephone wiretap revealed Thomas A. Aurelio thanking Costello for making him the Democratic nominee for judge of the New York Supreme Court (court of general, not appellate, jurisdiction) from Manhattan. Aurelio pledged "undying loyalty" to which "Francesco" responded: "When I tell you something is in the bag, you can rest assured" ("Frank Costello Dies of Coronary at 82" 1972). Despite a grand-jury probe, Aurelio was elected and served with distinction, without any hint of favoritism toward organized crime. Costello, it appears, was motivated more by ethnic than criminal interests. He had broken Irish domination over judicial appointments in Manhattan.

In 1949, Costello was asked to serve as vice-chairman of a Salvation Army fund-raising drive. He gladly accepted and held a fund-raising party at the Copacabana to which judges and other leading political figures were invited. The party raised $3,500, and Costello added another $6,500 of his own, sending the Salvation Army a check for $10,000. However, the newspapers found out about the party, and the public reaction was indignant (Talese 1965).

In 1951, Costello appeared before the Kefauver Committee[3] and was exposed on national television as a major crime figure. For the television viewers, however, only Costello's hands were seen; his lawyer had insisted that Costello not be televised. His evasive responses, coupled with a dramatic walkout, eventually led to an eighteen-month term for contempt of the Senate. In 1952, the government moved against him for income-tax evasion, for which he received a sentence of five years imprisonment in 1954. In 1956 his attorney, the noted criminal lawyer Edward Bennett Williams, proved that the conviction had been based on illegal wiretaps, and Costello was freed. Even while he was in prison, Costello's power continued unabated. While on a prison visit, Edward Bennett Williams mentioned to Costello that he wanted, but had been unable to purchase, tickets for the Broadway musical hit *My Fair Lady*. Later that same day, Williams reported, his doorbell at home rang: "A broad-shouldered man thrust an envelope in his hands and disappeared"; it contained four tickets for that evening's "sold out" performance ("Frank Costello Dies of Coronary at 82" 1972: 21).

Costello routinely travelled without any bodyguards. On May 2, 1957, he had an appointment to meet Anthony ("Tony Bender") Strollo, Family *caporegime* in charge of Greenwich Village. The meeting, at Chander's Restaurant on East Forty-Ninth Street, had been arranged by Vito Genovese, Family *sottocapo* (underboss). With Bender at the restaurant was Vincent Mauro (also known as Vincent Bruno). Mauro left but monitored Costello's movements by telephone. He spoke to an individual on a pay phone, outside of which a double-parked car was waiting for word that Costello was on his way home to his apartment on Central Park West. Costello rushed to the elevator of the luxury building when a passing fat man yelled: "This is for you Frank," and fired a revolver at Costello's face from a distance of six to ten feet. The bullet hit Costello in the head but caused only superficial damage. When questioned by the authorities, Costello insisted he did not recognize his assailant, the easily recognizable Vincent ("The Chin") Gigante, an obese ex-pugilist and Genovese gunman. Several months later, Albert Anastasia, Costello's close ally and boss of the Mineo Family, was murdered, and Costello retired. Vito Genovese became boss of the Luciano Family (Katz 1973).

The man who allegedly ordered the bungled attempt on Costello was born near Naples on November 27, 1897. At age fifteen he arrived in New York and lived with his family in the Little Italy of downtown Manhattan. Beginning as a street thief, Genovese graduated to working as a collector for the Italian lottery and eventually became an associate of Lucky Luciano. When his first wife died of tuberculosis in 1931, Genovese stated his intention of marrying Anna Petillo—she was already married. Twelve days later, Mr. Petillo was strangled to death, and Genovese married the widow Petillo. After twelve years of marriage, Anna Genovese sued him for support and denounced Vito in court as a racketeer with a huge income. The much-feared crime boss did nothing. Nicholas Gage (1972) reports that Genovese was too much in love with her to have her killed.

Genovese was becoming a power in organized crime and was making large profits from narcotics. In 1934, however, there was a bungled murder, that of Ferdinand ("The Shadow") Boccia, and Genovese was forced to flee to Italy in order to avoid prosecution; he took $750,000 with him. In Italy he was reputed to have been a confidant of Benito Mussolini—until the American invasion. At that time he gained the confidence of the American military authorities, for whom he acted as an interpreter. His position enabled him to become a major black marketeer, until he was identified as an American fugitive and returned to the United States to stand trial. While he was awaiting trial, a key witness was poisoned while in protective custody, and Genovese went free.

On April 14, 1959, Genovese, along with fourteen others, was convicted of conspiracy to violate narcotics laws and received a fifteen-year federal sentence. Ralph Salerno, a former New York City detective, says about the conviction:

> Oddly enough, several Bosses have gone to jail on evidence that knowledgeable people find questionable. One such case is that of Vito Genovese, a powerful New York family Boss who went to prison in April 1959 on a federal narcotics conviction. Genovese's family had indeed been involved in narcotics, but Nelson Cantellops, a narcotics courier, swore in court that he had personally met and talked with Genovese about details of the business. To anyone who understands the protocol and insulation procedures of Cosa Nostra, this testimony is almost unbelievable [Salerno 1969: 157].

On February 14, 1969, while serving his fifteen-year sentence, Genovese died. However, the group that he headed is still usually referred to as the *Genovese Family*, despite numerous changes in leadership.

The Mineo Family

Al Mineo (real name Manfredi) was a close ally of Masseria who was killed by Maranzano gunmen during the Castellammarese War. After the death of Masseria, Frank Scalise,[4] who had defected from the Mineo Family early in the war, was made boss of that same Family. He became a close confidant of Maranzano and after Maranzano's death was replaced as boss by Vincent Mangano. Bonanno (1983) states that this was done to appease Lucky Luciano. In 1951, Mangano disappeared—presumably murdered at the direction of Family *sottocapo* Albert Anastasia, who then became Family boss.

Albert Anastasia was born Umberto Anastasio in Tropea, Italy, on September 26, 1902. He entered the United States in 1919 and reportedly changed his name to save his family some embarrassment as a result of his 1921 arrest for murdering a fellow longshoreman (Freeman 1957: 12). His brother Anthony ("Tough Tony") Anastasio became the official ruler of the Brooklyn waterfront as head of Local 1814 of the International Longshoremen's Union (ILA); Albert became the unofficial ruler of these same docks. He was widely feared even among his associates and reportedly enjoyed the title "Executioner" (Berger 1957).

In 1923, Anastasia was sentenced to two years of imprisonment for possessing a firearm, although this did not prevent him from serving stateside in the United States Army during World War II. In 1955, he served a one-year sentence for income-tax evasion. Anastasia lived in a home along the Palisades in Fort Lee, New Jersey—a home with a seven-foot barbed wire fence, Doberman pinschers, and bodyguards. On October 25, 1957, he was getting his hair cut (some say it was a shave), when his bodyguard conveniently absented himself. Two gunmen entered, and the "Executioner" was executed. (The barbershop was located in the Park Sheraton, which in 1928 was known as the Park Central, the hotel where Arnold Rothstein was killed.) The death of Anastasia has been linked to the attempt on the life of Frank Costello, an act designed to thwart a retaliatory war; Anastasia was a close friend of Costello (Berger 1957). *Sottocapo* Carlo Gambino, believed to be in league with Vito Genovese, became the boss of the Family.

Carlo Gambino. Born in Palermo on August 24, 1900, Carlo arrived in the United States (an illegal alien) in 1921. He resided in Brooklyn, assisted by numerous relatives who had arrived earlier. In turn, he helped his brothers Paolo (Paul), born 1904, and Giuseppe (Joseph), born 1908, when they arrived in the United States. His boyhood friend from Palermo, Gaetano Lucchese, was already in the United States and rising in the ranks of organized crime, first under Masseria and then, as a defector, under Maranzano. Gambino, who was nominally on the side of "Joe the Boss," appears not to have actively participated in the Castellammarese War. He followed Lucchese into the Maranzano camp and after Maranzano's death moved into the ranks of the Mineo Family, eventually becoming a *caporegime* under Vincent Mangano.

After Prohibition, Gambino continued in the bootlegging business and in 1939 received a twenty-two-month sentence for conspiracy to defraud the United States of liquor taxes. Eight months later, the conviction was thrown out because the evidence had been based on illegal wiretaps. The Second World War made Gambino a millionaire; it also prevented him from being deported to Italy. Valachi testified before a Senate committee that Gambino "made over a million dollars from ration stamps during the war. The stamps came out of the O.P.A.'s offices. First Carlo's boys would steal them. Then, when the Government started hiding them in banks, Carlo made contact and the O.P.A. men sold him the stamps" (Gage 1975: 26). Paul Meskil (1973: 58) states:

> The wartime rationing of gasoline, meat, and groceries opened a nationwide black market that the American public patronized as eagerly as it had once bought bootleg booze. . . .
> Carlo went into the stamp-collecting business with his brother Paul and New Jersey mobster Settimo (Big Sam) Accardi. At first, they sent teams of safe-crackers to steal ration stamps from the vaults of the Office of Price Administration. Then they purchased the stamps directly from dishonest OPA officials.

When Albert Anastasia became Family boss, he made Gambino the *sottocapo*. When Anastasia was murdered in 1957, Gambino became the boss of reputedly the largest and most influential crime Family in the country. A strong family man, Gambino had one daughter, married to the son of Lucchese, and three sons, who operate trucking firms in the garment center. Gambino's wife died in 1971. In 1970 he was indicted for conspiracy to hijack an armored car carrying over $3 million, but the case was never brought to trial because of his poor health. In that same year, the Supreme Court upheld a 1967 deportation order, but once again ill health prevented any action.

In addition to his Family's illegal activities, from which he received an income, Gambino owned (directly or through fronts) many legitimate businesses, including meat markets, bakeries, nightclubs, linen-supply companies, and restaurants. His "SGS Associates Public and Labor Relations" firm had an uncanny knack for resolving labor disputes for its impressive list of clients, including Wellington Associates (real estate including the Chrysler Building), builder William Levitt, Bond Clothes, and the Flower and Fifth Avenue Hospital. The firm closed in 1965 after an investigation by state and federal authorities (Meskil 1973).

On October 15, 1975, Gambino died of natural causes in his Massapequa, Long Island, home. The Family he headed is still referred to as the Gambino Family.

The Reina Family

Gaetano ("Tommy") Reina headed one of the five Families in New York City "which formed spontaneously as Sicilian immigrants settled there" (Bonanno 1983: 84). Two of the leading men in the Reina Family were Gaetano Gagliano and Tommy Lucchese. Bonanno states that because of the power of Masseria, Reina had to be careful not to offend him, "and he generally toed the Masseria line" (1983: 85). At the start of the Castellammarese War, Reina apparently began talking (privately) against Masseria: "An informant within Reina's Family relayed these sentiments to Reina's *paesano* from Corleone, Peter Morello. And Morello reported it to Masseria" (Bonanno 1983: 106). On February 26, 1930, Reina was killed by the blast of a sawed-off shotgun. Bonanno reports that Masseria backed one of his own supporters, Joe Pinzola, to head the Reina Family. Gaetano ("Tommy") Gagliano formed a splinter group and challenged Pinzola and Masseria. He was joined by Tommy Lucchese, who was designated *sottocapo* of the (new) Gagliano Family. Gagliano emerged on the side of the victorious Salvatore Martanzano, and his leadership lasted until 1953, when he died of natural causes. Pinzola was killed during the Masseria-Martanzano conflict.

Lucchese was born in Palermo, Sicily, in 1900 and came to the United States in 1911. In 1919 he lost his right index finger in a machine-shop accident. His obituary in the *New York Times* states that the accident "apparently soured him on the workingman's life and steered him into a life of crime" (July 14, 1967: 31). As a result of the accident and his first arrest (for car theft in 1921), Lucchese was nicknamed "Three-Finger Brown," after a pitcher for the Chicago Cubs—the policeman who fingerprinted Lucchese was a fan of Mordecai ("Three-Finger") Brown and wrote that name down under the "alias" section of the fingerprint card. He was naturalized in 1943, despite the 1921 conviction, and in 1949 received a "certificate of good conduct" which restored his right to vote.

Virgil Peterson (1983: 403) states that Lucchese was very big in gambling, including numbers (illegal lottery) and bookmaking in Queens, New York. One of the principal members of his Family (and subsequent boss himself), Anthony ("Ducks") Corallo, was a major labor racketeer.[5] "Police officials listed eight dress firms in New York City in which Lucchese was a part owner, and he had similar holdings in Scranton, Pennsylvania." His firms in New York City were nonunion and, Peterson notes, "strangely, free from labor troubles." Lucchese was arrested for vagrancy on November 18, 1935—his last arrest.

Lucchese lived in an expensive home in Lido Beach, Long Island. His son Robert is a graduate of the United States Air Force Academy and an Air Force officer. Lucchese's daughter Frances went to Vassar College and later married the son of Carlo Gambino. Lucchese died of natural causes on July 13, 1967. His Family is, however, usually referred to as the Lucchese Family.

The Profaci Family

Joseph Profaci was born in Palermo on October 2, 1897; he came to the United States and never served a prison sentence. However, he did manage to owe the United States $1.5 million in income taxes. Profaci owned numerous (at least twenty) legitimate businesses and was the largest single importer of olive oil into the United States. In addition to his modest Brooklyn home, he owned a luxurious house in Miami Beach and a hunting lodge ("Profaci Dies of Cancer" 1962). Bonanno (1983) reports that at the outbreak of the Castellammarese War, Profaci was the boss of his own Family. While he sided with Maranzano, his Family did not participate in the conflict: "Maranzano urged Profaci to remain officially neutral and to act as an intermediary with other groups" (1983: 85).

Profaci, although clean shaven, was clearly a "moustache," faithful to Old World traditions. He was a devoted family man, devoid of any apparent extramarital romantic interests. A religious person, his profession notwithstanding, Profaci was a faithful churchgoer, a friend of the pastor, and a large contributor to church charities. One of the churches in the Bensonhurst–Bath Beach section of Brooklyn, where he lived, had a statue adorned with a crown of jewels worth several thousand dollars. Some reports state that Profaci had been the contributor of the crown. In any event, James ("Bucky") Ammino decided to steal the crown—an outrage Profaci ordered "corrected." Although the crown was returned, Bucky failed to restore three missing diamonds. His body was subsequently found, and lest the meaning of his death be misinterpreted, a set of rosary beads was wrapped around his neck (Martin 1963).

Profaci's traditionalism was viewed as despotic by some members of his Family; he apparently demanded a big percentage of all their illegal profits, and he placed "blood" and old friendships above business; old friends and relatives received larger shares of Family opportunities than the younger men in his ranks. In 1959, a policy (illegal lottery) operator, Frank ("Frankie Shots") Abbatemarco, was murdered on orders from Profaci. The contract was carried out by Joseph ("Joe Jelly") Gioielli, a short, obese, but vicious, killer and stalwart of the Gallo brothers, a Red Hook group that was part of the Profaci Family. The brothers, Lawrence ("Larry"), Albert ("Kid Blast"), and Joseph ("Crazy Joe") Gallo, expected to receive a large share of Abbatemarco's gambling operations. Instead, Profaci divided it up among his friends and relatives. The Gallo brothers fumed until February, 1961. Then, in one twenty-four-hour period, they abducted four of Profaci's closest associates, but the boss himself evaded capture. What transpired afterwards would rival the Roman plots in the days of the Caesars.

Profaci agreed to be more generous with the Gallo faction. However, several Gallo men secretly went over to the Profaci side, and on August 20, 1961, they lured Larry Gallo to the Sahara Lounge in Brooklyn. At an early hour in the morning, before the lounge had opened for business, Carmine ("The Snake") Persico and another man placed a rope around Larry's neck and slowly began to squeeze the life out of him. A police sergeant came into the lounge apparently only minutes before the victim would have expired—he had already lost control of his bowels and bladder. The officer noticed Larry's feet sticking out behind the bar, and he saw the two men dash from the darkened room out a side door. His patrolman driver waiting outside attempted to stop the two men; he was shot in the face and suffered a wound in the right cheek. Larry survived the ordeal, his neck badly scarred.

On that same day Joe Jelly was "put to sleep with the fishes"—his coat was dumped on the street near Gallo headquarters wrapped around several fresh fish. The "war" was on, but it was a rather one-sided affair; at least twelve men were killed, mostly Gallo loyalists. The Gallo group "took to the mattresses"—that is, they took refuge in their Red Hook, Brooklyn, headquarters at 49–51 President Street, a block away from the Union Street 76th Police Precinct House. A special squad of New York City detectives headed by Ramond V. Martin (who wrote a book on the subject, 1963) was assigned to maintain surveillance of the area, and it was the police who probably saved the Gallos from being completely wiped out by Profaci gunmen. During this period, the Gallos were responsible for saving several neighborhood youngsters from a building fire. They became local heroes, and the news media reported extensively on their exploits. On May 11, 1961, in an effort to replenish income that was dwindling as a result of the "war," Joey Gallo attempted to extort money from the owner of several bars. The victim refused, so Joey performed his best "Richard Widmark," explaining to the businessman that he could meet with an unfortunate "accident." It was no accident that two detectives were in the bar and Gallo received a lengthy prison sentence. In 1968, Larry Gallo died of cancer.

In 1962, Profaci died, and his place was taken by Joseph Magliocco, his brother-in-law. Magliocco died of natural causes at the end of 1963, and his place was taken by Joseph Colombo, Sr. A truce was finally arranged between the two factions in 1964. Ralph Salerno (with Tompkins, 1969) reports that one condition of the truce was that several top Gallo men were "made" (inducted as members of the Colombo Family).

While in prison, Crazy Joey continued to "raise hell." He so annoyed some of his fellow inmates in Attica that several of them threw him off a tier. Transferred to another prison, Joey befriended many black inmates, several of whom he recruited for his Brooklyn organization. In May, 1971, he was released from prison, and the intrigue reached new heights.

There appears to be general agreement over how Joseph Colombo was chosen to succeed Magliocco as boss of the Profaci Family. There was a plot to kill two other Family chieftains, Carlo Gambino and Thomas Lucchese, and Colombo informed Gambino of the plot. Some accounts say that the person who was supposed to effect the murders was Colombo, on behalf of Joseph Bonanno, boss of the Bonanno Family. Salerno (with Tompkins, 1969) reports that Bonanno and Joseph Magliocco, *sottocapo* of the Profaci Family, were behind the plot. Gay Talese (1971) places responsibility on Magliocco, and Bonanno (1983) denies any involvement. He blames his cousin, Stefano Magaddino, Buffalo, New York, Family boss, for "disseminating the story that Joe Bonanno wanted to kill Gambino and Lucchese. . . ." (1983: 235). In any event, Magliocco died, and Joseph Colombo was chosen by the "commission" to head the Profaci Family (Bonanno 1983).

In 1970, Colombo founded the Italian-American Civil Rights League and led in the daily picketing of New York FBI headquarters, generating a great deal of publicity. Colombo and the league succeeded in having all references to the "Mafia" or "Cosa Nostra" deleted from the script of *The Godfather* as well as the television series *The FBI*. Atty. Gen. John Mitchell and Gov. Nelson Rockefeller ordered their employees to refrain from using such references.

The league raised large sums of money through dues and testimonial dinners and held an "Annual Unity Day" rally which drew about 50,000 persons to Columbus Circle in New York. Nicholas Gage notes that the "rally conspicuously closed stores in neighborhoods controlled by the Mafia: New York's waterfront was virtually shut down . . . and almost every politician in the city joined" the 1970 celebration (1972: 172). There were articles in magazines and newspapers about Colombo and the league, and the boss began to portray himself as a civil rights leader who was simply misunderstood by the police.

Reports state that other Family bosses, particularly Carlo Gambino, did not look favorably on the activity of Colombo and the league, either because Colombo failed to share the financial fruits or because they resented the publicity—perhaps both. At the Second Annual Unity Day rally on June 28, 1971, in view of thousands, a lone black man, wearing a camera and apparently presenting himself as a newsman, approached Colombo, pulled out a gun, and shot him. The gunman, twenty-four-year-old Jerome A. Johnson, was immediately shot to death: "Johnson's killer escaped as professionally as he had carried out his mission, shooting Johnson three times even as police clustered around" (Gage 1972: 171). Colombo remained paralyzed until his death.

Interest focused on Jerome Johnson. He was never connected to organized crime, although he had a criminal record and was known as a violent person. Suspicion immediately centered on Joey Gallo; he had reason to dislike the Family boss and was known to have as his associates black criminals. The day after Colombo was shot, the *New York Times* stated (Gage 1971b: 21): "When Joseph Gallo was released in May from prison he was reported to have complained that the lot of his faction within the family had not improved much in his absence. He was also said to have questioned Colombo's involvement in the Italian Civil Rights League as drawing undue attention to the family." On April 7, 1972, Joey Gallo was dining at Umberto's Clam House in Lower Manhattan with his associate-bodyguard, Peter ("Pete the Greek") Diapoulas, Pete's girlfriend, Joey's fiancée and her daughter, and Joey's sister. Three Colombo Family gunmen entered the restaurant and shot Gallo to death; Diapoulas was wounded after he exchanged fire with the killers.

Despite the death of Joseph Colombo, the Family is usually referred to as the Colombo Family.

The Bonanno Family

We know more about Joseph ("Don Peppino") Bonanno than other crime figures because he was the subject of the biography by Gay Talese (1971) and authored his own autobiography (with Segio Lalli, 1983). Bonanno states that his father, Salvatore ("Don Turridu"), was the head of the Bonanno clan in Castellammare and a "man of honor" (*mafioso*). He left Sicily for the United States with his wife and three-year-old son, Giuseppe, in 1908 to avoid prosecution (Bonanno does not say for what crime). In 1911, at the request of his brothers in Castellammare, Don Turridu returned home with his wife and child. He died in 1915 of a heart attack.

Bonanno states that he was attending the nautical preparatory school in Trapani when Mussolini came to power. He claims that his anti-Fascist activities forced him to leave, and he entered the United States illegally in 1924. He quickly found help and refuge amongst friends and family from Castellammare. His cousin Stefano Magaddino was already a criminal power in Buffalo, and Bonanno eventually became involved in bootlegging with the Castellammare clan in Brooklyn under Salvatore Maranzano. During the Masseria-Maranzano conflict, Bonanno became an aide to Maranzano and was seen as a leader of the Castellammare group arrayed against Joe, the boss. After Maranzano's murder, a meeting of Family members was held, and Bonanno was elected Father (a term he uses for "boss") of what became known as the Bonanno Family. Bonanno successfully parlayed income received as boss of his own Family into legitimate enterprises such as garment and cheese manufacturing.

Although he had been arrested numerous times, until 1983 Bonanno never served a prison term. In 1945 he was convicted for a violation of the rent-control law and paid a $450 fine. In 1959, a federal grand jury indicted him for conspiracy to obstruct justice in the aftermath of the (in)famous meeting of Family bosses at Apalachin, New York. In that year, there had been an attempt on the life of Frank Costello, and Albert Anastasia had been murdered—events that apparently required a top-level conference. New York state police sergeant Edgar Croswell became suspicious of the activities at the home of Joseph M. Barbara, whom he knew to be an "organized-crime figure." Barbara was from Castellammare and had become the wealthy owner of a soda-pop distributing business and a bottling plant outside of Endicott, New York. His estate in Apalachin was about six miles away. The sergeant had discovered a number of expensive automobiles with out-of-state license plates parked at the Barbara estate. "There was nothing Croswell could legally do about Barbara's visitors, but by Saturday, November 14, 1957, with what he figured to be as many as seventy guests assembled, Croswell could no longer stifle his curiosity. He organized what few deputies he had and conducted a raid on Barbara's house, one merely, as he explained later, to see if anything criminal was going on or if Barbara's guests were wanted on any outstanding warrants" (Brashler 1977: 144). Ralph Salerno (with Tompkins) states that "within minutes dozens of well-dressed men ran out of the house and across the fields in all directions" (1969: 298). Using roadblocks and reinforcements, the police reportedly took sixty-three men into custody, although this figure is often disputed. Bonanno was reported to have been at the meeting, and his driver's license was confiscated, but he claims not to have been there but at a private meeting in a nearby motel. Frederic Sondern (1959: 36) reports: "One by one they were summoned to Sergeant Croswell's office, gave their names and addresses, took off their shoes, emptied their pockets as troopers searched and watched."

In 1959, Bonanno and other leading crime figures were indicted for refusing to answer questions as to the purpose of the meeting at Apalachin. Bonanno's case was separated from the others when he had a heart attack, but they were all found guilty. The verdict was later overturned on appeal. The court concluded that the people at the Barbara estate had been taken into custody, detained, and searched without probable cause that a crime had been committed.

In 1963 came the alleged plot against Gambino and Lucchese, and Bonanno sought, and was denied, Canadian citizenship. In February, 1964, while Bonanno was still in Canada, Family *capiregime* chose his son Bill *consigliere*.[6] The elevation of the young Bonanno was opposed from within and without the Bonanno Family. This act coupled with the plot against Gambino and Lucchese resulted in a "summons" for Joseph Bonanno to appear before the "national commission," of which he was one of the nine members; Bonanno declined. On October 21, 1964, Bonanno and his attorney were standing in front of a luxury apartment house in Manhattan, where they had sought shelter from the rain (1983: 260);

> . . . two men grabbed me from behind by each arm and immediately forced me toward the nearby street corner.
>   . . . "Come on, Joe, my boss wants you. . . . As they rushed me toward the corner, I heard Maloney [Bonanno's attorney] shouting after us. He was saying something about my being his client and they couldn't take me away like that. A pistol shot pinged the sidewalk. Maloney retreated.

Bonanno reports that he was kidnapped by two of his cousins, the son and brother of Stefano Magaddino, and held in a rural farmhouse for more than six weeks. Federal officials called it a hoax, an effort by Bonanno to avoid appearing before a grand jury investigating organized crime. Bonanno states that following his release, he remained in hiding in his Tucson home for more than a year. In the meantime, a revolt broke out within the Bonanno Family led by *caporegime* Gasper DiGregorio, Bill Bonanno's godfather and best man at the wedding of Fay and Joseph Bonanno.

On January 28, 1966, in an effort to reestablish unity, Bill Bonanno and several Family members loyal to his father went to Troutman Street in Brooklyn to meet with DiGregorio. The unity meeting turned out to be an ambush, and the young Bonanno narrowly escaped in an exchange of gunfire. On May 18, 1966, Joseph Bonanno reappeared and the war/revolt raged on. DiGregorio eventually withdrew, and the commission turned the Family over to Paul Sciacca. Joseph Bonanno retired to his Tucson home, leaving a three-man committee to fill the leadership until the "loyalists" could select a new boss. Despite Bonanno's retirement, the Family is still referred to as the Bonanno Family, something which Bonanno (1983: 292) decried:

> . . . it is improper for people still to refer to this Family as the Bonanno Family. It stopped being the Bonanno Family when I retired. In Sicily, a Family is sometimes likened to a *cosca*—an artichoke. The Family members are like the artichoke leaves and the Father is like the central stem on which they all hang. Remove the central stem and all you have is a lot of separate leaves. When I left New York to retire, all the separate leaves had to find themselves another stem.[7]

Jewish-Italian Cooperation: Murder, Inc.

In addition to the unparalleled level of criminal violence, Prohibition also encouraged cooperation among criminals across ethnic lines. By 1934, organized-crime leaders in the New York metropolitan area, Jewish and Italian, were meeting regularly to iron out differences and arrange business deals. Each recognized the interests of the others, the territory and/or enterprises each controlled. Out of this configuration emerged a unit of criminals dubbed by the press "Murder, Inc."

The setting is the East New York–Brownsville section of Brooklyn, a Jewish ghetto, and the adjoining neighborhood of Ocean Hill, an Italian ghetto. The story begins in the spring of 1930, when Abe ("Kid Twist") Reles, Martin ("Buggy") Goldstein, and Philip ("Pittsburgh Phil") Strauss decided to make some "easy" money by going into the pinball-machine business— renting the machines to candy stores and poolrooms. It was a good idea, but hardly original. In fact, the pinball business and criminal activities in that part of Brooklyn were controlled by the notorious Shapiro brothers, Irving, Meyer, and Willie. To deal with the anticipated problem, the boys from East New York–Brownsville teamed up with a crew of Italian criminals from Ocean Hill led by the Maione brothers, Harry ("Happy") and "Duke," and Frank ("The Dasher") Abbandando. They began to make inroads into the business controlled by the Shapiros, and with profits from the pinball machines they entered the loansharking business. The Shapiro brothers responded.

On June 11, 1930, one of the Reles group was killed, and he and Goldstein were wounded. Meyer Shapiro then abducted Reles's girlfriend, whom he beat and raped. The Reles group struck back—during 1930 and 1931 eighteen attempts were made on the life of Meyer Shapiro; he was killed on the *nineteenth*. Brother Irving followed, and Willie was abducted, severely beaten, and buried alive. The Reles group took over gambling, loansharking, and prostitution in the East New York–Brownsville and Ocean Hill sections of Brooklyn; their major specialty, however, became murder.

The "boys from Brooklyn" were used as staff killers by the confederation of organized-crime leaders that evolved in New York. In addition to their various criminal enterprises, the "boys" received a retainer to be "on call" whenever the occasion arose—and it arose often; in a ten-year period they murdered more than eighty persons in the borough of Brooklyn alone. They were so efficient that gang leaders from across the country made use of their services.

There were full-dress rehearsals; getaway routes were carefully checked; a "crash car" followed the stolen vehicle containing the actual killer (in the event of a police pursuit); guns were rendered untraceable, although ice picks and ropes were also used. One of the group's members described the "contract system" (Berger 1940: 5): The killer ("trooper") is merely directed to take a plane, car, or train to a certain place to meet "a man." The man points out ("fingers") the victim for the trooper, who kills him when it is convenient.

He then leaves town immediately, and when local hoodlums are questioned, their alibis are perfect. For the "boys from Brooklyn, murder was an art form. Pittsburgh Phil, for example, delighted in roping a victim like a little ball so that any movement pulled the line tighter and he eventually strangled himself (Turkus and Feder 1951).

Jenna Weissman Joselit (1983: 153) stresses the level of intergroup co-operation: ". . . the Jewish and Italian members of the gang worked side by side on a daily basis, physically molesting tardy borrowers and stubborn union leaders. Moreover, the gang took its orders from Albert Anastasia" even though Reles was considered the leader of the "boys from Brooklyn." Louis Capone was Anastasia's personnel representative and served as a buffer between the Reles and Maione parts of Murder, Inc.

In 1940 several of the "boys from Brooklyn" were indicted for the 1933 murder of Alec ("Red") Alpert. The nineteen-year-old had been "convicted" of talking to the authorities. Quite to the surprise of Burton Turkus, chief of the Homicide Bureau of the Brooklyn District Attorney's Office, one of the group's members who agreed to become a government witness was reputedly the toughest of the "boys." Abe Reles, upon being granted immunity from prosecution, began to disclose the sensational details of Murder, Inc., and seven men were eventually convicted and electrocuted, including Lepke Buchalter and Louis Capone. Before any case could be made against Albert Anastasia, Reles had an accident: on November 12, 1941, while under constant police guard, he fell out the sixth-floor window of a Coney Island hotel. His death remains unexplained.

---

[1] *Poolrooms* were places where lottery ("pool") tickets were sold. The drawings were held in the evenings, and the owners installed billiard tables to help customers pass the time while waiting for the lottery results (Katcher 1959).

[2] John ("Jack") Pullman was born in Russia in 1903. He was an associate of Lansky's during Prohibition and in 1931 served a fifteen-month sentence for bootlegging. He lived in Chicago, emigrated to Canada, and finally settled in Switzerland in 1960 (Petacque and Hough 1983).

[3] United States Senate Special Committee to Investigate Organized Crime in Interstate Commerce, Estes Kefauver of Tennessee, Chairman.

[4] Scalise (known as "Don Cheech") made his peace with Luciano and eventually emerged as the *sottocapo* of the Family headed by Albert Anastasia. On June 17, 1957, at age sixty-three, Scalise was shot to death in the Bronx. Joseph Valachi (Maas 1968) says that he was selling memberships—people were paying him up to $50,000 to be "made." This activity apparently infuriated Anastasia, who ordered Scalise's murder.

[5] Corallo received his nickname because of an ability to escape ("duck") assassinations and convictions. During the 1960s, this "ability" apparently faded. In 1961 he tried to bribe J. Vincent Keogh, a New York State supreme court judge, and Elliott Kahaner, chief assistant United States attorney for the Eastern District of New York, and received a two-year prison term. The case he was looking to "fix" involved James Marcus, commissioner of the New York City Department of Water Supply, Gas and Electricity, and Carmine De Sapio, head of Tammany Hall.

[6] Salvatore ("Bill") Bonanno and Joseph C. Bonanno, Jr., the sons of Joseph Bonanno, have served prison terms for conspiracy and extortion.

[7] In 1979, a federal grand jury indicted Bonanno and a commodities broker for obstructing justice. During the fourteen-week nonjury trial in 1980, the prosecutor maintained that Bonanno and his codefendant worked together to keep the records of several businesses from the grand jury. The FBI collected evidence by tapping Bonanno's telephone and retrieving his garbage for four years. (As in previous cases, the court ruled that garbage is not subject to rules governing privacy.) The defense objected to the introduction of notes in Sicilian fished out of Bonanno's garbage, contending that their translation into English was in doubt because there are no English equivalents to many of the terms used. Bonanno was found guilty and sentenced to a term of one year. He entered the federal prison at Terminal Island at the end of 1983.

chapter 9

Organized Crime In Chicago

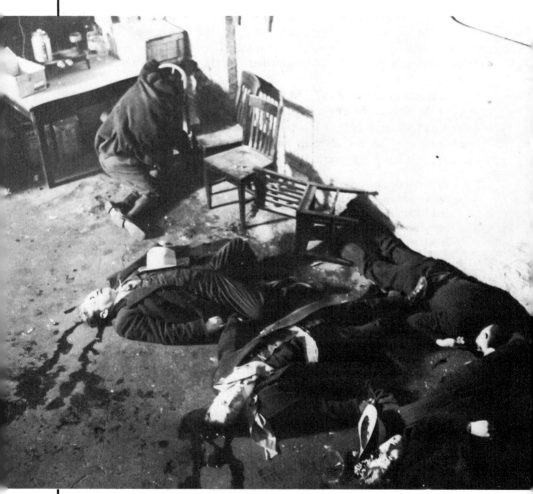

Used by permission of the Chicago Historical Society

H umbert Nelli (1969) traces the origins of organized crime in Chicago to the election of 1873, in which Michael Cassius McDonald backed Harvey Colvin for mayor. "In the mayoralty election of 1873, Mike McDonald, the gambling boss of Chicago, demonstrated that under effective leadership the gamblers, liquor interests, and brothel keepers could be welded into a formidable political power" (Peterson 1963: 31). Michael ("King Mike") McDonald was born in Niagara Falls, New York, around 1840 and left for Detroit when he was about fifteen. He held a number of menial jobs and spent a great deal of time gambling. In 1860, when he was about twenty, McDonald bought a bar in the heart of downtown Chicago. Bars in those days often included gambling and prostitution. His saloon was the center of a great deal of activity and was frequented by politicians who utilized McDonald as a "bagman," an intermediary for the collection of bribes (Klatt 1983).

After the great fire of 1871, McDonald opened "Our Store" (better known as just the Store), the city's largest liquor and gambling house. The lower floors had Mexican onyx wainscoting in the barrooms, while one huge bar was made of genuine mahogany and the floor was Roman mosaic. Wayne Klatt (1983: 30) points out:

> Until McDonald opened shop, gambling had been rather unorganized in Chicago—and so were politics. The city was fairly evenly divided between Democrats and Republicans; there were two aldermen per ward, and mayoral elections were every two years; and everything was a mess. The Democrats were interested only in winning aldermanic seats, and let the mayor be damned.

King Mike changed this by backing gambler Harvey D. Colvin. From then on until his death in 1907, McDonald controlled mayors, senators, and congressmen; his newspaper, the *Globe,* often influenced elections, and he also owned the elevated railroad line in Chicago (Wendt and Kogan 1943).

McDonald's Store was located in the Levee district of Chicago's notorious First Ward. The political "Lords of the Levee" (with McDonald's backing) were the "Mutt and Jeff" team of John ("Bathhouse") Coughlin, a powerfully built six-footer, and Michael ("Hinky Dink") Kenna, a diminutive organizational genius. Born in 1860, Coughlin began his career as a rubber in the exclusive Palmer Baths, where he met the wealthy and the powerful. These contacts helped him when he opened his own bathhouse, and soon others. Among his customers were important politicians, and he quickly became a Democratic precinct captain. On April 5, 1892, Coughlin was elected alderman from the First Ward, one of thirty-five into which the city was divided. The city council into which "the Bathhouse" (a nickname he enjoyed) entered was literally selling out the city of Chicago. The "boodles," schemes through which city privileges were sold, made the three-dollar-a-meeting alderman's position quite lucrative (Wendt and Kogan 1943).

"Hinky Dink" Kenna (who was reportedly named after a waterhole he swam in as a youngster) was born in the First Ward in 1858. He became a hardworking newsboy and eventually a successful saloon keeper and politician. He established a defense fund to which brothel keepers and gamblers contributed in order to secure the services of Kenna's lawyers, who were on retainer. Kenna eventually joined Coughlin as an alderman in the city council. The Bathhouse and the Hinky Dink became partners, and as their power grew it became necessary to be "licensed" by the Kenna-Coughlin team to do business in the Levee. Their ability to deliver votes was a mainstay—whether it was for their favorite mayoral candidate or for themselves. In 1897, the pair skillfully engineered the Democratic nomination for Carter Henry Harrison (the younger), whose father had been killed while he was mayor by a disgruntled job seeker. In the First Ward, Kenna and Coughlin delivered a vote of five to one. Their election techniques included the use of the Quincy Street Boys, a gang of vicious thugs who provided election day "services." Kenna was also something of a humanitarian; he provided food and lodging to large numbers of men made destitute during a depression. At election time these thankful men were brought into the First Ward, where they registered and voted for the Kenna-Coughlin ticket (Wendt and Kogan 1943).

The rise of Kenna and Coughlin coincided with the decline of Mike McDonald. He had grown rich, and by the time he died in 1907 his interest in ward politics had dwindled. While the Bathhouse and the Hinky Dink picked up part of his political mantle, King Mike's bookmaking operation was taken over by Mont Tennes, gambling boss of the North Side.

Mont Tennes

Writing in 1929, John Landesco (1968: 45), an investigator for the Illinois Association for Criminal Justice, stated: "The complete life history of one man, were it known in every detail, would disclose practically all there is to know about syndicated gambling as a phase of organized crime in Chicago in the last quarter century. That man is *Mont Tennes.*" In 1907, Tennes secured control of the wire service that transmitted the results of horse races throughout the country, and every bookmaker was dependent on the service. Without the wire service, a bookmaker is vulnerable to "past-posting"— placing a bet after the race is already over and the winner determined. The swindler sets up a relay system that transmits the results of a race to a confederate, who quickly places a bet on a horse that has already won. The bookmaker will accept the bet because regular channels have not informed him that the race has even started.

When some bookmakers balked at paying Tennes for the service, an outbreak of violence and police raids ensued. In retaliation, while walking with his wife, Tennes was attacked and badly beaten. Tennes responded with stepped-up police raids and bombings. By 1909, Tennes had an absolute control over racetrack gambling and handbooks in Chicago: "The Tennes ring at this time established systematic exclusion. Anyone wishing to enter the gambling business had to apply to the ring. The man and the location would be investigated, the leading gamblers in the city would be asked to approve the applicant, and if disapproved he would be placed upon the 'dead list' " (Landesco 1968: 54). Tennes paid the Payne Telegraph Service of Cincinnati, politicians, and the police; and gamblers who paid Tennes received race results immediately and protection from police raids. The Tennes syndicate paid half of the money lost to bettors who won from bookmakers, and received 50 percent of net receipts after racing sheets were balanced each day. Tennes's agents made rounds of subscribers checking betting sheets.

Tennes eventually established his own wire service, the General News Bureau, and a struggle ensued with the older Payne News Service. Disclosures resulting from the feud revealed that Tennes "had risen from king of Chicago gamblers to czar of all the race track gambling in the United States and Canada." His combine had a grip on the police in twenty American cities and enforced its dictates with dynamite. Cities from New York to San Francisco, Detroit to San Antonio paid for the Tennes wire service, which involved eighteen telephone and telegraph companies (Landesco 1968: 59).

With the advent of Prohibition, the level of violence in organized crime increased dramatically. Tennes sold his service to both George ("Bugs") Moran and his rival, Al Capone. In the end, Tennes became an associate of Jimmie Mondi, the Capone organization manager for gambling operations. Tennes withdrew from this "shotgun marriage" and retired in 1929 (Landesco 1968). Alson Smith (1962) states that Tennes retired, a millionaire, in 1927.

Big Bill Thompson

In order to fully understand and appreciate the climate that gave rise to Al Capone, we need to dwell on Chicago politics and the man William Hale ("Big Bill") Thompson, who was elected mayor in 1915.

The mayor of Chicago from 1911 to 1915 was Carter Harrison (the younger), who Charles Merriam (1929: 21) notes was opposed to the growth of boss-controlled "spoils and grafting machine." While not a leader of reform, Harrison "on the whole prevented the drift of the city into the hands of the spoilsmen of the worst type." In 1915, Harrison was opposed in the Democratic primary by a candidate backed by the Democratic organization, Robert M. Sweitzer, the county clerk (a patronage-rich office). Sweitzer won, and his prospects for victory in the general election were quite promising. The Republicans chose Thompson in their primary.

Thompson began his political career as a reformer, backed by the nonpartisan Municipal Voters' League in a successful race for alderman from the Second Ward in 1900. He was "a towering athlete with a snaggled front tooth who had brought glory to the Chicago Athletic Association in half a dozen sports" (Kobler 1971: 55). His father had been a wealthy real estate dealer, but the young Thompson (born in 1865) preferred the life of a cowboy and spent much of his youth out West. As mayor he often sported cowboy hats. He was a gifted orator—to call him demagogic would not be an exaggeration—who vilified real and imagined enemies such as the British and the king of England; such attacks gained him the support of German and Irish voters. In 1902 he was elected to the Cook County Board of Commissioners. His victory over Sweitzer in 1915 was based on demagogic appeals: in German neighborhoods he attacked the British; in German-hating Polish neighborhoods he attacked the Germans; in Irish areas he attacked the British; and when addressing Protestant audiences, he warned that a vote for Sweitzer was a vote for the pope. He promised the reformers strict enforcement of the gambling laws, and he promised the gamblers an open town. He received strong support in the black wards, and many Harrison Democrats deserted the party to support Thompson. Merriam (1929: 22) notes that, with the election of Thompson, "The spoils system swept over the city like a noxious blight, and city hall became a symbol for corruption and incompetence."

Jay Robert Nash (1981: 241) points out that Thompson had been elected even though he was known to be corrupt "and in the face of such an endorsement, Thompson felt he could act with impunity and did." John Kobler (1971: 57) notes that "within six months he had violated every campaign promise but one. He did keep Chicago wide open." Despite these excesses, Big Bill was reelected in 1919 (Nash 1981: 242):

> His 1919 campaign was all banner and slogan. Thompson organized the Chicago Boosters Club which put up huge posters everywhere reading, "A booster is better than a knocker." He extorted more than $1 million from business leaders for his war chest—he said it was "to help publicize Chicago"—by threatening not to renew their licenses. He led dozens of marches down the main streets while his paid henchman gave out the roaring chant, "All hats off to our mayor, Big Bill the Builder."

In 1923, Thompson was defeated by reform-minded William E. Dever. In 1927, running on a pledge to let the liquor flow again in Chicago, Big Bill was swept back into office for a third term: Mike Royko points out (1971: 35): "As much as Chicagoans wanted reform, they wanted their bootleg gin more, so after four years of Dever, they returned Thompson to power." In 1931, Big Bill lost to Anton ("Tony") Cermak.

Anton J. ("Tony") Cermak

Born in Kladno, Czechoslovakia, in 1873, Anton Cermak was brought to the United States by his parents when he was a year old. Like his father, Anton became a coal miner; in 1889 he moved to Chicago and obtained a job as a railroad brakeman. He became a member of a saloon-centered gang of young

Bohemians and excelled in the gang's two major interests: drinking and fighting. He opened his own business, which prospered, became a Democratic precinct captain, and was elected head of the "United Societies," a group representing liquor interests who were opposed to Sunday closing laws. In 1902 he was elected to the Illinois general assembly, and in 1921 he became president of the Cook County Board of Commissioners (Gottfried 1962). By 1929 he was the head of the Democratic organization of Cook County and a wealthy man. Royko (1971: 36) notes that Cermak "had sense to count up all the Irish votes, then he counted all the Italians, Jews, Germans, Poles and Bohemians." Cermak concluded that Irish domination of the Cook County Democratic Party did not make numerical sense. He organized instead an ethnically balanced slate of candidates and put together "the most powerful political machine in Chicago history." That machine ended the political career of Big Bill Thompson.

Harold Gosnell (1968) reports that Cermak was deeply involved with bootlegging interests, and Kenneth Allsop (1968: 217) states that, while Thompson's organization was corrupt, Cermak "systematized grand larceny." Fletcher Dobyns (1932: ix) reported that Cermak reached his position of wealth and power by joining with a group of men who "organized the denizens of the underworld and their patrons, political job holders and their dependents and friends, those seeking privileges and immunities, and grafters of every type. . . ." Alex Gottfried (1962), in his extensive biography of Cermak, portrays him as a dynamic and hardworking public figure; an honest man who literally went from "rags to riches" and power in accord with the American tradition of Horatio Alger.[1]

On February 15, 1933, a large crowd gathered in Miami's Bayfront park to greet President-elect Roosevelt. As Roosevelt and Cermak exchanged a few words, Guiseppe Zangara, an Italian immigrant residing in Hackensack, New Jersey, opened fire with a pistol. He managed to discharge five rounds before being seized. Five persons were wounded, including Cermak, who died several days later. Zangara was quoted as saying, shortly after he was arrested, "I'd kill every president." On his clothing he had several local newspaper clippings announcing Roosevelt's visit to Miami (Hagerty 1933: 1). Investigations into the incident revealed no evidence tying Zangara to any group, and it is generally believed that Roosevelt was the assassin's real target. August Bequai (1979: 38) states that on his deathbed Zangara "told the authorities that the syndicate had ordered the mayor's assassination." Royko (1971: 36) refers to Zangara as a would-be "mad" presidential assassin, and this is the generally accepted view.

From Colosimo to Torrio to Capone

James ("Big Jim" or "Diamond Jim") Colosimo arrived in Chicago from Calabria, Italy, in 1895 at age seventeen. As a street sweeper in the First

Ward (known as "white wings" because of their white uniforms), he organized his fellow sweepers into a successful labor and political bloc. He became a power among Italians in the ward and a precinct captain under Kenna and Coughlin. He later became a bagman for the Bathhouse and Hinky Dink, and eventually a successful "white slaver" with a string of brothels and gambling houses. He owned a nationally famous restaurant, Colosimo's Cafe, which attracted luminaries from society, opera, and the theater—such persons as George M. Cohan and Enrico Caruso (Nelli 1969; Kobler 1971). His bodyguard, Michael Carrozzo, eventually became the head of the "white wings" citywide and led twenty-five union locals in Chicago.

In 1909, Colosimo, like many other successful Italians, experienced Black Hand extortion threats.[2] In response, he brought John Torrio, age thirty-two, to Chicago. John Kobler (1971) refers to Torrio as Colosimo's nephew, while Jack McPhaul (1970) reports that he was a distant cousin of his wife, Victoria Colosimo, a former madam. In either event, he was the right man for the job. Torrio did not smoke, gamble, drink, or consort with women; he was, however, head of the notorious James Street Boys, an affiliate gang of Paul Kelly and his Five Pointers. His business partner was Frank ("Frankie Yale") Uale, a Sicilian racketeer whose specialty was murder by contract: "I'm an undertaker," he boasted (Kobler 1971: 29). Yale was also the national head of the *Unione Siciliana*. Shortly after he arrived in Chicago, Torrio lured three Black Handers into an ambush where they were shot to death.

Torrio's usefulness extended to overseeing brothels and gambling operations for Colosimo. He encountered trouble when a white-slave victim agreed to testify against him under the recently passed Mann Act, which made it a federal crime to transport someone over a state line for immoral purposes. White slavers had been luring young girls to Chicago with promises of legitimate employment. Upon arrival they were often dosed with knockout drops and removed to brothels. If they objected, they were raped and brutalized; some took their own lives. The potential witness against Torrio was in the custody of the FBI when she was murdered (McPhaul 1970).

When public opinion in Chicago turned against the red-light district of the Levee, the mayor, Carter Harrison, ordered the police to close down the brothels. Torrio moved the Colosimo operations into Burnham, a township of a thousand persons. He put the mayor and the chief of police on the payroll. Torrio was able to open a series of roadside brothels in rural Cook County by bribing both public officials and residents where the brothels were housed. He bought a four-story building a block away from Colosimo's Cafe, which became known as the Four Deuces because of its address, 2222 Wabash Avenue. The first floor had a saloon and Torrio's office, protected by a steel-barred gate. The second and third floors had gambling rooms with solid steel doors; the fourth floor housed a bordello. Back in New York, Frankie Yale hired a huge-fisted member of the Five Points Gang to deal with obstreperous customers. On one occasion, however, an offensive remark to a young girl in the saloon led to a four-inch scar, courtesy of her irate brother and his pocketknife. The young Five Pointer was prone to be somewhat overexuberant in carrying out his duties. A suspect in two murders, his third victim was on the critical list when Yale thought it best that Alphonse Capone leave for Chicago.

"Scarface" Al Capone

Capone's birthplace is the subject of debate; in addition to Brooklyn, various parts of Italy, other than Sicily, are mentioned (Albini 1971). Allsop (1968) maintains that he was born in Castel Amara, near Rome, on January 6, 1895. The *New York Times* states that he was born in Naples on January 17, 1899 ("Capone Dead" 1947). It appears, however, that Alphonse Capone was born and raised in the Navy Yard–Greenpoint section of Brooklyn. His parents, naturalized Americans, came from Naples in 1893.

Capone arrived in Chicago in 1919 and went to work as a bouncer for Johnny Torrio at the Four Deuces. Shortly after his arrival, Torrio sent Capone to teach some etiquette to someone who had had the temerity to slap and insult Jake Guzik, an important, but physically unimposing, Torrio aide. Temerity turned to outright stupidity; Capone too was insulted, and another man died. Capone fled to Burnham until the witnesses could be convinced of their mistaken identity. Meanwhile, Colosimo divorced his wife, and on April 17, 1920, he married Dale Winter, a young singer. Torrio was now in charge of all of Colosimo's operations, and he began to give Capone important responsibilities (McPhaul 1970).

Prohibition

With "the coming of Prohibition, the personnel of organized vice took the lead in the systematic organization of this new and profitable field of exploitation. All the experience gained by years of struggle against reformers and concealed agreements with politicians was brought into service in organizing and distribution of beer and whiskey" (Landesco 1968: 43). Colosimo, however, was fearful of federal enforcement efforts and wanted to stay away from bootlegging (McPhaul 1970). On May 11, 1920, Big Jim was found in the vestibule of his cafe—he had been shot to death. The murderer and the reason for his murder remain unknown. Speculation about the former centers on Frankie Yale. Infatuation with a young bride made Colosimo neglect business, and his murder has been ascribed to a reluctance to take full advantage of the new areas of profit offered by Prohibition. A second speculation concerns his ex-wife acting out the role of a "woman scorned." McPhaul (1970) reports, however, that Victoria had remarried and at the time of Colosimo's murder was in Los Angeles visiting her new in-laws. Colosimo was denied a Roman Catholic burial—he had been divorced and remarried.

The pallbearers and honorary pallbearers at Big Jim's funeral included ten aldermen, three judges, a congressman, and the Democratic leader of the state legislature (Wendt and Kogan 1943).

Nelli notes that "after Colosimo's death, John Torrio succeeded to the first ward based Italian 'syndicate' throne, which he occupied until his retirement in 1925. An able and effective leader, Torrio excelled as a master strategist and organizer and quickly built an empire which far exceeded that of his predecessor in wealth, power and influence" (1969: 386). This power is highlighted by an incident in 1921, when Torrio was arrested as a result of the white-slavery activities of Jake ("Greasy Thumb") Guzik (sometimes spelled Cusik—a Polish Jew). Guzik advertised for a housemaid, whom he subsequently imprisoned, had raped, and forced into working in a brothel. She was able to inform her brothers, who rescued her, and Guzik and Torrio were prosecuted. Before a verdict could be reached, however, the two were pardoned by Governor Len Small. Small had been indicted shortly after taking office, only to be saved by a Torrio enforcer who bribed and intimidated the jurors. The pardon was a reward for Small's acquittal (Kobler 1971).

Outside of the First Ward, various gangs ruled over sections of Chicago, where they combined crime and politics into wealth and power. On the Northeast Side, in the Forty-second and Forty-third Wards, was the gang headed by Dion O'Banion. He controlled the Irish vote much as Colosimo controlled the Italian vote in the First Ward. Despite his sordid background, including several shootings in public view, a banquet was held in O'Banion's honor by the Chicago Democratic Party in 1924. It seems that O'Banion had decided to switch his loyalty to the Republicans; the Democratic mayor at the time, Dever, was a reformer who insisted that laws against many of O'Banion's activities be enforced. The Democratic officials made speeches in his honor and even presented O'Banion with a platinum watch—all to no avail. O'Banion and the votes of the Forty-second and Forty-third Wards went to the Republicans (Coffey 1975). O'Banion was a regular churchgoer and loved flowers. This led him to purchase a florist shop and become gangdom's favorite florist.

Landesco (1968) points out that the O'Banion gang lacked the ethnic cohesion that bound together the dominant element in the Torrio-Capone organization. His gang included Samuel ("Nails") Morton, a Jew; Vincent Drucci, an Italian; and Earl Wajciechowski (better known as Hymie Weiss), a Pole. Other parts of Chicago also had their gangs: William ("Klondike") O'Donnell and his brothers Myles and Bernard were on the West Side; on the South Side was another group of O'Donnells, Steve, Walter, Thomas, and Edward ("Spike"); on the West Side were the Druggan-Lake or Valley gang headed by Terry Druggan. On the Southwest Side was the Saltis-McErlane gang headed by Joe Saltis and Frank McErlane. The latter is described as a "compulsive killer" by Kobler (1971), and Saltis is noted for having introduced the Thompson submachine gun ("tommy gun") into Chicago gang warfare. Until the 1920s, the tommy gun could be freely purchased by mail or in sporting-goods stores (Kobler 1971).

On the South Side were Ragen's Colts, whom John Landesco (1968: 169) selects as examples "of the genuine popularity of the gangster, home-grown in the neighborhood gang, idealized in the morality of the neighbor-hood." The gang began as a baseball team with Frank and Mike Ragen as star players. As the Morgan Athletic Club, they participated in amateur foot-ball, baseball, and rugby and stood high in their respective leagues. Around their activities centered many of the neighborhood's social events—picnics, dances, and an annual ball supported by business and professional men throughout the neighborhood. In 1908, the club's name was changed to the Ragen Athletic Association, and Frank Ragen remained president. He became a respected public figure and county commissioner, and eventually he an-nounced his separation from the club. In 1917, the club's New Year's Eve party was attended by more than five thousand persons. The group prided itself on patriotism, and five hundred members went into the armed forces during the First World War. Ragen's Colts were also active in the racial violence of 1919, which began when a black youngster drowned after being subjected to a rock-throwing crowd at a white beach.[3]

The Colts became "election specialists" during the years of Prohibition and were used for strong-arm work throughout Chicago. They eventually split into factions when various members joined opposing beer-running gangs that were then at war in Chicago. On August 4, 1927, the twelve remaining members met and voted to disband and sell their club headquarters (Landesco 1968).

In the "Little Italy" of the city's South Side were the "Terrible Gennas," six brothers known for their brutality but who, like Dion O'Banion, were regular churchgoers. Prohibition enabled them to become quite prosperous by organizing the Italian home stills that proliferated, or were encouraged by the Gennas, in Little Italy, and distributing the spirits with police and political protection (Kobler 1971). Just where politics ended and crime began was not always clear in Chicago, as the history of the Nineteenth Ward highlights.

Alderman's War in the Nineteenth Ward

John ("Johnny de Pow") Powers had been the ruler of the Nineteenth Ward since 1888, when the ward was predominantly Irish. The influx of Italian immigrants changed the ethnic makeup of the ward: by 1916 Italians held a majority of votes. In that year, Anthony D'Andrea announced that he would oppose Alderman James Bowler, the candidate of Johnny Powers. D'Andrea had been educated at the University of Palermo and was an accomplished linguist. He served as president of the International Hod Carriers' Union and was later business agent for the Macaroni Manufacturers' Union. He was also the head of the *Unione Siciliana* in Chicago. On February 21, 1916, the campaign began—a ward boss for Powers, Frank Lombardi, was shot to death in a Taylor Street saloon (the Gennas were suspected). D'Andrea, however, lost the election to Bowler, but the war had begun.

In March 1920, in an effort to secure Italian support, Powers had D'Andrea elected in his place as Democratic committeeman from the Nineteenth Ward. The Illinois Supreme Court, however, voided the election, and Powers regained the post. D'Andrea yelled "foul," and on September 28, 1920, a bomb exploded on the porch of Powers' house. In 1921, D'Andrea announced that he was a candidate for the aldermanic seat held by Johnny Powers—things heated up. Numerous bombings and killings followed as sluggers and gunmen from both camps patrolled the streets. In the end, Powers defeated D'Andrea by 435 votes, but the violence continued. On March 9, 1921, a Powers supporter was murdered, and another followed a short time later. The "Bloody Nineteenth" remained an armed camp, and D'Andrea announced his withdrawal from politics, but it was too late—on May 11, 1921, he was shotgunned to death (Landesco 1968; Kobler 1971).

"When You Smell Gunpowder, You're in Cicero"

By 1923, Torrio had expanded his beer operations well beyond his South Side stronghold. He moved out into the Cook County suburbs, and when a location was decided upon, the neighborhood people were canvassed. If they were agreeable, Torrio agents would provide rewards: a new car, a house redecorated or repaired. The local authorities were then approached and terms negotiated (Allsop 1968). Adjacent to Chicago's Far West Side, in the suburban city of Cicero (population 50,000), the saloons were associated with Klondike O'Donnell, and the only gambling was with slot machines owned by a local politician. At that time, the O'Donnells were opposed to prostitution; so when Torrio opened a brothel in Cicero, it was promptly raided. He opened a second, and it too was raided. Two days later, at Torrio's direction, a posse of deputy sheriffs entered Cicero and confiscated the slot machines—no whores, no slots. The outcome was an arrangement whereby the slot machines were returned, the O'Donnells continued to handle bootlegging, and Torrio was allowed to operate his bordellos and gambling houses (Allsop 1968).

In 1923, reform hit Chicago and the mayoralty went to a Democrat, William E. Dever, a judge and "by Chicago standards a decent man" (Royko 1971: 34). He ordered the police to move against the rampant vice in Chicago, but corruption was too deeply engrained to be easily pushed aside. Kenneth Allsop (1968: 201) states that "sporadically and trivially" Dever harassed some liquor deliveries and effected an occasional police raid. Although he was not corrupt, Dever apparently accomplished very little. However, with the Democrats in control of Chicago, the Republicans were fearful of a reform wave that would loosen their hold on the suburban areas of Cook County. As a result, a local Republican leader made a deal with Al Capone, while

Torrio was out of Chicago and on vacation. In return for helping the Republicans win reelection in Cicero, Torrio would be given a free hand in the city (Allsop 1968).

In the Cicero election of April 1924, the Capone brothers, Al and Salvatore (usually called "Frank")[4] led a group of some two hundred Chicago thugs into Cicero. They intimidated, beat, and even killed Democrats who sought to oppose the Republican candidates. Some Cicero officials responded by having a county judge deputize seventy Chicago police officers, who entered Cicero and engaged the Capone gangsters. In one incident, Chicago police saw the Capone brothers, Charley Fischetti (a Capone cousin), and Dave Hedlin standing by the polls with guns in their hands ushering voters inside. In the ensuing exchange of gunfire, Frank Capone was killed, but Joseph Z. Klenha, the Capone candidate, was reelected mayor of Cicero (Kobler 1971).

Capone moved his headquarters from Chicago and took over the Hawthorne Inn in Cicero with a little help from his friends, Myles O'Donnell and a gunman named James J. Doherty—they opened fire on the owner "while shopping housewives and local tradesmen threw themselves behind cars and into doorways in the horizontal position that was becoming an identifiable posture of Cicero citizens" (Allsop 1968: 62–63). At the Hawthorne Inn, Capone ruled Cicero with an iron hand. When Mayor Klenha failed to carry out one of his orders, Capone went to city hall, where he personally knocked "his honor" down the steps and kicked him repeatedly as a policeman strolled by (Allsop 1968). Mike Royko states that since the Capone organization took over Cicero, it has never completely let go: "It still has its strip of bars where gambling and whoring are unnoticed. The only thing they won't tolerate in Cicero are Negroes" (1971: 34).[5] The Torrio organization expanded its suburban operations into Forest View, a small town of about a thousand people south of Cicero, where they intimidated town officials into leaving. With their own chief of police in control, the Torrio organization turned Forest View into one large brothel and gang headquarters (Kobler 1971).

War in Chicago

Reform in Chicago had unexpected consequences; it created an unstable situation that encouraged competitive moves by various gang interests. When Thompson lost to Dever, the system of protection broke down, and in the ensuing confusion the South Side O'Donnells began to move into Torrio territory, terrorizing saloon keepers into buying their beer from the O'Donnell suppliers. On September 7, 1923, O'Donnell sluggers entered the saloon of Joe Kepka and began threatening him. The lights went out, shots rang out, and by the time the police arrived, the O'Donnells were short one young tough. Ten days later two more O'Donnell men were dispatched, and the O'Donnell brothers stopped bothering Torrio (Landesco 1968). This was apparently a wise move. Allsop (1968) reports that Al Capone had under his command an army of seven hundred men and among them were some of the most proficient gunmen in the country.

By 1924, Torrio was the head of a combine that included about a dozen Chicago gang leaders. Landesco (1968) reports that in a feudal arrangement, bootlegging was divided among the gangs and Torrio acted as an arbitrator in cases of disputes. The South Side O'Donnells were not included in the arrangement, and they began to move into the territory of the McErlane-Saltis gang, just as they had tried to move in on Torrio in 1923. They didn't do much better. In the *South Side Beer War* that resulted, the "take 'em for a ride" technique was inaugurated with the murder of Thomas ("Morrie") Keane by McErlane-Saltis gunmen. The war continued into 1918, and the O'Donnells suffered most of the losses. Kobler (1971) notes that it was against Spike O'Donnell on the evening of September 25, 1925, that Frank McErlane first used his tommy gun (at least on human targets). The shots went wild, and Spike escaped. There were, however, ten more attempts on his life, and he was wounded twice.

> "I've got a mob of blue-eyed Irish boys who are with me to stay," O'Donnell told police in 1928. "No Saltis is going to run us out." But Saltis had his Irishman too, in the person of Lefty Paddy Sullivan, a former Chicago police sergeant who reportedly joined his boss and two others in a blistering machine-gun attack on O'Donnell from a moving auto . . . on October 9, 1928. O'Donnell survived, returning their fire with his pistol and in the confusion shooting a policeman by mistake (Bowman 1983: 8).

Spike, leader of the O'Donnell brothers, withdrew from combat. He died of a heart attack in 1962, a few years after Joe Saltis, who also died a natural death.

The *West Side Beer War* began in 1924 when O'Banion began to feud with the Genna brothers: Allsop (1968) reports that the Gennas moved in on O'Banion territory, while Kobler states that it was O'Banion who was selling liquor in Genna territory (1971). In that same year O'Banion swindled Torrio by selling him his share of a brewery in which they were partners for $500,000—O'Banion knew that the Sieben Brewery was about to be raided (Allsop 1968). Emboldened by the lack of response from Torrio, apparently mistaking caution for fear, O'Banion went around boasting about how he had "taken" Torrio. He then hijacked a supply of Genna liquor, antagonizing the Gennas and indicating scorn for Torrio.

November 10, 1924, Albert Anselmi and John Scalise, Sicilian immigrants who worked for the Genna brothers and Torrio, and Mike Genna entered the O'Banion flower shop. O'Banion was busy preparing floral arrangements for the funeral of Mike Merlo, president of the *Unione Siciliana,* who had died of natural causes two days before. What the florist didn't know was that Merlo had been exerting his influence to keep the Gennas and Torrio from moving against O'Banion. Kobler (1971) reports that Merlo abhorred violence and also got along well with O'Banion—now he was dead. When the three entered the flower shop, O'Banion came out to greet them and shook hands with Genna; Torrio had placed an order for $10,000 worth of assorted flowers, and Capone had ordered $8,000 worth of roses. While shaking O'Banion's hand, Genna suddenly jerked him forward and seized his arms. Before he could wriggle free and reach for any of the three guns he always carried, O'Banion was hit by five bullets. A sixth, the *coup de grâce,* was fired into his head after he fell to the floor. The war that followed lasted more than four years and ended on St. Valentine's Day, 1929 (Kobler 1971; Allsop 1968).

The O'Banion forces, under the leadership of Hymie Weiss, struck back, and in 1925 they narrowly missed killing Capone. Afterwards Capone traveled in a specially built armored Cadillac limousine. To avoid the battle, Torrio pled guilty to a bootlegging charge and was sentenced to a nine-month term to begin five days from sentencing. On January 24, 1925, before he could surrender to begin serving the sentence, Torrio was critically wounded by O'Banion gunmen. He recovered from his wounds and retired from Chicago, leaving his organization to Capone (Kobler 1971).

During the war, four of the Genna brothers were killed, three by rival gangsters and one by the police. The remaining brothers fled Chicago. While Capone was busy fighting with the O'Banion forces under Weiss, the West Side O'Donnells (Klondike, Myles and Bernard) and their all-Irish gang began to move in on Capone operations in Cicero. On April 27, 1926, William H. McSwiggin, a twenty-six-year-old assistant state's attorney, stood in front of a Cicero saloon with two members of the West Side O'Donnells. Shortly afterwards a car drove up and machine-gunned the three to death. The murderers were never identified, but Capone was suspected. McSwiggin's reason for being in Cicero with gangsters has never been determined (Landesco 1968). His murder, however, resulted in a public outcry and raids on Capone's suburban empire by both police and vigilantes. Capone became a fugitive from a federal grand jury, although he eventually surrendered and avoided prosecution. On October 11, 1926, Hymie Weiss was shot down. At age twenty-eight, he left an estate of $1,300,000 (Allsop 1968).

Needless to say, gang wars are "bad for business," so that in the middle of the mayhem and murder, a truce was called, and the principals met at a Chicago hotel: the Hotel Sherman, according to Allsop (1968) and Kobler (1971); the Morrison Hotel, according to Landesco (1968). Allsop states that it took place on October 20, 1926; Kobler and Landesco say it was on the twenty-first of October. Allsop and Kobler agree that the meeting was initiated by Joe Saltis, who had pledged loyalty to Capone but who was secretly allied with O'Banion forces now led by George ("Bugs") Moran. Capone had discovered this treachery, but wanted peace more than he wanted revenge. The meeting was quite extraordinary, even for Chicago. The assembled gang chieftains divided up the city and county, with the largest shares going to the

Capone organization and the Moran-Drucci gang (Vincent Drucci was later killed by the police as they were driving him to the station house for "questioning"). Also receiving shares were representatives of the McErlane-Saltis gang (both men were in jail) and the Sheldon gang, now allied with Capone. The initial truce lasted seventy days, until a member of the Sheldon gang was killed on orders from Saltis. Sheldon complained to Capone, and two Saltis men were shot to death in their car—peace prevailed (Allsop 1968).

In 1927, supported by Capone and other criminal interests, and running on a pledge to let the liquor flow again in Chicago, Big Bill Thompson was swept back into office. During the election campaign, however, the peace treaty of October 20 or 21 came apart; there were a number of killings and an attempt on Capone's life. In one incident, four hired killers from out of town were themselves killed while trying to collect a $50,000 bounty that had been placed on Capone's head by his rivals. They were mowed down by machine guns only hours after arriving in Chicago (Kobler 1971).

In the Republican primary election for state's attorney (county prosecutor), held on April 10, 1928, there had been so much violence that it became known as the "Pineapple Primary" (named after the military exploding device, the hand grenade, of similar appearance). Fletcher Dobyns (1932: 1–4) describes what happened after the primary election:

> "Scarface Al" Capone sat in his grand headquarters in Chicago [at the Lexington Hotel]. The doors opened and past heavily armed guards moved the venerable figure of Frank J. Loesch, counsel for the Pennsylvania Railroad Company, president of the Chicago Crime Commission, and member of the National Commission on Law Observance and Enforcement [Wickersham Commission]. He had come by appointment and secretly to present to the all-powerful chief a humble petition that the people of Chicago be permitted to select their own State's Attorney—the official whose first and most imperative duty would be to hang Capone and every member of his gang. . . .

Capone agreed to help, and "it turned out to be the squarest and most successful election day in forty years. There was not one complaint, not one election fraud and not one threat of trouble all day."

> That the president of that [Crime] Commission knew that it would be useless to appeal to the Mayor, the Chief of Police, the State's Attorney or the Sheriff to prevent "hoodlums and cutthroats" from controlling the election of a State's Attorney shows that these officials were dominated by the criminal elements of the city. . . .
>
> The orderly election and the success of the candidate in whom Mr. Loesch was interested created not a ripple of excitement in Chicago's gangland. It was understood that whatever his intentions might be, he would be powerless. Capone knew this when he agreed to permit the people to elect him.

Prohibition had enabled Capone to rise from the ranks of common thugs to a place in the *Guiness Book of World Records*—highest gross income ever achieved by a private citizen in a single year, $105 million in 1927.[6] During the Great Depression, Capone used some of this money to open "soup kitchens" where he fed thousands of people daily.

Labor Racketeering

Harold Seidman (1938) points out that until 1929, labor racketeering was only a sideline for most top gangsters such as Capone. However, as the sale of liquor fell off with the onset of the Depression, gang leaders were faced with a restless army of young and violent men whom they were committed to pay anywhere from $100 to $500 per week. McPhaul (1970) states that Capone also recognized by 1928 that Prohibition would probably only last a few more years; new sources of income would be needed. Capone moved into racketeering on a grand scale. He took over many rackets then prevalent in Chicago: extortion from Jewish butchers, fish stores, the construction industry, garage owners, bakeries, laundries, beauty parlors, dry cleaners, theaters, sports arenas, even bootblacks. In 1928, the state's attorney of Cook County listed ninety-one Chicago unions and business associations under gangster control—these gradually came under the control of the Capone organization (Kobler 1971). Seidman (1938) points out that the gangsters who controlled racketeering in Chicago proved no match for the Capone forces. (It was the same in other cities; in Detroit, for example, the "Purple Gang" took over labor racketeering through a reign of terror.)

Capone's Victory and His Downfall

In 1928, Capone clashed with Frankie Yale. Kobler (1971) states that Capone had discovered that Yale—his onetime boss, president of the *Unione Siciliana,* and the person responsible for protecting Capone's liquor shipments as they were trucked west to Chicago—was actually behind a series of hijackings. According to Kobler, Yale had become friends with Capone's enemies, the Aiellos (Joseph and his eight brothers and numerous cousins), Sicilians who took over from the Genna brothers in the Little Italy of the Taylor Street area. Joe Aiello was aligned with the O'Banion gang headed by Bugs Moran. McPhaul (1970) provides a different version. He reports that Capone had been cheating some New York gangsters, especially Yale, over his beer shipments. Both Kobler and McPhaul agree that Yale was responsible for killing a Capone aide, James De Amato, who had been sent to spy on Yale in New York. On July 1, 1928, two weeks after De Amato's murder, a black sedan began following Yale's new Lincoln as it moved down a Brooklyn street. As the sedan drew near, shots were fired, and Yale sped off with the sedan in pursuit. The end came with a devastating blast of gunfire that filled Yale's head with bullets and buckshot ("Gangster Shot in Daylight Attack" 1928). Yale was thirty-five years old.

During the early part of 1929, while a peace agreement was in effect, at least in theory, Bugs Moran had been hijacking Capone's liquor, which he owned jointly with the Purple Gang. In addition, Pasqualino Lolardo, "a harmless old codger," who with Capone's efforts had been elected president of the *Unione Siciliana,* was murdered by the Aiellos—Joseph Aiello coveted the top office for himself (McPhaul 1970). Capone gave the orders and went off to enjoy the Florida sun in his fourteen-room palatial house on Miami's Palm Island. The house, shaded by a dozen palm trees, had been built in 1922 for Clarence M. Busch, the St. Louis brewer. Capone bought it a few years later. The house had a dock that could accommodate four vessels, one of which was Capone's plush, six-stateroom yacht, the *Reomar II,* built in 1924 for auto magnate R.E.Olds and acquired by Capone a few years later. On February 14, 1929, St. Valentine's Day, Capone was with more than 100 guests, gangsters, politicians, sports writers, and show-business personalities on Palm Island. They all enjoyed a hearty buffet and an endless supply of champagne (Galvan 1982). Meanwhile, back in Chicago. . . .

Six of Bugs Moran's men and Reinhardt Schwimmer, an optometrist who liked to associate with gangsters, were waiting at a warehouse at 2122 North Clark Street to unload a shipment of hijacked liquor from Detroit. A Cadillac stopped outside, and five men, two wearing police uniforms, entered the warehouse. Once inside, they lined up the seven men against the warehouse wall and systematically executed them with machine guns. Bugs Moran was not in the warehouse at the time, even though the "St. Valentine's Day Massacre" had been arranged in his honor. The police later learned that the killers thought Moran was among the victims; lookouts had mistaken one of the seven for the gang's leader[7] (Kozial and Estep 1983). The killers were never caught; it was suspected that they were brought in from Detroit or St. Louis (where Capone had ties with "Egan's Rats"). The affair was apparently arranged by South Side hit man Vincent Gebardi (Landesco [1968] states his name was James Gerbardi; Allsop [1968] says his name was James De Mora). In any event, this Capone bodyguard was better known as "Machine-gun Jack McGurn."[8] For a long time it was generally believed that *real* policemen were the actual killers (Kobler 1971). While the wrath of Bugs Moran continued, his gang withered. Moran eventually returned to more conventional crime; in 1946 he was sent to prison for robbing a tavern employee of $10,000 near Dayton, Ohio. He was released after ten years and several days later was arrested for bank robbery. On February 26, 1957, the *New York Times* reported that Moran died while serving his sentence in the federal penitentiary in Leavenworth, Kansas ("Bugs Moran Dies in Federal Prison" p. 59). Less than two months later, Johnny Torrio suffered a heart attack while in a barber's chair in Brooklyn, and on April 16, 1957, he died. His death went unnoticed by the media until May 8, when the *New York Times* ran the story: "Johnny Torrio, Ex-Public Enemy 1, Dies; Made Al Capone Boss of the Underworld." At the time of his death, Torrio was described as a real estate dealer.

In May of 1929, Capone decided to avoid the wrath of Bugs Moran and any number of Sicilians who had vowed to kill him (to avenge the deaths of John Scalise, Albert Anselmi, and Joe Giunta whom Capone suspected of disloyalty), by going to jail. He arranged to be arrested by a friendly detective in Philadelphia on a firearms violation. Although the maximum sentence was one year, Capone anticipated a sentence of about ninety days, enough time to let things settle down in Chicago. His arrest, however, generated a great deal of media attention, and the judge imposed the maximum sentence. Capone was released on March 17, 1930, two months early for "good behavior." His troubles, however, were just beginning.

The Depression severely reduced the income of the Capone organization. In addition, a special team of federal investigators headed by Elliot Ness and dubbed "The Untouchables" began to move against Capone distilleries, breweries, and liquor shipments (Kobler 1971). The most important event for Capone, however, was a United States Supreme Court decision *(United States v. Sullivan,* 274 U.S. 259) handed down in 1927. That decision upheld the Internal Revenue Service's contention that even *unlawful* income was subject to income taxes, the Fifth Amendment guarantee against self-incrimination notwithstanding. The tax-evasion case against Capone originated in 1929 with the Special Intelligence Unit of the Treasury Department headed by Elmer Lincoln Irey. It was a low-key agency that avoided publicity. In 1929, Secretary of the Treasury Andrew Mellon, acting under pressure from President Hoover, directed Irey to investigate Capone. J. Edgar Hoover and his FBI were apparently unwilling to take on Capone—the risk of failure was too high (Spiering 1976). Frank Wilson, a nearsighted special agent who never carried a firearm, was put in charge of the Capone investigation: he brought Capone down with a pencil.

Agents engaged in an intensive investigation, interviewing hundreds of persons, scanning bank records (Capone did not have a personal account) and Western Union records. The latter revealed that, while in Florida, Capone was receiving regular payments from Jake Guzik. "Some of the more daring investigators actually joined gangs controlled by Capone in Chicago, Cicero, and elsewhere" (Horne 1932: 1). Wilson also had an informant in the Capone organization, Edward J. O'Hare, a businessman who was involved with Capone in dog racetracks—O'Hare owned the rights to the mechanical rabbit.[9]

Capone stood trial for having a net income of $1,038,654 during the years 1924 to 1929, for which he failed to pay income tax. On October 17, 1931, he was found guilty of income-tax evasion and received sentences totalling eleven years. On May 3, 1932, his appeals exhausted, Capone entered the federal prison in Atlanta. He was released from prison in 1939 as a result of time off for good behavior, suffering from what is believed to have been an advanced case of syphilis. He died in 1947 of pneumonia following a stroke. He had been an invalid for many years before his death at his villa in Florida. Capone was buried in Mt. Olivet Cemetery on Chicago's Far South Side. His family subsequently had his remains transferred to Mt. Carmel

Cemetery in west suburban Hillside. In 1972, the simple stone that marked Capone's grave was stolen, and the family decided not to have it replaced ("Who Took the Stone of Alphonse Capone?" 1981).

The federal government was also able to convict other members of the Capone organization for income-tax evasion: Ralph Capone received a three-year sentence; Frank ("The Enforcer") Nitti received eighteen months; Sam Guzik received one year; while brother Jake was sentenced to a term of five years (Horne 1932).[10]

Capone in Perspective

Al Capone was the subject of a great deal of public admiration and even hero worship. He emphasized the "service" aspect of his activities, proclaiming: "All I do is to satisfy a public demand" (Nelli 1969: 389). Kobler states: "Ordinary citizens throughout the country tended to accept his own estimate of his activities" (1971: 292).

Harold Gosnell (1968: 8) states that dishonest, corrupt, and inefficient government in Chicago was actually promoted by business interests: "All factions, Republican and Democratic, were the handmaidens of the business interests. . . ." Dobyns supports this view (1932: 8): "Populous and efficient as the underworld is, it could not wield the influence it does if it were not for its financial and political alliance with the inhabitants of Chicago's upper world."

> The vast sums of money which gangsters use to control elections and bribe public officials are poured into their hands by the patrons of gamblers, prostitutes, dope sellers, bootleggers, smugglers, and racketeers. Gangsters, job hunters, from mayor to day laborer, and grafters, from millionaire social leaders seeking franchises, contracts and escape from taxation, down to the pettiest parasites, are organized into an invincible, political army, the object of which is to elect public officials who will permit each of its members to carry on his particular racket unmolested.
>
> The deal is that the underworld shall have a "liberal government" and a "wide open town" and its upper world allies shall be permitted to plunder the public treasury and appropriate wealth belonging to the people.

Allsop (1968: 244) concludes that the enormity of the piracy by public officials and businessmen in Chicago, businessmen such as Charles Tyson Yerkes, Jr., and Samuel Insull, placed the bootlegger and the gangster "in a state of relative grace."[11]

Chicago Organized Crime after Capone

Frank Nitti succeeded Al Capone and ran the Chicago organization, the Outfit, with the help of Jake Guzik, Capone's brothers, Ralph and Matt, his cousins Charles and Rocco Fischetti, Murray ("The Camel") Humphreys, Anthony

Capezio, Paul De Lucia (better known as Paul "The Waiter" Ricca), and Anthony ("Joe Batters" or "The Big Tuna") Accardo. In 1943, Nitti, fearing prosecution for extortion, apparently committed suicide. He had been involved in a scheme with Willie Bioff and George Browne extorting money from theater chains.

Bioff was a Chicago racketeer who had specialized in shakedowns of kosher butchers. He went into partnership with Browne, a local official of the International Alliance of Theatrical Stage Employees (IATSE), whose members also included motion picture projectionists and other movie theater employees. The two began extorting money from theater chains under the threat of "labor trouble." Nitti soon "muscled in" on the racket at a 50 percent and eventually a 75 percent partner. In 1932, Browne had unsuccessfully run for the presidency of the international union. In 1934, with the backing of Nitti, Browne received help from Lucky Luciano and Lepke Buchalter of New York and Longie Zwillman of New Jersey; he was elected president (Nelli 1976). Malcolm Johnson (1972: 329) states that the convention in Louisville that elected Browne was pervaded with "such an atmosphere of intimidation that opposition wilted." Browne appointed Bioff to a union position, and the two increased their extortion activities, this time on a nationwide scale. They were able to extort money from Hollywood film studios such as RKO and Twentieth Century–Fox under the threat of closing down theaters throughout the country (Johnson 1972).

The scheme came to an end in 1941. Joseph M. Schenck, the brother of Twentieth Century–Fox chairman of the board Nicholas Schenck, was indicted for income-tax evasion. In exchange for leniency, he disclosed the activities of Bioff and Browne. Bioff received a ten-year sentence, Browne eight years. As a result of their cooperation, other members of the Outfit, including Nitti, were indicted in 1943. Nitti, who had been in ill health, committed suicide. Others received long prison terms but, Ed Reid and Ovid Demaris (1964: 42) point out: "Three years later they were all paroled in a scandal that echoed all the way to Washington and affable Harry Truman in the White House." The Special Committee to Investigate Organized Crime in Interstate Commerce (better known by the name of its chairman, Senator Estes Kefauver of Tennessee) had this to say (1951: 51):

> The three mobsters [Paul Ricca, Louis ("Little New York") Campagna, Charlie ("Cherry Nose") Gioe] were released on parole after serving a minimum period of imprisonment although they were known to be vicious gangsters. A prominent member of the Missouri bar presented their parole applications to the parole board, which granted the parole against the recommendations of the prosecuting attorney and of the judge who had presided at their trial. In the opinion of this committee, this early release from imprisonment of three dangerous mobsters is a shocking abuse of parole powers.

In 1955 Bioff, using the name William Nelson, emerged as a friend of Sen. Barry Goldwater of Arizona—Bioff was living in Phoenix. In October

1955, Bioff returned from Las Vegas (where he was employed at a gambling casino) in Goldwater's private plane with the Senator and Mrs. Goldwater and Mrs. Bioff. Two weeks later, on November 4, 1955, Bioff left his Phoenix home and went into this pickup truck. A moment later Bioff and his truck went up in a tremendous explosion—a dynamite bomb had been wired to the starter. Reid and Demaris report that when Goldwater was questioned by people from the news media he replied that he did not know that William Nelson was the notorious Willie Bioff. "Later, the Senator changed his story. Bioff, he said, was helping him in his study of American labor, giving him special insight into union racketeering" (1964: 42–43).

With the death of Frank Nitti and the imprisonment of Paul Ricca, Anthony Accardo emerged as the leader of the Outfit. The former bodyguard for Al Capone was born in Chicago in 1906. He was a member of the Circus Cafe Gang, which later became affiliated with the Capone organization. Accardo was successful in avoiding any serious legal difficulties until 1955, when the Internal Revenue Service expressed dissatisfaction with his tax returns. Since 1940, Accardo had reported over 43 percent of his income as coming from "gambling and miscellaneous sources." The IRS considered this too vague, and prosecution was initiated for income-tax violations. Accardo was eventually convicted, but the conviction was reversed on appeal. Fearing further federal prosecution, Accardo and his aging partner, Paul Ricca, looked for someone to take over the day-to-day operations of the Outfit (Peterson 1962; Brashler 1977).

Enter Sam Giancana

Born Gilormo Giangona on May 24, 1908, in Chicago, Giancana was called "Mooney" and "Momo" by law-enforcement officials and fellow criminals, an apparent reference to his "crazy" behavior as a young man. He was raised by his immigrant parents in the notorious "Patch" (Taylor Street area), where Giancana became a member of the "42 Gang," a group that even other criminals of that day viewed as "crazy." Fellow members of the 42s, such as Sam ("Teets") Battaglia, Felix ("Milwaukee Phil") Alderisio, and Marshall Caifano (legally changed to John M. Marshall), would also gain prominence in the Outfit. While the gang was periodically involved in politics and union organizing as "muscle," its primary activities centered around conventional and often reckless criminality. Deaths, via the police or rival criminals, and imprisonment eventually brought an end to the 42s; Giancana was imprisoned for burglary (Brashler 1977).

Giancana's specialty was being a "wheelman," driving a getaway car. This eventually earned him a position as chauffeur for Paul Ricca. Despite his connection to the Outfit, in 1938 he was convicted of bootlegging and sentenced to Terre Haute. There he met Eddie Jones, a black numbers operator. In 1942, Giancana was released from prison, and Jones financed his entry into the jukebox racket. Giancana eventually double-crossed Jones; he had him kidnapped and muscled in on his numbers operation. In 1949, using his connections with Ricca, Giancana influenced the Outfit to take over the Jones numbers operation and to place him, Giancana, in charge. Terry Roe, a black numbers operator, refused to make way for Giancana, and the predictable occurred; in 1952, Roe was killed in a shotgun ambush (Brashler 1977).

Money from the numbers enabled Giancana to branch out into other enterprises, and his organizational skills allowed him to prosper. They also gained the attention of Tony Accardo and Paul Ricca. The two, fearful of federal investigations, placed Giancana in charge of Outfit operations. William Brashler points out (1977: 258): "The Chicago outfit had always been run more like a corporation than like a family."

Giancana lived a rather public social life, something that had become an anathema for the now modernized leaders of organized crime. He had a highly publicized romance with Phyllis McGuire (of the singing McGuire sisters) and a public friendship with Frank Sinatra. Giancana generated a great deal of publicity when he secured an injunction against the FBI's intensive surveillance of his activities. In 1965, he refused to testify in front of a federal grand jury, after being given immunity from prosecution, and was imprisoned for contempt from July 1, 1965, until May 31, 1966 (Peterson 1969). After his release, Giancana went into self-imposed exile in Mexico, where he remained until the Mexican government expelled him in 1974. His subsequent return to Chicago was apparently not welcomed by the Outfit; on June 19, 1975, he was shot to death at close range in his suburban Chicago home by someone he apparently knew and obviously trusted.

The death of Sam Giancana created a great deal of public interest because of his involvement with the Central Intelligence Agency (CIA). The CIA had apparently contacted Giancana and an associate, John Roselli (who was murdered the following year), in a bizarre plot to use syndicate assassins to kill Fidel Castro (Horrock 1975).

---

[1]William Roemer, Jr., a former FBI agent in Chicago and consultant to the Chicago Crime Commission, stated that, with respect to Chicago mayors and organized crimes, "Under some such as 'Big Bill' Thompson and Jane Byrne they have thrived. *Under some such as Tony Cermak they have been hard hit"* (Permanent Subcommittee on Investigations, *Organized Crime in Chicago* 1973: 203; emphasis added).

[2]The "Black Hand" was not the name of an organization, but referred to a method. Italian immigrants who had achieved some noticeable level of financial success would often receive a note threatening dire consequences unless a certain amount of money was paid to the (anonymous) extortionist(s). The note often contained a black hand or other symbols. "Black Handers" worked alone or in small groups, and "Black Hand" activity died out during Prohibition (when more lucrative opportunities presented themselves).

[3]The beach along Lake Michigan was segregated at Twenty-ninth Street, with blacks using one part of it and whites the other. On Sunday afternoon, July 27, 1919, some blacks crossed the unmarked boundary that separated the two groups and were chased away by whites. A rock-

throwing battle ensued. When a homemade raft with five black youngsters aboard floated into the white section, a seventeen-year-old was hit by a rock and drowned in the fifteen-foot water. A black policeman attempted to arrest the alleged rock thrower but was thwarted by a white policeman. Word of the white officer's actions resulted in a gathering of several hundred blacks near the beach. One of them fired into a group of police officers attempting to disperse the crowd. The police fired back and hit the man—the riot was on. It was joined by a number of white gangs, most notably Ragen's Colts. During the week of violence, thirty-eight people died; seven blacks (but no whites) were shot by the police (Bowman 1984).

⁴Capone had six brothers and two sisters. When his father, Gabriel, died, Capone brought his mother, sisters, and four of his brothers to live with him in Chicago.

⁵In 1965, Dr. Martin Luther King, Jr., highlighted his Chicago campaign for "open housing" by a march into Cicero. He became painfully aware of the futility of such a gesture, stating: "We can walk in outer space, but we can't walk the streets of Cicero without the National Guard." Jim Bishop, noting that shortly after entering Cicero the National Guard retreated, stated: "It was worse. Blacks couldn't march in Cicero *with* the National Guard" (1971: 444).

⁶When it comes to organized crime, however, the *Guiness Book* is not reliable, as evidenced by the perpetuation of the myth surrounding the death of Salvatore Maranzano and "40 allies." *Guiness* refers to this nonevent as America's biggest Mafia killing. The book also reports that the Mafia got its start in the United States in New Orleans in 1869. This assertion is probably based on a feud between two factions, Sicilian and Neapolitan, for control of stevedoring business in New Orleans. During the struggle David Hennessey, the chief of police, was murdered, and a number of Italians were tried for the murder. After their acquittal, a mob stormed the prison, and eleven of the defendants were lynched on March 14, 1891 (Gambino 1977).

⁷The warehouse on Clark Street was torn down in 1967 as part of a redevelopment project. George Patey, an entrepreneur from Vancouver, British Columbia, bought the wall from the company that demolished the building. He rebuilt the wall, brick by bullet-riddled brick, in the men's room of a "Roaring Twenties" banjo sing-along bar (Kozial and Estep 1983).

⁸On Valentine's Day seven years later, McGurn was himself machine-gunned to death in a Chicago bowling alley. The killers left a Valentine card next to his ruined body. McGurn, who is believed responsible for killing at least twenty-two people, used to place a nickel in the hands of his victims. He was responsible for the 1927 attack on comedian Joe E. Lewis during which his vocal cords were slashed and his tongue lacerated. Lewis, then a nightclub singer, had left McGurn's club for employment at another speakeasy. The Lewis story was told in the Frank Sinatra motion picture *The Joker Is Wild*.

⁹On November 9, 1939, Edward O'Hare was shotgunned to death in Chicago. In return for his father's service, Edward ("Butch") O'Hare, Jr., received an appointment to the Naval Academy at Annapolis. As a fighter pilot, on February 20, 1942, Butch shot down five Japanese bombers and was awarded the Congressional Medal of Honor. A year later, he was killed while pioneering night radar flights in the Pacific (Spiering 1976). Chicago's O'Hare Airport is named in his honor.

¹⁰Jake Guzik grew up in Chicago's Maxwell Street area, then a predominantly Jewish neighborhood. He started out as a waiter in a brothel and eventually became the financial genius of the Capone organization. Guzik ran a twenty-five–person auditing office for Capone which was once raided by the police. They found lists of customers, police officers, and public officials on the Capone payroll, leading Mayor William E. Dever to state: "We got the goods this time." The next day a judge impounded the lists, and they were returned to Capone. For his 1932 income-tax evasion convictions, Guzik served three years and five months at Leavenworth.

When he was arrested in 1946, Guzik told a policeman: "I've got more cash than Rockefeller, and there's twenty of us with more than I have." Until he died of a heart attack in 1956, at age sixty-nine, Guzik helped the organization run gambling operations. At his funeral, he was eulogized by Noah Ganze, rabbi of the Loop Synagogue, as a man who performed quiet charities and gave vast contributions to the synagogue (Bowman 1983b).

[11]Charles Yerkes is described by Jay Robert Nash (1981: 193) as "the fat thief who ran the street railways of Chicago," a man who "reveled in corrupting aldermen. . . ." Prior to arriving in Chicago, he had served two years in prison for misappropriating funds in Philadelphia—a fact he succeeded in hiding from the public in Chicago. Yerkes was finally driven out of Chicago by Mayor Carter Harrison, and he died in London in 1901 leaving an estate of $2.1 million. Samuel Insull avoided convictions for embezzlement and mail fraud after he was turned over to U.S. officials by Turkish authorities. He had fled to Turkey on his yacht after his financial empire—a mammoth interlocking directorate that operated hundreds of power plants throughout the United States—collapsed with the stock-market crash of 1929. At the height of this power, Insull was president of fifteen corporations, chairman of the board of fifty-six other firms, and a member of the board of eighty-one additional companies. The estimated worth of his holdings was in excess of $3 billion. Insull died a pauper in Paris in 1938, leaving debts of more than $14 million (Nash 1981; *The Concise Columbia Encyclopedia* 1983, S.V. Insull, Samuel).

chapter 10

Organized Crime
After World War II

Used by permission of AP/Wide World Photos

During the decades following World War II organized crime underwent considerable change. It became increasingly clear that OC was dominated mainly by Italians. There were formidable Irish gangs in the Boston area; Philadelphia was still under Harry Stromberg (better known as "Nig Rosen"; see Jenkins and Potter 1985); Longie Zwillman was a power in New Jersey. But the Irish and Jewish criminal organizations were failing to recruit new members; social mobility had led to their demise. The gangs, with dozens of gunmen, faded as competitive violence subsided. The Italian-American Families evolved into mature forms of modern organization, decentralized and characterized by a form of franchise—the *McDonald's*-ization of organized crime. Each member, or made-guy, became an individual entrepreneur linked to the Family by a network, at the center of which were the boss, the underboss, and a *consigliere* (as discussed in chapter 2).

The post-war era saw the formation of outlaw motorcycle gangs (discussed in chapter 3) and the evolution of some of them into sophisticated criminal organizations whose major business interest became trafficking in synthetic drugs such as methamphetamine. Drug trafficking provided a financial base and served as a catalyst for the formation of black and Hispanic organized criminal groups. In many respects the rise of black, Mexican, Cuban, and Colombian criminal organizations, whose business centers on heroin and cocaine trafficking, parallels the experience of other ethnic groups during the Prohibition era. Heightened ethnic awareness and organization resulted in Italian-American criminal operatives being forced out of many black and Hispanic areas.

Peter Reuter (1983: xi) notes the absence of armed retainers by Italian-American Families in recent times—the Capone organization during Prohibition is reputed to have had 700 gunmen—which leads him to state, "My analysis suggests that the Mafia may be a paper tiger, rationally reaping the returns from its reputation while no longer maintaining the forces that generated the reputation." He theorizes that having established a dominant position, an unchallenged monopoly of force, the Mafia can depend on its fearsome reputation, an asset that can be substituted for personnel costs that would be incurred by maintaining armed forces. He states that challenges to Mafia power in black and Hispanic communities have not "generated any effort by the Mafia to assert control through superior violence" (1983: 136). Reuter further theorizes that this may be based upon the lack of available force, or simply the result of a cost-benefit analysis that mitigates against its use—excessive violence attracts law-enforcement attention and is bad for business in general.

Reuter notes that challenges to the Mafia outside of black and Hispanic communities have not been noticeable. An appreciation of the structure of

Italian-American OC, as discussed in chapter 1, provides an explanation. Italian-American Families have undergone an evolutionary transition from primitive forms of quasi-military units to mature forms of modern organization. Business activities are decentralized, franchised, while violence is not. The Mafia is often "invisible"; that is, members usually avoid operating illegal enterprises such as gambling or marginal businesses such as "topless bars" or "strip joints." Instead, they often "license" such enterprises, sometimes receiving payments for restricting market entry or competition, sometimes providing no service—practicing simple extortion. How would a competing group set out to deal with this operation? The most obvious method would be a direct attack on Family members. But they do not reside, meet, or otherwise assemble in significant numbers, and they may be unknown to anyone except persons intimately involved in the local criminal underworld. The decentralized nature of the organization would render a frontal assault unproductive. While a number of members and associates could be killed here and there, the net effect would be analogous to punching an empty bag.

Any group with the temerity to undertake this challenge would require the resources to sustain an "army" in the field for an indefinite period of time. Elderly members of the Family would probably head for condominiums in south Florida and Palm Springs, California, but remaining behind would be a cadre of assassins whose sole function would be the murder of those mounting the challenge to the Family's supremacy. They could be reinforced by executioners from other Families. In addition, as Reuter notes (1983: 133): "Large numbers of young men in major American cities are willing to accept paid employment as violence disputants." Rational criminals with martial skill would be inclined to side with an organization that has already proven its staying power—the Mafia—rather than take a chance with a seemingly reckless new group.

Black Organized-Crime Groups

Heroin provided the vehicle by which black criminal operators were able to enter the ranks of organized crime. Resistance from already established Mafia entrepreneurs proved futile; emerging black criminal organizations revealed a willingness to use violence on a scale that neutralized otherwise formidable opposition. Certain blacks were leaders in this movement.

Frank Matthews

Born in Durham, North Carolina, in 1944 (Messick 1979) or 1946 (Goddard 1978), Matthews was raised by an aunt from the age of four, when his mother died. He spent a year in the state reformatory near Raleigh for hitting a (white) man with a rock—Matthews and his gang had been stealing the man's chickens. He was involved in the illegal numbers (lottery) in Durham and later found employment in Philadelphia as a numbers writer, for which he was arrested in 1963. Shortly afterwards, Matthews moved to the Bedford-Stuyvesant section of Brooklyn and became a collector for an Italian-owned numbers operation.

Matthews was introduced to the heroin business by "Louis Cirillo, considered one of the Mafia's major heroin distributors. . . ." (Messick 1979: 26). Matthews married a college graduate with a degree in accounting. Together, using money earned in the numbers business, they began to make a great deal of money from the drug business. In 1967, he decided to break with his Italian overlords who had a monopoly at the importation level. Matthews found the "French connection," which was controlled by Corsicans operating out of Marseilles. He used his old numbers network to distribute the drugs and recruited "home boys" from the Durham area to build an organization that spanned twenty states—all in three years.

Of course this activity inevitably came into conflict with Italian-American OC drug operations. Matthews refused to back down. From his fortified headquarters in Brooklyn he allegedly warned, "Touch one of my people and I'll load my men into cars and we'll drive down Mulberry Street [an Italian neighborhood in lower Manhattan] and shoot every wop we see" (Messick 1979: 27). In 1971 the "French connection" was broken. Matthews convened a conference of black drug dealers in Atlanta that was reportedly attended by more than forty prominent figures of the "Black Mafia." The agenda dealt primarily with ways of breaking the white syndicate's domination of heroin importation.

Matthews exhibited many of the characteristics of a figure of an earlier era. Like Al Capone, Matthews was flamboyant, displaying wealth and power that were more appropriate for the Chicago of the 1920s. In the New York of the 1970s it was reckless. In addition to expensive homes, cars, and a yacht, he used two credit cards in his own name for expensive purchases. The result was inevitable: he attracted attention and was indicted for income-tax evasion and drug violations. Matthews spent his twenty-ninth birthday in federal custody. In 1973, he was released on bail; his whereabouts, as of this writing, are unknown.

Charles Lucas

Like Matthews, Charles Lucas began working in numbers and moved into heroin wholesaling. He apparently had no connection to the white syndicate and established his own pipeline to suppliers in an area of Laos, Burma, and Thailand called the Golden Triangle. Lucas took advantage of the Vietnam experience of black veterans who had used their time abroad to gain entry into the world of Far Eastern heroin trafficking. The Lucas organization was a "Family" made up primarily of his relatives from North Carolina and a few trusted non-kin members (Schumach 1977). Lucas supplied his brothers Shorty and Larry, who operated in northern New Jersey and the Bronx, New York. He also supplied rings in Chicago, North Carolina, and Los Angeles. Rudy Langlais (1978: 14, edited) provides a description of how Lucas imported his heroin from Southeast Asia. Note that the figures are in terms of the value of the American dollar in 1974.

> A Lucas [importer's] agent leaves Kennedy Airport for Thailand in 1974 carrying $600,000 in brand new 50s and 100s. [This is already a violation of federal law which requires that all amounts over $5,000 entering or leaving the United States be declared.] In Bangkok he checks into a hotel and telephones the overseas source's agent. He offers a password and is given instructions on where to deliver the money. At the money drop he is informed of the shipping arrangements by an Oriental. The next day the importer's agent returns to New York and reports to Lucas. Shortly afterwards 150 kilos of heroin (retail value more than $50 million) is smuggled into Georgia in the footlocker and trunks of a soldier returning to Fort Gordon.
>
> The heroin is transported into New York by automobile with two back-up vehicles fore and aft. In New York it is secreted ("stashed") in one of the apartments rented throughout the city for this purpose. Lucas then arranges for the cutting and distribution. The Lucas operation runs all the way to the street level where his "salesmen" offer heroin marked with his own distinctive "Blue Magic" logo.

The Lucas downfall came in 1975 as the result of the trust he placed in a non-kin member of his organization, who subsequently became a government informer and eventually a murder victim. After receiving substantial federal sentences for drug trafficking, Lucas reportedly (Pileggi 1982) became a government witness, for which he was freed from prison.

Leroy ("Nicky") Barnes

After escaping prison for a host of criminal charges, weapons violations, bribery, and murder, Nicky Barnes was dubbed "Mr. Untouchable" by the news media and dominated the heroin trade in Harlem. Fred Ferretti (1977) reports that Barnes used Italian suppliers and was allowed to establish control over manufacturing and distribution throughout the metropolitan New York–New Jersey area. By 1978, however, his luck ran out. A joint FBI and Drug Enforcement Administration effort succeeded in placing informants into the Barnes organization. On January 19, 1978, he was sentenced to a term of life imprisonment. In 1982, like Lucas, he became a federal witness, and in 1985 appeared before a hearing of the President's Commission on Organized Crime wearing a black hood. At the hearing it was disclosed that another drug operator had emerged to control a major segment of the Barnes' organization (Browne, 1985).

The Royal Family

Ianni (1974: 158) reports that "prisons and the prison experience form the most important locus for establishing the social relationships that form the basis for partnerships in organized crime for both blacks and Puerto Ricans."[1] This is as opposed to the Italians, who "do not form their criminal relationships in prison, both because they do not go to jail as often as blacks and Puerto Ricans do now, and because they form their organized crime networks on the Mafia-oriented basis of kinship." The structure of black organized-crime groups, then, is usually more formal (artificial), tending toward the bureaucratic model of *Camorra* (which also developed in prison).

During the 1970s in the Stateville (Illinois) Penitentiary, thirty black inmates from Chicago formed the Royal Family, patterning themselves after popular renditions of Mario Puzo's *Godfather*. They formed close ties with members of traditional organized crime, the Chicago Outfit, acting as "muscle" and contract executioners in Chicago and elsewhere. They were also active in drug trafficking and armed robbery. In 1981, the leader of the Royal Family, Roger ("Cochise") Collins, and several members of his group were convicted of murder (Brodt 1981a: 5; 1981b: 14).

Jeff Fort and the El Rukns

The best-known black organized-crime group in Chicago is the El Rukns headed by Jeff Fort (born 1947)[2] who as a teenager was the leader of the notorious Blackstone Rangers. In 1966, his organization, then called the Black P. Stone Nation, was successful in securing a federal grant of $1 million from the Office of Economic Opportunity for an elaborate grass-roots learning program. Mayor Richard Daley was outraged, and in 1968 and 1969 the grant was the subject of a United States Senate investigation. Fort was eventually imprisoned for embezzling $7,500 in federal funds.

While in prison, Fort founded the El Rukns, a "Moorish" religious organization, and dubbed himself Prince Malik. His South Side headquarters became the Grand Major Temple. After serving two years of a five-year sentence, Fort was paroled, and his organization soon came to dominate large areas of the black community. He purchased a home in Milwaukee for his wife and children but spent most of his time on Chicago's South Side riding in a chauffered limousine with his bodyguards. Fort is a physically imposing individual who usually wears braids, fur coats, and funny-looking Chinese coolie-type triangular hats. He grants no interviews and rarely speaks to anyone not part of his organization. When seen by this writer in court in 1982, Fort was accompanied by a large entourage and two attorneys.

Fort and the El Rukns are reputed to be involved in extensive narcotic operations in Chicago and elsewhere. His operations inevitably came to the attention of the Outfit. The Italian syndicate overlord for the South Side "sent" for Prince Malik. In the back of an Outfit restaurant, Fort was subjected to a diatribe of threats and abuse—he remained silent. After "putting the nigger in his place," the overlord ordered Fort out. That evening several members of Fort's organization returned, and the restaurant was put to the torch. The Outfit was told to get out—or be carried out—of the South Side. The "advice" was heeded.

The El Rukns have been involved in politics (an old Chicago tradition for criminals in that city). During the summer of 1982 they organized a voter-registration drive, Operation Grassroots. On August 24, 1982, Fred Giles, a "general" in the El Rukns, led a group of about 200 persons to the City Hall office of the Board of Elections to register to vote. In 1983, members of the El Rukns were involved in the reelection campaign of Mayor Jane Byrne.[3] In a speech at Chicago's City Hall on February 9, 1984, presidential candidate Jesse Jackson thanked the El Rukns for the help he was receiving from them in his Chicago campaign.

Jeff Fort, a native of Mississippi, was convicted of participation in a drug conspiracy in that state and is currently serving a federal prison sentence.

Hispanic Organized-Crime Groups[4]

While black OC groups are a home-grown phenomenon, Hispanics imported some of their criminal organizations along with the drugs they purveyed. Most active among them were groups based in Mexico and Colombia; Cuban exiles were also involved.

Mexican Groups

The best-known organized-crime group in Mexico, the Herrera Family, has been headed by a former Mexican state judicial police officer, Jaime ("Don Jaime") Herrera-Nevarez (born 1924). The headquarters of the organization is Durango, Mexico, a city of about 200,000. An analysis of accounts in Mexican banks in 1977–78 by American officials revealed that the Family has deposits in excess of $200 million. The Herrera Family is reputed to control the production and distribution of Mexican "brown heroin," from opium-growing plots in the Sierra Madre Occidental Mountains to the streets of Chicago—from "farm to arm."

American officials estimate that there are three to five thousand members of the Herrera Family, actually an organization that consists of six interrelated family groups. All the members are tied together by blood or marriage, making infiltration very difficult. The younger members of the Family are responsible for distribution in Chicago and wholesaling to groups in such cities as New York, Boston, Philadelphia, Detroit, and Louisville. "Efficient organizational management is maintained by some twenty-six executive-level directors, and a vast array of 'field representatives' in a number of American cities. This network is held together through the Herrera organization's Chicago 'offices' and through constant communications and trips back to the organization's headquarters in Durango" (Lupsha and Schlegel 1980: 7).

In 1983, when his youngest son was married, Don Jaime invited a thousand guests, including high-ranking politicians and police officials, plus a contingent of Colombian cocaine dealers who are believed to be using the Herrera pipeline into Chicago. The scope of corruption in Mexico, where it is referred to as *mordida* ("a little bite"), is highlighted by the case of Arturo Durazlo-Moreno, chief of police for Mexico City. He accumulated a fortune estimated to be worth $12.5 million and, among other crimes, is reputed to have provided protection for the drug-smuggling operations of the Herrera family. In 1982, Durazlo-Moreno became the subject of a worldwide manhunt.

Cubans and Colombians

When Fidel Castro took control of Cuba, he expelled American gangsters who worked under Meyer Lansky and operated gambling casinos in Havana. Many of their Cuban associates fled to the United States, settling primarily in the New York–New Jersey and Miami areas. They began to look for new sources of income. Many Cuban exiles were organized and trained by the Central Intelligence Agency (CIA) to dislodge Castro. After the 1961 Bay of Pigs debacle, members of the Cuban exile army were supposed to disband and go into legitimate business. However, as Donald Goddard (1978: 44) points out, they "had no lawful business." Elements in these two exile groups (they often overlapped) began to enter the drug market.

Until the early 1970s, the importation of marijuana, cocaine, and counterfeit Quaaludes[5] into the United States was largely a Cuban operation whose sources of supply were Colombians. The Colombians harvest marijuana, manufacture "Quaaludes," and make cocaine crystals out of cocaine paste they import from Bolivia, Peru, Ecuador, and Brazil. During the latter half of the 1960s, Colombians began migrating to the United States in numbers sufficient to establish communities in New York, Miami, Chicago, and Los Angeles. Many were illegal immigrants brought in through the Bahamas carrying such false documents as phoney Puerto Rican birth certificates or forged immigration papers of high quality. The Colombians became highly organized both in the United States and back at home. By 1973, independent foreign nationals could no longer "deal drugs" in Colombia. In 1976, the Colombians became dissatisfied with their Cuban agents in the United States. The latter were reportedly making most of the profits and shortchanging the Colombians. Enforcers, often young men from the Guajira Peninsula of Colombia, were sent in, and Cubans were executed in Miami and New York. According to government officials, Colombians now dominate both importation and distribution—the Cubans work for the Colombians.

Colombia, a nation of about 26 million, is the only South American country with both Pacific and Caribbean coastlines. Colombia has been torn by political strife and civil war—*La Violencia*—which has cost the lives of hundreds of thousands of persons. Kathleen Romoli (1941: 37) notes: "At the root of Colombia's easy violence is an extraordinary indifference towards death." She points out that since "death has small significance, human life has little importance." In this political/social atmosphere, bandits roamed freely, engaging in a combination of brigandage, terrorism, and revolution. In the north—Barranquilla, Santa Marta, and La Guajira—smuggling *(contrabandista)* groups have operated for decades. Bandits, *contrabandistas,* and Guajiran Indians, often backed and financed by businessmen in Bogotá, have emerged as crime "families." They are usually related by blood, marriage or *compadrazgo* (fictional kinship), and in many respects they resemble Sicilian *mafia* groups.

There are some rather striking similarities between the Colombian and the Sicilian. In both groups the nuclear family unit is patriarchal, with the father or oldest male having absolute authority. In the Colombian family, however, in the absence of the father, the mother may occupy this position. This may account for the dramatically different roles that women play in Italian crime families and their Colombian counterparts. For the southern Italian, organized crime is strictly a man's business, excluding traditionally female roles in prostitution and related activities. However, some Colombian crime families have been headed by women. Like the southern Italian, the Colombian family is extended by ritual godparenthood, and duty to family, including *compadres* (ritual kinsmen), is *the* primary responsibility. The Colombian stresses *dignidad,* which is inadequately translated as "dignity." It actually shares some relationship with the Italian concern for *rispetto.* The Colombian concept of *hombría,* inadequately translated as "manhood," actually resembles the Sicilian concept of *omertà.*

In the Colombian crime families, a division of labor has emerged that parallels roles in Italian-American crime Families. Roles such as "enforcer" and "corrupter" have been identified by law-enforcement agencies. The latter role is of prime importance in Colombia, where the "cooperation" of officials is vital to drug operations. In the United States, where the Colombian community in general, and crime Families in particular, have been almost impossible to penetrate, the position is less important. Enforcers, however, are necessary in both Colombia and the United States. Many have come from the Guajira Peninsula, between the Sierra Nevada and the Gulf of Venezuela, where Colombia's northern coast juts out into the Caribbean Sea. An area of desperate poverty, hot, dry, remote, and primitive, it has few natural resources besides a marijuana crop and access to the sea. The area has a large Indian population and has traditionally been a smuggler's paradise. About thirty years ago, Levantine traders moved into the Guajira and married into powerful Indian families. They organized and developed the smuggling trade into a sophisticated business enterprise. Because the Guajiro Indians identify with the upper strata rather than the lower classes of Colombian society, they have been able to relate easily to the cocaine entrepreneurs of Bogotá (Aschmann 1975). Robert Coram (1981: 8) describes the Guajira as "Hostile. Hot. Alien. A place beyond the conception of most Americans. A combination of Dodge City, the Barbary Coast, Oz, and Transylvania. A place where gun battles are common, unsolved murders number in the hundreds, and civilization is far, far away." Marguerite Michaels (1980: 4) describes the town of Riohacha, on the west coast of the Guajira:

> Twice a year the town of Riohacha, Colombia, erupts. A bootlegged bottle of Johnny Walker Black Label goes for as little as $3, a weekend with a high-class prostitute for as much as $5000. The streets are lined with Ford Rangers and Mercedes guarded by men carrying submachine guns. The whole city is an armed camp. Police either turn their backs or get killed.
>
> The marijuana crop is in.

Pico Iyer (1985) states that Colombian cocaine trafficking became big business in the late 1970s when major crime bosses entered the trade. Until then profits had come largely from the smuggling of automobiles, liquor and electronic appliances into the country and from illegally exporting cattle, emeralds and coffee. Then a businessman and a major smuggler teamed up to take advantage of the profits from dealing in cocaine. The two took over the domestic industry and sent enforcers into the United States to seize control of the U.S. wholesale market. Mark Whitaker (1985: 19) notes that the cocaine industry is controlled by a small clique of overlords—*coqueros*—who "are almost as rich and powerful as the Colombian government itself." Melinda Beck (1985: 23) states that important Colombian operators "are settling down in U.S. communities—particularly those with large Latin populations or wealthy resorts where they can live inconspicuously."

One of the leading *narcotraficantes,* Carlos Enrique Lehder Rivas ("Joe Leather" and "Joe Lemon") is the son of a German engineer who moved to Colombia. Lehder entered the U.S. at age eighteen and in 1973 was arrested in Detroit for smuggling stolen cars from South America. After jumping bail, he fled to Florida where he was arrested in Miami with 200 pounds of marijuana. Lehder served two years in federal prison and in 1975 was released and immediately deported to Bogotá. In 1979 he emerged in the Bahamas with a 3,300–foot runway protected by radar, bodyguards and attack dogs. The air strip was used by his private fleet of aircraft to smuggle cocaine from Colombia into the U.S. In 1981, Lehder was indicted by a U.S. grand jury for cocaine smuggling. He moved his base of operations back to Colombia. Among his other eccentricities is a fascination for Adolph Hitler, who Lehder considers a hero. He has organized an extreme right-wing political party whose paramilitary wing is reputed to be responsible for the deaths of dozens of leftists.

In 1984 the Justice Minister, who had been crusading against the cocaine smugglers, was machine-gunned to death on a Bogotá street. The public uproar resulted in a pledge by the president to enforce Colombia's 1982 extradition treaty with the U.S. Carlos Lehder went into hiding. On January 6, 1985, four middle-ranking drug traffickers were extradited to the U.S. On March 16, 1985, Marcos Cadavid became the first Colombian to be convicted in the U.S. under the extradition treaty. Eleven Americans had already been convicted of participating in a drug trafficking conspiracy with Cadavid who, until he fled to Colombia, had been operating out of Miami and Washington, D.C.

In the United States, officials have identified a small number of Colombian Families who dominate the importation of marihuana, cocaine and counterfeit Quualudes into the U.S. The Cubans have apparently become aligned with these Families who are tied to patrons back in Colombia. The core of each Family is an extended kinship network with members related by blood, marriage or fictional kinship. Each Family is ruled by a patriarch and is hierarchical. In addition, a rudimentary division of labor has evolved. According to knowledgeable federal officials, these Families do not yet exhibit the discipline of their Italian-American counterparts. Until late 1978, the Families exhibited a great deal of cooperation. For example, if five hundred tons of marihuana were needed to effect a deal with a wholesaler, they would pool their resources. Financing was often cooperative, and the Families even shared couriers and used the same enforcers. The latter are justifiably feared in the Hispanic community; their favorite weapon is a lightweight submachine gun, although executions with smaller weapons or by slitting throats are not uncommon. The routine murder of women and children is something that distinguishes Colombian violence from that of Italian-American Crime Families.

According to Internal Revenue Service officials, the Colombians usually do not file income-tax returns (they may be illegal aliens) and merely hide the money, here or in Colombia. Luxury housing has been bought in south Florida by men who can barely speak English and who pay with cash delivered in shopping bags. The crime families are reported to have patrons in Bogotá, sophisticated international businesspersons. As a result, drug money has been funneled into the nearby Antilles and other places with bank-secrecy laws, where investment corporations controlled by the Colombians "launder" the money and invest it in legitimate businesses. In one incident, fifty agents from the Internal Revenue Service, Customs, and the Drug Enforcement Administration stormed two banks in Miami. They seized bank records and found enough evidence to arrest Isaac Kattan Kassin, a Colombian who had deposited $7 million during the week preceding his arrest.

At the end of 1978, for reasons that are not clear, the cooperation among the Colombian crime Families was replaced by internecine warfare on a scale that parallels Chicago of the Prohibition era. In one incident, a delivery van drove into a crowded Miami shopping mall. Two men exited and walked into a liquor store, where they opened fire with submachine guns, escaping in the pandemonium that followed. Two persons were killed and two were wounded. One of the dead men was reputed to be the head of a Colombian crime Family. In New York, four persons, a man and his wife and their two children, were found slain in an automobile.on Long Island. Orlando Galvez, thirty-two, one of the deceased, was reported to be a leader in a Colombian crime family. In his Queens, New York, apartment the police found 140 pounds of cocaine, an arsenal of weapons, and $1 million in cash.

Japanese Organized-Crime Groups

Most Americans have heard of the Mafia, Lucky Luciano, Al Capone, and their "soldiers," but what about the Yamaguchi-gumi, Kazuo Taoka, Hideomi Oda, and their *yakuza* (pronounced YAHK-za)? The Yamaguchi-gumi is a criminal organization with more than 10,000 members who hold sway over the industrialized, densely populated region extending from Kyoto through Osaka to Kobe, as well as Tokyo and most other major centers in Japan. They are largest of the *Boryokudan*, organizations which constitute Japanese organized crime. These organizations have been in existence for about 300 years and date back to the Tokugawa period when Japan united under a central system of government. With the end of Japanese feudalism, many *samurai*, or knights, lost their role in life (Rome, 1975). The *yakuza* were originally a mixture of outcast *samurai* and peasants who, under the leadership of their *kumi-cho* (boss), were able to exert control over sections of Japan's urban areas. Present-day *yakuza* view themselves as modern *samurai*, maintaining exotic rituals including extensive tatooing that virtually covers their entire bodies from neck to ankles, and clipped fingers that have been self-amputated with a short sword as a sign of contrition for mistakes.

Clyde Haberman (1985: 6) notes that the term *yakuza* "is derived from an old card game . . . whose object was to draw three cards adding up as close as possible to 19 without exceeding it." This would be similar to our game of "21" or blackjack. "Ya-ku-za represents the Japanese words for 8, 9, 3, which total 20, a useless number. Basically, yakuza means 'good for nothing'. " Like many of their American counterparts, the *yakuza* "were born into poverty and graduated from juvenile delinquency into organized crime" (Kirk, 1976: 93). The "Al Capone" of Japan, Kazuo Taoka, was, like Capone, born into a poor family, and he began his criminal career as a bouncer in Kobe, much as Capone filled this capacity in Brooklyn before going to Chicago. Taoka, like Capone, played a major role in the gang conflicts of the day, and both men rose to prominence because of their talents with violence and organization. In 1981, Taoka, sixty-eight, died of a heart attack. His funeral in Kobe (a city about 275 miles southwest of Tokyo) was attended by more than 1,200 persons. "Taoka's friendships and contacts extended to the highest levels of government, with two former prime ministers . . . among his friends. That kind of relationship reflected not only Taoka's personal success but also historic ties between gangsters and prominent government figures . . ." (Kirk, 1981: 17). Like many of their American counterparts, the *yakuza* are conservative, hawks on matters of foreign policy and vigorously anticommunist. This has endeared them to many right-wing politicians.

Sadahiko Takahashi and Carl Becker (1985: 3) report that the *Boryokudan* groups "form closed societies in their individual groups, but the groups are inter-linked through a wide-spread underworld syndicate." They describe the structure of the *Yamaguchi-gumi* (1985: 4):

> It includes 578 sub-groups and [in 1982] 13,063 members, divided into 51 lineal "family" (staff) organizations. Each of these 51 "family" bosses has their own groups with one to eleven subordinate bosses (called "grandchildren"), and some of these subordinate bosses in turn have gang bosses under them. Thus the Yamaguchi mafia headquarters has 51 staff groups under it, which in turn control 149 "grandchildren" gang bosses, and there are another 11 "great-grandchildren" bosses on a level under them, forming a total of 211 "recognized" (dues-paying) groups.
>
> All 211 groups pay dues . . . to the Yamaguchi headquarters, and additional fees determined by headquarters . . .; they are passed vertically up through their respective channels until they reach the staff at headquarters. When the members of a given local group cannot collect the money which their boss owes, the boss often pays the dues from his own private sources. This in turn places his group members in debt to him, which they must repay by becoming assassins, scapegoats . . .

The self-image of the *yakuza* stands in some contrast to that of their American counterparts. The *Yamaguchi-gumi,* for example, publish a membership newsletter. In 1981, when Masahisa Takenaka was installed as the head of the *Yamaguchi-gumi,* it was seen on national television. Likewise, his funeral in 1985 (Takenaka was gunned down by rival members of his *Boryokudan*) was carried on national television. When a rival for leadership, Hiroshi Yamamoto, seceded from the clan, he announced it at a news conference (Haberman, 1985).

Yakuza have been reported operating in Hawaii, California, Nevada, and Colorado (see, for example, Lindsey 1985). Interestingly, many of these gangsters may have entered the United States in order to avoid a crackdown by Japanese law-enforcement agencies, much as *mafiosi* entered the U.S. during the 1920s to escape Mussolini.

---

[1]Ianni could have included Chicanos (Mexican-Americans) and such groups as *La Nuestra Familia* (NF), a criminal organization that, like several similar groups of varying ethnicity—Aryan Brotherhood, Brown Bears, Black Guerillas—originated in the California prison system.

Like the outlaw motorcycle gangs, NF reportedly has a rigid hierarchy, written rules of conduct, sponsorship requirements, and initiation rituals for new members. Like the *Camorra* of Naples, NF has extended its criminal activities well beyond the prison walls.

[2]Information about Jeff Fort is from news reports carried by the *Chicago Tribune,* the *Chicago Sun Times,* television, and radio, as well as private law-enforcement sources.

[3]On April 25, 1984, the *Chicago Tribune* (section 2: 3) reported that Robert Brown, twenty-nine, an enforcer for the El Rukns, was convicted of murdering a South Side man on June 18, 1983. Brown helped in a voter-registration drive that distributed turkeys for the benefit of Jane Byrne.

[4]Unless otherwise stated, information in this section is from the *New York Times,* the *Chicago Tribune,* the *Chicago Sun-Times,* the *Miami Herald,* government reports, and law-enforcement officials.

[5]*Quaalude* is a brand name for a sedative (methaqualone) used to treat insomnia when barbiturates are medically contraindicated or have failed. Despite earlier beliefs to the contrary, addiction can develop to methaqualone as easily and as rapidly as to barbiturates. Its effects are similar to those of barbiturates except that there is a greater loss of motor coordination, which explains why it is sometimes referred to as "wallbanger."

The Business of Organized Crime

We believe that organized crime by gangsters is in large measure based upon the law of supply and demand. We as a nation have failed in our attempt by legislation to make the physical man and the moral man identical.—Report of the Committee on Mercenary Crime 1932[1]

Herbert Packer (1968: 264) argues that when we consider translating morality into law, we should inquire whether there exists any significant body of dissent from the proposition that the conduct in question is indeed immoral. If a social group will be offended, "then prudence dictates caution in employing the criminal sanction." Unfortunately, as Prohibition taught us, when it comes to questions of "morality," prudence is not often the dictator. Packer, with a great deal of insight, concludes (1968: 279):

> Regardless of what we think we are trying to do, when we make it illegal to traffic in commodities for which there is an inelastic demand, the effect is to secure a kind of monopoly profit to the entrepreneur who is willing to break the law. In effect, we say to him: "We will set up a barrier to entry into this line of commerce by making it illegal and, therefore, risky; if you are willing to take the risk, you will be sheltered from the competition of those unwilling to do so.

Thus, translating morality into a statute backed by the criminal sanction does not provide for greater morality; it merely widens the scope of the law and creates both temptation and opportunity for a particular set of social actors. As in any business, the better organized are usually the more successful, and organized crime is basically a business enterprise.

Organized crime is often described as simply a provider of "goods and services" that just happen to be illegal. Back in 1931 Walter Lippmann (1962: 60) stated that organized crime "performs a function based ultimately upon a public demand." Contemporary criminologists have tended to emphasize the "goods and services" aspect of OC. Thus, George Vold states: "The syndicate is in the business of providing forbidden and illegal services or commodities desired by customers who are able and willing to pay for what they want. Illicit sex, drugs, alcohol, loans, and gambling are the main staples sold to willing customers at prices high enough to give substantial profit to management after meeting the cost of carrying on the business" (1979: 347). Joseph Albini (1971) states that organized crime continues to exist because it performs a function for those who want goods and services that the government defines as illegal. The (federal) Task Force on Organized Crime (1967: 1) states: "The core of organized crime activity is the supplying of illegal goods and services—gambling, loansharking, narcotics, and other forms of vice—to countless numbers of citizen customers."

Thomas Schelling (1971) dissents from the "goods and services" view of organized crime. Instead, he argues that organized crime has a relationship with the purveyors of illegal goods and services that is extortionate; *the business of organized crime is extortion, and those criminals who provide goods and services are its victims.* Thus, Schelling points out, a bookmaker operating in an area dominated by an OC unit will be required to pay for the "privilege" of doing business—or suffer from violence (or perhaps a raid by corrupt police). The OC unit merely "licenses" the business, and the bookmaker requires a "license" to avoid being beaten or killed (or subjected to police raids).

Actually, OC may provide services for the illegal entrepreneur. It may limit market entry—competition—and enforce uniform setting of gambling odds (the "line," to be discussed shortly). Rubinstein and Reuter (1978a: 64) note that a distinctive service provided by Italian-American OC is arbitration:[2] "In an economy without conventional written contracts, there is obviously room for frequent disagreements. These are hard to resolve. Many bookmakers make payments to 'wise-guys' to ensure that when disputes arise they have effective representation." In 1985 the writer met with a successful bookmaker in New York. He stated that he always keeps a "wise-guy" on the payroll at a cost of between $200-300 per week. This is insurance—it prevents other criminals from placing bets and then refusing to pay, using their status as "made-guys" to protect them. It also keeps other criminals from trying to "shake-down" the bookmaker, i.e., extort money from him. The "wise-guy" will also assist in the collecting of bets, keeping half of whatever he collects for the bookmaker. In northwestern Indiana, Ken ("Tokyo Joe") Eto,[3] the bolita (lottery) kingpin, paid thousands of dollars a month in "street taxes" to the Outfit in order to remain in business. On one occasion, an Eto lieutenant was beaten up by a syndicate thug. Eto complained to his Outfit overseer, Ross Prio, and the man was murdered (O'Brien 1983).

Schelling (1971: 648) reports that OC needs victims who cannot easily hide, persons with fixed places of business:

> Even if one can find and recognize an embezzler or jewel thief, one would have a hard time going shares with him, because the embezzler can fool the extortionist if he can fool the firm he embezzles from, and the jewel thief needn't put his best prizes on display.

Schelling underestimates members of OC—they spend a great deal of time on the prowl for information and opportunity. Bartenders, fences, prostitutes, and a host of legitimate and illegitimate persons are often eager to provide the "wise-guy" with information, to be on his "good side"; they may owe him favors or money. Albert Seedman (1974: 70-74), former chief of detectives in New York City, taped a conversation between "Woody," who had swindled $500,000 from Mays Department Store in Brooklyn, and Carmine ("The Snake") Persico, an enforcer for the Profaci Family. In this edited version, Woody wants to know why he is being asked to pay a rather large share of the money he had stolen to Persico, who had played no part in the scheme.

> PERSICO: When you get a job with the telephone company, or maybe even Mays Department Store, they take something out of every paycheck for taxes, right?
> WOODY: Right.
> PERSICO: Now why, you may ask, does the government have the right to make you pay taxes? The answer to that question, Woody, is that you pay taxes for the right to live and work and make money at a legit business. Well, its the exact same situation—you did a crooked job in Brooklyn [in the territory of the Profaci Family]. You worked hard and earned a lot of money. Now you have got to pay your taxes on it just like in the straight world. Why? Because *we* let you do it. We're the government.

The jewel thief deals in expensive merchandise, and he needs a fence who can provide large amounts of cash on very short notice. The jewel thieves studied by this writer (Abadinsky 1983) would fence their jewels the same night they were stolen. A fence connected to OC can be relied upon to have, or be able to raise, large amounts of cash on short notice. Dealing with a "connected" fence also provides insurance for the thief. It guarantees that he will not be "ripped off" by other criminals (since this would raise the ire of the OC unit). Thus, OC can provide an umbrella of protection to independent criminals who might otherwise be at risk from other criminals.

For Vincent Teresa (1973), an associate of the New England Crime Family headed by Raymond Patriarca, what started out as a "service" ended up as extortion. Joseph ("The Animal") Barboza, a vicious ex-fighter of Portuguese ancestry, was an unaffiliated criminal operating in Massachusetts with his own band of thugs. They became nasty in the Ebbtide, a legitimate nightclub, beat up the owners, and threatened to return and kill everybody. The owners went to Teresa for help, and he went to Patriarca's underboss, who agreed to help—for a price. After being "called in," Barboza agreed not to bother the Ebbtide—it was now a "protected" club. This gave Teresa an idea (1973: 123-24): "We sent Barboza and his animals to more than twenty nightclubs. They would go into these places and tear the joints apart. . . . These people would come running to us to complain about Barboza, to ask for protection."

When it comes to "goods and services," then, the picture is mixed. Many of those who provide gambling and other goods and services such as loan-sharking have a relationship with OC that is forced upon them; others find the OC connection useful to their enterprise, and sometimes, the "made-guy" is a bookmaker, numbers operator, or (more frequently) a loanshark. With this in mind, let us review the "goods and services" of organized crime.

---

[1] Source: MacDougal 1933: 342.

[2] The concept of *rispetto* enables a "made-guy" to act as an arbitrator. If, at the request of an aggrieved party, a *uomo di rispetto* is asked for assistance, he can summon the accused to a "sitdown" or Table, an informal hearing at which he presides. Robin Moore (1977: 64) notes: "Anyone in the community, mob-connected or not, who had a legitimate complaint against someone else was entitled to ask for a Table hearing. . ." and "any ranking Mafioso or man of respect could be prevailed upon to preside at a Table." To refuse to appear, or to disregard a decision made, at a Table would indicate disrespect with attendant consequences that are life-threatening. As noted by Reuter (1983) and Abadinsky (1983), the arbitrator will receive a fee for this service when the disputants are nonmember criminals.

[3] Eto (born in 1920 of Japanese ancestry) was convicted on January 18, 1983, of operating a bolita business that grossed nearly $6 million between May 4, 1980, and August 20, 1980 ("2 Convicted of Gambling Charges" 1983). On February 10, 1983, Eto was shot in the head and left for dead by two Outfit killers, Jasper Campise and John Gattuso, a Cook County Deputy Sheriff. Eto survived. On July 12, 1983, the bodies of Campise and Gattuso were found in the trunk of a car with multiple stab wounds—apparently the penalty for botching the murder of Ken Eto.

chapter 11

Gambling and Loansharking

Used by permission of AP/Wide World Photos

The Task Force on Organized Crime (1967: 1) states that "the core of organized crime activity is the supplying of illegal goods and services—gambling, loan sharking, narcotics, and other forms of vice—to countless numbers of citizen customers." In this chapter, and the next three chapters, we will be examining a variety of "goods and services" that have traditionally been associated with OC.

As already noted, however, Thomas Schelling (1971) argues that the *real* business of OC is extortion from illegitimate (and sometimes legitimate) entrepreneurs. In fact, OC is *both* a provider and an extorter. At certain times and in certain places an OC unit will provide illegal goods or services; at other times and in certain places it will merely extort "protection" money without providing any service.

There are also OC activities such as labor racketeering and the scams that do not easily fall into the categories of goods, services, or extortion. OC also responds to changing market conditions. For example, during the oil crisis in 1973, for the first time persons involved in OC began to hijack gasoline trucks. During the 1980s, members of OC became involved in the counterfeiting of designer-label goods such as Calvin Klein jeans and Izod shirts (Rehfeld 1984).

Bookmaking

Bookmakers "book" bets on two types of events—horse (and sometimes dog) races and sporting events like football, basketball, and boxing. In earlier days "horse parlors" or "wire rooms," neighborhood outlets, were often set up in back of a legitimate business, where results were posted on a large chalkboard. Many bettors would wait for race results to come in over the wire service. Today, most bets are placed by telephone (see fig. 11.1). To maintain security, some bookmakers change locations frequently, often monthly. Others may use a "call-back" system. The bettor calls an answering service or answering machine and leaves his number. The bookmaker returns the call, and the bet is placed. A more elaborate system is the "black box" or "backstrap." The telephone company installs telephones in a vacant apartment rented by the bookmaker, who runs an extension wire to a second location where the wire room is set up. A police raid on the telephone location will turn up only an empty apartment and several telephones. By the time the extension wire is traced and a new search warrant secured, the bookmaker has left to set up in a new location. (Cheeseboxes are similar devices no longer in use).

Bets are usually written down and may also be tape-recorded by a machine attached to the phone. This may avoid any discrepancies over what arrangements actually transpired over the phone. The bookmaker usually employs clerks and "sheetwriters" or "runners." The clerks handle the telephone, record the bets, and figure out the daily finances. The runners call the clerks and are given the day's totals for the bets they booked; based on this information, they either collect or pay off. The runners receive a portion of the winnings, usually half, and they must also share in the losses. Rubinstein and Reuter explain how (1977: 10):

> . . . if his customers win in the first week a total of $1000, then the bookmaker will give the sheetwriter $1000 to pay them. This will give the sheetwriter a "red figure" of $1000. In the next week, let us assume that the sheetwriter's customers lose $400; then the red figure will be reduced by that amount, to $600. In the next week assume the customers lose $2000. The sheetwriter will pay the bookmaker the remaining $600 of the red figure plus half of the $1,400 which represents the net winnings, a total of $1300. His risks are the same as the bookmaker's but he invests no money.

Horse-race Wagering[1]

Although the oldest of the major bookmaking activities, horse-race wagering today ranks behind sports and numbers wagering in terms of illegal activity. The typical bettor is middle age or beyond and wagers amount from two to ten dollars per selection.

Information as to the horses running on a given day may be obtained from a local newspaper, a "scratch sheet" (such as the *Armstrong Daily News Review, Turf and Sports Mirror,* or *Illinois Sports Journal*), or the *Daily Racing Form.* Voluminous data are available in the *Daily Racing Form,* and the scratch sheets provide information on the time and nature of each race, the jockeys, the post positions, the weights carried, the probable odds, and the handicapper's estimate of the horses' finishing position. Such information, especially that in the scratch sheet, is the basic information needed by the bookmaker in handling wagers.

Payoffs at the track are, except where a bookmaker's limits are reached, the basis for the bookmaker's payoffs. The bookie's cut is obtained in this manner: before the track makes a payoff under the parimutual system (in which the track acts as a broker to pay the winners from moneys it collects from the losers), it deducts for taxes and its operational expenses. The bookmaker, by keeping wagers roughly equal to the track's, percentagewise, realizes a profit from that portion which, at the track, goes to expenses and taxes. Since this deduction is generally from 15 to 20 percent, there is comfortable room for maneuvering. A bookmaker who has too much money on a horse, vis-à-vis the track, lays off the excess. This layoff process continues wherever lack of balance exists until it reaches the top layoff operations, which have their agents stationed near major tracks. Upon being given their orders they make an ultimate layoff by placing large wagers at the track's parimutuel window. In the event that the wager is a winning one, money to

Figure 11.1
The Wagering Process

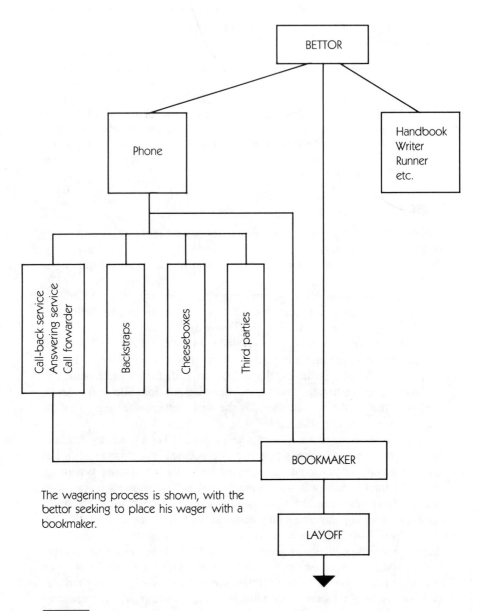

The wagering process is shown, with the bettor seeking to place his wager with a bookmaker.

SOURCE: Kier T. Boyd, *Gambling Technology,* Washington, D.C.: United States Government Printing Office, 1977

assist in making payoffs comes from track winnings. Also, by placing large wagers at the track, the track's potential payoff, and consequently the bookmaker's, is reduced.

The bookmaker cannot, of course, know precisely what percentage of money will be wagered on each horse at the track; however, information supplied by the scratch sheet or the *Daily Racing Form* is generally an acceptable guide and, in the event of a high track payment, the bookmaker invokes limits (generally 15 to 1 or 20 to 1 for a "win" bet, 6 to 1 or 8 to 1 for a "place" bet, 3 to 1 or 4 to 1 for a "show" bet, and 50 to 1 for two-horse events such as the "daily double").

Wagers. Shown below are the common wagers together with ways in which they may be recorded by a bookmaker. The bookmaker will generally record the bettor's identity, the racetrack, the identity of the horse, the type of wager, and the amount of the wager. The name of the track is almost always abbreviated (either by name or location).The identity of the horse may be written out fully or represented by its post position number or the handicapper's number as found on the scratch sheet.

Win—choose the horse which will finish first.

1 NY JOEY BOY 2/1
6 L # 8 5-0-0

(First race, New York (e.g., Aqueduct), $2 to win on Joey Boy) (Sixth race, Laurel horse with post position or handicap number 8, $5 to win)

Place—choose the horse which will finish first or second.

4 GS MARY MARY X-10-X

(Fourth race, Gulfstream, $10 to place on Mary Mary)

Show—choose the horse which will finish first, second, or third.

9 5/A 6 5/3

(Ninth race, Santa Anita, horse #6, $5 to show)

Combo (Across-the-Board)—a single bet encompassing equal amounts for win, place, and show.

B 6 2 2-2-2

(Sixth race, Bowie, horse #2, $2 to win, $2 to place, $2 to show)

Sports Wagering

"From a gross dollar volume standpoint, sports wagering is the king of bookmaking" (Boyd 1977: 13). Kier Boyd notes that, as in other forms of bookmaking, the sports bookmaker acts as a broker, *not a gambler*. "In order to achieve an equality between teams, one which the bookmaker hopes will attract like sums of money on each contestant; a 'handicapping' process takes place" through the use of a *line* (Boyd 1977). R. Phillip Harker explains (1977: 2):

> The line theoretically functions as a handicap to balance the relative strengths of the opposing teams. It consists of points either added to the underdog teams' final scores or subtracted from the favorite teams' final scores. Then again, theoretically having balanced the relative strengths of the teams, wagers are accepted by bookmakers usually at 11-10 odds. Thus, for instance, if a bettor desires to bet $500 on the Washington Redskins at -6 (meaning Washington is favored by 6 points, and 6 points are subtracted from Washington's final score to determine the result of the wager), he would actually risk $550 to the bookmaker's $500.
>
> As stated above, the line is only *theoretically* a balancing of the strengths of the teams. However, as a practical matter, the line is really a number of points, either added to the underdogs' scores or subtracted from the favorites' scores, which the bookmakers feel will tend to attract relatively even amounts of wagering on both sides of the contest. If the bookmaker achieves an even balance of wagering on a game and he has no gamble or risk, his profit is assured of being 10 percent, the "juice" or "vigorish" of the losing wages.

Harker explains how the line is derived (1977: 3-5):

> To a great extent the line is developed in Las Vegas, Nev. Not only may the line be formulated legally there and posted publicly in legal bookmaking establishments, but Las Vegas is the recognized hub of wagering and the clearinghouse for much of the intelligence information used to develop the line. Persons there, who are instrumental in line development, have vast sources of information about the games, as well as knowledge of major trends or "moves" in game wagering, especially by the so-called "smart" or knowledgeable bettors. Each week in Las Vegas, the football line is developed, legally printed, and published. Thereafter, line information is disseminated almost instantaneously, usually via telephone, to various persons throughout the country.
>
> Every bookmaker, by necessity, has a source for the Las Vegas line. The line may come directly from Nevada, from Nevada indirectly through one or more other cities, or from other local bookmakers who obtain it from sources ultimately obtaining it from Las Vegas. This accessibility is necessary for several reasons: First, as indicated above, the Las Vegas gambling community is considered extremely knowledgeable in all aspects of line development; and second, since other bookmakers and bettors are also aware of this line, the individual must start out using the Las Vegas line as his basis lest he become immediately out of balance, and hence, unable to lay off. For example, if the bookmaker felt the proper line on a game should be Team A favored by 4 points and used this line for taking bets, and if other bookmakers used the Las Vegas line of 12 points, our bookmaker would find immediately that no one would bet with him on the underdog getting only 4 points; whereas everyone would bet with him on the

favorite giving up only 4 points rather than 12. Thus, he would experience a tremendous imbalance of betting on the favorite, which we have indicated is not a desirable situation. Moreover, he could not lay off with other bookmakers, since he must lay off with them at *their* line, which would be 12 rather than 4. And if he should lay off with the other bookmakers on the favorite giving up 12 points when his imbalance is at 4 points, and if the final score showed Team A winning by more than 4 points but less than 12 points, he would then lose not only his imbalance of bets on the favorite at 4 points, but his layoff bets at 12 points—a very dismal situation generally referred to as being "middled."

When the bookmaker obtains *the* line, he then often adjusts it to suit his needs or makes up *his* line. He may well know his usual bettors and be able to anticipate what volume on various games he can expect. If the line he receives is 4 and he knows that his bettors are likely to bet heavily on the underdog (the hometown favorite, perhaps), he might decide to use 3 or 3½ as his line. Then, as wagering progresses during the wagering period, such as often from Tuesday until Sunday on professional football games, he may vary his line upwards or downwards one-half point at a time to tend to attract betting, or conversely, to discourage betting on the other side, in order to balance the betting. The traditional thought is that the use of half points stems from the bookmakers' desires to eliminate "pushes" (or ties) when the bet is a draw. Although half points do have this effect, the real purpose is to facilitate varying the line by small increments. There is a tremendous difference between a line of 3 and 3½ points, but very little practical difference between 25 and 25½ points.

The bookmaker must know not only the Las Vegas opening line, but he must get frequent updates in the line. A change in the Las Vegas line does not mean that Las Vegas has changed its collective mind as to the anticipated final score (as if the line were a true power rating); it means that there has been an influx of wise money on the game. The bookmaker must be wary of the same influx. Also, the Las Vegas books may either "scratch" a game or "circle" it. To scratch a game means to eliminate further betting or to take it off the board. To circle it means literally to draw a circle around the game on the line sheet, resulting in a limitation of wagering on the game. Bookmakers may take no betting on a circled game or may accept only a limited amount of wagers on it, such as a maximum of $100. In either case, scratching or circling arises because of some unusual factors developing after the opening of betting. These factors include critical injuries, rumors of a fix in the game, or extremely unusual patterns of wagering. This type of information is of vital importance to every bookmaker because by the time he learns of the scratching or circling, he frequently will have been besieged with bets by bettors who have also been privy to the information.

It is worth noting that contrary to popular thought, a crucial injury occurring *after* the opening of betting cannot effectively be handicapped. Bookmakers cannot change the line enough to reflect the value of the loss of a good quarterback, such as possibly 6 or 7 points, or else the bookmaker would be in the position of possibly being "middled," as indicated above. All he can then do is stop further betting and hope for the best.

Likewise, other changes in factors, such as weather and internal disputes, cannot affect the line *after* its opening. These things only cause the game to be scratched or circled. The only factor affecting the line after opening is solely the volume of the wagering.

The question frequently arises as to why a bookmaker cannot use line information published fairly regularly in many newspapers. He cannot for two reasons. First, the bookmakers only trust money. If they could go to the newspapers and bet on the line appearing in it, then they could trust it. However, as far as a bookie is concerned, a line is only a line if he can place bets on it. And second, whatever appears in the newspaper is not timely enough for the bookmaker; he must be able to learn of the changes in the line immediately and not the next day, at which time he may have already been inundated by smart money.

Baseball. In football, basketball, and hockey, handicapping takes the form of points added to the underdog or subtracted from the favorite for wagering purposes. Except in rare cases, handicapping in baseball is done by varying the amount of money a bettor must put up to obtain a wager of a stated denomination. Thus, if the Pittsburgh Pirates are favored over the St. Louis Cardinals, and Briles may be pitching, the line might be quoted as "Pirates 6½-7½, Briles 135-145," or simply "Pirates 7½, Briles 145." The first quotation, 6½-7½, would be the "point" or "twenty-cent" line. Wager mechanics would be as follows:

> Wager on Pirates: Risk $7.50 to win $5.00
> Wager on Cardinals: Risk $5.00 to win $6.50

It will be seen that with a five dollar wager on each team the bookmaker will keep one dollar if the Cards win and break even if the Pirates win. This vigorish of one dollar (the difference between what he collects from the favorite and pays to the underdog) is the source of the bookmaker's profit.

Just as in sports handicapped by point spreads, there is an area where the baseball bookmaker can achieve balance (i.e., make a profit regardless of which team wins). However, this is not so easy a matter to determine since it depends upon the precise line quoted. For the line given above, Pirates 6½-7½, the balance limits would be determined as follows:

Maximum percentage of money on the Pirates

$$X + \frac{5.00}{7.50} X = 100$$

$$12.5 X = 750$$

$$X = 60\%$$

Maximum percentage of money on the Cards

$$Y + \frac{6.50}{5.00} Y = 100$$

$$11.5 \ Y = 500$$

$$Y = 43.478\%$$

It follows that as long as the bookmaker retains between 56½% and 60% of his wager money on the favorite, he is in balance (the ideal balance would be approximately 58% of the wager money on the Pirates, where the bookmaker would win close to $3.50 per $100 in wagers regardless of which team won).

The second line quoted above, Briles 135-145, is called the "pitching" or "ten-cent" line and will culminate in a wager only if the named pitchers are the starters. The wager mechanics are as follows:

Wager on Briles: Risk $145 to win $100
Wager on other pitcher: Risk $100 to win $135

On this line, the balance limits would be approximately 57½% and 59% on Briles.

Added to the considerations above is the fact that there is no standard method of quoting the baseball line. For some the base is $5, for others $10 or $100. Thereafter variations may arise as to whether or not either or both the lay and take figures start with the base and/or end with it. Some examples of regional variations on the basic line quoted are set forth:

Basic odds: 7 to 5 Pirates

1. 6½-7½ (explained above).
2. 135-145 (explained above).
3. 7-8 ($10 to win $7 on favorite, $8 to win $10 on underdog).
4. ⅔-1³⁄₁₀ ($15 to win $10 on favorite, $10 to win $13 on underdog).
5. 5-3; 5-6 ($5 to win $3 on favorite, $5 to win $6 on underdog).

From the above it may be seen that layoff wagers from one section of the country to another frequently involve communication problems (What system is the other party using?) and conversion problems (What are the applicable equivalents and how nearly do they conform with my balance limits?). Use of a conversion chart is essential.

With a low margin of potential profit, narrow and complex balance limits, and convertibility problems when dealing with distant bookmakers, it is small wonder that baseball bookmaking is for the stout of heart.

Straight wagers may be written a number of ways. Some of the most common are listed below:

PIRATES - 7½ 100

BRILES - 29°

BRILES - 145- 100

FOSTER 200 -270

CARDS 13/10 200

PIRATES ⅔ 150

Occasionally when a contest is so one-sided that a money line will not attract bettors, a point-spread type of line is used. Also in a very few areas (e.g., Honolulu) a point-spread type line is used exclusively.

Aside from straight wagers, the baseball bets may include over-and-under wagers and parlay wagers. Although baseball parlays may be computed, bookmakers almost always rely on a chart to determine the payoff amounts.

Just as in football, wager records of a baseball bookmaker may be distinguished from those of a mere bettor by the appearance of multiple wagers on the same team, self-defeating wagers (i.e., wagers on both sides of the contest where, when the line is reduced to a common base, the vigorish is on the bookmaker's side), and the presence of bettors' names or coded identities [Boyd 1977].

Because of the use of the point spread (line), when there are attempts to "fix" games, the approach is to have key players "shave points." That is, their play will reflect the need to keep the score within the point spread. The National Football League has been extremely outspoken in its opposition to the legalization of sports betting. Pete Rozelle, speaking for the NFL, stated (quoted in Tuite 1978: B21):

> The league believes legalized gambling on professional sports will dramatically change the character of the fan interests in the sports. No longer will sports fans identify their interests with the success or failure of their favorite teams, but with the effect of their team's performance in the winning or losing of bets.

The NFL's real fear, of course, is that "legalized gambling will greatly multiply the security problems confronting all professional sports" (Tuite 1978: B21).

The NFL sued the state of Delaware, which experimented briefly with football betting in 1976. The NFL lost the suit, but the league's chief security officer, Jack Danahy, explains why the suit was brought: "We are not naive. We are not unaware of the fact that there is a great deal of gambling going on, but we don't think that the state or any governmental authority rightfully should come in and impose a gambling situation on our game" (Marshall 1978: 21). Interestingly, Eliot Marshall reports that Delaware "gave it up after it found that state officials were less adept at setting odds than the underworld. Professional gamblers realized they could take advantage of Delaware's inexperience in bookmaking and collect a lot of easy money" (Marshall 1978: 21). (For an inside look at the effect of gambling on college basketball, see Rosen 1978.)

A sports betting line may appear in the daily press, such as fig. 11.2, from the *Miami News*.

Organized Crime Involvement in Bookmaking

In an earlier period bookmaking was an important source of income for organized crime. The latter either ran the operation directly or "licensed" syndicate bookmakers. As we have seen, in chapter nine, the wire service was an important source of organized-crime control over bookmaking. However, most wagering today involves sports, as opposed to horse racing, and uses the telephone; the quick results provided by the wire service are no longer vital. In addition, the almost exclusive use of the telephone provides greater security and has reduced the need for police protection, often another important syndicate service. Rubinstein and Reuter (1978a and 1978b) report that their research in New York City revealed very little syndicate involvement in bookmaking.

Bookmaking, without the need for a wire service and elaborate police payoffs, is a relatively easy-entry enterprise. This easy entry has made it impossible to maintain monopolistic control. In addition, the profit margin is only between 4.5 and 5 percent; only a large operation would be of financial interest to an organized-crime syndicate. Independents, as long as they did not get too big or compete seriously with a syndicate operation, could continue unmolested.

Lotteries: Numbers, Policy, and Sports Pools

Henry Chafetz notes that the "American colonies were floated on lotteries." In 1612, King James I authorized a lottery to promote the colony of Virginia. The colonies themselves used lotteries, and such outstanding men as George Washington bought and sold lottery tickets (1960: 20-21). The lottery was used (unsuccessfully) to help finance the Revolutionary War. Many of America's outstanding institutions of higher learning were supported through the use of lotteries—Brown (Rhode Island College), Columbia, Harvard, Uni-

Fig. 11.2
A Typical Sports Betting Line

AMERICAN LEAGUE

Favorite	Odds	Underdog			
BALT.	× 1½-2	Seattle	ST. LOUIS	8-9	Atlanta
BOSTON	2-2½	Oakland	HOUSTON	+ Even-6	Chicago
NEW YORK	7-8	California	SAN DIEGO	++ Even-6	Montreal
DETROIT	Pick 'em	Milwaukee	SAN FRAN.	7½-8½	New York
CHICAGO	5½-6½	Kansas City	LOS ANG.	5½-6½	Phila.
MINN.	6½-7½	Cleveland	+ Vs. Rick Reuschel, otherwise		
× Both games of doubleheader			Astros 6½-7½		
			++ Vs. Rogers, otherwise Padres		
			6½-7½		

NATIONAL LEAGUE			SOCCER (NASL)		
Favorite	Odds	Underdog	Favorite	Odds	Underdog
PITT.	6-7	Cincin.	Tampa	5½-6½	ROCH.
			Home Team in CAPS		

The Greek Line

Jimmy Snyder's Odds

AL - BALTIMORE (McGregor and Martinez) 11-5 over Seattle (Bannister and Jones) (both games); BOSTON (Eckersley) 3-1 over Oakland (Morgan); NEW YORK (Tiant) 7-5 over California (Aase); Milwaukee (Travers) 6-5 over DETROIT (Underwood); MINNESOTA (Koosman) 7-5 over Cleveland (Wise); Kansas City (Gale) 6-5 over CHICAGO (Kravec)

NL - PITTSBURGH (Kison) 7-5 over Cincinnati (Norman); ST. LOUIS (Vuckovich) 8-5 over Atlanta (Brizzolara); HOUSTON (Forsch) 6-5 over Chicago (Reuschel); SAN DIEGO (Perry) 6-5 over Montreal (Rogers); LOS ANGELES (Hooton) 6-5 over Philadelphia (Lerch); SAN FRANCISCO (Montefusco) 8-5 over New York (Kobel)

(CAPS indicate home team)

SOURCE: The *Miami News*

versity of North Carolina, William and Mary, and Yale (Chafetz 1960).

During the nineteenth century, lotteries under state license or control were found throughout the United States. Because of the negative publicity surrounding problems with the Louisiana Lottery, in 1890 the United States enacted legislation prohibiting lotteries from using the mails and even prohibited newspapers that carried lottery advertisements from using the mails (Chafetz 1960). This prohibition opened the way to illegal exploitation of bettors through such devices as numbers and policy.

Numbers and Policy

In numbers and policy a player selects one, two, or three digits from zero to nine, with the odds of winning thus running from 10 to 1, 100 to 1, and 1,000 to 1. For a single-digit ("single action") play, the payoff is 6 or 7 to 1; for two digits ("boledo" or "bolito") the payoff is between 50 and 64 to 1; for three digits the payoff is between 550 and 600 to 1. On certain popular numbers—e.g. 711—the payoff may be reduced to 500 to 1 or even lower. A player can also "box" numbers—bet all the possible three-digit combinations. While this increases the chances of winning, it also reduces the payoff to about 100 to 1.

There are several schemes for determining the winning numbers in addition to simply using the results of a state-run lottery. For example, the first digit is determined by adding what the horses coming in first, second, and third (win, place, show) paid on a two-dollar bet in the first race; the second digit is a repeat for the second race; and the third digit is determined using the third race, all at a particular racetrack.

	Win	Place	Show	Totals
First race	58.80	26.80	10.40	96.00
Second race	11.00	5.40	2.80	19.20
Third race	10.20	5.60	4.20	20.00

The final three numbers are determined by reading the first digit to the left of the decimal point from the top down: 6 9 0.

Another widely used system is the last three digits of the daily total gross receipts ("handle") of a designated racetrack, e.g., $2,534,940. The winning number is: 9 4 0. Other methods include the last three digits of the daily balance of the United States Treasury, stocks traded, or agricultural prices for eggs or other commodities, amounts generally reported in the daily press. When the numbers are determined by a drawing (lottery), the game is usually called *policy* and the places where the drawings conducted are referred to as *wheels,* after the container from which the lottery balls are drawn. However, *policy* and *numbers* are terms often used interchangeably, as are *wheels* and *numbers banks.*

During the 1930s, an extremely popular form of gambling was the "Italian lottery," which was played throughout the United States, almost exclusively by persons of Italian birth or descent. Weekly income for the lottery in 1935 was estimated at $2 million a week in the New York metropolitan area alone. The winning numbers were reportedly drawn from a wheel by a blind boy every Friday in eight different Italian towns and cities. One letter and five numbers, from 1 to 1,000, are drawn in each of the eight locations; thus:

B	7	41	17	86	48
E	78	22	9	38	6
H	16	39	28	63	81
J	96	7	18	53	59
L	2	78	61	24	8
M	12	71	3	46	89
Q	83	6	4	66	3
V	31	14	51	9	72

If a player has correctly guessed a letter with two of the numbers (out of five) next to it, there is a payoff of 250 to 1; if three numbers, the payoff is 5,000 to 1; four numbers win 50,000 to 1. The winning letters and numbers were cabled from Italy and printed on Saturday in a variety of handouts and publications ("$2,000,000 Lottery Unmolested Here" 1935).

In an affidavit supporting a search warrant, an Asheville, North Carolina, police officer describes a version of the numbers game called *bolita:*

> I am Sgt. L. Williams, having been employed by the Asheville Police Dept. for 29 years. It has been my responsibility to enforce gambling laws and, more recently, to initiate gambling investigations. This affidavit describes "Bolita," which is a numbers game and wagering system; Bolita employs strips of paper which are numbered 1 through 100 and sold by individuals on a daily basis. Each slip of paper or number which is sold has a value assigned by the seller, usually 25 cents, 50 cents, or $1.00. If $1.00 is invested on a winning number, the holder of that number would be paid $80.00. The winning number is determined on a daily basis at a designated time in the following manner; several subjects stand at various locations in close relation to one another, at this time a bag is passed around which contains small balls numbered 1 through 100. When this bag is passed to a designated person, he or she grasps one ball from the outside of the bag and it is tied off. The rest of the balls are then removed from the bag. The ball remaining in the grasp of the designated person represents the winning number (which is the number appearing on the ball). Having arrested or assisted in the arrests of more than 100 persons for possession of Bolita strips and interviewing many of them, I believe the above description is accurate in describing the gambling system known as "Bolita."

Fig. 11.3 shows a copy of a sheet of bets seized in a raid on a policy bank. Lasswell and McKenna explain the notations (1972: 87):

Figure 11.3
A Sheet of Bets Seized in a Raid on a Policy Bank

612 - 25 (1.50	564 - 15	263 - 1.5 (.30
261 - 1.00	673 - 15	800 - 30 (.30
166 - 25 (.30	148 - 15	580 - 25
186 - 25 (.30	516 - 15	120 - 25
575 - 25 (.30	109 - 10	111 - 25
938 - 20 (.30	320 - 10	729 - 25
832 - 20 (.30	230 - 10	445 - 25
902 - 20 (.30	666 - 25	061 - 25
604 - 20 (.30	222 - 25	318 - 25
500 - 20 (.30	054 - 10	544 - 25
940 - 5 (.60	579 - 10	568 - 25
923 - 5 (.60	112 - 10	625 - 25
157 - 5 (.60	209 - 10	418 - 25
186 - 5 (.60	165 - 10	302 - 5 (.30
316 - 5 (.60	243 - 10	045 - 5 (.30
317 - 5 (.60	276 - 10	597 - 5 (.30
813 - 5 (.60	369 - 10	121 - 5 (.30
225 - 25 (.15	520 - 10	092 - 5 (.30
989 - 25 (.15	358 - 10	116 - 5 (.45
	942 - 10	823 - 25
		427 - 15
		526 - 15

The sheet contains three columns of numbers. Each column shows a three-digit number (the number bet upon separated by a hyphen from the number or numbers indicating the amount of the wager). Some amounts on the wager side of the column have the letter C before them which indicates the number was bet as a combination. A combination bet means that any of the six possible combinations of the original three-digit number was also being bet.

The first series of numbers in the first column are 612-25 C 1.50 which mean 612 was bet individually for 25¢ and again as a combination for $1.50. Thus, if any combination of 612 (621, 126, 162, 216, 261, and 612) became the winning number, the bettor would collect on a 25¢ bet (1.50 divided six ways).

Note on the lower part of the paper the designation "D.B.Q." This is the code name for the runner turning those bets. The sheet of bets represented by this page is usually turned into the bank in an envelope bearing the code designation for the controller for whom the runner is working.

Numbers Organizational Structure[2]

At the bottom of the hierarchical totem pole is the person who accepts wagers directly from the bettors. These are known as writers, runners, sellers, etc., and generally are individuals with ready access to the public (e.g., elevator operators, shoeshine boys, newspaper vendors, bartenders, waitresses). Customarily they are paid a percentage of the wagers they write (unlike sports bookmaking, numbers wagering is done on a cash basis), usually from 15 to 30 percent, and frequently they are given a 10 percent tip from bettors receiving payment for hits. In only a very few places do writers furnish their customers with a written record of the wager.

The number writer is strictly a salesman and assumes no financial burden for the numbers he writes. It is essential, therefore, that his wagers reach trusted hands before the winning number or any part of it is known. Sometimes this is done by telephone; other times the wager records (commonly known as work, action, business, etc.) are physically forwarded to a higher echelon by a pickup man (frequently a taxi driver, vending machine serviceman, etc.).

In a small operation the wagers may go directly to the central processing office (commonly called the bank, clearinghouse, countinghouse). More often, in large enterprises they are given to management's field representative (known as the field man, controller, etc.), who may be responsible for making a quick tally to determine the existence of any heavily played numbers which should be laid off. At such levels of operation one frequently finds charts consisting of 1,000 spaces numbered 000 to 999 where tallies can be made for all wagers or only for certain wagers meeting a minimum dollar value.

Near the top of the totem pole is the bank, the place where all transactions are handled. During the collection process the bank will be making decisions as to whether or not to lay off certain heavily played numbers. After the winning number is known the bank will meticulously process the paperwork to determine how much action has been written, how many hits are present, and the controllers and/or writers involved. Provision will be made for the payment of hits. Frequently, if the hits are small the payment will be made directly by the writer and deducted from the amount he owes the bank. In other cases, particularly large hits, payment will first be made to the writer by the bank or the controller.

Numbers wagers produce a large volume of records, hence the bank will seldom keep the recorded wagers for much longer than a week. Some retention is necessary in case of claims arising by bettors or writers. Not infrequently a winning number may be missed by the bank's clerical personnel, resulting in a claim for an "overlook."

Behind the bank and at the top of the totem pole is the financial backer who may or may not be associated with the day-to-day operations. He will frequently provide the funds to furnish bond and legal counsel to employees who are arrested.

Settlement with the writers may be on a daily basis, but more frequently it is done on a weekly basis. The bank will prepare a "tape" (i.e., adding machine tape showing the gross action written, deductions for the writer's commission plus any payment for hits he has made from his own funds, and ending with the amount due from the writer to the bank) advising the writer how much to pay the collector, controller, or other person who represents the bank [Boyd 1977].

The paper used to record bets may be deliberately treated with chemicals so that it is quite flammable and thus easily destroyed in order to avoid arrest and prosecution. Records of bets may be made on metal strips which can be swallowed and later retrieved; in New York's Chinatown, bets are recorded on rice paper which can be easily swallowed.

Groups of writers or runners transfer their bets to a controller who receives about 10 percent of the bets while the writer receives 25 to 30 percent. The controller transfers the bets to the bank, a central operating location. After the number is determined ("comes out"), the bank calculates the winnings to be paid out, and this is returned to the writer through the controller. The writer is the only contact with the player, and he or she makes the payoff. If payments exceed collections, the writer may be in "debit" and thus not receive any commissions until accounts are even. This situation is compensated, somewhat, by receiving the usual 10 percent of any "hits" as tips from winning players.

Sports Pools

The *sports pool* has several versions, but the essentials are the same. A series of "tips" are placed on a "tip-board" or in some container. Each tip bears two three-digit numbers, with the last two digits of each number representing a major league baseball (or other) team. Players purchase a tip, which they select blindly; if this tip bears the two numbers representing the two teams which scored the most runs (points, goals, etc.) that day, they are winners. In a baseball pool there are 153 different combinations (tips), and the payoff is usually 120 times the amount wagered.

In this form of lottery the seller receives about 10 percent of the wagers he or she collects, while payoffs come from the bank through the seller. Between the bank and the seller is often a tip-board salesperson, someone who does not solicit bets but who sells the tip-boards for the bank and receives a 10 percent commission.

Several aspects of lotteries help to enhance the game. Desmond Cartey, for example, points out that the writer often provides valuable information to the player on matters ranging from vacant apartments for rent to securing stolen merchandise at discount prices (1970: 35).

Casino Gambling and Related Activities

Illegal casino gambling (with a wide array of games of chance including roulette, chuck-a-luck, blackjack, and craps) requires a great deal of space, personnel, and funding (legalized gambling is dealt with in chapter 19). In the past, casino gambling was available in "wide-open towns" such as Newport, Kentucky, and Phenix City, Alabama,[3] where the operations would be safe from law enforcement. In some cities there is a tradition of holding "Las Vegas Nights." These events are often run by organized-crime elements using the legitimate front of a religious or charitable organization. The operators provide the gambling devices, personnel, and financing, and they share some of the profits with the sponsoring organization.

Organized-crime operatives may also organize or sponsor card or dice games, taking a cut of every pot for their services. These may be in a permanent location—e.g., a social club or a veterans' hall—or for security reasons may float from place to place. The games may be operated in the home of a person in debt to a loanshark as a form of paying off the loan. Gambling activities not operated under OC protection, "outlaw games," run the risk of being raided by the police or being held up by independent criminals or robbery teams sponsored by an OC unit. Vincent Siciliano (1970: 50), an armed robber with OC connections, reports: "The organization knows there is this game and when some friend in the police needs an arrest, to earn his keep as a protector of the people against the bad gamblers, the organization guy tells the police and off they go with sirens wailing." During the raid, Siciliano notes, the police can also help themselves to much of the game's proceeds. He points out that even the dumbest thief knows which are syndicate games and recognizes the consequences. Greenberg (1980: 93) quotes one man who expressed his concern with robbing a "connected" operation: "I didn't think the Mafia'd read me my rights and let me go consult with an attorney. And I said [to his partners], 'Is this thing connected?' I said, 'Look, if this is the Mafia's money I don't want any part of it. I don't want some guys to come gunnin' for me.'"

In many states, bingo, purportedly to raise funds for charitable causes, is a source of profits for OC; they may run the operations for the front (charity) or merely be connected through "licensure." Gary Bowdach, an enforcer and executioner for OC Families, before a U.S. Senate Committee (Permanent Subcommittee on Investigations 1978, part 1: 157-58):

MR. BOWDACH: The operation was owned by a gentleman, I don't know his name, I met him on one occasion. He was a little old Jewish fellow who was moved in on by the organization run by Carlo DiPietro [member of the Genovese Family] and the organization run by Eddie Coco [*caporegime* in the Lucchese Family]. They had cut themselves into this operation.

SENATOR CHILES: Was he legitimate at the time he was running the organization and the mob moved in on him? How did that work?

MR. BOWDACH: What happened is that the Coco organization moved in on him first for a certain percentage of his receipts. They started getting a little bit out of hand. They wanted more and more and he went out to seek help, and ended up with the help of Carlo DiPietro, and losing the bigger end of it, had he had [sic] given it to Eddie Coco.

SENATOR CHILES: When you say somebody moved in on him, do you mean they just kind of went to see him and said, "We would like to buy part of your business?" How does "moved in" work?

MR. BOWDACH: You move in, you tell him you are going to protect his operation from anybody else moving in, the bingo operation in Florida has grown to a pretty good sized business today. So they offer protection. If they don't take, the place is burned down or bombed.

Gambling profits can also be generated by the *fixing* of the outcome of sporting events. Teresa (1973: 158) states: "There was hardly a race track in New England where the mob didn't put the fix in at one time or another. . . . I should know," he adds, "I helped fix enough races." There is a history of fixing (actually "shaving of points" to stay within the "line") in college basketball (see Cohen, 1977, and Hill, 1981, for examples). However, legalized gambling in Nevada has been a lucrative source of profits for OC.

The Las Vegas Connection

In 1931, the state of Nevada, desperate for tax revenue, legalized gambling and established a licensing procedure for those wishing to operate gambling establishments. Bugsy Siegel was the first important criminal to recognize the potential from legalized gambling in Nevada. He had been operating in California, and

> from about 1942 until the time of his death, Siegel controlled the race-wire service in Las Vegas through Moe Sedway, an ex-convict, gambler, and long-time associate of many New York mobsters, who Siegel brought to Las Vegas. Through a control of the wire service, Siegel controlled the operation of all handbooks operating in Las Vegas. He refused wire service to any book unless he or his agents actually operated and managed it [Special Committee to Investigate Organized Crime 1951: 91]

With financing from OC leaders throughout the country, Siegel built the Flamingo Hotel, the first of Las Vegas's elaborate gambling establishments.

Since Siegel's death in 1947, the Flamingo and a number of plush Las Vegas hotels have been controlled (through hidden interests) by OC units. Typically, funds are "skimmed" before they are counted for tax purposes. The skimmed money is distributed to OC leaders in proportion to their amount of (hidden) ownership. According to federal officials, from 1973 to 1983, at least $14 million was skimmed from just one hotel, the Stardust. In 1983 several Stardust employees were prosecuted and the owners (of record) forced to sell the hotel. The Stardust was originally licensed to Moe Dalitz of the Cleveland syndicate, who sold it to Howard Hughes in 1967. In 1983, two Kansas City, Missouri, OC figures and an executive of the Tropicana Hotel-Casino were sentenced to long prison terms for skimming operations (Turner 1984).

Usury and Loansharking

The Bible (Deuteronomy 23: 20-21) admonishes, "Unto a foreigner thou mayest lend upon interest; but upon thy brother thou shalt not lend upon interest." Thus, Hebrews could not charge interest on a loan to another Hebrew, and later the Christian Church adopted a similar interpretation: Christians could not charge interest on a loan to another Christian.[4] In 1596, William Shakespeare depicted the unsavory Shylock in his *Merchant of Venice*, a money-lending Jew who demanded a pound of flesh from a desperate borrower as repayment for a delinquent loan. The term *Shylock* became slurred by illiterate criminals into "shark," and the word *loanshark* was born.[5] Ronald Goldstock and Dan Coenen (1978: 2) note that loansharking embodies two central features: "the assessment of exorbitant interest rates in extending credit and the use of threats and violence in collecting debts." Sometimes such credit is called "juice" loans.

Between 1880 and 1915 a practice known as "salary lending" thrived in the United States. This quasi-legal business provided loans to salaried workers at usurious rates. The collection of debts was ensured by having the borrower sign a variety of complicated legal documents that subjected him or her to the real possibility of being sued and losing employment. Through the efforts of the Russell Sage Foundation, states began enacting small-loan acts to combat this practice, first in Massachusetts in 1911. These laws, which licensed small lenders and set ceilings on interest, eventually led to an end of salary lending, and credit unions, savings banks, and similar institutions began to offer small loans. However, it also led to the wholesale entry of organized crime into the illicit credit business (Goldstock and Coenen 1978).

As was noted in part 3, as Prohibition was drawing to a close, and with the onset of the Great Depression, persons in organized crime began searching for new areas of profit. These criminals found themselves in the enviable position of having a great deal of excess cash in a cash-starved economy, and this condition gave them a new source of continued income. Goldstock and Coenen (1978: 4) point out:

Contemporary loansharking is marked by the dominance of organized crime. This pervasive influence is hardly surprising. Syndicate access to rich stores of capital allows the underworld to pour substantial amounts of cash into the credit market. The strength and reputation of organized operations lends credence to threats of reprisals, thus augmenting the aura of fear critical to success in the loansharking business. Moreover, organized crime's aversion to competition militates strongly against successful independent operations.

Members of OC often insulate themselves from direct involvement in loansharking by using nonmember associates. For example, Gambino Family member Tony Plate employed—actually funded—Charles ("The Bear") Calise. Calise, in turn, employed others as lenders and collectors. The connection with Tony Plate gave the whole operation an umbrella of protection from other criminals. Without this connection, a borrower who was a "made-guy" in a Crime Family could very easily refuse to pay back the loan; and violence used to collect would bring retaliation from the Family. Many loansharks provide loans to other criminals. Rubinstein and Reuter (1978b: Appendix, 3-5) state, "There is strong evidence for specialization by loansharks. Some deal with legitimate businessmen only, some with illegal entrepreneurs. One medium level loanshark specialized in fur dealers, though he might make loans to other small businessmen. Some specialize in lending to gambling operators." Joseph Valachi (Maas 1968) worked as a loanshark and reported that most of his customers were themselves involved in illegal activities, such as numbers and bookmaking. Rubinstein and Reuter (1978b: 53) report that loansharks "frequently provide capital for a bookmaker who is in financial difficulty."

Individual gamblers may also borrow from a loanshark. The latter may stay around card and dice games or accept "referrals" from a bookmaker. In one case familiar to this writer, a young gambler borrowed from a loanshark to pay his bookmaker. He continued to gamble and borrow and eventually was unable to repay his loanshark. As a result, he embarked on a series of illegal activities that eventually led to a prison term. Among his activities were running high-stakes poker games, at which his wife played hostess, and securing fraudulent loans from numerous banks. On one occasion, he decided to use some of his money to continue gambling and missed his loanshark payment. A severe beating in a parking lot ensued, leaving him with two black eyes and a broken nose. For collecting debts, the loanshark obviously has means not usually used by other lending institutions and is thus more willing to lend money to otherwise "poor risks." However, loansharks are not in the "muscle" business; they are in the money business, and thus "they lend money to customers whom they expect will pay off and eventually return as customers again. The loanshark is not attempting to gain control of the customer's business"[6] (Rubinstein and Reuter 1978b: 3-4). But this sometimes happens, as Valachi notes (Maas 1968). He lent money to a legitimate businessman, the owner of a dress and negligee company, and became a partner when the loan could not be repaid. With Valachi's financial backing and his ability to keep unions from organizing the factory, the business prospered. Rubinstein and Reuter, as a result of their research in New York, note (1978b: 4):

> . . . collection very rarely involves violence, or even the threat of violence. Loansharks are interested in making credit assessments in the manner of legitimate lenders. Often they secure collateral for the loan, though it may be of an illiquid form. Sometimes a borrower will have to produce a guarantor. In many cases the loan is very short term, less than a month, and collection is simply not an issue. Repeat business is the backbone of those operations we have studied. A good faith effort to make payments will probably guarantee the borrower against harassment, particularly if he has made substantial payment of interest before he starts to have repayment problems.

There are two basic types of usurious loan: the *knockdown* and the *vig*. The knockdown requires a specified schedule of repayment including both principal and interest—e.g., $1,000 might be repaid in fourteen weekly installments of $100. The vig is a "six for five" loan: for every five dollars borrowed on Monday, six dollars is due on the following Monday. The one-dollar interest is called *juice*, and loansharking is often referred to as the "juice racket." If total repayment of the vig loan, principal plus interest, is not forthcoming on the date due, the interest is compounded for the following week. Thus, a loan of $100 requires repayment of $120 seven days later. The debt will increase at the following rate on the original $100:

Week 1—$120.
Week 2—$144.
Week 3—$172.80.
Week 4—$207.36.

The insidious nature of the vig loan is that the borrower must keep paying interest until the principal plus the accumulated interest is repaid at one time. It is quite easy for the original loan to be repaid many times without actually decreasing the principal owed; the loanshark is primarily interested in a steady income and is quite willing to let the principal remain outstanding for an indefinite period.

---

[1] Unless otherwise cited, material in this section has been edited from Boyd (1977).

[2] Unless otherwise cited, material in this section is from Boyd (1977).

[3] Newport was run by the Cleveland syndicate headed by Moe Dalitz, Morris Kleinman, Sam Tucker, and Louis Rothkopf. Located just across the Ohio River from Cincinnati, Newport is a city of only 1.5 square miles with a population of about 25,000 located in Kentucky's Cambell County. In 1961, as part of a reform effort, George Ratterman, a former professional

football player, agreed to run for sheriff of Cambell County. In a rather famous incident, Ratterman was drugged and, with the cooperation of the Newport police, was arrested with a striptease dancer and taken to police headquarters wearing only a bedspread. The ploy failed; Ratterman was elected and the town was "closed" (Messick 1967).

On June 15, 1954, Albert L. Patterson, a Phenix City reformer who had been nominated Alabama attorney general, was murdered. His son was elected governor of Alabama, and Gordon Patterson declared martial law in Phenix City and sent in the National Guard to "close it down." These events inspired the movie *The Phenix City Story* (Wright 1979).

[4] This led to a paradoxical situation. Within organized Jewish communities, the Hebrew Free Loan Society developed; it loaned money to Jews without interest. On the other hand, laws and regulations restricting their ability to purchase land and enter guilds resulted in Jews becoming moneylenders to Christians. Shakespeare's Shylock is based on this historical irony.

[5] At the time Shakespeare was writing, there were no Jewish moneylenders in England— Jews had been expelled from that country in 1290. In Hebrew, the term for interest is *neshech*, literally "to bite," something for which sharks are noted.

[6] A loanshark who wanted to be in a legitimate business obviously would use the money for that purpose. Loansharking, however, requires very little time and can be engaged in by those with limited intelligence and ability. While some persons in OC are obviously quite bright, many others would lose an argument with a fire hydrant.

chapter 12

Drug Trafficking

Used by permission of United Press International Inc.

As was noted in part 2, trafficking in controlled substances parallels that in alcohol during Prohibition. There are, however, some important differences. The plants from which heroin and cocaine are derived are not grown in the United States, and so these substances must be smuggled into the country. Because of the clandestine nature of drug use (there are no equivalents to the speakeasy), trafficking in drugs is difficult to monopolize—it is a relatively easy business to enter. In addition, the market is so extensive and profits so huge that efforts to control market entry would simply not be cost-effective for an OC unit. It should be noted that, while many Italian-American OC units, particularly in New York, are involved in drug trafficking, others, such as the Chicago Outfit, avoid this business. Aside from any ethical considerations ("drugs are dirty"), dealing drugs makes the organization quite vulnerable to law-enforcement efforts. It automatically means that the Drug Enforcement Administration will be making arrests, and this increases the likelihood of informants' jeopardizing the members and business interests of the OC unit. Generally, a "made-guy" or associate involved in drug trafficking will be required to stay away from other (non-trafficking) members. While he will be expected to provide a portion of his earnings to the Family hierarchy, the Family will not protect him with respect to his drug operations nor will they intervene on his behalf with the criminal justice system—he is on his own.

For purposes of discussion, this section will divide controlled substances into four parts:

1. Heroin.
2. Cocaine.
3. Cannabis.
4. Synthetic drugs.

Heroin

Heroin is a chemical derivative of opium, from the Greek word *opion,* meaning juice of the poppy (Bresler 1980). Opium, which has a sedating effect on the user, was consumed by the Sumerians in 4000 B.C., and ancient art relics depict its use in Egyptian religious rituals as early as 3500 B.C. (Inverarity, Lauderdale, and Feld 1983). The poppy *(Papaver somniferum)* was grown in the Mediterranean region as early as 300 B.C. and has since been cultivated in countries around the world, including Hungary, Yugoslavia, Turkey, India, Burma, China, and Mexico. It grows best in moist climates at elevations above 2,000 feet.

The milky fluid that oozes from incisions in the unripe seedpod has since ancient times been scraped by hand and air dried to produce opium gum. A more modern method of harvesting is by the industrial poppy straw process of extracting alkaloids from the mature dried plant. The extract may be in either liquid, solid, or powder form *(Drugs of Abuse* 1979: 11).

Opium was brought to China from India by Portuguese seamen, and its sale was banned by the Ch'ing Emperor in 1729. The ban proved ineffective, and British merchants took over the trade. In 1773, the British East India Company was granted an exclusive monopoly over the entire Indian poppy crop by the government of British India. Faced with a massive balance-of-payments deficit with China, England began to expand the export of opium from India to China. At this time tobacco smoking was introduced, and the widespread smoking of opium followed. The Chinese government, alarmed over the widespread addiction to opium, attempted to stop importation. This resulted in the First Opium War (1839–42), in which Britain defeated China, forced it to cede Hong Kong to colonial rule, and opened China to an unbridled opium trade. Further attempts by the Chinese to curtail drug imports led to the Second Opium War (1856–58), the loss of more of their territory, and no cessation of the opium trade.

In 1806, a German pharmacist added liquid ammonia to opium, and the result was a new drug which he named after the Greek god of dreams, *Morphius*. Morphine was born. Many times more powerful than the raw opium, morphine suppresses anxiety and alters the perception of pain, producing a form of euphoria (incorrectly) referred to as a "high" (since it is actually a "low"). It also reduces hunger and the sex drive while inducing lethargy. As a result of the primitive state of medicine, opium and morphine were widely used to deal with the symptoms of dozens of maladies, mental and physical, minor and serious. They were readily available in the United States in "patent medicines," which were sold without any restrictions in drugstores or through the mails. In 1856 the hypodermic method of injecting drugs directly into the bloodstream was introduced to American medicine. The extensive use of morphine during the years of the Civil War (1861–65) resulted in widespread addiction, which was referred to as the "Soldier's Disease."

In 1874, a British chemist experimenting with morphine synthesized diacetyl-morphine.

Commercial promotion of the new drug had to wait until 1898 when the highly respectable German pharmaceutical combine Bayer, in perfectly good faith but perhaps without sufficient prior care, launched upon an unsuspecting world public this new substance, for which they coined the trade name "heroin" and which they marketed as—of all things—a "sedative for coughs" [Bresler 1980: 11].

Heroin is the most powerful of the opium derivatives.

Opiates, including morphine and heroin, were readily available in the United States until five years before the Volstead Act and the onset of Prohibition. Edward Brecher (1974: 3) refers to the United States during the nineteenth century as a "dope fiend's paradise." He points out that, while the use of opiates was frowned upon by some as immoral—it was never socially acceptable in the United States—it was not the subject of the sanctions, legal or social, that are experienced today. An employee was not fired for being an addict, and children were not taken away from their addicted parents and placed in foster care. Indeed, there were prominent opium users in those days, one being Dr. William Stewart Halsted (1852–1922), one of America's greatest surgeons and a founder of Johns Hopkins Medical School.

As a result of international pressures over the opium trade, in 1912 the Hague Convention agreed that each contracting nation would adopt laws regulating opium and opium products. In the United States, as a result of the Hague agreement, the Harrison Act was passed in 1914. Brecher stresses that the focus of this law was the international and not the domestic problems with opium (the act also dealt with cocaine, which was mistakenly deemed a narcotic). The original intent of the Harrison Act was to license and thus control domestic drug traffic. However, as Edwin Schur (1965: 130) points out, restrictive federal regulations and harassment from drug-enforcement officials "effectively and severely limited the freedom of medical practitioners to treat addict-patients as they see fit—in particular, to provide addicts with drugs when that is believed medically advisable." After the Harrison Act was passed, the Federal Bureau of Narcotics arrested thousands of medical doctors for dispensing narcotics to addict-patients. In 1922, the United States Supreme Court decided the case of the *United States* v. *Behrman* (258 U.S. 280), which involved an obvious abuse by a medical doctor who had given an addict a huge quantity of narcotics to use as he pleased. The Federal Bureau of Narcotics interpreted this decision to mean that regardless of the medical intent, treatment of addicts involving the administration of narcotics was prohibited. Federal agents moved to close down narcotics clinics and arrested thousands of doctors for supplying opiates. This spawned a flourishing, albeit illegal, traffic in drugs.

The Business of Heroin

The business of heroin begins outside the United States, mainly in the Middle East, Asia, and Mexico. At one time Turkey was the major American supplier of both legal and illegal opium. In Turkey farmers grow the poppy legally and sell it to a government monopoly, which exports it for medical use. Because of a lack of adequate controls, up until the 1970s, Turkish farmers on average each diverted three to five kilos (a kilo is 2.2046 pounds) to the black market. Illegal opium dealers collected the raw opium from the numerous farmers until they accumulated about 1,000 kilos, enough to produce about 100 kilos of heroin. The raw opium was moved across minefields blocking the Turkish border and into Syria, where it was converted into base morphine. It was then shipped to Aleppo and then on to Marseilles or Sicily, where it was converted into heroin in clandestine laboratories. Then it was smuggled into the United States. During the 1970s American pressure on Turkey caused the government to reduce the amount of poppy cultivation and institute strong inspection measures, which significantly reduced the illegal diversion of opium. However, this merely stimulated opium production in other parts of the world.

The *Golden Triangle* refers to approximately 150,000 square miles of forest-covered highlands made up of the western fringe of Laos, the four northern provinces of Thailand, and the northeastern parts of Burma, including the semiautonomous Shan States. It is an area noted for growing poppies and private armies. Burma became independent from British rule in 1948 and continues to have difficulty establishing its sovereignty over the Shan States. In this region the Shan United Army (SUA), consisting of remnants of the Shan separatist movement, maintains an impressive military presence supported by trafficking in opium. A U.S. Senate committee report describes the headquarters of the SUA (Permanent Subcommittee on Investigations, *International Narcotics Trafficking* 1981: 413–14):

> Situated in the hill country of northern Thailand, approximately eight kilometers from the Burmese border, the Shan United Army headquarters is a growing city, dwarfing the surrounding villages by comparison. Built on the narcotics profits of the Shan United Army, Ban Hin Taek boasts new housing developments, a hospital, two jails, and a radio intercept facility, capable of collecting Burmese army transmissions. Total population of the village is approximately 1,400, including 200 Thai citizens who are not direct Shan United Army dependents.
>
> The city is clearly well armed and well protected. In Ban Hin Taek itself, there are 600 to 650 men armed with M-16 rifles. Another 50 men are equipped with 30-caliber machine guns. Additional rifles and bazookas are stored within the city. . . . All these troops are well-led, well-trained, and well-armed.
>
> With a total strength estimated to be near 5,000 armed men, the Shan United Army is, by any standard, a substantial military force.

A second private army in the Golden Triangle has its origins in the Communist revolutionary victory in mainland China. With the defeat of Chiang Kai-Shek's forces there during the late 1940s, two of his armies, the Third and the Fifth, stationed in the remote southern province of Yunnan, escaped over the mountainous frontier into the Shan States. With support from the United States, the Nationalists were rearmed and resupplied; with recruits from hill tribesmen, they attempted to invade China in 1951 and 1952. When the attempts failed, U.S. interest and support waned. The Nationalists turned to drug trafficking. In 1961 and 1969 there were U.S.-backed airlifts of Nationalist troops to Taiwan, and that was the last official contact between the Nationalist remnant on the mainland and the Chiang Kai-Shek government. The remaining troops, about 4,000 strong, became known as the Chinese Irregular Forces (CIF). Despite the fact that they are financed by trafficking in opium, the CIF is tolerated by the government of Thailand as a force against Communist insurgents.

The third major private army in the area is that of the Burmese Communist Party (BCP), consisting of between 10,000 and 12,000 well-armed men. In the past, the BCP received support from the People's Republic of China. After Peking cut off this aid in order to improve relations with Burma, the BCP went into the opium business.

(During the Vietnam War, the Central Intelligence Agency financed Meo tribesmen in Laos in efforts against the Communists. The Meo economy is based on the cultivation of the poppy.)

Whether the source is the SUA, the CIF, the BCP, or Meo tribes, the morphine base is converted into heroin in laboratories near Bangkok. Major transactions involving Golden Triangle heroin are accomplished in Bangkok, and the brokers are usually ethnic Chinese (Bresler 1980).

The *Golden Crescent* of Southwest Asia covers areas of Iran, Afghanistan, and Pakistan. Like northern Turkey, the region has the limestone-rich soil, climate, and altitude ideal for poppy cultivation. In Pakistan, the typical poppy farmer is in tribal areas outside the direct control of the central government in Karachi. In northwest Pakistan's Karakorum Mountains one acre of poppies will yield about a dozen kilos of opium gum; ten kilos of opium gum will be converted into a kilo of base-morphine. The wholesaling is accomplished in lawless border towns such as Landi Kotal, which is about three miles from the Afghan border. Jonathan Broder (1984: 12) describes his visit to a heroin merchant in the bazaar town of Bara, Pakistan (edited):

> He carefully unfolded a small brown paper packet to reveal the off-white heroin powder that he was eager to sell.
>
> "Taste it," he encouraged. "By the prophet's beard, it is nearly 100 percent pure. I don't lie. I have made the pilgrimage to Mecca twice. Allah has made me rich because I don't lie. Go ahead and taste it."
>
> He didn't lie. A fingernail dab of this heroin, more than 90 percent pure, packed enough wallop to dull the senses and induce vomiting for hours. He was rich too.
>
> His fortresslike stone house, surrounded by hard dirt fields, was the size of a small school. In one large room, brown bales of raw opium were stacked to the ceiling. Another room was cluttered with bottles of chemicals and plastic bowls for converting opium into heroin.

Most of the poppy farmers in this region are Pathan tribesmen (Islamic Afghans), many of whom actively oppose the Soviet-backed regime in Kabul. The Soviet invasion of Afghanistan disrupted normal drug-trade routes into Iran and Turkey. As a result, morphine-base was moved through the Khyber

Figure 12.1
Major Asian Opium Regions

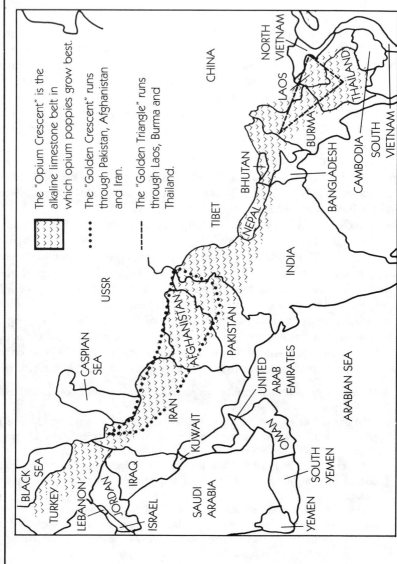

The "Opium Crescent" is the alkaline limestone belt in which opium poppies grow best.

The "Golden Crescent" runs through Pakistan, Afghanistan and Iran.

The "Golden Triangle" runs through Laos, Burma and Thailand.

SOURCE: Levins 1980: 115.

Pass into Karachi or on to Delhi or Bombay. Broder (1984) reports that the Russians and Soviet-backed regime in Afghanistan have stopped interfering with the Pathan tribesmen's drug trafficking—as long as they do not get involved in resistance activity. American officials see this as an effort to placate the rural tribesmen who have been waging a guerilla war since 1979.

Up until the 1970s, morphine-base from Turkey, the Golden Triangle, and the Golden Crescent would often be shipped to Marseilles, a French port noted for smuggling. There, clandestine laboratories would convert it into heroin. This "French Connection" is no longer important. Asian dealers are either converting the base-morphine into heroin themselves or shipping it to Italy, where Mafia and Camorra groups convert it and arrange for the heroin to be smuggled into the United States. How this is accomplished is explained by Albert Camille Gillet (Raab 1984), a courier for a Sicilian Mafia group.

Gillet was born in Belgium in 1921. He worked for a shipping company in Antwerp and for ten years had helped to smuggle cigarettes into Italy for a Mafia group. In 1979 they switched to exporting heroin into the United States. Gillet, a pudgy man with thinning brown hair and thick horn-rimmed glasses, was the perfect courier—a quite ordinary-looking man in the shipping business. From July 1979 to May 1980, he made twenty-four flights from various points in Europe (to avoid flying from Sicily, which would have raised suspicion) to New York with fifty-six kilos of heroin altogether. He returned to Europe with partial payments from the American importers—Gambino and Bonanno Family members—totaling $3 million.

Gillet collected packages of heroin at the home of a Mafia member in Palermo and usually secreted them in suitcases with false bottoms. The packages were sprayed with a pepper-based perfume to thwart detection by dogs used to sniff out drugs at airports. He received $10,000 for each trip and 3 percent commission for exchanging the U.S. dollars into Swiss francs or Italian lire—dollars attract attention in Italy.[1]

Mexico is the source for brown heroin which, as noted in chapter 2, is dominated by the Herrera Family. The Mexican producers gained a place in the American drug market during the early 1970s when the French Connection was disrupted—it had been importing Turkish (white) heroin through Marseilles. The poppy is not native to Mexico but was brought into the country at the turn of the century by Chinese laborers who were helping to build the railroad system (Wiederich 1984).

Lebanon has become another source of heroin for the United States and Canada. On August 18, 1983, the Royal Canadian Mounted Police, working in cooperation with the U.S. Drug Enforcement Administration, arrested three Libyans and one Lebanese in a Detroit parking lot with 2.5 kilos of heroin destined for Windsor, Ontario (Kessel 1983). According to U.S. officials, about a ton of pure heroin enters the country each year from mobile processing laboratories in Lebanon's Bekaa Valley. More than half winds up in Detroit, which, like Windsor, has a large Arab population (Blum 1984).

The Economics of Heroin

Importation is the highest level of operation in heroin; the actual smugglers ("mules") take much of the risk, while the organizers who arrange for the importation and wholesale distribution avoid physical possession. David Durk, the New York City detective partner of Frank Serpico, points out (1976: 49): "The key figures in the Italian heroin establishment never touched heroin. Guys who were in the business for twenty years and had made millions off it had never seen it. After all, does a commodities trader in Wall Street have to see hog bellies and platinum bars?" After importation the drugs are "stepped on," diluted, often several times. The wholesaler, basically a facilitator, arranges for the cutting (diluting) of the almost pure heroin. The actual physical work is often done by women brought together for the task. Between ten and twenty women cut anywhere from ten to fifty kilos in an apartment rented for this purpose. Under guard, often working without any clothes on (as a precaution against their stealing any of the precious powder), wearing surgical masks to avoid inhaling heroin dust, they mix the heroin with quinine, lactose, and dextrose, usually four or five parts of the dilutant to each one of heroin. They work through the night, receiving about $2,000 each, making the risks and embarrassment worthwhile.

When the cutting is complete, jobbers (fig. 12.2), who have been waiting for a telephone call, arrive with the necessary cash, which they exchange for the cut heroin, now packaged in glassine envelopes of the kind used by stamp collectors. The jobbers move it to retail outlets, where it is usually cut again. From there it moves to street wholesalers and eventually to addicts.

The enormous profits available to those involved in drug trafficking explain its popularity. For example, in 1984 a kilo of morphine-base cost Italian importers about $12,500. Converted into almost pure heroin, it is sold to an importer in New York for about $130,000. The importer sells it to a wholesaler for about $200,000. When the original kilo reaches a final street level, its value has increased to between $1.5 and $2 million (depending on how many times it has been stepped on). The relative level of purity, usually between 3 and 6 percent, is based on market fluctuations, and gives an indication of the amount of heroin entering the country, and, concomitantly, the level of competition—capitalism in its purest form. When heroin is sold at the street level it often carries a name or logo for addicts interested in "brand names." At stages below the *wholesaler* level, heroin is an easy-entry business requiring only a source and funds. Various informal groups, friends, street gangs, and associated individuals who come together only to "deal drugs" are part of the business. Traditionally, Italian OC units operated only at the importer level, while black organizations have operated all the way down to the street. The latter form of organization, while increasing profits enormously, makes the hierarchy more vulnerable to law-enforcement efforts.

Figure 12.2.
Heroin Distribution Organization

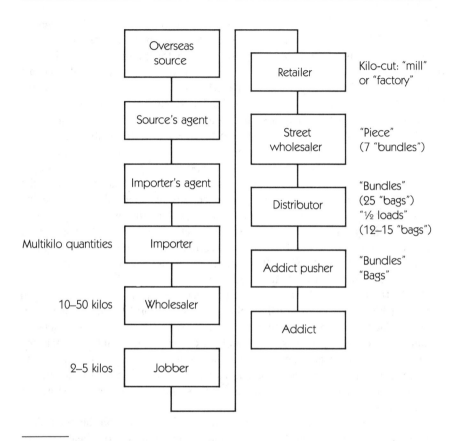

SOURCE: Adapted from Lasswell and McKenna 1972: 94.

Cocaine

Cocaine is an alkaloid found in significant quantities only in the leaves of two species of the coca shrub; one species grows in the Andes of Ecuador, Peru, and Bolivia, and the other is found in the mountainous regions of Colombia, along the Caribbean coast of South America, on the northern coast of Peru, and in the dry valley of the Marañón River in northeastern Peru. (For maps of Latin America, see fig. 12.3.) Human experience with cocaine dates back at least 5,000 years, and to the Incas coca was a plant of divine origin reserved for those who believed themselves descendants of the gods. European experience with coca chewing coincided with Spanish exploration of the New World. Despite enthusiastic reports about the effects of coca on Indians, the chewing of coca leaves was not adopted by Europeans until the nineteenth century. In 1855, a German chemist isolated alkaloidal cocaine from the coca leaf. Other scientists began experimenting with the substance, noting that it had an effect opposite of that caused by morphine, which depresses the central nervous system. At first it was used to treat morphine addiction, but the result was often a morphine addict who was now dependent also on cocaine (Van Dyke and Byck 1982).

In 1884, Sigmund Freud began taking cocaine and soon afterwards began to treat his friend Ernst von Fleischl-Marxow, a morphine addict, with cocaine. The following year, von Fleischl-Marxow suffered from toxic psychosis as a result of taking increasing amounts of cocaine, and Freud wrote that the misuse of cocaine hastened his friend's death. While Freud continued the recreational use of cocaine as late as 1895, his enthusiasm for its therapeutic value waned (Byck 1974). However, enthusiasm for cocaine spread across the United States.

"By the late 1880s, a feel-good pharmacology based on the coca plant and its derivative, cocaine, was hawked for everything from headaches to hysteria. Catarrh powders for sinus trouble and headaches—a few were nearly pure cocaine—introduced the concept of snorting" (Gomez 1984: 58). One very popular product was coca-wine. *Vin Mariani,* which contained two ounces of fresh coca leaves in each pint of Bordeaux wine, received the praise of prominent persons such as Sarah Bernhardt and John Philip Sousa, as well as three popes and sixteen heads of state. *Peruvian Wine of Coca* was available for one dollar a bottle through the Sears, Roebuck catalog in 1902. The most famous beverage containing coca, however, was first bottled in 1894. The cocaine was removed from Coca-Cola in 1903 after a presidential commission criticized the use of habit-forming drugs in soft drinks (Gomez 1984). Cocaine remained readily available in the United States up until the Harrison Act of 1914.

Coca leaves are legally imported into the United States by the Stepan Chemical Company in New Jersey, which extracts the cocaine for pharmaceutical purposes; the remaining leaf material is prepared as a flavoring for

Figure 12.3
Latin America

Scale of Miles
200 0   400   800

Coca-Cola. Cocaine has use as a local anesthetic, mostly for ear, nose, and throat surgery. Synthetic drugs have, for the most part, replaced cocaine as a local anesthetic, e.g., procaine (Novocain). The (illegal) recreational use of cocaine is usually in the form of a hydrochloride salt that is sniffed. Cocaine is readily absorbed through mucous membranes and enters the bloodstream, producing a euphoria ("high") that lasts from fifteen to thirty minutes. "Cocaine can also be introduced intravenously, or it can be absorbed through the lungs by smoking the alkaloidal substance, which users call free base" (Van Dyke and Byck 1982: 139).

Jane Brody (1984: 18) reports: "Cocaine, a euphoriant drug that is the most potent natural stimulant yet discovered, is said to make occasional users feel full of energy, self-confidence, control, sexuality, drive and willpower." However, Craig Van Dyke and Robert Byck (1982: 140) point out:

> Chronic use of a drug can have both social and pharmacological consequences. If a person becomes totally involved in the acquisition and consumption of a drug, his entire life may change. When cocaine is taken regularly, it can cause sleeplessness and loss of appetite; after high doses or chronic consumption the user may experience an anxious paranoid state . . . [T]here is increasing evidence that hallucinations and paranoia can result if the drug is taken frequently in high doses.

The Business of Cocaine

Coca, the basic ingredient of cocaine, grows in several Latin American countries, although the primary exporters are Colombia, Peru, Bolivia, and Ecuador where cocaine and politics are often intertwined. In Colombia coca grows in remote mountain areas that are often dominated by insurgent guerilla groups. In Peru the coca is cultivated in obscure jungle areas where there is little government control. In 1984, for example, the U.S. government's cocaine-eradication program in Tingo María, a valley between the Andes and the Peruvian jungles, had to be suspended as a result of raids by guerillas of Shining Path, a Communist group favoring a Chinese-style political system in Peru. The guerillas took advantage of antigovernment attitudes among the area's coca growers (Simons 1984a).

In Bolivia, the major supplier for the U.S. market, coca is grown legally and sold openly at street markets. It has been chewed by Indians for centuries and is also used as a poultice for wounds and as a tea that will cure the headache of a tourist suffering from the 12,000-foot altitude of La Paz. The coca is diverted for the illegal export trade with little interference from law-enforcement authorities—corruption abounds. In 1983, in an effort to overcome enforcement problems in Bolivia, the United States spent $5 million to train and equip a special 300-member strike force known as the Leopards. The Bolivian government, however, apparently fearful of upsetting the estimated 25,000 peasant families who depend on the coca harvest, kept the Leopards confined to their barracks in La Paz. On June 30, 1984, the Leopards (allegedly) abducted the Bolivian president as part of a coup. Although President Hernán Siles Zuazo was rescued, the attempted coup was an embarrassment for the United States. (Opponents of President Zuazo have suggested that he was not really kidnapped).

Between 200 and 500 kilos of coca leaves are made into a one-kilo paste, which is converted into one kilo of cocaine base, a malodorous, rough, greenish yellow powder of more than 66 percent purity. One kilo of cocaine base is synthesized into one kilo of cocaine hydrochloride, a white crystalline powder that is about 95 percent pure. In the United States, the cocaine hydrochloride is diluted ("cut") for the "street sale" by adding sugars such as lactose, inositol, manitol; and local anesthetics such as lidocaine. After cutting the cocaine has a purity of about 15 percent.

Wherever it originated, until 1984 most cocaine hydrochloride smuggled into the United States was shipped from laboratories in the Colombian outback (see fig. 12.4). In 1984, however, Colombian justice minister Rodrigo Lara Bonilla was assassinated by drug traffickers, and the president, Belisario Betancour, ordered a major crackdown. As a result, there was an increase in the smuggling of cocaine base directly from Peru and Bolivia to laboratories in the United States. In August of 1984, for example, 2,700 pounds of cocaine base, hidden in hollowed-out aluminum pulleys, was seized at Miami International Airport.

In Colombia, according to the Drug Enforcement Administration, there are eight major "Cocaine Families" whose operations resemble those of a medium-sized corporation (see fig. 12.5). The head of the Family is surrounded by an inner group, often relatives by blood or marriage, who protect and direct the organization's Colombian operations. At the American end are distribution organizations usually headed by Colombians, but sometimes a Cuban or even an American will fill this spot. The American organization is responsible for distribution. Colombian and American organizations are tied together by brokers, Colombian middlemen. The cocaine organizations are not as disciplined as Italian-American OC units. There is a great deal of turnover of personnel, with persons entering, leaving, and switching organizations. Cocaine buyers may also avoid the American-based broker by travelling to Colombia. This lack of discipline has produced a great deal of violence in south Florida and New York. While Colombians clearly dominate the cocaine trade, Bolivians and Peruvians have been known to avoid the "Colombian Connection" by smuggling the drug directly into the United States.

As with heroin, the cocaine business reflects the law of supply and demand. For example, in 1982 and 1983, a kilo ("key") of cocaine, which sold for about $20,000 in Colombia, cost as much as $75,000 in Miami. This added up to a final "street value" of $600,000 to $800,000. In 1984, however, a "key of coke" could be purchased in Miami for about $25,000. In 1985 it jumped to more than $35,000.

Like heroin, at the distribution level cocaine is an easy-entry business;

Figure 12.4
Major Cocaine-Smuggling Routes (Air, Land, Sea).

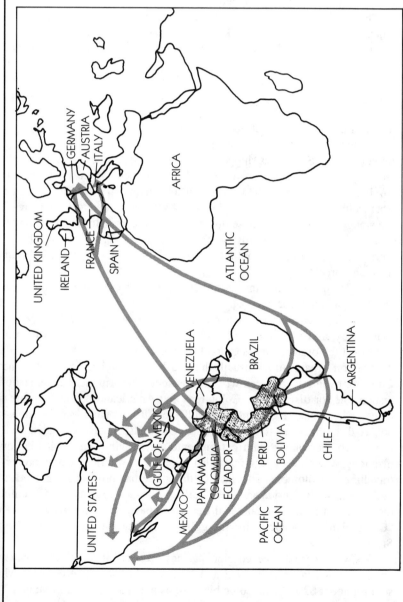

SOURCE: U.S. Drug Enforcement Administration

Figure 12.5
Typical Colombian Cocaine Organization

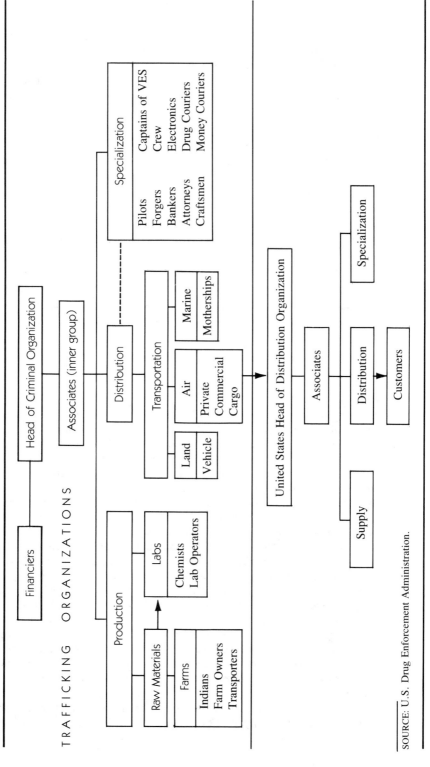

SOURCE: U.S. Drug Enforcement Administration.

cash and a "connection" are the only requirements. As opposed to heroin, persons trafficking in cocaine often have had no prior criminal involvement. The so-called New Age Syndicates spring up among young persons in business, athletics, the arts. In 1982, for example, the Drug Enforcement Administration uncovered a cocaine operation that centered around the world of stock-car racing. It involved seventy persons, including four drivers. One cocaine ring is known as the "Veggie Group" because they run a string of vegetarian restaurants on both coasts. Another, the "Remodelers," uses drug money to restore houses. In many college and resort towns, the boom in chic restaurants and other related businesses is part of a "trail dusted with white powder" (Browning 1982: sec. 2: 2). A variety of cocaine syndicates have evolved in the South among persons of working-class backgrounds; they have been referred to as the "Dixie Mafia" or the "Hillbilly Mafia." Whatever their backgrounds, cocaine profits obviously act as an irresistible magnet for many persons.

Like heroin, cocaine is smuggled into the United States in a variety of ways: in diplomatic pouches, in condoms secreted in the stomachs of "mules," in suitcases with false bottoms. Larger quantities are brought in by small, private high-speed aircraft flying at altitudes of about 500 feet to avoid detection by radar.

Cannabis

Cannabis sativa L., the hemp plant, grows wild throughout most of the tropic and temperate regions of the world. It is a single species. This plant has long been cultivated for the tough fiber of the stem, the seed used in feed mixtures, and the oil as an ingredient of paint, as well as for its biologically active substances, most highly concentrated in the leaves and resinous flowering tops.

The plant material has been used as a drug for centuries. In 1839 it entered the annals of western medicine with the publication of an article surveying its therapeutic potential, including possible uses as an analgesic and anticonvulsant agent. It was alleged to be effective in treating a wide range of physical and mental ailments during the remainder of the 19th century.

. . . Cannabis products are usually smoked in the form of loosely rolled cigarettes ("joints"). . . . The effects are felt within minutes, reach their peak in 10 to 30 minutes, and may linger for two or three hours. A condensed description of these effects is apt to be inadequate or even misleading, so much depends upon the experience and expectations of the individual as [well as] the activity of the drug itself. Low doses tend to induce restlessness and an increasing sense of well-being, followed by a dreamy state of relaxation, and frequently hunger, especially a craving for sweets. Changes of sensory perception—a more vivid sense of sight, smell, touch, taste, and hearing—may be accompanied by subtle alterations in thought formation and expression. Stronger doses intensify these reactions.

. . . The term marihuana (or marijuana) is used in this country to refer to the cannabis plant and to any part or extract of it that produces somatic or psychic changes in man. A tobacco-like substance produced by drying the leaves and flowering tops of the plant, marihuana varies significantly in its potency, depending on the source and selectivity of plant material used. Most wild U.S. cannabis is considered inferior because of a low concentration of THC [*delta-9-tetrahydrocannabinol,* the ingredient believed responsible for psychoactive effects], usually less than 0.5 percent. Jamaican, Colombian, and Mexican varieties range between 0.5 and 4 percent. The most select product is reputed to be Sinsemilla (Spanish, *sin semilla:* "without seed"), prepared from the unpollenated female cannabis plant, samples of which have been found to contain up to 6 percent THC. Southeast Asian "Thai sticks," consisting of marihuana buds bound onto short sections of bamboo, are also encountered infrequently on the U.S. illicit market.

The Middle East is the main source of *hashish.* It consists of the drug-rich resinous secretions of the cannabis plant, which are collected, dried, and then compressed into a variety of forms, such as balls, cakes, or cookie-like sheets. Hashish in the United States varies in potency as in appearance, ranging in THC content from trace amounts up to 10 percent. . . .

Hashish Oil. The name comes from the drug culture and is a misnomer in suggesting any resemblance to hashish other than its objective of further concentration. Hashish oil is produced by a process of repeated extraction of cannabis plant materials to yield a dark viscous liquid, current samples of which average about 20 percent THC. In terms of its psychoactive effect, a drop or two of this liquid on a cigarette is equal to a single "joint" of marihuana" [*Drugs of Abuse* 1979: 34–37].

In the United States the use of marijuana was closely associated with Mexican immigrants: "Chicanos in the Southwest were believed to be incited to violence by smoking it" (Musto 1973: 65). State laws against marijuana were often part of a reaction to Mexican immigration, and by 1930 sixteen western states had antimarijuana laws. In 1936, the movie *Reefer Madness* was released, frightening many Americans about the "evils" of marijuana use. Although the film is quite outrageous, it helped to generate support for the passage of the Marihuana Tax Act of 1937, which put an end to the lawful recreational use of the drug.

Marimba, as marijuana is known in Colombia, is referred to as "Colombian Gold" in the United States because of its high level of THC. Most of the marijuana entering the United States comes from Colombia, carried by way of the Guajira Peninsula in boats and planes. *Ganja,* as marijuana is called in Jamaica, accounts for between 10 and 15 percent of the marijuana used in the United States. Marijuana is also a domestic crop that is cultivated in many states, most heavily in northern California, Oregon, and Hawaii. A cover story in *Newsweek* referred to "Guns, Grass and Money: America's Billion-Dollar Crop" (October 25, 1982).

There is little or no pattern to marijuana trafficking in the United States. It is an easy-entry business, as exemplified by the "Black Tuna Gang." The leaders of this group, Robert J. Meinster and Robert E. Platshorn, were in

1974 a used-car dealer and a gadget seller at fairs, respectively. Both were in their late thirties when they bought 2,500 pounds of Colombian marijuana. At the time of their indictment in 1979, they headed a group of forty men and women including pilots, boat captains, communications experts, and enforcers. By 1977, "Black Tuna had successfully imported its first million pounds of marijuana worth $250 million wholesale" (Volsky 1979: 26). Another group called "The Company" was made up of college graduates and men with Vietnam military experience. After pooling their resources and assets, only a Colombian connection was necessary, which one of the men who joined The Company had (Permanent Subcommittee on Investigations 1981, *International Narcotics Trafficking,* 27–28):

> I had a contact in Colombia who had contacts with three men who could supply all the marihuana The Company could use. Orders were placed with me by the president of The Company. I would call in the orders collect to my Colombian connection from a pay phone in Florida, telling him the time and date we wanted to make the pickup.
>
> The Colombians would then contact the army colonel in the area and other key military people to obtain clearance for a shipment of marihuana to be made for the given time and place in the Guajira Peninsula. The colonels we dealt with were on a fixed retainer and were paid an additional certain amount for each load we shipped out of Colombia.

Between 1976 and 1978 The Company made thirty-seven trips to Colombia, where they purchased marijuana for between $50 and $70 a pound. They sold approximately two hundred thousand pounds of it in the United States for $300 per pound.

Synthetic Drugs

There are three general categories of synthetic controlled substances: (1) depressants, (2) stimulants, (3) hallucinogens.

Depressants

Heroin Analogues   Among the first category are several drugs similar to heroin. Fentantyl, for example, which is often used in major surgery, works exactly like the opiates: kills pain, produces euphoria, and, if abused, leads to physical dependency. The substance is relatively easy to produce for persons skilled in chemistry. Fentantyl compounds are often sold as "China White," the street name for the finest Southeast Asian heroin, to addicts who often cannot tell the difference. These compounds are quite potent and difficult for street dealers to cut properly, which can lead to overdose and death. Another heroin substitute found on the street, *methadone,* was developed by the Germans during World War II when their access to morphine was cut by the

Allies. Methadone effects can last up to twenty-four hours, thereby permitting administration only once per day in maintenance programs for heroin addicts; it can be taken orally or injected. Methadone has been diverted into drug trafficking, and many deaths have been reported from overdoses.

Barbiturates are sedatives derived from barbituric acid. Small therapeutic doses tend to calm nervous conditions, and larger doses cause sleep twenty to sixty minutes after oral administration. As with alcohol, also a depressant, individuals may experience a sense of excitement before the onset of sedation. Barbiturates are classified according to how long it takes for the substance to activate. The short-acting and intermediate-acting barbiturates are most sought after by abusers: phenobarbital (Nembutal), secobarbital (Seconal), and amobarbital (Amytal). Habitual use of barbiturates results in a buildup of tolerance, and dependence on them is widespread (*Drugs of Abuse* 1979).

Quaaludes is a brand name for a sedative (methaqualone) used to treat insomnia when barbiturates are medically contraindicated or have failed. Their effects are similar to those of barbiturates except that they produce even greater loss of motor coordination, which explains why they are sometimes referred to as "wallbangers." Imitation Quaaludes are manufactured in Colombia and smuggled into the United States.

Stimulants

Many stimulant drugs are legal; they include such substances as nicotine in tobacco products and caffeine in coffee and soft drinks. Such substances tend to relieve fatigue and increase alertness. The more potent synthetic stimulants, such as amphetamine and methamphetamine, are used to treat narcolepsy (a rare disorder resulting in an uncontrollable desire for sleep), hyperkinetic behavioral disorders in children, and certain cases of obesity as a short-term adjunct to a restricted diet. Their illicit use closely parallels that of cocaine in short-term and long-term effects. As noted in the first chapter, outlaw motorcycle gangs often traffic in methamphetamine.

Hallucinogenic Drugs

Hallucinogens may be either natural or synthetic. Both distort the perception of objective reality. They induce a state of excitation of the central nervous system, manifested by alterations of mood, usually euphoric, but sometimes severely depressive. Under the influence of hallucinogens, the pupils dilate, and body temperature and blood pressure rise. The senses of direction, distance, and time become disoriented. A user may speak of "seeing" sounds and "hearing" colors. If taken in a large enough dose, the drug produces delusions and visual hallucinations [*Drugs of Abuse* 1979: 28].

Natural hallucinogens are found in the peyote cactus (which contains mescaline), used legally in religious ceremonies by the Native American Church, and psilocybe mushrooms, which have also been used for centuries in traditional Indian rites.

LSD, the abbreviation for lysergic acid diethylamide, was first synthesized in 1938. Its psychotomimetic effects were discovered in 1943 when a chemist accidentally took some LSD and experienced what became known later as a "trip." LSD is a very potent substance that causes effects in the user that imitate certain aspects of psychosis. It is taken orally, and higher doses can cause the effects to last for ten to twelve hours.

PCP, the abbreviation for phencyclidine and related drugs, was investigated in the 1950s as an anesthetic, but because of its side effects, confusion and delirium, its development for human use was discontinued. It was used in the 1960s in veterinary medicine, but the manufacturer stopped production in 1978. Often referred to in the illicit trade as "Angel Dust," PCP is taken orally in tablet, capsule, powder, or liquid form, or applied to leafy material, such as parsley, oregano, or marijuana, and smoked. A moderate amount results in a sense of detachment, distance, and estrangement from one's surroundings. Numbness, slurred or blocked speech, and a loss of coordination may be accompanied by a sense of strength and invulnerability. "Auditory hallucinations, image distortion as in a fun-house mirror, and severe mood disorders may occur, producing in some acute anxiety and a feeling of impending doom, in others paranoia and violent hostility" (*Drugs of Abuse* 1979: 30).

---

[1]There are, obviously, many ways of smuggling heroin into the country. The French Connection shipped automobiles loaded with secreted heroin, and diplomats have been discovered using their immunity to move drugs through customs. In 1982, for example, with the cooperation of Thai officials, Thailand's vice-counsul in Chicago was arrested for smuggling heroin into the United States, and 7.5 pounds were confiscated. In the same year, the Dominican Republic's second-ranking representative to the United Nations was seized at New York's Kennedy Airport with a kilo of heroin (O'Connor and Possley 1982). On January 8, 1983, an Iranian aide to Ayatollah Ruhollah Khomeni was seized at Düsseldorf airport with four pounds of raw opium. He claimed diplomatic immunity and was freed by the West German authorities (Markham 1983).

chapter 13

"Old-Style" Crime:
Theft, Scam, and Sex

Used by permission of AP/Wide World Photos

Small-time crime is not rewarding enough to attract much attention from the large criminal organizations. It tends to be messy, dangerous, and not particularly lucrative. However, under certain circumstances OC does become involved in theft, scam, and sex—including both prostitution and pornography.

Theft and Fencing

Members of OC do not usually engage directly in theft, burglary, or robbery. However, wise-guys will provide the financing and sometimes the information or expertise necessary to carry out such predatory crimes as payroll robberies, large-scale commercial burglaries, hijackings, thefts of stocks and bonds; they will finance frauds, swindles, and any conventional criminal activity that can bring in a profit substantial enough to make the effort worthwhile. They will help to market stolen merchandise such as securities, checks, and credit cards. Members of OC are in a unique position to provide these "services." Their widespread connections to both legitimate and illegitimate outlets provide a link between more conventional criminals and the business world. Organized crime serves as a catalyst for a great deal of "disorganized" crime.

Stolen Securities.

During the late 1960s and early 1970s there was a dramatic increase in the volume of securities being traded, and this provided a lucrative source of income for OC. Patrick V. Murphy, New York City Police Commissioner, before a congressional committee, explains (Permanent Subcommittee on Investigations 1971, *Organized Crime and Stolen Securities,* part 1: 36–39, edited):

> Let me begin by offering some background to the problem. Although thefts of securities are by no means a recent phenomenon, occurrences of this type have increased substantially in the last few years and have involved growing amounts of money. The year 1966 serves as a convenient time to begin.
>
> In that year, Wall Street was rocked by several large losses from brokerage houses. For instance, on August 16 of that year, a messenger was accosted in broad daylight on the street in the financial district of New York City and relieved of $375,000 in stock certificates. The messenger was subsequently found murdered in an alleyway in Brooklyn. After an investigation lasting over a 2-year period, six persons were arrested and convicted of criminal possession of stolen property, but the case of the homicide still remains unsolved.

In addition to reported thefts,

> . . . as incredible as it may sound, brokers and banks frequently are totally unaware that hundreds of thousands of dollars worth of securities have been furtively removed from their vaults. These stolen certificates, thus, are not the subject of reports—except, that is, when a detective or FBI agent who has recovered them in the course of another investigation traces them back to the victimized house and alerts the victim to the fact that the securities had been stolen, perhaps months earlier. Incidents like this have occurred.

The questions immediately arise: What factors led to the recent dramatic upsurge in securities thefts, and why have law-enforcement agencies chalked up only modest success in dealing with this problem? The answers to these questions are complex, but I shall offer what seem to me some of the explanations.

When, in 1966 or so, the frequency of securities thefts began to intensify notably, the volume of trades in the stock market was at an alltime high, beyond the capacity of brokers, traders, and banks to handle clerically. Paperwork became hopelessly bogged down. Great numbers of young workers, low paid and virtually unscreened, were brought in to serve in back offices.

Inventory audits were sporadic and inaccurate. "Fails" were commonplace. Stock certificates or bonds, thus, could disappear without being detected, or at least without raising the suspicion of criminal behavior. Even when someone noted that certificates were missing, complainants were frequently unable to tell the investigators where the missing securities were supposed to have been stored, and who might have had access to them.

Reports of losses themselves were in many cases delayed for weeks or months, and by that time the missing securities had been sold, and frequently resold, in the market. Investigators encountered reluctance to cooperate on the part of subsequent purchasers as brokerage houses, banks, and investors claimed the legal status of innocent and unknowing "holders in due course," without any direct, practical interest in the fact that the certificates were stolen.

There are two major methods used for converting stolen (or counterfeit) securities into cash:

1. The stolen (or counterfeit) securities are taken out of the United States to banks in countries whose secrecy laws protect such transactions, such as Panama or the Cayman Islands. The securities are deposited in the bank, which issues letters of credit. The letters of credit are used to secure loans or to purchase legitimate securities, which are then sold for cash.

2. They are used for bank loans. An operative presents the stolen (or counterfeit) securities at a bank, usually to a "cooperative" loan official, and secures a loan, which is defaulted. Or, the securities may be "rented." For a pictorial version of this process see fig. 13.1. Murray J. Gross, Manhattan Assistant District Attorney, told the Permanent Subcommittee on Investigations (1971: 75):

Figure 13.1
Conversion of Stolen Securities

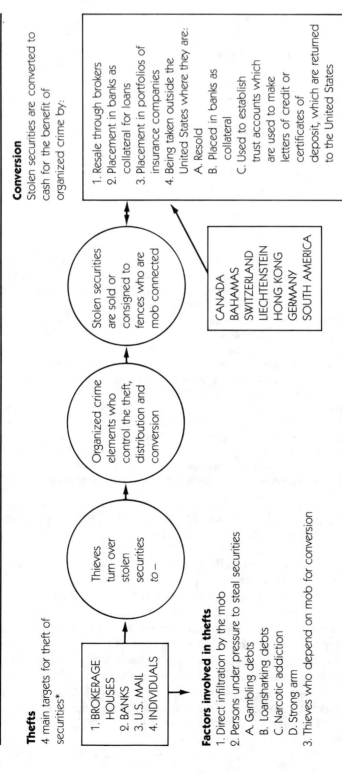

Thefts

4 main targets for theft of securities*

1. BROKERAGE HOUSES
2. BANKS
3. U.S. MAIL
4. INDIVIDUALS

Factors involved in thefts

1. Direct infiltration by the mob
2. Persons under pressure to steal securities
   A. Gambling debts
   B. Loansharking debts
   C. Narcotic addiction
   D. Strong arm
3. Thieves who depend on mob for conversion

Thieves turn over stolen securities to –

Organized crime elements who control the theft, distribution and conversion

Stolen securities are sold or consigned to fences who are mob connected

CANADA
BAHAMAS
SWITZERLAND
LIECHTENSTEIN
HONG KONG
GERMANY
SOUTH AMERICA

Conversion

Stolen securities are converted to cash for the benefit of organized crime by:

1. Resale through brokers
2. Placement in banks as collateral for loans
3. Placement in portfolios of insurance companies
4. Being taken outside the United States where they are:
   A. Resold
   B. Placed in banks as collateral
   C. Used to establish trust accounts which are used to make letters of credit or certificates of deposit, which are returned to the United States

*Securities which are stolen include corporate stocks and bonds and U.S. notes and bonds. These securities are either in "street name," bearer instruments or in name of companies or individuals.

SOURCE: Permanent Subcommittee on Investigations 1971.

A legitimate businessman who finds himself temporarily short of capital after exhausting his available credit with legitimate institutions, may seek out a loan-shark. Most often he will receive money; however, sometimes the loanshark has an alternate proposition to suggest. He may "rent" stolen securities to the businessman who then uses them as collateral for a loan.

In a recent case, the businessman "rented" $1¼ million worth of stolen securities for $70,000. The criminal is therefore not directly exposed and although his profit is less on the individual transactions, the securities become a reusable stock-in-trade which may be "rented" repeatedly.

The borrower, on the other hand, is less apt to be compromised since he is then a legitimate businessman with a longstanding relationship with the bank or factory.

It should be borne in mind that the intention of the parties is that the loan be repaid. Nevertheless, the element of risk of exposure still exists for the businessman; if he were unable to repay the loan, the true nature of the collateral would become known and immediately traceable to him.

A still more conservative method has been evolved. The "rented" securities may instead be used to bolster up a sagging financial profile. The businessman calls in a reputable accounting firm, and presents among his assets, these "rented" securities. He obtains a certified statement of his apparently sound business, and on the basis of that statement is able to obtain a line of credit.[1]

There was no central clearinghouse collecting and disseminating information on stolen certificates, and, thus, they could be peddled without serious likelihood of challenge.

Insurance companies, for their part, did not require their insured brokerage houses to report their losses to the police department. When approached by our investigators, they were reluctant to identify their clients.

Many of the victimized banks and brokerage houses declined to cooperate with investigators, either on the advice of legal staffs or simply out of concern for their images. These are not crimes of violence; and since losses are generally insured, prospective complainants sometimes placed concern about adverse publicity above the desire to see the crimes solved.

The most insidious factor that contributed to the rise in thefts was the intrusion of organized crime into this area. Attracted by the possibility of high profits and uniquely qualified to dispose of stolen securities throughout the nation and abroad, the organized professional criminals quickly learned how to capitalize on the industry's vulnerability.

. . . I would like to concentrate for a few moments on the involvement of organized crime in the theft of stocks and bonds. Organized crime has assumed a major role, particularly in the disposition of stolen securities, because it can provide the organizational framework without which thefts of securities would be ineffectual.

Although many people may have access to valuable securities, few can put stolen securities into immediate use. Hundreds of back-office clerks can pilfer stock certificates—for example, 100 shares of IBM stock or a $100,000 Treasury bill—but converting such highly valuable commercial paper into cash is an integral part of the planned theft, and the average clerk lacks the contacts to accomplish it directly.

Organized-crime groups serve as the intermediate link in the criminal enterprise. Bookmakers and loansharks who may have exerted the pressure that induced the thief to take the securities frequently serve as the conduit by which the stolen securities get into the hands of other organized-crime figures. The original recipient, whether bookmaker, loanshark, or fence, cannot make direct use of the securities, so he will dispose of them within the underworld system. Passing upwards through the ranks of organized crime, the stolen securities will eventually reach the hands of someone who does have the expertise, the capital, and the personnel to effect a profitable disposition.

Ironically, the actual thief normally obtains only a tiny slice of the illegal profit that is made possible by his theft. The securities commonly pass through a number of hands between the original theft and their final disposition, and in the process, each participant generally obtains a profit. The bulk of the gain is made by those who actually dispose of the securities; the thief generally gets relatively little.

Stolen Cars, Jewels, Consumer Goods

There is often an indirect relationship between theft and fencing on the one hand and organized crime on the other. Edward D. Hegarty, special agent in charge of the Chicago office of the FBI, points out that, when it comes to stolen cars and OC,

> . . . they don't really get involved in the day-to-day management of the theft of automobiles from parking lots or from garages or from streets. They get involved to the extent that they extort the lower level organized crime groups that are continually involved in the theft of automobiles and the chopping of automobiles, and they impose upon them a street tax.
>
> Many of the murders which have been committed in the Chicago area in recent years arose from automobile theft and chop shop activity. Generally these murders resulted from a failure, inability, or cheating by lower level organized crime figures on their La Cosa Nostra superiors. They were cheating on the street tax which is imposed upon criminal cartels of the lower strength, the lower power base, that you have in and around the Chicago area [Permanent Subcommittee on Investigations 1983, *Organized Crime in Chicago* 33–34].

In other words, car thieves and their chop shop employers are tied to OC in an extortionate relationship.

The *fence* provides a readily available outlet for marketing stolen ("hot") merchandise. He thus provides an incentive to thieves and may also organize, finance, and direct their operations. In her research into fencing, Marilyn Walsh (1977: 13) found that about 13 percent of the fences she studied were part of organized crime: "For these individuals fencing appeared to be just another enterprise in a varied and totally illegal business portfolio." In addition to fencing, she notes, these persons were active in loansharking, and gambling, and some were enforcers. OC involvement in fencing can merely be serving as an intermediary. In the Genovese Family, for example, Anthony ("Figgy") Ficcorata (or Ficarotta), among other criminal activities, forced jewel thieves to deal only with certain fences, from whom Ficcorata would receive a percentage of the proceeds. In Chicago, eight "independent" burglars "were murdered for refusing to dispose of their loot through syndicate-connected fences" (Nicodemus and Petaque 1981: 5). Because of his connections with criminals and (otherwise) legitimate businesses, the "wise-guy" is in a unique position to arrange for the disposition of stolen goods.

Scam

The scam is a bankruptcy fraud that victimizes wholesale providers of various goods. The business used as the basis for a scam may be set up with the scheme in mind, or it may be an established business that has fallen into OC control as a result of gambling or loanshark debts. Edward De Franco (1973) notes that scam operations are popular in industries with merchandise that has a high turnover potential, is readily transportable, and is not easy to trace. There are three basic variations of the scam (De Franco 1973: 5–7).

Three-Step Scam

A new corporation is formed, managed by a front man, or "pencil," who has no prior criminal or bankruptcy record. An initial large bank deposit, known as the "nut," is made to establish credit. (This money, plus other money subsequently deposited, is later withdrawn.) A large store is rented, and orders for merchandise are placed with as many companies as possible. The size of these orders appears to indicate a successful operation to the suppliers. Then the owners deal with suppliers in three steps:

1. Smaller orders are placed during the first month, and such orders are almost always paid for in full.

2. During the second month, larger orders are placed, and about a quarter of the balance due on such orders is paid.

3. During the third month, using the credit established as a result of payments made for the previous orders, very large orders are placed. Items easily converted into cash, such as jewelry and appliances, usually constitute a large proportion of these orders. Thereafter, merchandise is converted into cash through a fence or a surplus-property operator, normally one with a sufficiently large legitimate inventory to easily intermix the scam merchandise into the normal inventory. The company is then forced into bankruptcy by creditors since, according to plan, all cash has been appropriated by the scam operator.

One-Step Scam

Since the three-step scam requires several months for completion, the more rapid one-step scam is more frequently used.

A successful business with good credit references is purchased. No notice of the change in management is provided to Dun and Bradstreet or other credit agencies, thus enabling the new management to trade on the previous owner's good credit reputation. Manufacturers are approached in person or at trade shows to arrange for the purchase of merchandise. The orders are usually of a large quantity, and suppliers who did not sell to the company previously are very politely informed by the scam operator that if they do not want to fill the order, some other company will be glad to do so. This technique is known as the "sketch." Orders often include many items not previously purchased by the company.

After the orders have been received, the merchandise is sold, as in the three-step scam. The money is milked from the business, and the company is forced into bankruptcy, just as the scam operator had planned.

Same-Name Scam

This is a variation of the one-step scam. A company is organized with a name deceptively similar, and often almost identical, to that of a successful company in the same area. Large orders are placed with suppliers who fill them, assuming the legitimacy of the company based on the similarity in firm names. The merchandise is then sold in the same fashion as with the other types of scam.

A popular time for the scam operator is just before a seasonal increase in the popularity of particular merchandise, when rush deliveries are commonplace and thorough credit checks often overlooked. In some scams, arson is the final step: the business is "torched" for the insurance instead of declaring bankruptcy.

The Business of Sex

OC involvement in sex as a money-maker has changed with the times. Because of the liberalization of sexual mores among the population as a whole, sex for pay—prostitution—is no longer in as much demand as it once was.

Pornography, however, is big business. Even though it has largely been legalized, the profits to be made have attracted OC money and muscle to this field of endeavor.

Prostitution

House prostitution (whorehouses, or bordellos) was an important social phenomenon during the days of large-scale immigration. Immigrants were most often males, single or travelling without their wives. Commercial sex, usually confined to infamous ("red-light") vice districts in urban areas, was a target of social and religious reformers. The campaign against this activity became known as the war on the white slave trade. In a book with that title (Bell 1909: 48), Edwin W. Sims, U.S. attorney for Chicago, stated:

> The recent examination of more than two hundred "white slaves" by the office of the United States district attorney at Chicago has brought to light the fact that literally thousands of innocent girls from the country districts are every year entrapped into a life of hopeless slavery and degradation because parents in the country do not understand conditions as they exist and how to protect their daughters from the "white slave" traders who have reduced the art of ruining young girls to a national and international system.

There was an elaborate system for procuring and transporting girls between New York, Milwaukee, St. Louis, and Chicago (Landesco 1968). The constant transfer of girls provided "new faces" and was good for business. This type of interstate activity, and incidents of actual "white slavery," the use of force to recruit or maintain prostitutes, led to the passage of the "White Slave Traffic Act" of 1910, called the Mann Act after its sponsor, Congressman James R. Mann of Illinois. "White slave" was actually something of a misnomer; many of the girls were Orientals, particularly on the West Coast, who were sold by their families in China and smuggled into the United States. During the 1920s and early 1930s, madams arranged for opening a brothel, attracting prostitutes and customers and securing protection from the police. The madam also acted as a "housemother," preventing quarrels and providing advice; she was both a friend and an employer: "Her work made it almost inevitable that she would assume traditionally maternal functions" (Winick and Kinsie 1971: 98). In Chicago, as we have seen in chapter 3, brothels were often owned and managed by men such as Johnny Torrio, who went on to become important gangsters during the Prohibition era.

OC interest in prostitution waned during Prohibition—so much money could more easily be made in bootlegging. With Prohibition drawing to a close, and with the advent of the Great Depression, OC groups began looking for new areas of income. In many cities they "organized" independent brothels, and the madams paid OC middlemen for protection from the police and from violence. If the madam did not pay, there would be violence. Gangsters such as David ("Little Davie") Betillo, a member of the Luciano Family, organized previously independent brothels in New York City.

Charles Winick and Paul Kinsie (1971) note that the brothel industry reached its peak in 1939. During the war, and more significantly after 1945, the importance of brothels as a source of income for OC steadily declined but did not entirely disappear. In New York City, Salvatore ("Sally Crash") Panico, a "wise-guy" whom this writer once had on parole, controlled a territory extending from the Upper East Side to the lower end of Manhattan in which he extorted money from brothels. The owners usually advertise in sex-oriented publications such as *Screw*, which is how Panico could monitor who was operating in his territory. An owner would be visited by Panico and his men—guns, threats, and robbery soon brought the brothels into line. The scheme ended when Panico appeared on closed-circuit television threatening an FBI agent who was playing the role of a bordello manager (Post 1981).

In some American cities there are "massage parlors" and other types of establishments fronting for brothels, and some are either controlled or have been financed by OC groups. Prostitution, however, is for the most part unorganized, with pimps, usually black or Hispanic, having a "stable" of from three to eight girls working for them. These pimps usually dress in a "uniform" of flashy, often outlandish, clothes and drive equally outlandish automobiles—"pimpmobiles," pink Cadillacs and Lincolns with real leopard upholstery, for example. Only Nevada has legalized prostitution, on a county-option basis; elsewhere in the United States it is a misdemeanor (although pandering can be a felony). In Nevada, brothel prostitutes are fingerprinted and carry official identification cards. They are required to have periodic medical examinations and are usually prohibited from leaving the brothel to mingle with community residents.

Pornography

Pornography, like prostitution, is apparently suffering from a great deal of "amateur" involvement. Pornography, which at one time was a product of organized crime, is widely available throughout the United States. Liberal court decisions have virtually legalized pornography, and legitimate entre-preneurs have entered the market. This has resulted in a proliferation, and substantial improvement in the quality, of pornographic movies. In 1978, members of the New York City Police Department, acting officially, produced a pornographic film. The idea behind the production was to gather information and evidence about OC. The film, however, was of such poor quality that the undercover police officers were unable to find any buyers.

Rick Kogan and Toni Ginnetti of the *Chicago Sun-Times* report that the "porno classic" *Deep Throat* was backed—financed and distributed—by Anthony Peraino and his sons, all reputed to be members of the Colombo Family (1982a). The Task Force on Organized Crime (1976: 227) reports how OC became involved with the successful porn movie *Behind the Green Door:*

> Organized crime figures approached the producers concerning distribution rights, which the producers continuously refused to grant, despite threats of piracy. Within a short time, hundreds of pirate versions appeared all over the country. The producers lost several key markets—Las Vegas, Miami, and Dallas among them. Also, because the pirated versions were often of poor quality, the movie got a bad reputation, which further reduced its market.

Organized-crime involvement in pornography, however, can often simply be extortion, as in Los Angeles, where the entire hierarchy of the Dragna

Family was convicted of, among other crimes, extorting money from the owners of porno shops. Kogan and Ginnetti (1982b: 14) quote the owner of one of the few independent adult bookstores in Chicago: "This business is all Outfit. It's simply impossible to operate without dealing with these guys. They've got a lock on the industry." The "lock" was achieved with the assistance of the police, who closed down many bookstores, and violence: warehouses were firebombed; men wearing ski masks smashed peep machines and dumped paint over books and magazines. In the early 1970s the Apache Film Corporation, owned by Harry Goodman, was the major distributor of pornographic films in Chicago. A rival firm was established by Patrick Ricciardi, a reputed loanshark and cousin of the late Felix ("Milwaukee Phil") Alderisio, a power in the Chicago Outfit. Goodman sold out to Ricciardi—after his home was bombed four times in two years.

---

[1] For a journalistic account of an elaborate conspiracy involving organized crime and Vatican officials to use counterfeit "blue chip" stocks to cover losses by the *Instituto per le Opere di Religione* (known as the Bank of the Vatican), see Richard Hammer (1982).

chapter 14

Organized Crime in Labor and Business

Used by permission of AP/Wide World Photos

The conflict generated by the rise of organized labor and the consequent reaction of American business often provided a fertile ground for the seeds of racketeering and organized crime. The leaders of OC provided mercenary armies to unions in need of violence to organize workers and thwart strikebreakers. In the spirit of "ideological neutrality," OC also provided private violence to meet the needs of business in its efforts against organized labor.

A third form of OC involvement in business is to run it directly. Profits from illegal activities must be invested somewhere; often a legitimate business is a profitable outlet for these funds—especially if it then does business with the mob or is backed up tacitly by the power of OC. A legitimate business can also be a convenient means to "hide" illegal profits so as to counter any government investigators who might be looking for evidence against OC leaders.

Labor Racketeering

In part 2, we reviewed the excesses of some early American capitalists who became known as the "Robber Barons." At the bottom of their world was labor, an amorphous collection of immigrants who, if they spoke English, often did so with a variety of foreign accents. They labored twelve hours a day, six days a week. Their struggles for better working conditions and wages resulted in what Sidney Lens calls *The Labor Wars* (1974: 4):

> The labor wars were a specific response to a specific set of injustices at a time when industrial and financial capitalism was establishing its predominance over American society. In a sense the battles were no different from the hundreds of other violent clashes against social injustices, as normal as the proverbial apple pie in the nation's annals.

From the early days of industrialization until 1937 (the year the Supreme Court upheld the Wagner Labor Relations Act), labor confrontations with employers often took on a particular scenario: Company spies, often from the Pinkerton Private Detective Agency, would identify union leaders, who were then fired by management. The guard force would be increased and strikebreakers secured. Company lawyers would secure injunctions from friendly judges prohibiting a strike. The union would organize "flying squadrons" to guard against the influx of strikebreakers and plan for mass picketing. If the Pinkerton guards proved inadequate, deputy sheriffs, policemen, and National Guard troops would be used to deal with union strikers.

In the early days, labor unions provided their own "muscle" from the ranks of their membership to deal with Pinkertons and strikebreakers. In 1909, however, a large number of women in the garment trades participated in strikes, and they required protection. Benjamin ("Dopey Benny") Fein, who was everything but dopey, became the chief supplier of sluggers for the International Ladies Garment Worker's Union. Fein formed alliances with such New York City street gangs as the Hudson Dusters, assigning territories and working out businesslike agreements and patterns of operation. He also assisted the union in keeping its members in line. It would soon become clear, however, that it was easier to hire gangsters than it was to fire them (Seidman 1938).

In order to avoid the problem of company spies reporting to management, which then fired union leaders, unions employed the "walking delegate" or business agent, who was often empowered to call a strike without any formal vote by the union membership. As an employee of the union, he was immune from management intimidation, and his power was instrumental in allowing the union to strike quickly and at the most opportune time. The men chosen for this position were usually tough, and it was this quality, rather than intelligence or integrity, that abounded in business agents. Before long, some of these men began abusing their power, calling needless strikes and engaging in extortionate practices (Seidman 1938). Employers hired gangsters to prevent unionization, and labor unions responded by making deals of their own with criminal elements. During struggles over jurisdiction and representation between the American Federation of Labor (AFL) and the Congress of Industrial Organizations (CIO), both sides resorted to "muscle" from organized crime.[1]

But as Harold Seidman noted back in 1938, they were "playing with the devil," and some unions were delivered into the hands of organized crime. Forty-four years later, a congressional committee concluded (Permanent Subcommittee on Investigations 1982, part 1: 5):

> At least four international unions are completely dominated by men who either have strong ties or are members of the organized crime syndicate. A majority of the locals in most major cities of the United States in the International Brotherhood of Teamsters (IBT), Hotel and Restaurant Employees Union (HRE), Laborers International Union of North America (Laborers), and International Longshoremen's Association (ILA) are completely dominated by organized crime.

The Laborers International Union, Michael Kilian (et al. 1979: 247) notes,

> is classic Chicago old-time unionism. It was headed for years by Peter Fosco, an Italian immigrant whose association with Capone-era hoodlums did not prevent him from winning public office and once earning an Italian-American award at a dinner addressed by Richard Nixon. . . . The Laborers Union has always had a healthy treasury, kept brimming with hard-working workers' dues.

In Chicago, members of the Outfit have held important positions in the Laborers Union: Vincent Solano, president of Local 1, and Alfred Pilotta, president of Local 5 until he was convicted in 1982 for his role in a kickback scheme involving the union's welfare benefit plan. The "De Cavalcante Tapes"[2] contain conversations involving New Jersey family boss Sam De Cavalcante, during which he discussed how control of Laborers Union locals enabled him to "shake down" building contractors who wanted to avoid using expensive union labor.

The Hotel Employees and Restaurant Employees International Union (HEREIU) was established in Chicago in 1891 (Permanent Subcommittee on Investigations 1982, part 1: 4):

> At first, only workers from pubs and restaurants were represented. Yet as America's cities began to grow so did the international, and soon hotel workers as well as food and beverage workers were represented. Thwarted only by prohibition in the 1920's, the international became the fastest growing union in the United States in the 1930's. By 1941 the international was the seventh largest union in North America.
>
> Today the international is the largest service union in the United States. Approximately 235 locals from 48 states and 8 provinces in Canada are affiliated with the international. . . .

Many of the HEREIU locals are reputed to be under the domination of OC Families. Local 450 in Chicago was chartered by Joey ("Doves") Aiuppa, a top leader of the Outfit, in 1935. Local 54 in New Jersey has about ten thousand members employed in the Atlantic City casino business, and the local is reputedly controlled by the Philadelphia crime Family. As a result, Family members were able to force hotels in Atlantic City to buy supplies and provisions from companies they owned.

As noted in part 3, Neapolitan Paola Antonio Vaccarelli, better known as Paul Kelly, leader of the Five Points Gang, became vice-president of the International Longshoremen's Association. Before assuming his position with the ILA, Kelly organized the ragpickers and served as their business agent and "walking delegate," a position he used to extort money from real estate and property agents. Until the twentieth century, about 95 percent of the longshoremen in the New York City area were Irish. By 1912, Italians comprised about 35 percent, and by 1919 they accounted for about 75 percent of the area's longshoremen. The Irish kept control of the West Side docks, while the Italians dominated the East Side, Brooklyn, and New Jersey docks. With the able assistance of men such as Paul Kelly, the ILA, which was organized in the 1890s, gained complete control over the waterfront by 1914 (Nelli 1976).

For poorly educated and often illiterate immigrants, such as this writer's maternal grandfather, the waterfront provided attractive employment opportunities. It was also attractive to racketeers for its lucrative illegal opportunities. The "shape-up," vividly portrayed in the Academy Award-winning film *On the Waterfront*, provided corrupt officials with kickbacks from workers eager for a day's wage. Loansharking, large-scale pilfering, smuggling, and deals with employers eager for "labor peace" enriched the criminals who dominated the waterfront.

In 1927, Thomas P. Ryan became president of the ILA; he stayed in that position until 1953. Under his reign OC solidified its control of the New York–New Jersey waterfront.[3] On September 23, 1953, the AFL convention voted to revoke the charter of the ILA. In November, Ryan, while under indictment for misappropriating union funds, stepped down and was given a $10,000 annual pension. William V. Bradley was elected president, and the AFL unsuccessfully attempted to wrest control from the ILA by setting up a rival union, the International Brotherhood of Longshoremen (IBL). In 1955, the AFL and CIO merged into the AFL-CIO. In 1959, the IBL and the ILA merged, and shortly afterwards the ILA was admitted to the AFL-CIO. Bradley apparently failed to cooperate with OC, and taped conversations between leading waterfront racketeers indicate he "was visited by mob members who told him he'd have to give up his position to Teddy Gleason or he'd be killed" (Permanent Subcommittee on Investigations 1981, *Waterfront Corruption*: 447). On July 17, 1963, after Bradley declined to run for reelection, Thomas ("Teddy") Gleason was unanimously elected president of the ILA.

In1953, the states of New York and New Jersey passed legislation creating a bistate Waterfront Commission, which became a reality when it won the approval of Congress and the authorizing legislation was signed by President Dwight D. Eisenhower on August 12, 1953. The commission was empowered to license stevedoring concerns and regulate waterfront employees. Those with serious criminal records were banned from the docks. The commission was given subpoena and investigative authority in New York and New Jersey. Thus began a movement to "clean up" the New York–New Jersey waterfront, an effort aided by federal investigations into the ILA.

Donald Goddard (1980: 66) notes that as a result of more stringent law-enforcement efforts in the ports of New York and New Jersey, ILA racketeers moved operations to Florida, where they plundered the Port of Miami. The ILA shifted from exploiting its members to "carving up the cargo traffic among the port's stevedores and 'taxing' them on their shares." Goddard points out that shipowners, agents, stevedores, contractors, and service companies were caught up in a web of corrupt practices with the ILA—and few wanted to escape. "They had only to pay their 'rent' in order to enrich themselves with guaranteed profits." Special Agent Louis J. Freeh of the FBI notes (Permanent Subcommittee on Investigations 1981, *Waterfront Corruption*: 183):

> You do not have extortion, you do not have threats, you do not have violence. What you have is a businessman who is as corrupt as the ILA official who he pays looking for additional business, looking for an advantage against his competitors and using his organized crime connection . . . to have that union official contact another businessman to extend an economic advantage.

The FBI's UNIRAC investigation (1975–79) resulted in the conviction of several ranking members of the ILA, including Anthony Scotto, who is married to the niece of Albert Anastasia and is reputed to be a *caporegime* in the Gambino Family. The investigation revealed that ports along the East Coast from New York to Florida were divided between the Genovese and Gambino Families into spheres of interest. In addition to the ILA officials, several members of these Families were convicted of a number of corrupt practices, including:

1. Payoffs in lieu of employer contributions to ILA pension and welfare benefit plans.
2. Payoffs to secure "labor peace" and avoid adhering to ILA rules which (amounted to "featherbedding") were costly.
3. Payoffs by businessmen to secure union contracts which were necessary to qualify for maritime work in ports under ILA control.
4. Payoffs to help firms secure new business and to keep the business they had without competitive bidding.

The International Brotherhood of Teamsters (IBT) is the largest labor union in the United States, with 7,000 officers and business agents in 742 locals representing 2.3 million workers (Brill 1978). In 1898, the Team Drivers International Union received a charter from the AFL for its membership of 1,200 drivers. In 1902, Chicago members of the Team Drivers established a rival Teamsters National Union with 18,000 horse handlers. The following year Samuel Gompers, president of the AFL, arranged for a merger of the two, which became the IBT with a membership of 50,000. Although the Teamsters remained a relatively weak and ineffective union, by 1933 they had about 125,000 members concentrated mostly in industrial centers such as Detroit and Chicago. In 1907, Dan Tobin became IBT president and served without any major scandal until 1952, when he was succeeded by Dave Beck of Seattle, who controlled the Western Conference of Teamsters. Because of the support he received from Jimmy Hoffa, head of the Teamsters in Detroit, Beck rewarded Hoffa with an IBT vice-presidency. In 1957, Beck was convicted of embezzling union funds and income-tax violations in Seattle federal court and sentenced to five years' imprisonment. At the 1957 IBT convention in Miami, James R. Hoffa, who had been accused of dozens of improper activities by the McClellan Committee,[4] was elected president. That same year the IBT was expelled from the AFL-CIO (Moldea 1978).

Jimmy Hoffa

Hoffa was born in Brazil, Indiana, on February 14, 1913, and moved to Detroit with his family in 1924. A school dropout, Hoffa eventually became a warehouse worker and developed a reputation as a tough street fighter who always stood up for his fellow workers against management. Because of this,

Hoffa was fired from his warehouse job and hired as an organizer by Local 299 of the IBT. He and other IBT organizers battled management goons in their organizing efforts throughout Detroit. In 1941, after he had risen to a leadership position in Local 299, Hoffa found himself in a battle with the CIO which began a "raid" to represent Detroit teamsters. The CIO action was backed by a small army of goons, and the IBT was literally being beaten in the streets of Detroit. Jimmy Hoffa turned to some friends in the Detroit underworld and secured the assistance of the powerful Meli Family; Dan Moldea points out (1978: 38): "The CIO raiders were defeated by the end of the year. And considering the new players on Hoffa's team, it was a miracle that the CIO survived at all in Detroit." As Moldea (1978: 38) notes, the victory was not without cost:

> The CIO's defeat, brought about by Hoffa's ringers, became the major factor in his rapid plunge from union reformer to labor racketeer. His pact with the underworld, no matter how tenuous at the time, took him out of the running as a potentially great leader of the Teamsters' rank and file.

Hoffa's road to power and the presidency of the IBT is strewn with scandal, such as his alliance with Anthony ("Tony Pro") Provenzano (Brill 1978: 125):

> The Hoffa-Provenzano alliance was typical of the bargains Hoffa struck with gangsters around the country; they helped push him to the top, and he helped them use their union posts for a series of money-making schemes: extortion from employers, loan-sharking, pension-fund frauds, and anything else that control of union muscle and money offered.

Anthony Provenzano was born in 1917 to Italian immigrants on the Lower East Side of New York. He dropped out of school at age fifteen to become a truck helper and later a driver, with aspirations of becoming a prizefighter. His reputation for violence brought him to the attention of a next-door neighbor, Anthony Strollo, better known as "Tony Bender" (born 1899), a *caporegime* in the Genovese Family and a powerful waterfront racketeer. As a result of Bender's patronage, Provenzano became a member of the Genovese Family and an organizer for IBT Local 560 in New Jersey. In 1959, with help from Jimmy Hoffa, Provenzano was elected president of the local. In 1960, Hoffa appointed Provenzano to fill a vacancy among IBT vice-presidents.

In 1963, Provanzano's union salaries totalled $113,000—he was the highest paid union official in the world. That same year he was convicted of extorting $17,000 from the Dorn Trucking Company to end a discipline problem the firm was having with its union employees. During the 4½ years he was in prison, and for the five years he was disqualified from holding union office (as per the 1959 Landrum-Griffin Act), his brothers Salvatore ("Sammy") and Nunzio headed the local, while Tony ran its affairs. Opponents of the Provanzanos in the union found themselves subjected to threats, beatings, or (in at least one instance) murder. In 1978, Tony was convicted for the 1961 slaying of Anthony Castellito, a union official who had defied him, and sentenced to twenty years' imprisonment. In 1981, Nunzio Provenzano, president of Local 560, was sentenced to ten years' imprisonment. He had been convicted on April 30 of accepting $187,000 from four interstate trucking companies for "labor peace." He permitted the companies to avoid contract rules for hiring Local 560 drivers. Sammy Pro became president of Local 560.

"Paper Locals." In 1956, elections were scheduled to choose officers for the IBT's Joint Council 16 in New York City. If Hoffa could affect the outcome of the Joint Council 16 elections, he would pave the way for winning control of the IBT presidency. In 1955 Hoffa had seven new Teamster charters issued to a union friend of John ("Johnny Dio") Dioguardi,[5] a member of the Lucchese Family. Along with Anthony ("Tony Ducks") Corallo (later Boss of the Lucchese Family) Dioguardi filled the locals with a variety of gangsters who could then vote in the 1956 election. Five of the seven locals did not have a single member—they were "paper locals." Corallo had already gained control of five other Teamster locals, although he held office in only one, Local 239, whose president, Sam Goldstein, took orders from Corallo. Walter Sheridan (1972) reports that Dioguardi and Corallo brought into the newly chartered locals some forty men with an aggregate record of 178 arrests and seventy-seven convictions.

While Hoffa was interested in winning over the locals and their votes, Dioguardi and Corallo were interested in financial rewards. The newly "elected" officers would approach various non-union employers with an offer they could not easily refuse: "Pay the union fees and membership dues for your employees (who often would not even know they were union members), and you keep your business free of all labor problems, including demands by legitimate unions; fail to pay, and labor problems, or worse, will result." By the time Hoffa gained control of the IBT in New York, twenty-five of these men had already been convicted of new charges, including bribery, extortion, perjury and forgery. Those convicted included Sam Goldstein and Harry Davidoff, the IBT boss of Kennedy International Airport.

Allen Dorfman. Allen Dorfman was born in 1923 and was awarded the Silver Star during his World War II service with the Marine Corps. In 1948 he was a physical education teacher at the University of Illinois earning $4,000 a year. By 1953 he was a millionaire.

Paul ("Red") Dorfman, Allen's stepfather, was a former professional boxer and close friend of Anthony Accardo, boss of the Chicago Outfit. In 1940 the founder and secretary-treasurer of the Chicago Waste Handlers Union was murdered. Red Dorfman, who had never been a member of the union or a waste handler, showed up at a union meeting, paid his dues and on the same night became the secretary-treasurer. In 1928 he had been indicted for rigging election ballots and terrorist tactics in a local election—there is apparently no record of the disposition. In 1942 he was arrested again as the result of a dispute with the chairman of the waste handlers employers' association—the two disagreed over wages to be paid for men in Dorfman's union. Dorfman, using brass knuckles concealed in a glove, severely beat the man in his office. The charges were dropped when the victim refused to prosecute. In 1949 Dorfman assisted Jimmy Hoffa by introducing him to important people in the Outfit, gaining their help in his organizing drives for the IBT (Brill 1978).

> In 1949 Allen Dorfman formed the Union Insurance Agency.
>
> In 1950 and 1951, Hoffa successfully maneuvered the insurance business of the teamsters health and welfare funds to the Dorfmans. Hoffa entered into a collusive arrangement with the head of Union Casualty Company, and Paul and Allan Dorfman [sic] to assure the placing of the Central States Insurance business with Union Casualty Company, with the understanding that Allan Dorfman would be named the broker on this lucrative account. Evidence indicated that Union Casualty placed its bid based on more favorable factors than those of its competitors, and when another company did offer a lower bid, it was rejected on baseless grounds. Subsequently, Allan, Paul, and Rose Dorfman, all of whom had absolutely no experience in the insurance field, received more than $3 million in commissions and service fees on teamsters insurance over an eight year period [Permanent Subcommittee on Investigations 1983; *Organized Crime in Chicago:* 83].

In 1955, Jimmy Hoffa negotiated the IBT's first pension plan, into which each employer would contribute two dollars per week per IBT employee. By June 1983, despite being subjected to a great deal of plundering, the Central States, Southeast and Southwest Areas Pension Fund and Health and Welfare Fund (usually referred to simply as the Central States Pension Fund) had assets of $4.685 billion (Wallace 1983). Appointed as a consultant to the fund's board of trustees was Allen Dorfman, who turned it into "a bank for the underworld and their cronies in the 1960s and early 1970s" (Frantz and Neubauer 1983: 1). He had the trustees lend millions of dollars to Las Vegas casinos, mob-connected resorts, and speculative hotel and land ventures, projects that conventional lending institutions would not finance. In 1972, Dorfman was convicted for taking a $55,000 kickback for securing a pension fund loan of $1.5 million; he served ten months in a federal prison. In 1974, he was indicted with Irwin Weiner, a mob associate, Joseph ("Joey the Clown") Lombardo, and Anthony Spilotro, members of the Outfit, on charges of fraud in connection with another pension fund loan. They were subsequently acquitted after the chief government witness was gunned down outside of his business establishment. In 1977, the federal government forced the trustees of the Central States Pension Fund to relinquish financial control to an independent management firm (Frantz and Neubauer 1983).

On December 15, 1982, Dorfman, Joseph Lombardo, and Teamster president Roy L. Williams were found guilty of attempting to bribe U.S. senator Howard Cannon of Nevada in return for his help in delaying legislation that substantially deregulated the trucking industry. The three were scheduled for sentencing on February 10. On January 20 Dorfman was walking with Irwin Weiner in a parking lot of the suburban Lincolnwood Hyatt Hotel just outside of Chicago. Two men approached Dorfman from behind. One carried a sawed-off shotgun under his coat, and the other drew a .22-caliber automatic with a silencer attached and fired five shots, point blank, into Dorfman's head. The two men then pulled on ski masks and fled in a car driven by a third person. The car plates and firearm were found several days later in a trash can. The plates had been stolen in August, and the .22 automatic was traced to a shop in Florida that had been out of business for years.

Hoffa versus Kennedy

> *From the day that James Hoffa told Robert Kennedy that he was nothing but a rich man's kid who never had to earn a nickel in his life, Hoffa was a marked man.* [Professor Monroe Freedman; quoted in Navasky 1977: 395. Emphasis added.]

The first clash between Hoffa and Kennedy occurred when the latter was chief counsel to the McClellan Committee, 1957–59. In his sometimes blunt, sometimes evasive answers in testimony before the committee, Hoffa at times referred to Kennedy as "Bob" or "Bobby." In the following exchange Kennedy asked Hoffa about the vice-president of IBT Local 239, Anthony Corallo [McClellan 1962: 50]:

> KENNEDY: He has been arrested twelve times, ranging from robbery, grand larceny, and narcotics. He was identified before the committee as an important figure in narcotics, and he was a close friend of Johnny Dioguardi. My question is, Have you made any investigation of him? . . . Have you taken any steps against Mr. Tony Ducks Corallo?
> HOFFA: As of now, no.

In 1957, FBI surveillance cameras recorded Hoffa giving $2,000 to John C. Cheasty, a New York attorney who was cooperating with the government, to pass on confidential McClellan Committee documents. Hoffa had recruited Cheasty to serve as a plant on the committee. When FBI agents arrested Hoffa the following day, he had confidential committee reports on him. In a jury trial, Hoffa was acquitted. In 1958, Hoffa was tried for illegally wiretapping the phones of some Teamster officials. The first trial resulted in a hung jury; the second in an acquittal. In 1960, John F. Kennedy was elected president of the United States and Robert Kennedy was appointed attorney general. Robert Kennedy made the Labor and Racketeering Unit, a subdivision of the Organized Crime Section of the Criminal Division of the Department of Justice, his personal "Get-Hoffa Squad." It was headed by former FBI Special Agent Walter Sheridan, who was actually on the attorney general's payroll as a "confidential assistant" (Navasky 1977).

Soon after Kennedy became attorney general, federal grand juries across the country began investigating the IBT. Several important convictions were secured, including that of Anthony Provenzano. In 1962, Hoffa was charged with a conflict-of-interest violation of the Taft-Hartley law—a misdemeanor. Victor Navasky (1977: 417) comments: "Never in history had the government devoted so much money, manpower, and top-level brainpower to a misdemeanor case." The trial lasted two months and ended in a hung jury—seven to five for acquittal. This case, which was tried in Nashville, Tennessee, resulted in a second trial in Chattanooga—Hoffa was accused of trying to bribe jurors in the Nashville case. The second trial was moved to Chattanooga on a Hoffa motion for a change of venue based on adverse newspaper publicity. On March 4, 1964, Hoffa was convicted of jury tampering and sentenced to eight years' imprisonment.

On December 21, 1971, Hoffa was released from prison after President Richard Nixon approved his application for clemency (the IBT had supported Nixon for president). By 1975, Hoffa was actively seeking the Teamster presidency. Teamster officials loyal to him were holding fund-raising dinners to prepare for the campaign. Hoffa began attacking Frank Fitzsimmons, the man who had replaced him as IBT president. Ironically, Hoffa criticized Fitzsimmons as being the tool of organized crime. On July 30, 1975, Hoffa arrived at the Machus Red Fox Restaurant to meet with several persons, including Anthony ("Tony Jack") Giacalone, a *caporegime* in the Detroit Family and a friend of Hoffa, and Anthony Provanzano. Giacalone had arranged the meeting ostensibly to mediate differences between Provenzano and Hoffa over the latter's quest for the IBT presidency. None of the principals were at the Red Fox, and Hoffa has not been seen since.

Business Racketeering

Business racketeering usually involves some form of restraint of trade—limiting competition—but it need not involve organized crime (as it has been defined in this book). The "Great Electrical Equipment Conspiracy," for example, involved executives of major corporations, including General Electric and Westinghouse, in a bid-rigging scheme (Richard A. Smith 1961a, 1961b). The conspiracy began just before World War II and climaxed in 1961. In that year forty-five persons representing twenty-nine corporations were indicted. They were accused of price fixing by rigging bids and dividing the available market through a secret cartel that dealt with electrical equipment worth $1.7 billion annually. To effect the conspiracy, the defendants used secret codes and clandestine meetings in a variety of hotel rooms. The defendants pleaded guilty: twenty-four received suspended sentences; twenty-one were imprisoned for as much as *thirty days*. In 1980, thirty-seven manufacturers were accused of being part of an eighteen-year nationwide conspiracy to fix the prices of corrugated containers and sheets, a multibillion-dollar scheme; they settled out of court.

Back in 1931, Walter Lippmann (1962: 61) noted that "racketeering in many of its most important forms tends to develop where an industry is subjected to excessively competitive conditions." Companies "faced with the constant threat of cutthroat competition are subject to easy temptation to pay gangsters for protection against competitors." As noted in chapter 3, Lepke Buchalter and Gurrah Shapiro were invited into the fur industry in order to "police" illegal business practices that limited competition. There are two basic variables that characterize an industry susceptible to racketeering:

1. Entry into the industry is relatively easy, requiring few skills and only a limited financial investment.
2. Demand for the industry's goods and/or services is inelastic.

The solid-waste collection industry in many areas has been associated with racketeering. Typically, there are too many small firms with from one to twenty trucks servicing a limited number of customers. Competition for a customer's business drives down profits until, at some point, with or without help from OC, an association is formed. Association members divide up the industry, usually allocating geographic areas (territories) or specific customers, and each gets a share. The members (illegally) agree not to compete for the business of any other member. Each is therefore free to charge whatever the market will bear for its services. Organized crime will become involved if there is a need to police the (illegal) agreements. Peter Reuter (et al. 1983: 11) reports that in New York City:

> Racketeers play a continuing role in the operation of this agreement. That role comes mainly through the need to constantly mediate the disputes that inevitably arise in a conspiracy that involves the allocation of over 100,000 customers between 300 carters. The "grievance committees" that settle these disputes, using the basic rule that whoever serviced the site first has continuing rights to any customer that occupies the site, include at least one Mafioso. While there is little evidence of either threats or actual violence, it seems reasonable to infer that the racketeers provide a credible continuing threat of violence that ensures compliance with the rulings of the committee.

In 1976, in an effort to secure evidence of organized crime activity in the refuse-carting business in the Bronx, the FBI went into the solid-waste removal business. Several agents, using some old Army sanitation trucks, opened the American Automated Refuse Company. While they were able to secure a number of accounts, the service that they provided was so poor that they ran into trouble—not with OC but with the New York City Consumer Protection Agency. In response, the FBI purchased four well-conditioned trucks and began to make a profit; they also attracted the attention of the carters' association under Joseph Gambino, cousin of Carlo Gambino. Gambino and his associate visited the office of American Automated and explained that they would have to pay a fee in order to operate in the Bronx. When the firm's (agent) "owner" demurred, he was subjected to a(n on camera) beating. Gambino, who entered the United States illegally in 1957, received a sentence of ten years (Block and Scarpitti, 1985).

A business association that engages in racketeering without an OC connection is vulnerable. In New Jersey, for example, the organizer of a waste-haulers association that effectively controlled competition found himself being pushed out by an emissary from Gerardo ("Jerry") Catena, who ran New Jersey operations for the Genovese Family. The head of the association told the writer about his response: "I had a feeling, *fear,* that if I did not just put my tail between my legs and allow myself to be pushed out, they would find another way to get me out" (Abadinsky 1981: 39).

In New York City, the Grinders Association is made up of firms engaged in the cutlery-grinding business; they supply knives and other commercial cutlery equipment, freshly sharpened on a regular basis, to various customers such as butcher shops and restaurants. The cutlery is owned by the grinder, whose fee for sharpening also includes a rental charge. This is an easy-entry business, and the association had divided up the industry among its membership.

In 1961, a firm run by Salvatore Gugliemini and Paul Gambino—cousin and brother, respectively, of Carlo Gambino and members of his Family— effectively competed with members of the Grinders Association. Under more normal circumstances, the association would probably have undercut the prices of outside competition, or even threatened violence, to drive the competitor out of business. Given the nature of the new competition, however, neither approach was particularly attractive to association members. Instead, they pooled their financial resources and bought out the Gugliemini-Gambino firm (New York State Commission of Investigation 1970).

Business/Labor Racketeering

There is often a very thin, nearly nonexistent, line between labor racketeering and business racketeering. In a great many instances they are merely flip sides of the same coin. Earlier in this chapter, for example, it was noted that the International Longshoremen's Association engaged in collusive relationships with shipping and stevedoring firms. Jonathan Kwitny (1979) describes the machinations of racketeer-extraordinary Moses ("Moe") Steinman, who dominated the wholesale meat industry in New York City. Because of his connections with such important OC figures as John Dioguardi and Paul Castellano (a relative of Carlo Gambino and later boss of the Gambino Family), Steinman was able to deal with racketeer-controlled unions and thus affect labor relations in the meat industry. This ability secured for him a position as a supermarket-chain executive who led industrywide negotiations with meat-industry unions. In this strategic position, he effected under-the-table payments to the union leaders, and he could determine from whom the supermarkets bought their meat. Supermarket officials would buy from firms recommended by Steinman, overpaying for their beef, and receive kickbacks. Steinman, in addition, would be paid handsome commission fees from the beef companies for these sales.

Steinman's greatest achievement was his relationship with Currier J. Holman, founder of Iowa Beef, the largest meat-processing firm in the world. The midwestern patrician business executive and the hard-drinking, inarticulate New York racketeer had something in common—greed. In return for opening up New York markets for Iowa Beef and assisting the company with "labor relations," Iowa Beef gave millions of dollars to Steinman and his friends and relatives.

Legitimate Business

In addition to a plethora of illegal business activities, persons involved in organized crime often have legitimate business enterprises. One of the popular activities of government officials, who often provide the grist for journalistic mills, has been to decry the "infiltration" of organized crime into legitimate business. Michael Maltz (1975: 83), however, points out that "the alternative to penetration of legitimate business is the reinvestment of the ill-gotten gains into the same criminal enterprises, which may cause greater social harm." Annelise Anderson (1979: 77) points out, however, that funds from illegal business enterprises cannot easily "be profitably reinvested in illegal market enterprises without aggressive expansion of the territory controlled by the group." Thus, members of OC may be in the position of having an oversupply of illegal funds which they cannot profitably use to expand illegal activities. Maltz (1975) concludes that the penetration of OC into legitimate business can be viewed as the equivalent to the legitimation of family fortunes by the robber barons, as described in part 2.

Anderson provides six reasons for organized criminal involvement in legitimate business. We will review each of them.

1. *Profit.* In a conversation from the "De Cavalcante Tapes," Anthony Russo, an underboss in Long Branch, New Jersey, complained to Sam De Cavalcante that the *amici nostri* ("friends of ours"; OC members) could not even support themselves. In another incident, De Cavalcante arranged for the

removal of a local union official, who was also a *caporegime* in his Family, because he was not providing *legitimate* employment to the *amici nostri* as construction laborers. Jimmy Fratianno's 531-page autobiography (Demaris 1981), *The Last Mafioso,* contains very little discussion of his business activities. Indeed, it appears that Fratianno's most successful enterprise was a legitimate trucking business he owned in California.

   2. *Diversification.* A legitimate business provides the OC member with security of income. While it may be subject to market and other business conditions, a legitimate enterprise is usually not a target of law-enforcement efforts.

   3. *Transfer.* Illegitimate enterprises are difficult, if not impossible, to transfer to dependents (particularly if they are female).

   4. *Services.* An OC member with a legitimate business is in a position to act as a patron for persons in need of legitimate employment—for example, persons on probation or parole, or relatives he wants to shield from the stigma and risks associated with criminal enterprises.

   5. *Taxes.* A legitimate business can provide a tax cover, thereby reducing the risk of being charged with income-tax evasion. As noted earlier, funds from the illegitimate activities can be mixed with those from the legitimate business; the latter need not be profitable.

   6. *Front.* A legitimate business can provide a front or a base of operations for a host of illegal activities: loansharking, gambling, drug trafficking, to name a few.

   Obviously, these categories are not mutually exclusive. It is quite likely that OC involvement in legitimate business involves a combination of these six reasons.

"Laundering Dirty Money"

Ever since Al Capone was imprisoned for income-tax evasion, financially successful criminals have sought ways to launder their illegally secured money. Some use a "cash business," such as a vending-machine firm, to mingle legitimate and illegitimate money on which they can pay income tax. In more elaborate schemes, the first step is usually to convert large quantities of cash into one or more cashier's checks. In addition to being easier to carry, they are difficult to trace since they do not have the receiver's name or address. The cash can also be Telexed overseas. Under the Bank Secrecy Act, banks must identify the depositor and the source of money for cash transactions of $10,000 or more. These currency transactions must then be reported to the Internal Revenue Service.[6] Obviously, launderers require a bank with "cooperative" officials, or they may even buy their own bank. In 1985, for example, it was revealed that the Bank of Boston, that city's oldest and biggest bank, had helped to "launder" money for the underboss, and subsequently boss, of the Patriarca crime Family. From 1979 to 1983 Jerry Angiulo and his brothers would convert paper bags stuffed with tens of thousands of dollars into $100 bills and more than $7 million in cashiers' checks. None of the transactions were reported to the Internal Revenue Service (IRS) as required by federal law. Two real estate companies controlled by the Anguilos in the Italian neighborhood of Boston's North End, had been placed on the "exempt" list, which meant their cash transactions in excess of $10,000 did not have to be reported to the IRS. The only businesses legally entitled to such exemptions are retail outlets such as supermarkets which do large amounts of cash business. Penny Lernoux (1984: F8) points out that "the only certain criteria for denying an outsider the right to buy or acquire substantial shares in an existing United States bank is whether the buyer is in jail at the time the application is processed."

Whether it is in cash or a cashier's check or Telexed, the funds must reach an overseas bank in a country that has strict bank-secrecy laws (Permanent Subcommittee on Investigations 1983 *Staff Study:* 7):

> For years, Switzerland has been a major sanctuary for funds whose owners wish to remain anonymous. Swiss bank secrecy, reinforced by strong criminal penalties, dates back to the Hitler-ascendancy days of 1934 when the Swiss enacted a law to prevent the Nazis from forcing Swiss banks to disclose deposits by Jewish customers from Germany who had opened accounts there. Since then, Switzerland and other European countries such as Luxembourg and Liechtenstein have been host to thousands of secret bank accounts and corporations and trusts of unrevealed ownership. In recent years, similar accommodations have become available across the board in Caribbean and South Atlantic countries [such] as the Bahamas and the Cayman Islands.
>
> In addition to providing secrecy, these countries impose no taxation or low taxes on foreign funds. Thus, they do not recognize tax evasion as a crime and are loathe to assist in any investigation of a U.S. citizen suspected of evasion. Indeed, their generous complement of attorneys, accountants and bankers will overnight construct a framework of corporate paper designed to hide true ownership or, if it becomes necessary, to satisfy any inquiries from our Internal Revenue Service.
>
> Except with Switzerland, the United States has no treaty arrangements with any secrecy jurisdiction for the extradition of offshore banking or corporate information. The taxation treaties which the U.S. does have with many secrecy countries provide only for information exchanges aimed at eliminating double taxation of the respective citizens of the treaty partners.
>
> U.S. law-enforcement authorities have occasionally resorted to other recognized means to obtain information, such as letters rogatory, a time-consuming process involving diplomatic and judicial channels. As noted above, the U.S. has risked generating international friction by obtaining subpoenas against U.S. branch offices of foreign banks for the production of records in other offshore branches or of the headquarters banks themselves. The underlying philosophy is that a foreign bank operating in the U.S. must play by our rules.
>
> What are viewed in some offshore countries as U.S. encroachments on their

sovereignty or the good order of their commercial systems have been met with certain backlash actions. In 1976 the Cayman Islands, which had strict bank secrecy before, tightened its laws by adding more substantial sanctions against persons who divulged banking and commercial information. This tightening was a reaction to *United States* v. *Field* 532 F.2d 404 (5th Cir. 1976), in which a U.S. court directed a Cayman resident to give grand jury testimony even though the testimony would violate Cayman bank-secrecy laws and subject him to limited criminal penalties.

In 1984, however, the United States and Great Britain signed an agreement that gives American officials investigating drug cases information about secret bank accounts in the Cayman Islands, which are a British colony (Thomas 1984).

In 1984, federal tax amendments extended cash-reporting requirements to anyone who receives more than $10,000 in cash in the course of a trade or business. Up until then, only banks, financial institutions, stockbrokers, and currency exchanges had been required to inform the Internal Revenue Service when they received more than $10,000 in cash.

As part of the laundering process, a "paper" company is registered in one of a number of countries which have privacy laws—for example, Panama, which has over 200,000 companies registered, or the Cayman Islands, which has about 13,600—about one for every resident (Pileggi 1983). The funds to be laundered are deposited in an account that belongs to the "paper" company. In the final stage, the "paper" company returns the money to its owner in the United States in the form of a loan. Not only does the criminal get the money back, but it is augmented by a tax write-off for the interest on the loan.

---

[1] For a first-person account of the violence involved in union organizing and jurisdictional disputes, see the autobiography of Max ("The Butcher") Block (1982). Block was a professional boxer, a union organizer, and an international vice-president of the Amalgamated Meat Cutters and Butcher Workmen of North America.

[2] During the 1960s the FBI bugged the office of Sam ("The Plumber") De Cavalcante (sometimes spelled DeCavalcante or de Cavalcante), boss of a small New Jersey crime Family, for almost four years. On June 10, 1969, as a result of De Cavalcante's trial, some of the results of the bugging were made public. Known as the "De Cavalcante Tapes," the material is actually a document based on transcripts of conversations overheard by four microphones and summarized by FBI agents, with some verbatim transcriptions.

[3] On the West Coast, Australian-born Alfred Reuton ("Harry") Bridges withdrew from the ILA and organized the International Longshoremen and Warehousemen's Union (ILWU), which became part of the CIO. Bridges, who was born in 1900, came to the United States as a merchant seaman in 1920 and went to work as a longshoreman in San Francisco. He reactivated a dormant ILA local and led a successful strike in 1934. The strike was opposed by Ryan, and Bridges was attacked for his leftist views and close association with Communists (Lens 1974). The ILWU, in marked contrast to the ILA, has been free of OC influence.

[4] U.S. Senate Select Committee on Improper Activities in the Labor or Management Field, created on January 30, 1957, and chaired by Sen. John L. McClellan of Arkansas. Sen. John F. Kennedy was a member of the committee, and Robert Kennedy was chief counsel.

In 1984, for example, twenty-one persons were indicted for a conspiracy to dominate private carting on Long Island. The Private Sanitation Industry Association of Nassau/Suffolk and its fifteen member firms were accused of illegally assigning collection territories, setting prices, rigging bids, and using coercion to intimidate carters who declined to join the conspiracy. Tony Corallo, boss of the Lucchese Family, and Paul Castellano, boss of the Gambino Family, were said to have split quarterly payments of more than $50,000 for their services, which included settling disputes that arose among member firms ("21 People Indicted on L.I. As Carting Plot Is Charged," 1984: 20).

[5] John Dioguardi was born on the Lower East Side of Manhattan on April 29, 1914. The nephew of James Plumeri (better known as "Jimmy Doyle"), a *caporegime* in the Lucchese Family, Dioguardi became a member of his Family. His first conviction was in 1937 for extorting money from the trucking industry. In 1956 he was indicted for the acid-throwing attack that blinded labor columnist Victor Riesel. The charges were dropped when a witness refused to testify. In 1967 Dioguardi received a five-year sentence for bankruptcy fraud ("scam"), and when he finished that term he was convicted for stock fraud involving a car-leasing company. Dioguardi died in prison on January 14, 1979 (Kihss 1979).

Anthony Corallo was described by Robert F. Kennedy (1960: 84) as "an underworld figure of great influence whose unusual nickname stems from his reputation for 'ducking' convictions in court cases in which he is arrested. Tony Ducks, whose police arrest list includes drug and robbery charges and who is on the Treasury Department's narcotics list, lost only one bout with the law. In 1941 he was sentenced to six months for unlawful possession of narcotics." In 1962, however, Corallo received a two-year sentence for bribing a judge in a fraudulent bankruptcy case. In 1968 he was convicted for his part in a kickback scheme that involved James L. Marcus, a close confidant of New York City mayor John V. Lindsay and commissioner of the Department of Water Supply, Gas and Electricity. Corallo received a three-year sentence and Marcus, who eventually cooperated with the authorities, was sentenced to fifteen months.

[6] The Federal government's means of monitoring large cash transactions and the export and import of large amounts of cash is the Currency and Foreign Transactions Reporting Act of 1970, popularly known as the Bank Secrecy Act. Under this Act and its regulations: (1) a bank or other financial institution is required to file a currency transaction report (CTR or form 4789) with the IRS for each deposit, withdrawal or exchange of currency or monetary instruments in excess of $10,000; (2) a person must immediately file a report (CIMR or form 4790) with the Customs Service when physically transporting into or out of the United States any currency or monetary instruments exceeding $10,000; and (3) a person who owns or controls a foreign financial account must declare such ownership or control on that person's federal income tax return and also file form 90-22.1 with the Treasury Department [Permanent Subcommittee on Investigations 1983, *Staff Study:* 114; personal communication, Henry Ristic, U.S. Customs Service].

Laws and
Law Enforcement

Organized crime presents a formidable problem to law enforcement. As opposed to many other forms of lawbreaking, OC is usually rational, reasoned, and exceptionally well informed. While local authorities are able to arrest and successfully prosecute low-level operatives in gambling and drug trafficking, penetrating the core of an OC unit requires an enormous expenditure of resources—money and personnel—and a willingness to work for long periods without immediate results. In general, it is usually enforcement agencies at the federal level that have such resources. Efforts at every level, however, are complicated by the multiplicity of agencies and jurisdictions—and by the continuing problem of corruption. Law enforcement is also handicapped by the very civil liberties it is sworn to defend.

In chapter 14 we will examine the difficulties encountered by law enforcement and discuss how the fight against OC is managed. Chapter 15 outlines the provisions of the statutes on which law-enforcement efforts against OC are based. Chapters 16 and 17 will delve into the techniques used in combatting OC and the laws and regulations that shape them. Finally, in chapter 18, we will deal with society's perceptions and the resulting policies regarding OC—how they evolved, where they may be heading, and some of the options available to us in the effort to contain the activities of OC.

chapter 15

Problems in Combatting Organized Crime:
Complexity and Corruption

Used by permission of AP/Wide World Photo

Of the major problems besetting U.S. law-enforcement agencies fighting organized crime, one is, in a sense, self-imposed: the complexity of the system, its checks and balances, makes it unwieldy. The other major problem, corruption, may have its origin outside the agencies, but in a sense it too is in the nature of the task; fighting OC exposes law-enforcement personnel to the possibility of large (and illegal) personal gains.

Complexity

In the United States, government is fragmented into four levels: federal, state, county, municipal; and three branches: executive, legislative, judicial. Each level of government has its own law-enforcement agencies, such as the FBI, state police, county sheriff, municipal police. The deliberate fragmenting of government was an effort by the founding fathers to ensure against tyranny. While a more unified system of government—for example, a single national police force—would obviously be more efficient, it would also carry with it the danger of totalitarianism. To further protect the people from governmental power and its abuse, the United States Constitution provides for civil liberties that protect each citizen—the law-abiding and the criminal. Thus, in the United States, the control of crime and criminals often requires considerably more sophistication than in nations whose system of government provides law enforcement with great unity and authority. We share with other systems, however, the problem of corruption of government.

Local Police

General police responsibility is a function of the "full-service" municipal department—there is no national police force, and the primary responsibility of state police forces is highway traffic enforcement. Most of the resources of a municipal police department go into uniformed services such as patrol; only a small portion goes into plainclothes or detective units. In larger cities, such units include specialties such as "vice" (gambling and prostitution) and drug enforcement. In this function, local police do apprehend some of the "troops" of organized crime. OC, however, is rarely a priority item for a municipal department. Resources devoted to dealing with it reduce the department's ability to respond to citizen demands for police services. Justine J. Dintino and Frederick T. Martens (1980: 67) point out:

> Few local police departments have the luxury of developing a sophisticated organized crime control program. Obviously, the daily realities of police work at the grass-roots level mitigate against a well-developed execution of an organized

crime control strategy. Since organized crime is often synonymous with vice enforcement—gambling, prostitution, narcotics, and loansharking—there are few incentives for a police administrator to allocate limited and valuable resources toward this particular form of criminality. Often the investment of personnel to enforce laws which govern "consensual relationships" between customer and supplier are met with judicial indifference and public apathy; and as demonstrated through numerous studies and investigations, it is highly questionable from a purely cost-benefit analysis whether the benefits outweigh the costs incurred.

Accordingly, most law-enforcement efforts against OC are found at the federal level.

Federal Law Enforcement

But even in the national government, there is no single agency responsible for dealing with the problem. Instead, responsibility is shared principally by the Federal Bureau of Investigation (FBI); the Drug Enforcement Administration (DEA); and the Internal Revenue Service (IRS); along with the Customs Service; the Secret Service; the Marshals Service; the Bureau of Alcohol, Tobacco and Firearms (ATF); the Immigration and Naturalization Service; the Postal Inspection Service; the Department of Labor; the Department of Agriculture; the Coast Guard; and, at times, the military.

These agencies have few means of cooperating with one another and often do not coordinate their activities. To mitigate this problem, agencies have evolved the device of the ad hoc cooperative strike force, discussed in chapter 17.

Despite all these problems, the agencies do at times manage to perform remarkably well. Even with all their resources, many top figures in organized crime have in the end been caught in the law-enforcement net.

Civil Liberties

The due process guarantees that protect citizens from abuses of the justice system also limit the ability of law enforcement to deal with OC. For example, efforts to gather evidence are circumscribed by various legal protections of privacy—such as the necessity for search warrants and the restrictions on electronic eavesdropping, which will be discussed at length in chapter 16. Law-enforcement personnel who penetrate into criminal organizations must beware, not only of the criminals they are pursuing, but of violating laws against entrapment.

If legally admissible evidence is found, indictments must be obtained through a grand jury. When there are indictments, a case must go to trial— a highly regulated process. Defendants, for example, may refuse to testify by invoking Fifth Amendment protections against self-incrimination. Court proceedings are discussed in chapter 17.

Corruption

In this book, corruption is defined as *an illegal act that involves the abuse of a public trust or office for some private benefit.* Lawrence Sherman (1978: xxiii) points out: "Virtually every urban police department in the United States has experienced both organized corruption and a major scandal over that corruption." Furthermore, "the assertion may even be true for just the period since World War II."

American police development was fostered by the British experience, particularly the reforms of Sir Robert Peel in 1829, from whom the "Bobbies" get their name. However, the American experience differed from the British. The police in most major urban areas depended on political appointments for their jobs and for promotions. James Richardson (1975: 20) highlights problems in the New York system: "The tensions and antagonisms which required an improved police system for New York made the creation of such a system more difficult." There was disagreement over what laws should be enforced, how they were to be enforced, and who would enforce them. "Those who provided such sought-after but illegal services as gambling, prostitution, and saloons that opened on Sunday wished to limit police activities in these areas. Those who were morally opposed to such services pressed the police to be as energetic as possible in suppressing them."

Herbert Packer (1968: 262) states that the police must be sure of their role—that what they are doing reflects the "common consensus." He suggests: "The way to keep these processes recurring at peak efficiency is to ensure that those who operate them are convinced that what they are doing is right." He argues, "If the criminal sanction is widely used to deal with morally neutral behavior, law-enforcement officials are likely to be at least subconsciously defensive about their work, and the public will find the criminal law a confusing guide to moral, or even acceptable behavior." This point of view is reinforced by a statement from Patrick V. Murphy, former New York City Police Commissioner and president of the Police Foundation (Murphy and Plate 1977: 44): "I am unable to regard gambling as a mortal sin; I also felt, somewhat intuitively, that gambling enforcement is demeaning and quite possibly beneath the dignity of the police. And, as a practical matter, the law against gambling was utterly impossible to enforce, even by the most professional, assiduous police action."

Edwin Schur (1969: 196) points to a serious functional problem involved in enforcing statutes concerning activities most closely associated with organized crime—the absence of a complainant. He argues that the lack of a complainant-victim lies at the heart of the unenforcibility of statutes outlawing so-called victimless crime. (Such crimes as drug violations, gambling, and prostitution obviously have *victims*—but the victim does not usually view himself or herself as such.) The lack of a complainant-victim leads to the need to engage informants, usually persons involved in criminal activity. Law-enforcement personnel dealing with organized crime must often maintain personal contact with criminals, either as undercover operatives or by dealing with informants. This contact is potentially corrupting. It is often only a small step from using drug traffickers as informants to entering into business with them. Edward Epstein (1977: 105) notes, for example, that in 1968 it was discovered "that a number of federal agents in the New York office [of the Bureau of Narcotics] were in the business of selling heroin or protecting drug dealers and that the bureau itself had been a major source of supply and protection in the United States." David Durk (Durk and Silverman 1976: 36) notes:

> By 1969, there were two major marketing operations of heroin in New York City. One operated out of Pleasant Avenue [an Italian neighborhood in Harlem]; the other operated out of the fourth floor of the First Precinct station house in lower Manhattan—the headquarters of the Special Investigations Unit of the police department's Narcotics Division.

Durk (Durk and Silverman 1976: 33) states that the police acted as enforcers for the larger drug dealers by arresting their competition. They also kept dealers in line: a narcotics dealer "who wasn't 'cooperating' might be locked in a car trunk, and left there for several hours. When a dealer 'really had to be taught a lesson,' a snake was put in the car trunk with him." (The widely acclaimed motion picture *Prince of the City* avoids these ugly details in its treatment of the Special Investigations Unit.)

The potentially corrupting influence when dealing with OC is often given as a reason why J. Edgar Hoover steered the FBI away from OC investigations. Sanford Unger (1975: 391) states that

> the Director was simply clever enough to steer clear of the toughest problems— the ones less likely to produce prompt and stunning results, that might test conflicts of loyalty among agents, or that would require them to be exposed to the seamier side of life (and, as with many policemen, tempt them into corruption).

Fred J. Cook (1979) notes that the first FBI agent ever convicted of a felony accepted a $10,000 bribe from a syndicate bookmaker. In 1985, an FBI agent pleaded guilty to receiving $850,000 from cocaine traffickers he was assigned to investigate. The agent had been teamed up with a drug informant in an undercover operation designed to break up a ring which distributed cocaine from Miami to other parts of the country.

James Q. Wilson offers a conceptual framework for explaining corruption in drug-law enforcement. Narcotic officers/agents "know with reasonable confidence that one or more persons has committed or is about to commit a crime; their task is to observe its commission, usually by creating under controlled conditions a suitable opportunity" (1978: 57). Wilson refers to such agents as *instigators* (not meant in a derogatory sense) as opposed to conventional investigators who act after being informed of a crime, i.e., after receiving a complaint, usually from the victim. He points out that investigators and instigators "are exposed to opportunities for corruption, but the latter far more than the former":

> The detective [investigator], were he to accept money or favors to act other than as his duty required, would have to conceal or alter information about a crime already known to his organization. The instigator can easily agree to overlook offenses known to him but to no one else or to participate in illegal transactions (buying and selling drugs) for his own rather than the organization's advantage.

In addition to the problem of being proactive, drug-law enforcement is susceptible to corruption because of the enormous profits generated at the importation and wholesale levels. An investigation into the Sonal Organization, a travel and money-exchange agency with branches in Miami and Colombia, provides some indication of these profits. Sonal was used by Colombian drug dealers to "launder" their money (Permanent Subcommittee on Investigations, *Crime and Secrecy,* 1983: 62–65):

> . . . since the inception of the Sonal account, the deposits had been almost entirely cash deposits made daily, in amounts ranging from $500,000 to $2 million. These dollars were primarily in denominations of $5's, $10's, and $20's, packed in paper bags, cardboard boxes and suitcases.
> . . . On August 19–20, 1981, $7,012,799 in cash was delivered to the Sonal office by various Latin couriers who did not remain to count their delivery or accept any type of receipt. The cash was delivered without any security, in large brown cardboard boxes, grocery bags, and a Samsonite travel bag.
> . . . It shows that during the period of January through August, an 8-month period . . . [Sonal] received in Miami, $242,238,739 as a result of . . . transactions in Colombia with 29 Latin individuals. None of these individuals were found to reside or engage in legitimate business in the United States.

The problem of corruption with respect to drug trafficking has affected sheriffs in a number of southern states. During 1982–84, four sheriffs in rural eastern Tennessee were convicted of crimes ranging from sale of drugs to taking bribes from drug importers. Sheriffs in Mississippi, Georgia, and Texas have been indicted or convicted of federal drug-related charges (Schmidt 1984).

The Task Force on Organized Crime stated in 1967: "All available data indicate that organized crime flourishes only where it has corrupted local officials" (1967: 6). Anthony Simpson (1977: 88) refers to the task force statement and notes: "This point should be well-taken as support for it is generated throughout the literature." However, there is a difficulty with viewing the problem as simply *organized crime corrupts officials.* In part 3 we noted that the line between organized crime and corrupt officials is often unclear, at times nonexistent. Indeed, at times, *it was public officials who were organized crime;* they ran the organized criminal activities, gambling, and prostitution. In other instances—for example the case of Harry Gross—it was actually the police who organized handbooks into a syndicate. Gross was a smalltime handbook—a bookmaker with no fixed business location—in Brooklyn when he met James E. Reardon, a New York City plainclothes police officer. Reardon not only protected the Gross operation but acted as "muscle" by physically threatening or arresting competitors: "Rival bookies were given the choice of going out of business or joining the Gross combine" (Mockridge and Prall 1954: 33–34). Reardon was kicked out of plainclothes and put back in uniform because of his activities; so he quit the force to work with Gross. However, Gross began to gamble himself, and he lost heavily to a syndicate headed by Frank Erikson (a partner of Frank Costello). In fear for his safety, Gross fled to California, leaving the business to Reardon. Reardon kept the business together; he went to other police officers who were able to secure more than $100,000 through Joseph Doto (better known by his nickname "Joe Adonis"[1]), enabling Gross to return from California and head up the police-organized syndicate. By the time he was arrested on September 15, 1950, Gross and his syndicate were paying about $1 million annually for police protection.

---

[1] Born Giuseppe Antonio Doto near Naples in 1903, Joe Adonis worked for Frankie Yale and was part of the organization headed by Joe Masseria. When Yale was killed in 1928, Adonis took over his operations. His Brooklyn restaurant, Joe's Italian Kitchen, was a rendezvous spot for major politicians, and Adonis became a conduit between Brooklyn politics and OC, much as his close friend Frank Costello had done in Manhattan. Adonis was the proprietor of a Ford auto dealership and the owner of a large cigarette-vending-machine company whose products were installed in bars, restaurants, and hotels throughout Brooklyn. He was the major shareholder of a firm that conveyed Ford automobiles assembled at a plant in New Jersey to nine states and the District of Columbia. He was able to avoid serious encounters with the law until 1951, when he pled no contest to a charge of conspiracy to violate gambling laws in New Jersey and received a sentence of two to three years. In 1953, Adonis told a New Jersey grand jury that he was born in Passaic, New Jersey. He was convicted of perjury, and on January 3, 1956, was deported to Italy.

chapter 16

Federal Statutes
and Their Enforcement

Used by permission of AP/Wide World Photos

The "business of organized crime" involves the violation of numerous laws. Many of these statutes are routinely enforced by municipal police departments—for example, laws against gambling, prostitution, assault, and murder. While local agencies may be successful in arresting and prosecuting lower-level criminals, the penetration of an OC unit requires resources that in most cases are beyond the ability of local agencies.

Amendment X of the Constitution is known as the "reserve clause," and it states: "The powers not delegated to the United States by the Constitution, nor prohibited by it to the States, are reserved to the States respectively, or to the people." In order to provide federal jurisdiction for dealing with OC, special statutes have been enacted, while other laws have been applied in unique ways.

Chief among the federal statutes used to combat OC are the Internal Revenue Code; the Controlled Substances Act; the Hobbs Act; the Racketeer Influenced and Corrupt Organizations (RICO) statute; the Consumer Credit Protection Act; and statutes against conspiracy. Which statute(s) an enforcement agency chooses to invoke depends on what is discovered in the course of an investigation. Federal agents will gather evidence on a suspected OC unit and then the prosecutor (U.S. attorney) will decide to invoke RICO, the tax laws, conspiracy statutes, or one or more other federal statutes, depending on the nature of the evidence.

The Internal Revenue Code

In 1927 the United States Supreme Court decided the case of *United States v. Sullivan*, 274 U.S. 259, which denied the claim of self-incrimination as an excuse for failure to file income tax on illegally gained earnings. This decision enabled the federal government to successfully prosecute Al Capone and members of his organization.

As taxpayers, management-level organized-crime figures can be prosecuted for several acts:

1. For failing to make required returns or maintain required business records.
2. For filing a false return or making a false statement about taxes.
3. For willful failure to pay federal income tax or concealment of assets with intent to defraud.
4. For assisting others to evade income taxes.

Earl Johnson points out, "Acts which do not comprise a violation or attempt to violate any of these substantive sections may be punishable as part of a conspiracy 'to impair, defeat, and obstruct the functions of the Commissioner of Internal Revenue' by concealing matters relevant to collection of federal taxes" (1963: 17). An employer can be prosecuted for not complying with social security withholding requirements relative to employees. Thus, the manager of an illegal enterprise, a gambling operation for example, can be prosecuted for such evasions.

> In the Internal Revenue Service there are a national office, seven regional offices, and fifty-eight district offices. The Intelligence Division [now called Criminal Investigation Division] has approximately 2,600 Special Agents who investigate and report criminal violations of the Internal Revenue Code to the Department of Justice.
>
> Additional income for criminal tax purposes is established by both direct and indirect methods. The direct method consists of the identification of specific items of unreported taxable receipts, overstated costs and expenses (such as personal expenses charged to business, diversion of corporate income to office-stockholders, allocation of income or expense to incorrect year in order to lower tax, etc.), and improper claims for credit or exemption. The advantage of using this method is that the proof involved is easier for jurors and others to understand [Committee on the Office of Attorney General 1974: 49-50].

Organized-crime figures have devised methods for successful evasion of taxes—dealing in cash, keeping minimal records, setting up fronts. This is countered by the indirect method known as the *net worth theory:* "The government establishes a taxpayer's net worth at the commencement of the taxing period [requires substantial accuracy], deducts that from his or her net worth at the end of the period, and proves that the net gain in net worth exceeds the income reported by the taxpayer" (Johnson 1963: 17-18).

In effect, the Internal Revenue Service reconstructs the total expenditures by examining the standard of living and comparing it with reported income (see table 16.1). The government can then maintain that the taxpayer did not report her or his entire income; the government does not have to show a probable source of the excess unreported gain in net worth. Earl Johnson points out that the Capone case taught many criminals a lesson: management-level members of organized crime have scrupulously reported their income—at least the part of it that they spend (1963: 18).

The Internal Revenue Service explains its various investigative methods as follows (Committee on the Office of Attorney General 1974):

Table 16.1
Net Worth Statement, John and Mary Roe, Dayton, Ohio

Assets	12–31–65	12–31–66	12–31–67
1. Cash—First National Bank	$ 4,500.00	$ 150.00	$ 2,500.00
2. Cash on hand	25.00	25.00	25.00
3. Inventory, Liquor Store	4,800.00	13,000.00	29,000.00
4. U.S. Savings Bonds	–0–	3,750.00	–0–
5. Note Receivable, Frank Roe	–0–	–0–	300.00
6. Note Receivable, Roger Jones	–0–	–0–	16,000.00
7. Accounts Receivable, Doc's Market	–0–	1,600.00	–0–
8. Lot on Dayton Road	1,000.00	1,000.00	1,000.00
9. Ohio Tourist Camp	12,000.00	12,000.00	12,000.00
10. Residence, 1100 Vine Street	2,800.00	2,800.00	–0–
11. 30 Acre Farm, East Dayton	–0–	7,400.00	7,400.00
12. 150 Acre Farm, North Dayton	–0–	–0–	7,000.00
13. Equipment—Liquor Store	800.00	800.00	800.00
14. Buick Automobile	2,800.00	2,800.00	2,800.00
15. Farm Truck	–0–	–0–	800.00
16. Farm Equipment	–0–	1,250.00	2,250.00
17. Livestock on Farm	–0–	900.00	1,300.00
Total Assets	$28,725.00	$47,475.00	$83,175.00
Liabilities			
18. First Federal Savings & Loan Assn.	$ 2,400.00	$ 1,800.00	$ –0–
19. First National Bank	2,900.00	2,700.00	–0–
20. Depreciation Reserve	2,500.00	3,200.00	4,300.00
Total Liabilities	$ 7,800.00	$ 7,700.00	$ 4,300.00
NET WORTH	$20,925.00	$39,775.00	$78,875.00
Less: Net Worth of Prior Year		20,925.00	39,775.00
Increase in Net Worth		$18,850.00	$39,100.00
Adjustments			
Add:			
21. Living Expenses		$ 2,500.00	$ 2,500.00
22. Life Insurance Premium		300.00	500.00
23. Federal Income Taxes Paid		750.00	900.00
Less:			
24. Long-Term Capital Gain on Sale of Residence (50%)		–0–	(500.00)
25. Inheritance		–0–	(10,000.00)
Adjusted Gross Income		$22,400.00	$32,500.00
Less: Standard Deduction		1,000.00	1,000.00
Balance		$21,400.00	$31,500.00
Less: Exemptions (4)		2,400.00	2,400.00
Taxable Income		$19,000.00	$29,100.00
Less: Taxable Income Reported		6,100.00	6,400.00
Taxable Income Not Reported		$12,900.00	$22,700.00

SOURCE: Internal Revenue Service Agent's Manual.

The net worth method is an indirect method of computing income during a year by determining net worth increases and other outlays. Any change in net worth is adjusted to allow for non-taxable receipts and for reported income—the balance being unreported income. The formula here is: assets minus liabilities equals net worth; ending net worth minus beginning net worth equals net worth increase; net worth increase plus other expenditures plus (or minus) tax adjustments equals adjusted gross income; adjusted gross income minus deductions and exemptions equals corrected taxable income; and corrected taxable income minus reported taxable income equals additional taxable income.

Another indirect method is the expenditures method—related to net worth, but expressed differently. Funds are measured by their flow during the year, rather than by observing changes in net worth from the beginning to the end of the year. The formula here is: non-deductible applications of funds minus nontaxable sources equals adjusted gross income; from there, the formula is the same as for the net worth method. Note that the starting point for the beginning of the first year must be established in order to eliminate reasonable doubt that subsequent expenditures did not come from conversion of existing assets.

Another indirect method is the bank deposits method. This one is unlike the net worth and expenditures methods, which measure income at the point of its outflow—here, income is measured at the time of receipt. In this method, the three immediate dispositions of receipts for the year are determined: how much was deposited into banks; how much was spent without going through banks (cash expenditures); and how much was stored in other places (increases in cash on hand). The formula is: total deposits, plus cash expenditures, minus nonincome items, equals gross receipts.

The stages in an IRS investigation are as follows: Information is received by the Intelligence Division relating to an allegation of violation. Each information item is evaluated by the Chief of the Intelligence Division of the district involved, or by his designated representative, to determine whether it indicates a criminal violation. If criminal potential is apparent, the allegation may be assigned to a special agent for an investigation.

Steps taken by the special agent in a tax evasion case are outlined below. Whether or not any of the following steps are taken, and the order in which they occur in an investigation, vary according to the facts of the particular case involved. The special agent scrutinizes the tax returns for the years under investigation. A certificate of assessments and payments for the years involved in the investigation, and for prior years, if pertinent, is obtained. If returns were prepared by someone other than the principal, the person who prepared the return is interviewed concerning the circumstances surrounding the preparation of the returns. The books and records are reconciled with the returns, and differences are noted. Documents (invoices, canceled checks, receipted bills, etc.) supporting amounts shown on records and returns are examined, if available. The principal is questioned regarding his assets, liabilities, and personal expenditures. This information is of the utmost importance in a case where there are no books and records or where the records are incomplete or inadequate.

Where a corporation is involved, the agents may also analyze the officers' personal accounts to determine the source and disposition of funds credited or charged thereto. If a partnership is involved, the agents will examine the capital accounts and the personal drawing accounts of the partners to determine the source and disposition of funds. For the same purpose, the personal and proprietorship accounts of a sole proprietorship are also examined.

If the taxpayer has not maintained adequate books and records, the agents may list and analyze all the canceled checks and classify them into business expenses, capital expenditures, personal items, and nondeductible expenditures. The agents may examine records of deposits to bank accounts.

During the course of the investigation information may be obtained from: banks; customers of the principal; other persons who have had business transactions with the principal; records of the principal; public records; and newspapers, etc., regarding sources of the principal's income. The agents may interview, and obtain records from, persons who have had, or have knowledge of, transactions with the principal to determine what payments the principal received and the purposes thereof. Transactions involving purchases or sales of property may be examined. Information relative to those matters may be obtained from the purchaser or seller, from real estate agencies, and from public records. Information regarding the principal's personal and financial history is obtained from the principal, from those who know him, and from documents. This includes determining whether or not the principal has a record of prior violation of federal, state, or local laws.

If the case is based on a net worth computation, evidence must be obtained to support the value of each item appearing in the net worth statement. The principal will be questioned regarding whether all assets and liabilities are included, especially in the beginning and ending computations of net worth. He also may be questioned about inheritances and gifts, both during the period under investigation and in prior years. Further questions will be asked about the taxpayer's assets and liabilities at the beginning and end of each year which is included in the investigation and of any prior year pertinent to the case. The principal will be given an opportunity to explain the alleged discrepancies, and his explanations will be verified to whatever extent is possible. In the examination of records and during interviews with witnesses, the special agent is constantly alert for any facts or circumstances that cast light on the principal's intent, that is, any conduct the likely effect of which would be to mislead or to conceal.

Where a violation involves a failure to file a return, the agent obtains from the District Director or Service Center a certificate stating that a search of the files failed to disclose a return in the name of the principal. The special agent also will question the principal concerning whether or not he filed a return and the reasons for his failure. If the principal alleges that he has filed a return, evidence is obtained to prove or disprove his statement. In other respects the investigation of a failure to file a return proceeds in much the same manner as that of a case involving a willful attempt to evade or defeat income tax.

In many instances, other methods of determining income may be used to corroborate the method on which the case is primarily based. For example, in a case based on proof of specific items of omitted income, a net-worth computation may be used as corroborative proof; to show that the additional income was used to increase the financial position of the principal rather than to pay deductible expenses which were not claimed on the return but which the principal now alleges were incurred. At the conclusion of the investigation, the special agent writes a report setting forth the history of the principal, the evidence of additional income and willful intent, the principal's explanation and defense, and any evidence obtained to prove or disprove the defense. The special agent also sets forth in the report conclusions regarding specific portions of evidence and concerning the case as a whole, together with recommendations regarding criminal prosecution and the assertion of the appropriate civil penalties.

The district group manager is responsible for the initial technical review of all prosecution case reports prepared by special agents under his supervision. The purpose of the review is to determine whether the special agent's report is complete, logically presented, clear, concise, accurate, and that statements made in the report are supported by the facts and evidence. The Chief, or his designated representative, also reviews all prosecution case reports. The Chief must forward to the Regional Counsel for review all cases in which a recommendation for prosecution has been made by the special agent and approved by the chief, except for certain type cases which may be sent directly to the United States Attorney. If the chief does not concur in the recommendation of the special agent that a completed investigation of the special agent be forwarded for prosecution or closed as a non-prosecution case, he will request a written opinion and recommendation from the Assistant Regional Commissioner (intelligence) (ARC-I). After receipt of the opinion and recommendations from the ARC-I, the Chief, as the representative of the District Director, will make the final decision as to the disposition of the case.

In regional level case processing, the ARC-I is responsible for providing technical assistance to districts within the region. The Chief will notify the ARC-I in writing when he desires technical assistance. In rendering technical assistance, the ARC-I, through his representative, will assure objectivity and regionwide uniformity in the application of Service policies. The regional representative will examine evidentiary material to the extent necessary to make an evaluation of prosecution potential. He may suggest alternative or additional investigative steps and make recommendations concerning the special agent's final report.

The regional counsel performs a legal review of the case. If the Regional Counsel concurs in the recommendation for prosecution, he forwards the case to the Department of Justice. If the Regional Counsel does not concur with the recommendations for prosecution in a case, he will confer with the Chief, intelligence, in an effort to resolve the difference of opinion.

If the Department of Justice approves the recommendation for prosecution, the case is forwarded by the Department to the United States Attorney for the district in which the case is to be tried. If the Department of Justice does not approve the recommendation for prosecution, the case is returned to the Internal Revenue Service for disposition as a civil case. Procedure by the U.S. Attorney in criminal tax cases is the same as that for any other criminal case, namely, presentation to a grand jury or the filing of a criminal information (statement of charges). Appeals may be taken to the Circuit Courts of Appeals and to the Supreme Court.

Informants furnish information regarding alleged violations for a variety of reasons. Treasury Decision 6421, adopted October 23, 1959, provides for the payment of rewards for information relating to violations of the internal revenue laws. The amount of the reward depends upon the value of the information furnished in relation to the facts developed by the investigation. Informant's communications are forwarded to the Intelligence Division for evaluation and appropriate action. Information that indicates a violation of the internal revenue laws, discovered by officers of other federal, state, and local law enforcement agencies during their investigations, is forwarded to the Intelligence Division for evaluation and appropriate action.

The sections of the Code under which taxpayers are most frequently prosecuted in connection with violations of income-tax laws are Section 7203 of Title 26, U.S.C., relating to the willful failure to file, and Section 7201 of Title 26, U.S.C., relating to willful attempts to evade or defeat any taxes. Section 7201 of the Internal Revenue Code of 1954 provides as follows: "Any person who willfully attempts in any manner to evade or defeat any tax imposed by this title or the payment thereof shall, in addition to other penalties provided by law, be guilty of a felony and upon conviction thereof, shall be fined not more than $10,000, or imprisoned not more than 5 years, or both, together with the cost of prose-cution."

It is the question of what is the willful attempt in any manner to evade taxes that is the primary concern in determining whether or not there is proof of fraud. Willfulness is one of the crucial elements of the offense of attempted evasion and involves a specific intent, "the tax evasion motive." The attempt to defraud the government must be made intentionally. The phrase "willfully attempt in any manner" as provided in this section of the code has been the subject of many court decisions. These decisions have established certain acts and circumstances as indicia of fraud. The most frequently quoted Supreme Court decision on the subject of willful attempts to evade or defeat is that of *Spies* v. *U.S.*, in which the Court states as follows:

> Congress did not define or limit the methods by which a willful attempt to defeat and evade might be accomplished, and perhaps did not define lest its effort to do so result in some unexpected limitation. Nor would we by definition constrict the scope of the Congressional provision that it may be accomplished in any manner. By the way of illustration and not by way of limitation, we would think affirmative willful attempt may be inferred from conduct such as keeping a double set of books, making false entries or alterations, or false invoices or documents, destruction of books or records, concealment of assets or covering up sources of income, handling of one's affairs to avoid making the records usual in transactions of the kind, and any conduct, the likely effect of which would be to mislead or conceal. If the tax-evasion motive plays any part in such conduct, the offense may be made out even though the conduct may also serve other purposes such as concealment of other crime.

This decision has briefly enumerated some of the taxpayer's actions which in the court's opinion would be indicative of fraud.

It is also apparent from this quotation that neither Congress nor the Supreme Court has attempted to in any way limit the circumstances of conduct of the taxpayer which may be interpreted as indicative of an attempt to evade tax.

It is important to distinguish between tax evasion and tax avoidance. Tax avoidance, as distinguished from tax evasion, implies that the taxpayer has only availed himself of all legal means of reducing his tax liability without the intent to evade or without the practice of intentional deception.

As a consequence of the Tax Reform Act of 1976, the Internal Revenue Service has been severely restricted with respect to the information that it can disclose even to law enforcement agencies that have a bona fide need to know. The IRS cannot even disclose if the person actually filed an income tax return as required by law. Information from IRS can only be secured with a federal court order.

Under federal statutes, all persons operating a gambling business must purchase an occupational tax stamp. This Special Income Wagering Tax Stamp costs $500, and the business is liable for an excise tax of 2 percent on the gross income.

Criminal and civil sanctions available to the IRS are summarized in table 16.2.

Table 16.2
Internal Revenue Service Sanctions

I. Criminal sanctions

A. Title 26 United States Code

Code Section	Maximum Sentences/Fines
7201—Evasion	5 years/$10,000
7203—Failure to file	1 year/$10,000
7206(1)—Signing a false return	3 years/$5,000
7206(2)—Preparation of false return	3 years/$5,000
7207—False returns altered documents	1 year/$1,000

B. Title 18 United States Code

Code Section	Maximum Sentences/Fines
287—False claims	5 years/$10,000
1001—False statements	5 years/$10,000
1621—Perjury	5 years/$2,000
2—Aiding and abetting	Same as substantive violation
371—Conspiracy	5 years/$10,000

II. Civil sanctions
  A. 50% fraud penalty (e.g., if taxpayer's liability is determined to be $100,000 he or she would owe $150,000).

  B. Seizure of real property (land, buildings) and personal property (auto, boat, bank accounts, cash, etc.).

  C. Jeopardy or termination assessments used in ongoing examination or Criminal Investigation Division investigations, when at least one of the following conditions is present:

    1. Taxpayer is, or appears to be, designing to quickly depart from the United States or to conceal himself/herself.

    2. The taxpayer is, or appears to be designing to quickly place his/her/its property beyond the reach of the government either by removing it from the United States, or by concealing it, or by transferring it to other persons, or by dissipating it.

    3. Taxpayer's financial solvency is or appears to be imperiled. (This does not include cases where the taxpayer becomes insolvent of virtue of the accrual of the proposed assessment of tax and penalty, if any.)

SOURCE: Internal Revenue Service, *Special Agent's Manual.*

The Controlled Substances Act

The legal foundation for the federal response to dealing with the illicit use of controlled substances is Title II of the Comprehensive Drug Abuse Prevention and Control Act of 1970 (Public Law 91-513), usually referred to as the Controlled Substances Act (CSA). Under the provisions of the CSA there is a set of criteria for placing a substance in one of five schedules, shown in table 16.3. Penalties for trafficking in the five classes of drugs are shown in fig. 16.1. For simple possession of a controlled substances, first offenders may receive up to one year's imprisonment and/or a $5,000 fine; these penalties double for second offenses. Persons under twenty-one may receive probation. Drugs are classified by schedule in fig. 16.2.

There are three basic strategies in drug-law enforcement: interdiction, buy and bust, and conspiracy.

Table 16.3
Substances of Abuse

Schedule I

A. The drug or other substance has a high potential for abuse.
B. The drug or other substance has no currently accepted medical use in treatment in the United States.

C. There is a lack of accepted safety for use of the drug or other substance under medical supervision.

Schedule II

A. The drug or other substance has a high potential for abuse.
B. The drug or other substance has a currently accepted medical use in treatment in the United States or a currently accepted medical use with severe restrictions.
C. Abuse of the drug or other substances may lead to severe psychological or physical dependence.

Schedule III

A. The drug or other substance has a potential for abuse less than the drugs or other substances in Schedules I and II.
B. The drug or other substance has a currently accepted medical use in treatment in the United States.
C. Abuse of the drug or other substance may lead to moderate or low physical dependence or high psychological dependence.

Schedule IV

A. The drug or other substance has a low potential for abuse relative to the drugs or other substances in Schedule III.
B. The drug or other substance has a currently accepted medical use in treatment in the United States.
C. Abuse of the drug or other substance may lead to limited physical dependence or psychological dependence relative to the drugs or other substances in Schedule III.

Schedule V

A. The drug or other substance has a low potential for abuse relative to the drugs or other substances in Schedule IV.
B. The drug or other substance has a currently accepted medical use in treatment in the United States.
C. Abuse of the drug or other substance may lead to limited physical dependence or psychological dependence relative to the drugs or other substances in Schedule IV.

SOURCE: Drug Enforcement Administration.

Figure 16.1
Federal Penalties for Trafficking in Controlled Substances

CSA Schedule	Type of Drug	First Offense			Second Offense		
		Max. Imprison.	Max. Fine	Min. Parole	Max. Imprison.	Max. Fine	Min. Parole
I	Narcotic	15 yrs.	25 k	3 yrs.	30 yrs.	50 k	6 yrs.
	Nonnarcotic	5 yrs.	15 k	2 yrs.	10 yrs.	30 k	4 yrs.
II	Narcotic	15 yrs.	25 k	3 yrs.	30 yrs.	50 k	6 yrs.
	Nonnarcotic	5 yrs.	15 k	2 yrs.	10 yrs.	30 k	4 yrs.
III	Narcotic	5 yrs.	15 k	2 yrs.	10 yrs.	30 k	4 yrs.
	Nonnarcotic	5 yrs.	15 k	2 yrs.	10 yrs.	30 k	4 yrs.
IV	Narcotic	3 yrs.	10 k	1 yr.	6 yrs.	20 k	2 yrs.
	Nonnarcotic	3 yrs.	10 k	1 yr.	6 yrs.	20 k	2 yrs.
V	Narcotic	1 yr.	5 k	0	2 yrs.	10 k	0
	Nonnarcotic	1 yr.	5 k	0	2 yrs.	10 k	0

For simple possession of any controlled substance: First offenders may receive up to one year, $5,000 fine, or both, and if under 21 may receive up to one-year probation and thereafter motion court for expungement of all records; second offenders may receive up to 2 years, $10,000 fine, or both.

SOURCE: U.S. Drug Enforcement Administration.

Interdiction

The government tries to intercept drugs being smuggled into the United States by private aircraft, vessels at sea, motor vehicles, mail, or on the person or in the luggage of travelers. Dealing with smuggling by private aircraft is the responsibility of the Customs Service assisted by the Department of Defense. The Coast Guard is responsible for interdicting drugs smuggled by sea, and it receives some assistance from the Navy. Smuggling at airports and other ports of entry is the responsibility of Customs, while the use of the mails is the responsibility of Postal Inspectors. Interdiction results in the seizure of only a small fraction of the drugs smuggled into the country. In addition, the person or persons arrested are usually "mules," unimportant couriers who are easily replaced without disrupting the drug organization.

Buy and Bust

Drugs that have already been smuggled into the country or are grown or manufactured domestically are the responsibility of the Drug Enforcement Administration (DEA). The FBI has been given extended jurisdiction and can now work drug cases that their agents uncover. While DEA agents often patrol airports supplementing Customs, their basic tactic involves a "controlled buy," the purchase of illegal drugs by undercover agents. This usually involves an informant who introduces the undercover agent to the drug seller. The informant, James Q. Wilson notes, is "indispensible in virtually all DEA cases" (1978: 61). Typically, the agent buys a small amount and then attempts to move further up the organizational ladder by increasing the amount of the purchases. "The agent prefers to defer an arrest until he can seize a large amount of drugs or can implicate higher-ups in the distribution system or both" (Wilson 1978: 43).

The use of informants is problematic. The most useful informants ("snitches") are those involved in criminal activity. Their cooperation is usually an attempt to "work off a beef"—avoid prosecution or a lengthy prison term. Cooperation may also earn the snitch a "license" to practice his or her "trade" without fear of arrest and prosecution. In 1977 the FBI agreed to drop an investigation into several robberies committed by an ex-convict, Michael Orlando, in return for the suspect's cooperation. Orlando became a paid informant for which he received $53,167 over a three-year period. He provided the FBI with information about hijacking and narcotic conspiracies involving organized crime and implicated the U.S. Secretary of Labor, Raymond J. Donovan, in a conspiracy to defraud the government. His information enabled the FBI to secure a court order for an electronic surveillance that lasted six months. While working for the bureau, Orlando committed at least one murder and numerous other crimes—which were apparently unknown to the FBI (Raab, 1985).

Figure 16.2
Controlled Substances, Classified by Type and by Federal
Schedule Number

	Drugs	Schedule	Trade or Other Names
NARCOTICS	Opium	II, III, V	Dover's Powder, Paregoric, Parepectolin
	Morphine	II, III	Morphine, Pectoral Syrup
	Codeine	II, III, V	Codeine, Empirin Compound with Codeine, Robitussin A-C
	Heroin	I	Diacetylmorphine, Horse, Smack
	Hydromorphone		Dilaudid
	Meperidine (Pethidine)	II	Demerol, Pethadol
	Methadone		Dolophine, Methadone, Methadose
	Other Narcotics	I, II, III, IV, V	LAAM, Leritine, Levo-Dromoran, Percodan, Tussionex, Fentanyl, Darvon*, Talwin*, Lomotil
DEPRESSANTS	Chloral Hydrate	IV	Noctec, Somnos
	Barbiturates	II, III, IV	Amobarbital, Phenobarbital, Butisol, Phenoxbarbital, Secobarbital, Tuinal
	Glutethimide	III	Doriden
	Methaqualone	II	Optimil, Parest, Quaalude, Somnafac, Sopor
	Benzodiazepines	IV	Ativan, Azene, Clonopin, Dalmane, Diazepam, Librium, Serax, Tranxene, Valium, Verstran
	Other Depressants	III, IV	Equanil, Miltown, Noludar Placidyl, Valmid

SOURCE: U.S. Drug Enforcement Administration.

	Drugs	Schedule	Trade or Other Names
STIMULANTS	Cocaine†	II	Coke, Flake, Snow
	Amphetamines	II, III	Biphetamine, Delcobese, Desoxyn, Dexedrine, Mediatric
	Phenmetrazine	II	Preludin
	Methylphenidate		Ritalin
	Other Stimulants	III, IV	Adipex, Bacarate, Cylert, Di-drex, Ionamin, Plegine, Pre-Sate, Sanorex, Tenuate, Tepanil, Voranil
HALLUCINOGENS	LSD		Acid, Microdot
	Mescaline and Peyote	I	Mesc. Buttons, Cactus
	Amphetamine Variants		2, 5-DMA, PMA, STP, MDA, MMDA, TMA, DOM, DOB
	Phencyclidine	II	PCP, Angel Dust, Hog
	Phencyclidine Analogs	I	PCE, PCPy, TCP
	Other Hallucinogens		Bufotenine, Ibogaine, DMT, DET, Psilocybin, Psilocyn
CANNABIS	Marihuana	I	Pot, Acapulco Gold, Grass, Reefer, Sinsemilla, Thai Sticks
	Tetrahydrocannabinol		THC
	Hashish		Hash
	Hashish Oil		Hash Oil

Conspiracy

An agreement by two or more persons to violate the law, plus an overt act in furtherance of the agreement, is a crime—conspiracy. Thus, persons who arrange for the importation and distribution of heroin or cocaine, even though they have never had physical possession of either substance, can be prosecuted for conspiracy to violate the Controlled Substances Act. We will review the use of conspiracy statutes in greater depth later in this chapter.

The Hobbs Act

The earliest federal statutes designed to deal with "racketeering" are collectively known as the *Hobbs Act* (18 U.S.C. Sections 1951-55). Since their enactment in 1946 they have been amended several times. The Hobbs Act makes it a federal crime to engage in behavior that interferes with interstate commerce:

> Whosoever in any way or degree obstructs, delays, or affects commerce or the movement of any articles or commodity in commerce, by robbery or extortion or attempts or conspires so to do, or commits or threatens physical violence to any person or property in furtherance of a plan or purpose to do anything in violation of this section shall be fined not more than $10,000 or imprisoned not more than twenty years, or both.

The statute has been broadly interpreted so as to permit the successful prosecution of more than sixty Chicago police officers for extorting payoffs from the owners of saloons. The six-year investigation (1970-76) by the U.S. Department of Justice was based on the Hobbs Act (Beigel and Beigel 1977: 7):

> It made extortion that in any way affected interstate commerce a federal crime. . . . Attorneys reasoned that because taverns sold beer and liquor, much of which was either delivered from or manufactured in states other than Illinois, extortion of a tavern owner would be a violation of the Hobbs Act.

The Hobbs Act also prohibits foreign or interstate travel or the use of interstate facilities—e.g., mail or telephone—to advance illegal activities such as gambling, drug trafficking, extortion, and bribery. Section 1954 defines as criminal a union official who misuses an employee benefit plan: An official who

> receives or agrees to receive or solicits any fee, kickback, commission, gift, loan, money, or thing of value because of or with intent to be influenced with respect to, any of the actions, decisions, or other duties relating to any question or matter concerning such plan or any person who directly or indirectly gives or offers, or promises to give or offer, any fee, kickback, commission, gift, loan, money, or thing of value prohibited by this section, shall be fined not more than $10,000 or imprisoned not more than three years, or both. . . .

RICO

The Racketeer Influenced and Corrupt Organizations statute (18 U.S.C. Sections 1961-68), usually referred to as RICO, is Title IX of the Organized Crime Control Act of 1970, (Public Law No. 91-452, 84 Stat. 941). RICO defines "racketeering" in an extremely broad manner, and it includes many offenses that do not ordinarily violate any federal statute; "any act or threat involving murder, kidnapping, gambling, arson, robbery, bribery, extortion, or dealing in narcotic or other dangerous drugs, which is chargeable under State law and punishable by imprisonment for more than one year. . . ." In addition here are a "laundry list" of federal offenses that are defined as "racketeering":

- Hobbs Act violations.
- Bribery.
- Sports bribery.
- Counterfeiting.
- Embezzlement from union funds.
- Loansharking.
- Mail fraud.
- Wire fraud.
- Obstruction of (state or federal) justice.
- Contraband cigarettes.
- White slavery (Mann Act).
- Bankruptcy fraud (scam).
- Drug violations.

In order to be violation of RICO there must be a "pattern of racketeering":

"pattern of racketeering activity" requires at least two acts of racketeering activity, one of which occurred after the effective date of this chapter and the last of which occurred within ten years (excluding any period of imprisonment) after the commission of a prior act of racketeering activity. . . .

The substantive provisions of RICO are contained in Section 1962.

(*a*) It shall be unlawful for any person who has received any income derived, directly or indirectly, from a pattern of racketeering activity or through collection of an unlawful debt . . . to use or invest, directly or indirectly, any part of such income, or the proceeds of such income, in acquisition of any interest in, or the establishment or operation of, any enterprise which is engaged in, or the activities of which affect, interstate or foreign commerce. A purchase of securities on the open market for purposes of investment, and without the intention of controlling or participating in the control of the issuer, or of assisting another to do so, shall not be unlawful under this subsection if the securities of the issuer held by the purchaser, the members of his immediate family, and his or their accomplices in any pattern of racketeering activity or the collection of an unlawful debt after such purchase do not amount in the aggregate to one percent of the outstanding securities of any one class, and do not confer, either in law or in fact, the power to elect one or more directors of the issuer.

(*b*) It shall be unlawful for any person through a pattern of racketeering activity or through collection of an unlawful debt to acquire or maintain directly or indirectly any interest in or control of any enterprise which is engaged in, or the activities of which affect interstate or foreign commerce.

(*c*) It shall be unlawful for any person employed by or associated with any enterprise engaged in, or the activities of which affect interstate or foreign commerce, to conduct or participate, directly or indirectly, in the conduct of such enterprise's affairs through a pattern of racketeering activity or collection of unlawful debt.

(*d*) It shall be unlawful for any person to conspire to violate any of the provisions of subsections (*a*), (*b*), (*c*) of this section.

The criminal penalties for violating RICO are substantial: "Whoever violates any provision of section 1962 of this chapter shall be fined not more than $25,000 or imprisoned not more than twenty years, or both. . . ." In addition are civil sanctions requiring the violator to

. . . forfeit to the United States (1) any interest he has acquired or maintained in violation of Section 1962, and (2) any interest in, security of, claim against, or property or contractual right of any kind affording a source of influence over, any enterprise which he has established, operated, controlled, conducted, or participated in the conduct of, in violation of Section 1962.

(*b*) In any action brought by the United States under this section, the district courts of the United States shall have jurisdiction to enter such restraining orders or prohibitions, or to take such other actions, including, but not limited to, the acceptance of satisfactory performance bonds, in connection with any property or other interest subject to forfeiture under this section, as it shall deem proper.

(*c*) Upon conviction of a person under this section, the court shall authorize the Attorney General to seize all property or other interest declared forfeited under this section upon such terms and conditions as the court shall deem proper. If a property right or other interest is not exercisable or transferable for value by the United States, it shall expire, and shall not revert to the convicted person. All provisions of law, relating to the disposition of property, or the proceeds from the sale thereof, or the remission or mitigation of forfeitures for violation of the customs laws, and the compromise of claims and the award of compensation to informers in respect of such forfeitures shall apply to forfeitures incurred, or alleged to have been incurred, under the provisions of this section, insofar as applicable and not inconsistent with the provisions hereof. Such duties as are imposed upon the collector of customs or any other person with respect to the disposition of property under the customs laws shall be performed under this chapter by the Attorney General. The United States shall dispose of all such property as soon as commercially feasible, making due provision for the rights of innocent persons.

RICO also has provisions by which private citizens can sue for damages: "Any person injured in his business or property by reason of a violation of section 1962 of this chapter may sue therefore in any appropriate United States district court and shall recover threefold damages he sustains and the cost of the suit, including a reasonable attorney's fee." This provision has resulted in some rather outlandish legal actions. For example, when Seka, known to pornography aficionados as the "Platinum Princess," was sued by her agent for breach of contract, her attorney (a former OC prosecutor) responded with a RICO suit. It is doubtful that Congress intended to provide the star of *Lust at First Bite* with a vehicle for seeking treble damages from her agent.

Problems with RICO

The Organized Crime Control Act of which RICO is a part, fails to define *organized crime;* likewise, RICO fails to define *racketeer.* The lack of precision coupled with penalties of twenty years on each count has made RICO a tempting tool for federal prosecutors. However, it often gives the appearance of using a cannon to hunt rabbits. When the statute first went into effect, federal agents swept down on gamblers and made hundreds of arrests (1,532 in 1972, for example). However, only half the defendants were convicted, and of these only 20 percent were sentenced to imprisonment. The courts were apparently unwilling to invoke such harsh penalties against minor operators or persons only tangentially involved in organized gambling (Rubinstein and Reuter 1978b). RICO significantly expanded the scope of federal enforcement authority and the discretionary powers of U.S. attorneys. The act has often been used against persons with no ties to organized crime, but who fall under the statute's very broad category of "racketeering." In an editorial, the conservative *Chicago Tribune* had this to say about RICO (January 18, 1985: 26):

> The trouble is that it was drafted so loosely that prosecutors and private lawyers have been able to stretch it all out of shape. It has been used by prosecutors as a pressure device in cases that fit no definition of organized crime but the statute's. And private lawyers have used the law as the basis of civil suits in the ordinary business context. The penalties of the law are so grave that it really ought to be limited to extreme situations.

While the civil sanctions available under RICO can be a valuable law-enforcement tool, they can easily be subjected to abuse. Instead of the rather high level of proof necessary for a determination of guilt in a criminal proceeding, "beyond a reasonable doubt," a civil defendant can be found liable based on a "preponderance of the evidence." In a civil matter the defendant is not entitled to an attorney if he or she cannot afford to hire one, and the right to remain silent (Fifth Amendment) can be negated by a grant of (criminal) immunity, thus forcing the defendant to testify against herself or himself.

The Consumer Credit Protection Act

The 1968 Consumer Credit Protection Act (18 U.S.C. Sections 891-94, 896) was designed to combat loansharking. It provides a definition of a loanshark debt, an extortionate extension of credit:

> any extension of credit with respect to which it is the understanding of the creditor and the debtor at the time it is made that delay in making repayment or failure to make repayment could result in the use of violence or other criminal means to cause harm to the person, reputation, or property of any person.

Ronald Goldstock and Dan T. Coenen (1978: 65) point out that the statute "chose the term 'understanding' in an obvious effort to catch the many loansharks who operate purely on the basis of implication and veiled suggestion." The critical element of the offense is the "understanding" that violence "could result" if repayment is not timely. The statute even provides for an alternative to direct evidence, the prima facie case (not requiring further supportive evidence). To prove such a case, first,

> the state must show the debtor's reasonable belief that the creditor had used, or had a reputation for using, extortionate means to collect or punish nonpayment. Second, if direct evidence of this sort is unavailable (as when the victim is dead or too frightened to testify) and certain other prerequisites are met, the court may allow evidence tending to show the creditor's reputation as to collection practices to show the understanding element [Goldstock and Coenen 1978: 110-11; edited].

The statute also contains a provision intended to make it possible to prosecute upper levels of the OC hierarchy who often are the original source of funding for extortionate credit transactions, made directly by underlings (18 U.S.C. Section 893):

> Whoever willfully advances money or property, whether as a gift, as a loan, as an investment, pursuant to a partnership or profit-sharing agreement, or otherwise, to any person, with the reasonable grounds to believe that it is the intention of that person to use the money or property so advanced directly or indirectly for the purpose of making extortionate extensions of credit, shall be fined not more than $10,000 or an amount not to exceed twice the value of the money or property so advanced, whichever is greater, or shall be imprisoned not more than 20 years, or both.

This coincides with the penalties for the person, loanshark, actually making the extortionate extension of credit (18 U.S.C. Section 894):

Whoever knowingly participates in any way, or conspires to do so, in the use of any extortionate means

(1) to collect or attempt to collect any extension of credit, or
(2) to punish any person for the nonrepayment thereof, shall be fined not more than $10,000 or imprisoned not more than 20 years, or both.

Conspiracy Laws

Back in 1925 the eminent jurist and legal scholar Learned Hand referred to the use of the criminal conspiracy charge as that "darling of the modern prosecutor's nursery" (Campane 1981a). Jerome Campane, a special agent with the FBI's Legal Counsel Division, notes: "Federal prosecutors generally will include a conspiracy charge whenever a case involves multiple defendants" (1981a: 24). He points to three reasons for the popularity of the charge (1981a: 24-25):

[1] The crime of conspiracy permits the intervention of criminal law at a time prior to the commission of a substantive offense. . . .
[2] A conspirator is not allowed to shield himself from prosecution because of a lack of knowledge of the details of the conspiracy, or its intended victims, or the identity of his co-conspirators and their contributions. . . .
[3] Under the co-conspirator exception to the hearsay rule, an act or declaration by one conspirator committed in furtherance of the conspiracy is admissible against each co-conspirator. . . . Under the theory of complicity, a conspirator is liable for the substantive crimes of his co-conspirators and can be punished for both the conspiracy and the completed substantive offense. Even late joiners to an ongoing conspiracy can be liable for prior acts of co-conspirators if the agreement by the latecomer is made with full knowledge of the conspiracy's objective.

Conspiracy can be defined as an agreement by two or more persons to commit an act, which if committed would be in violation of some criminal statute. Thus, it is the agreement itself that becomes the corpus of the crime, and the crime is committed even though the object of the illegal undertaking is not committed. Earl Johnson (1963: 2) notes that the charge of criminal conspiracy is particularly effective against upper-echelon OC figures: "The fundamental essence of a conspiracy obviates the necessity of establishing that the organization leader committed a physical act amounting to a crime or that he even committed an overt act in furtherance of the object of the conspiracy. It is sufficient if he can be shown to have been a party to the conspiratorial agreement." The following incident provides an example of a situation in which only a charge of conspiracy could be used against an important OC figure:

Two young men entered an Italian restaurant and approached the table of an elderly gentleman who was sipping anisette with a large burly individual. After he acknowledged them, the two sat down. They were members of a powerful OC Family; he was the boss. The young men explained that they had discovered a large-scale gambling operation that was not tied to OC—an "outlaw" game. They wanted to "license" the operation and asked for his approval. The Boss gestured with his hands and face, saying nothing, but conveying approval. The two young men, assisted by two other members of the Family, proceeded to assault and threaten the owner of the gambling operation, extorting several thousand dollars from him. They shared the money with their Boss who knew nothing of the details of what had occurred.

Robert W. Johannesen, Jr.,[1] provides a summary of some of the legal aspects of conspiracy:

1. During the development of a conspiracy, statements by one of the co-conspirators in furtherance of the conspiracy [are] binding on the other members of the conspiracy.
2. A co-conspirator *need not* have joined the conspiracy at its *inception*. Upon joining the conspiracy *each* co-conspirator is therefore *bound* by the prior acts and statements of his/her co-conspirators which were made in furtherance of the conspiracy.
3. To be *guilty* of a conspiracy violation, a defendant must be proven to have had *knowledge* of the conspiracy and its essential *objective*. It is not sufficient merely to show that he furthered the conspiracy, even through commission of unlawful acts, or that he associated himself with other members of the conspiracy.
4. Statute of Limitations (five years) does not begin to run until the commission of the *last* overt act.
5. Regarding withdrawal, a defendant who claims to have withdrawn from the conspiracy prior to the indictable period, *has* the burden of presenting affirmation proof that he did, in fact, actually withdraw. This means some affirmation action, *not* just inactivity.
6. *Venue* in a conspiracy prosecution generally lies in *any* judicial district (or jurisdiction) in which the agreement was made or in which one of the overt act(s) has been committed, including where a telephone call is made between two jurisdictions, district or state, assuming such a call can be said to have been an overt act in furtherance of the conspiracy.
7. Generally, a *party* to a conspiracy is responsible for any substantive offense committed by a co-conspirator in furtherance of the conspiracy even though he did not participate in such substantive offense and even though he had no actual knowledge of it.

There are actually three types of conspiracy: "wheels," "chains," and "enterprise" (Myers and Brzostolwski 1981; edited):

Wheel Conspiracies

In a "wheel" conspiracy, one person at the "hub" conspires individually with two or more persons who make up the "spokes" of the wheel. Unless the persons forming the spokes are aware of each other and agree with each other to achieve a common, illegal goal, the wheel is incomplete—it lacks a "rim" tying everyone together into the pursuit of one objective.

Wheel conspiracies are very hard to prosecute because a common agreement between the spokes is difficult to prove. Without good evidence of a "rim," there can be no conviction of the whole wheel. Also, without good evidence of a rim, the government is prohibited from even trying all the members of the wheel in one proceeding. This forces prosecutors to try a series of smaller conspiracies, each consisting of the hub and one of the spokes. As a result, only the person at the hub faces responsibility for all the crimes of the organization. Each spoke escapes responsibility for the crimes of the other spokes.

Chain Conspiracies

When a criminal goal is absolutely dependent upon the successful participation of every member of a group, a chain conspiracy exists. By definition, each member, or "link," understands that the success of the scheme depends upon everyone in the chain, either because of the nature of the goal or by actual knowledge.

Chain conspiracies are relatively easy to prosecute, as long as the members can be shown to have one common, interdependent goal, such as drug smuggling. But if an organization engages in a variety of crimes having different goals (arson, murder, loansharking, drug trafficking, etc.), holding everyone responsible for all the organization's activities becomes very difficult. And without evidence that everyone has one common goal, all the members cannot be tried together in one proceeding.

Enterprise Conspiracies

RICO avoids the practical limitations on proving wheel and chain conspiracies by creating a new offense: "enterprise conspiracy."

Section 1962(d) makes it a separate crime to conspire to violate any of the three substantive offenses found in RICO (18 U.S.C. 1962a, b, c). In effect, it defines as a new crime *an agreement to participate in an enterprise by engaging in a pattern of racketeering activity.*[11]

The enterprise may have a variety of different goals, so everyone is not in one chain. All of its members, or spokes, may not be aware of each other's various illegal activities; so there is no rim for the wheel. It does not matter. All that need be shown is each member's agreement to participate in the organization—the "enterprise"—by committing two or more acts of racketeering.

Enterprise conspiracy uses mass trials. Everyone charged with conspiracy to participate in a RICO enterprise can be prosecuted together in one criminal proceeding. In addition, enterprise conspiracy imposes separate, additional criminal liability for agreeing to join a criminal organization.

Prosecuting criminal conspiracy cases can be problematic. In the 1974 case *United States* v. *Sperling* (506 F.2d 1323, 1341, 2d Cir.) the court noted that

> it has become all too common for the government to bring indictments against a dozen or more defendants and endeavor to force as many of them as possible to trial in the same proceeding on the claim of a single conspiracy when the criminal acts could more reasonably be regarded as two or more conspiracies, perhaps with a link at the top.

This creates the risk of "guilt by association" wherein a jury, confronted by a large number of defendants and a great volume of evidence, is unable to give each defendant the individual consideration that due process requires. In such situations, a finding of guilty brings with it the risk of being reversed on appeal. Campane (1981b: 30) notes that constitutional guarantees of a fair trial "make it imperative to determine whether the evidence establishes one large conspiracy as opposed to multiple smaller ones."

Another considerable problem is that conspiracy cases usually require direct testimony of eyewitnesses; these are often participants in the conspiracy who agree to testify ("flip") against their coconspirators in exchange for leniency or immunity from prosecution. Thus, Campane (1981b: 29) advises:

> An investigator should therefore be prepared to locate witnesses (often immunized coconspirators) who are willing to testify and are able to explain the complicated or intricate nature of the unlawful activity, and as a consequence, the stake in the venture or mutual dependence each participant has with each other.

The complexity of a conspiracy case, for both the prosecutor and the jury, can be seen in feature inset 16.1, showing *United States* v. *Frank Matthews* (and eighteen other defendants); Matthews is the black drug dealer discussed in part 2.

Feature Inset 16.1
United States v. Frank Matthews

UNITED STATES DISTRICT COURT
EASTERN DISTRICT OF NEW YORK
. . . . x
UNITED STATES OF AMERICA

-against-

FRANK MATTHEWS, a/k/a "Pee Wee,"
  "Big Book," "Frank McNeil,"
  "Mark IV Frank,"

Crim. No. _____
(T.21, U.S.C., §§173, 174, 812
841(a)(1), 843(b), 846
952(a), 960(a)(1), 963)

BARBARA HINTON, a/k/a "Barbara
   Matthews,"
GATTIS HINTON, a/k/a "Bud," "Slim,"
   "Joseph Jackson,"
WILIAM BECKWITH, a/k/a "Mickey,"
   "McGill," "Miguel,"
DONALD CONNER
ROBERT CURRINGTON, a/k/a "Pedro,"
CHARLES WILLIAM CAMERON, a/k/a
   "Swayzie,"
JAMES WESLEY CARTER, a/k/a "Brother
   Carter," "Big Head Brother," "Big B,"
JOHN DARBY, a/k/a "Pop," "John Smith,"
THELMA DARBY, a/k/a "Flossie,"
   "Thelma Reese,"
DAVID CLEMENT BATES, a/k/a "Rev,"
WALTER ROSENBAUM
ERNEST ROBINSON, a/k/a "Ernie,"
JAMES E. MARTINEZ,
SCARVEY MC CARGO,
FRED BROWN,
LUCY MATHEWS,
MARZELLA STEELE WEBB,
         Defendants.
. . . . x

The Grand Jury Charges:

Count One

From on or about September, 1968, and continuously thereafter up to and including the date of the filing of this indictment, within the Eastern District of New York and elsewhere, the defendants FRANK MATTHEWS, a/k/a "Pee Wee," "Big Book," "Frank McNeil," "Mark IV Frank," BARBARA HINTON, a/k/a "Barbara Matthews," GATTIS HINTON, a/k/a/ "Bud," "Slim," "Joseph Jackson," WILLIAM BECKWITH, a/k/a "Mickey," "McGill," "Miguel," DONALD CONNER, ROBERT CURRING-TON, a/k/a "Pedro," CHARLES WILLIAM CAMERON, a/k/a "Swayzie," JAMES WESLEY CARTER, a/k/a "Brother Carter," "Big Head Brother," "Big B," JOHN DARBY, a/k/a "Pop," "John Smith," THELMA DARBY, a/k/a "Flossie," "Thelma Reese," DAVID CLEMENT BATES, a/k/a "Rev," WALTER ROSENBAUM, ER-NEST ROBINSON, a/k/a "Ernie," JAMES E. MARTINEZ, SCARVEY MC CARGO, FRED BROWN, LUCY MATHEWS, and MARZELLA STEELE WEBB together with Emerson Dorsey, Nathaniel Elder, a/k/a "Nat," Donald James, John Edward Jones, a/k/a "Liddy Jones," George Mosley, Ana Ramos, Jorge Ramos, James Aubrey Scott, and John Thorp, a/k/a "Pete," named herein as coconspirators but not as defendants, and others known and unknown to the Grand Jury, wilfully, knowingly and unlawfully did combine, conspire, confederate, and agree to violate prior to May 1,

1971, Sections 173 and 174 of Title 21, United States Code, and to violate on and after May 1, 1971, Sections 812, 841(a)(1), 952(a), and 960(a)(1) of Title 21, United States Code.

1. It was part of said conspiracy that prior to May 1, 1971, the defendants and co-conspirators fraudulently and knowingly would import and bring into the United States large quantities of heroin and cocaine, narcotic drugs, contrary to law.
2. It was further a part of said conspiracy that prior to May 1, 1971, the defendants and co-conspirators wilfully, knowingly, and unlawfully would receive conceal, buy, sell, and facilitate the transportation, concealment, and sale of large quantities of heroin and cocaine, narcotic drugs, after the narcotic drugs had been imported and brought into the United States knowing the same to have been imported and brought into the United States contrary to law.
3. It was further a part of said conspiracy that on and after May 1, 1971, the defendants and co-conspirators knowingly and intentionally would import large quantities of heroin and cocaine, Schedule I and Schedule II narcotic drug controlled substances, into the United States from places outside thereof.
4. It was further a part of said conspiracy that on and after May 1, 1971, the defendants and co-conspirators knowingly and intentionally would distribute and possess with intent to distribute large quantities of heroin and cocaine, Schedule I and Schedule II narcotic drug controlled substances.
5. It was further a part of said conspiracy that the defendants and coconspirators would obtain large quantities of mannitol, quinine, glassine envelopes, and other paraphernalia in order to enable defendants and co-conspirators to adulterate, dilute, process, and package the narcotic drugs for unlawful distribution.
6. It was further a part of said conspiracy that the defendants and co-conspirators would conceal the existence of the conspiracy and would take steps designed to prevent disclosure of their activities.

In furtherance of the conspiracy and to effect the objects thereof, the following acts, among others, were committed within the Eastern District of New York and elsewhere;

Overt Acts

1. In or about the middle of 1969 the defendant CHARLES WILLIAM CAMERON and others met in Brooklyn, New York.
2. In or about Summer, 1971, the defendant WILLIAM BECKWITH met with co-conspirator John Thorp and others in Brooklyn, New York.
3. On or about January 31, 1972, the defendants FRANK MATTHEWS, SCARVEY MC CARGO, JAMES E. MARTINEZ, and co-conspirator Nathaniel Elder met in Brooklyn, New York.
4. On or about June 5, 1972, the defendant JAMES WESLEY CARTER made a telephone call to the defendant FRANK MATTHEWS.
5. On or about June 22, 1972, the defendant WALTER ROSENBAUM caused

to be transported from Genoa, Italy, to Philadelphia, Pennsylvania, a quantity of mannite.

6. In or about June, 1972, the defendant GATTIS HINTON received 11 kilograms of cocaine from co-conspirator Jorge Ramos in New York, New York.

7. On or about July 8, 1972, the defendants FRANK MATTHEWS and DAVID CLEMENT BATES had a telephone conversation.

8. On or about August 1, 1972, the defendants FRANK MATTHEWS received six (6) kilograms of cocaine from co-conspirator Jorge Ramos in New York, New York.

9. On or about September 5, 1972, the defendants FRANK MATTHEWS, WILLIAM BECKWITH, and JOHN DARBY had a telephone conversation.

10. On or about September 16, 1972, the defendants BARBARA HINTON and THELMA DARBY had a telephone conversation.

11. On or about January 16, 1974, the defendants DONALD CONNER, JOHN DARBY, and ERNEST ROBINSON met in Brooklyn, New York.

12. On or about March 1, 1974, the defendants FRED BROWN and LUCY MATHEWS had a conversation in Newark, New Jersey. (Title 21, United States Code, Sections 173, 174, 846 and 963.)

Count Two

On or about the 8th day of July 1972, within the Eastern District of New York and elsewhere, the defendants FRANK MATTHEWS, a/k/a "Pee Wee," "Big Book," "Frank McNeil," "Mark IV Frank," and DAVID CLEMENT BATES, a/k/a "Rev," knowingly, intentionally, and unlawfully did use a communication facility, to wit, the telephone, in committing and in causing and facilitating the commission of the conspiracy set forth in Count One of this indictment. (Title 21, United States Code, Section 843(b)).

Count Three

On or about the 8th day of July 1972, within the Eastern District of New York and elsewhere, the defendants FRANK MATTHEWS, a/k/a "Pee Wee," "Big Book," "Frank McNeil," "Mark IV Frank," and DAVID CLEMENT BATES, a/k/a "Rev," knowingly, intentionally, and unlawfully did use a communication facility, to wit, the telephone, in committing and in causing and facilitating the commission of the conspiracy set forth in Count One of this indictment. (Title 21, United States Code, Section 843(b)).

Count Four

On or about the 1st day of September 1972, within the Eastern District of New York and elsewhere, the defendants JOHN DARBY, a/k/a "Pop," "John Smith," and BARBARA HINTON, a/k/a "Barbara Matthews," knowingly, intentionally, and unlawfully did use a communication facility, to wit, the telephone, in committing and in causing and facilitating the commission of the conspiracy set forth in Count One of this indictment. (Title 21, United States Code, Section 843(b)).

Count Five

On or about the 5th day of September 1972, within the Eastern District of New York, the defendants FRANK MATTHEWS, a/k/a "Pee Wee," "Big Book," "Frank McNeil," "Mark IV Frank," and JOHN DARBY, a/k/a "Pop," "John Smith," knowingly, intentionally, and unlawfully did use a communication facility, to wit, the telephone, in committing and in causing and facilitating the commission of the conspiracy set forth in Count One of this indictment. (Title 21, United States Code, Section 843(b)).

Count Six

On or about the 6th day of September 1972, within the Eastern District of New York, the defendants FRANK MATTHEWS, a/k/a "Pee Wee," "Big Book," "Frank McNeil," "Mark IV Frank," WILLIAM BECKWITH, a/k/a "Mickey," "McGill," "Miguel," and JOHN DARBY, a/k/a "Pop," "John Smith," knowingly, intentionally, and unlawfully did use a communication facility, to wit, the telephone, in committing and in causing and facilitating the commission of the conspiracy set forth in Count One of this indictment. (Title 21, United States Code, Section 843(b)).

Count Seven

On or about the 7th day of September 1972, within the Eastern District of New York and elsewhere, the defendants FRANK MATTHEWS, a/k/a "Pee Wee," "Big Book," "Frank McNeil," "Mark IV Frank," and JOHN DARBY, a/k/a "Pop," "John Smith," knowingly, intentionally, and unlawfully did use a communication facility, to wit, the telephone, in committing and in causing and facilitating the commission of the conspiracy set forth in Count One of this indictment. (Title 21, United States Code, Section 843(b)).

Count Eight

On or about the 11th day of September 1972, within the Eastern District of New York and elsewhere, the defendants FRANK MATTHEWS, a/k/a "Pee Wee," "Big Book," "Frank McNeil," "Mark IV Frank," and JOHN DARBY, a/k/a "Pop," "John Smith," knowingly, intentionally, and unlawfully did use a communication facility, to wit, the telephone, in committing and in causing and facilitating the commission of the conspiracy set forth in Count One of this indictment. (Title 21, United States Code, Section 843(b)).

Count Nine

On or about the 16th day of September 1972, within the Eastern District of New York and elsewhere, the defendants BARBARA HINTON, a/k/a "Barbara Matthews," and THELMA DARBY, a/k/a "Flossie," "Thelma Reese," knowingly, intentionally, and unlawfully did use a communication facility, to wit, the telephone, in committing and in causing and facilitating the commission of the conspiracy set forth in Count One of this indictment. (Title 21, United States Code, Section 843(b)).

A TRUE BILL.

_____

Foreman.

_____
UNITED STATES ATTORNEY

_____

_____

[1] Robert W. Johannesen, Jr., is a special agent of the Drug Enforcement Administration who specializes in conspiracy cases. He was an instructor at a training institute at the North Carolina Justice Academy, "Investigating Organized Crime," attended by the writer.

chapter 17

Gathering Information about Organized Crime

Used by permission of AP/Wide World Photos

Because of the nature of their enterprises, OC units must keep their activities hidden. This obviously presents a challenge to the law-enforcement community. Actually, useful information may be found in such public and quasi-public sources as newspapers, court files, and utility company records. Newspaper clippings are part of the records kept by agencies interested in OC. Information may also be obtained from ordinary citizens, although criminal informants are a more likely source. Information is secured directly from criminal suspects through wiretapping and electronic surveillance ("bugging"). These two approaches, although often indispensible, tread a narrow line along the boundaries of privacy and civil liberty; for that reason they are heavily regulated. Wiretapping and bugging are also extremely expensive techniques—another reason for limiting their use. When OC operations cross national boundaries, law enforcement agencies may utilize the services of INTERPOL.

The collection of information about OC, its evaluation, collation, analysis, reporting, and dissemination are collectively referred to as *intelligence* (Dintino and Martens 1984). It is laborious and usually unexciting work that requires a great deal of expertise.

Intelligence

The *American Heritage Dictionary* (1981) defines intelligence (in the sense that we are using it) as the work of gathering secret information about an enemy, but experts such as Drexel Godfrey and Don Harris (1971), and Justin Dintino and Frederick Martens choose to avoid defining the term. Dintino and Martens (1984: 9) conceive of intelligence as simply "(1) a process through which information is managed which (2) will hopefully increase our knowledge of a particular problem (3) resulting in preventive and/or informed public policy."

Intelligence data are collected for two main purposes—tactical and strategic; at times these two categories overlap (Godfrey and Harris 1971). *Tactical intelligence* is information that contributes directly to the achievement of an immediate law-enforcement objective, such as arrest and prosecution. *Strategic intelligence* is information that contributes to producing sound judgment with respect to long-range law-enforcement objectives and goals. The information is collected over time and put together by an intelligence analyst to reveal new (or newly discovered) patterns of organized criminal activity. The information may be unsubstantiated ("raw") data and require further investigation for confirmation (thus becoming "hard" data).

Collecting Intelligence Data

Robert Stewert (1980: 54) notes the common sources of intelligence data:

- Court records.
- Other public agency documents such as real estate, tax, and incorporation records.
- Business records.
- Old case records in the [intelligence unit's] agency files.
- Investigative and intelligence files of other law-enforcement agencies.
- Newspapers and periodicals.
- Utility company records.
- Documents and items recovered during searches or subpoenaed by the grand jury, administrative agencies, and legislative committees.
- Electronic surveillance evidence.
- Material produced voluntarily by citizens.
- Statements and/or testimony obtained from accomplices, informants, victims, and law-enforcement personnel.[1]

This material can be collected overtly or covertly. Covert collection involves the acquisition of information from subjects who are unaware that they are being observed or overheard. Since this type of collection is usually quite expensive in terms of the manpower required, it is usually tied directly to the goal of securing evidence that can be used in prosecution; that is, it is more tactical than strategic.

Processing Intelligence Data

Stewert (1980: 79) notes the importance of properly *processing* intelligence data:

> Regardless of how a particular item of information was obtained—whether through informant interview, grand jury testimony or any of the other potential sources mentioned earlier—it must be processed and stored in a manner which makes it (1) legally useful and (2) easily retrievable. Obviously, if one hundred informants have been interviewed over a six-month period and the interview notes are filed in the folders of each, no single detail about any particular suspect will be available unless the particular interrogator happens to remember where to locate it in the mass of notes.

Drexel Godfrey and Don Harris (1971) refer to *analysis* as the "heart" of the intelligence system. An analyst uses the methods of social science research,[2] and central to this approach is the hypothesis. The analyst develops a hypothesis, simply makes an "educated guess," about the relevance of the information that has already been collected, collated, and stored. The investigators are then told to seek data that will permit "hypothesis testing." If the hypothesis does not withstand an adequate test, alternative hypotheses must be developed and tested. A hypothesis that has been supported by the data after rigorous testing becomes the basis for an *intelligence report*. The report will serve to guide tactical and/or strategic law-enforcement efforts. The storage and analysis of intelligence data have been greatly enhanced by computer and information-retrieval technology.

Problems of Intelligence

The collecting and storing of intelligence data, however, are problematic for at least two reasons. (1) Intelligence gathering lacks many of the exciting aspects of law enforcement—there are no television series based on the adventures of intelligence analysts. The results produced by strategic intelligence are never immediate and seldom dramatic. It fails to impress those who allocate funds for law-enforcement agencies, and intelligence personnel often have little status in such agencies as the DEA. (2) There have been abuses (Task Force on Organized Crime 1976: 122):

> A basic principle in collecting information for a criminal intelligence file is that such information should be restricted to what an agency needs to know in order to fulfill its responsibility to detect and combat organized crime in its jurisdiction. The ethnic origin or the political or religious beliefs of any individual, group, or organization should never be the reason for collecting information on them. Criminal activities or associations must be the key factors. If associations are found not to be criminal in nature, the data collected on them should be dropped from the files.

For several decades this was not the practice. In many urban police departments and the FBI, extensive intelligence efforts were directed against political groups and personalities. "Red squads" would sometimes "leak" raw data whose source was untrustworthy. However, when such data move through a respected law-enforcement agency, there is a "cleansing" effect, and the now-laundered information takes on new importance. Restrictions on what information may be kept in intelligence files and "Freedom of Information" statutes have resulted from these abuses.

The Law Enforcement Intelligence Unit (LEIU)

In 1956, the *Law Enforcement Intelligence Unit* (LEIU) was formed in San Francisco at a meeting of representatives of twenty-six law-enforcement agencies from seven western states. The LEIU was subsequently expanded to include agencies from states across the nation. The purpose of the new group was "to promote the gathering, recording, and exchange of confidential information not available through normal police channels, concerning organized crime." Chip Berlet (1981: 34) argues that "the unofficial purpose was to establish a national criminal intelligence network independent of the Federal Bureau of Investigation, whose agents frequently refused to share information with local law-enforcement officers." LEIU is a private, nongovernmental organization, and agencies requesting to join must meet standards for integrity and information security set by LEIU. In 1978, a member agency from Nevada compromised intelligence information and was expelled from the organization. LEIU has been criticized for failing to verify information in its files and for maintaining noncriminal information on political activists. The main purpose of LEIU is not to maintain intelligence information but to act as a clearinghouse providing member agencies with access to each other's intelligence information.

Regional Information Sharing Systems (RISS)

Since 1980 the U.S. Department of Justice has funded six regional information sharing systems (RISS Projects) which provide services to 150,000 sworn state and local law enforcement officers in 1,658 criminal justice agencies in all fifty states and the District of Columbia. The projects support efforts to combat major criminal conspiracies. Two primary services are provided by RISS to each of the member agencies in the six regions:

1. A computerized law enforcement data base. Data base entries are made by member agencies relating to major criminals for which they have information they are willing to share with member agencies. The collection, storage and dissemination of this information is regulated by 28 Code of Federal Regulations, Part 23. As a prerequisite of membership in RISS, agencies must agree to abide by these regulations which prohibit remote access to the computerized data base. All information must be relayed telephonically (call-back system) or in writing.

2. Investigative analysis products. The latter includes such services as link charts for telephone toll analysis and assessments of criminal activity.

In addition to these primary services, RISS provides investigative equipment on loan, confidential funds, timely bulletins of criminal information, training, technical assistance, referrals, and access to a telecommunications system.

One of the six regional projects is known by the acronym MAGLOCLEN: Middle Atlantic-Great Lakes Organized Crime Law Enforcement Network which covers agencies in Delaware, the District of Columbia, Indiana, Maryland, Michigan, New Jersey, New York, Ohio and Pennsylvania. Membership is limited to those agencies with units dedicated to gathering intelligence on or investigating organized-criminal activities. Agencies applying for membership must be sponsored by a member agency from their state. Applications are screened by a review committee which must verify the agency's integrity. If the application is approved by the MAGLOCLEN policy board, the agency must undergo a six-month probationary period before being accepted as a member. The Executive Director has a staff of 23 and is responsible to a policy board of representatives from members' agencies. The MAGLOCLEN mission is to encourage and aid in the investigation of major interstate conspiracies.

MAGLOCLEN maintains a computerized data base on more than 13,000 "organized criminals" whose criminal acts occur within the eight-state region. The data base utilizes a "pointer system" that refers (points) an inquirer back to the member agency which submitted the requested information. The project targets persons involved in the manufacture and distribution of controlled substances, auto theft rings, chop shops, outlaw motorcycle gang criminal activity, arson for profit, economic crime, and toxic/hazardous waste violations. (Source: various RISS publications.)

INTERPOL

The International Criminal Police Organization, now known as INTERPOL, was founded in 1923. The United States became a member in 1938. During the 1930s, when it was known as the International Criminal Police Commission, INTERPOL was headquartered in Austria—its founder was Johannes Schober, the Vienna chief of police. When the Nazis declared Austria a German province, Gestapo agents occupied INTERPOL headquarters and control went to arch-Nazi Rheinhard Heydrich in Berlin. He used it to help capture fleeing Jews. As foreign police agencies began to realize that the Germans were only interested in political enemies, INTERPOL went silent until the end of the war. In 1946, police representatives from thirty-eight nations met in Brussels, adopted the name INTERPOL, and moved the headquarters to St. Cloud, a Paris suburb. J. Edgar Hoover was elected a vice-president, but the United States remained an inactive member until 1958, when Congress voted to permit the attorney general to authorize official membership for the Treasury Department. In 1977, the attorney general was named permanent representative to INTERPOL, and the secretary of the treasury was named alternate representative, a compromise that was designed to end conflict between Justice and Treasury.

INTERPOL has more than 130 members; a country merely announces its intention to join in order to become a member. The Soviet Union and most satellite states are not members, but Yugoslavia and Romania are. Cuba stopped paying dues and is considered a nonmember. No country can be expelled from INTERPOL, although South Africa was allowed to resign.

> Interpol is a two-tiered structure consisting of a headquarters called the General Secretariat and a network of national central bureaus (NCBs), one in each member country. . . . The central core of the entire organization is the Police Coordination Division, one of the three divisions of the Secretariat. (The other two divisions are for administrative and support services and for research.) The Police Coor-

dination Division manages the criminal records systems, conducts liaison with
the NCBs, and operates units specializing in categories of offenses reflecting
world law enforcement's major concerns: murder and personal violence, counterfeiting, property crimes, fraud and financial crimes, and drug trafficking
(Fooner 1983: 911).

INTERPOL has detailed files on more than 3 million international criminal suspects and is sometimes criticized for making inquiries about innocent
people. Once a person is on file with INTERPOL, it is almost impossible to
have his or her name removed, and this can hinder an international traveler.
Under its charter, INTERPOL can only be involved in criminal, not political,
racial, or religious matters. A request for assistance must meet this qualification, which is not always easy to discern (Laytner 1980). Until recently,
INTERPOL did not get involved in terrorism cases, largely because of the
problem of international politics. However, this policy was recently changed,
and the resolution recently adopted by the General Assembly concerning
terrorism made official a practice unofficially used for years by the organization. In fact, the difficult point is to conciliate the necessities of cooperation
and respect of INTERPOL's constitution, whose Article III forbids any involvement in political cases. The Organization does now provide information
in cases of terrorism which are clearly of a "criminal" nature. ("Interpol,"
1985: 9). A law-enforcement official of any member nation can initiate a
request through that country's NCB, which transmits the request directly to
the foreign country or through the general secretariat in St. Cloud. This ensures
greater speed and efficiency than would moving the request through normal
diplomatic channels.

The United States National Central Bureau (USNCB) is located in the
U.S. Department of Justice, 9th and Pennsylvania Avenue NW, Washington,
D.C. 20530 (tel. 202/633-2867).

> The broad range of offenses and requests for investigative information received
> by the USNCB include those pertaining to crimes of murder and robbery; large-
> scale violations involving narcotics, fraud, and counterfeiting; and the location
> and apprehension of international fugitives. Such cases often involve arrests and
> extraditions to the countries where the crimes were committed (Simpson 1984:
> 32).

One such case involved the arrest of Arturo Durazlo-Moreno, the corrupt
former police chief of Mexico City. He was taken into custody by FBI agents
in San Juan, Puerto Rico, in 1984.

Wiretapping and Electronic Surveillance

Probably that area of organized crime information gathering that can generate
the hottest debate is wiretapping and electronic surveillance—"bugging." The

technology available to investigators in this area is continually becoming more powerful and sophisticated.

Regulation

There is a strong temptation to use such powerful technology to learn things that are none of one's business. Legal definitions of just what may be part of law enforcement's business have been evolving since the first wiretap case confronted the United States Supreme Court in 1928. In *Olmstead* v. *United States* (277 U.S. 438 S.Ct. 564), telephone wiretaps were used to prosecute persons involved in large-scale Prohibition violations. The interception of Olmstead's telephone line was accomplished without trespass. Chief Justice William Howard Taft, writing for the majority, determined that since telephone conversations are not tangible items, they cannot be the subject of an illegal seizure, and thus wiretapping is not prohibited by the Fourth Amendment. Shortly after the *Olmstead* decision, Congress prohibited interception of telephonic communication without judicial authorization.

The first bugging case to reach the Supreme Court was *Goldman* v. *United States* (316 U.S. 129, 62 S.Ct. 993), in 1942. The Court, consistent with *Olmstead*, ruled that a detectaphone placed against an office wall did not violate the Fourth Amendment since there was no trespass. In *Silverman* v. *United States* (365 U.S. 505, 81 S.Ct. 679), in 1961, a foot-long spike with a microphone attached was inserted under a faceboard and into the wall until it made contact with a heating duct that ran through Silverman's house. The Court found this activity unconstitutional, not because of trespass but based upon actual intrusion into "a constitutionally protected area." This set the precedent for the most important decision on this matter, *Katz* v. *United States* (389 U.S. 347, 88 S.Ct. 507, 1967).

In violation of the Hobbs Act, Katz regularly used a public telephone booth to transmit wagering information (McGuiness 1981: 27):

> In *Katz*, the Government, acting without a warrant or other judicial authorization, intercepted defendant's end of telephone conversations by means of two microphones attached by tape to the top of two adjoining public telephone booths from which Katz regularly made calls. Katz was subsequently prosecuted for the interstate transmission of wagering information by telephone in violation of a Federal statute, and tape recordings of the intercepted telephone calls were introduced in evidence over his objection. The Government argued that since no physical intrusion was made into the booth and since it was not a "constitutionally protected area" (the defendant having no possessory interest as such in the booth), a search for fourth amendment purposes did not occur. In holding that there was a search, the Court stated that it was erroneous to resolve questions of fourth amendment law on the basis of whether a constitutionally protected area is involved, "[f]or the Fourth Amendment protects people, not places." This being the case, the reach of the "Amendment [also] cannot turn upon the presence or

absence of a physical intrusion into any given enclosure." The Court thus concluded that the Government's activities "violated the privacy upon which [the defendant] *justifiably relied* while using the telephone" (emphasis added), and hence a search within the meaning of the fourth amendment had taken place.

Robert L. McGuiness (1981) notes that the key to understanding *Katz* and subsequent decisions concerning surveillance and the Fourth Amendment are the terms: "reasonable expectation of privacy," or "legitimate expectation of privacy," or "justifiable expectation of privacy."

Kevin Krajick (1983: 30) notes:

Numerous Congressional committees and criminal court judges in the 1960s found that the FBI and local police had for decades used illegal electronic surveillance to supplement their investigations. And, worse, they had used taps and bugs to spy on and disrupt the activities of law-abiding citizens and organizations. Civil rights leader Martin Luther King, Jr., for one, was the subject of extensive electronic surveillance in the 1960s.

As a result of this activity, and in order to bring some uniformity into the use of electronic surveillance and wiretapping, Congress enacted Title III of the Omnibus Crime Control and Safe Streets Act in 1968 (18 U.S.C. Sections 2510–2520). This law authorizes federal officials, and prosecutors in states that conform to the federal statute, to petition for court authorization to intercept wire or oral communications provided that:

1. There is probable cause for belief that an individual is committing, has committed, or is about to commit a particular offense that is enumerated in Title III; and
2. There is probable cause for belief that particular communications concerning that offense will be obtained through such interception; and
3. Normal investigative procedures have been tried and have failed, or reasonably appear unlikely to succeed if tried, or are too dangerous; and
4. There is probable cause for belief that the facilities in which, or the place where, the oral communications are to be intercepted is being used, or is about to be used, in connection with the commission of such offense, or is leased to, listed in the name of, or commonly used by persons believed to commit such offenses.

The court order terminates in thirty days or less, unless extended by the judge:

No order entered under this section may authorize or approve the interception of any wire or oral communication for any period longer than necessary to achieve the objective of the authorization, nor in any event longer than thirty days.

Extensions of an order may be granted, but only upon the application for an extension made in accordance with subsection (1) of this section [essentially the material listed above]. . . . The period of extension shall be no longer than the authorizing judge deems necessary to achieve the purposes for which it was granted and in no event for longer than thirty days. Every order and extension thereof shall contain a provision that the authorization to intercept shall be executed as soon as practicable, shall be conducted in such a way as to minimize the interception of communications not otherwise subject to interception under this chapter, and must terminate upon attainment of the authorized objective, or in any event in thirty days.

Title III requires that the target(s) of the court order be notified of the order within ninety days after its termination. Although Title III regulates the interception of wire and oral communications, Congress did not explicitly provide authority for the surreptitious placement of a listening device ("bug") to intercept oral communication—a "black bag job." Federal courts remained in conflict over the issue until *Dilia* v. *United States* 441 U.S. 238 (1979). FBI agents had pried open a window in the New Jersey office of Lawrence Dilia in order to install a bug in his ceiling. As a result of the intercepted conversations, Dilia was convicted of violating the Hobbs Act by receiving property stolen from an interstate shipment. The Supreme Court concluded that a Title III warrant for eavesdropping implicitly grants authority for covert entry.

Title III is sometimes criticized by law-enforcement officials because of the extensive investigation and documentation required to secure a warrant, although there are emergency exceptions built into the statute:

. . . any investigative or law enforcement officer, specially designated by the Attorney General or by the principal prosecuting attorney of any State or subdivision thereof acting pursuant to a statute of that State, who reasonably determines that—

(a) an emergency situation exists with respect to conspiratorial activities threatening the national security interests or to conspiratorial activities characteristic of organized crime that requires a wire or oral communication to be intercepted before an order authorizing such interception can with due diligence be obtained, and
(b) there are grounds which an order could be entered under this chapter to authorize such interception

may intercept such wire or oral communication if an application for an order approving the interception is made in accordance with this section within forty-eight hours after the interception has occurred, or begins to occur.

Any wire or oral communication may be intercepted legally without a court order if one of the parties to the communication gives prior consent.

Thus, law-enforcement officers and informants may be "wired" to secure incriminating conversation without a court order. In 1979, the United States Supreme Court (by a 5–3 vote) ruled that the police do not need a search warrant to record the numbers dialed from a particular telephone. In *Smith* v. *Maryland* (78-5374), the Court affirmed the robbery conviction of a man linked to the crime by a pen register which, when installed at a telephone company switching office, can record the numbers dialed from a particular telephone.

Costs

Monitoring requirements also make electronic surveillance and wiretapping costly. The receiving device must be monitored at all times, in addition to being recorded. Certain communications are privileged—those between doctor and patient or attorney and client, for example. If the monitoring agent should hear a privileged conversation, she or he must discontinue the interception. Agents usually wear earphones, and these must be taken off and placed where the conversation cannot be overheard—usually in a box provided for that purpose. Personal conversation unrelated to the warrant, between husband and wife, for example, cannot be intercepted. Each time such a conversation comes across the wire the agent is permitted to listen only briefly, long enough to establish if the nature of the conversation is outside the scope of the court order. A monitoring agent who falls asleep and causes the recording of a privileged conversation can jeopardize the results of the investigation.

Since Title III was enacted in 1968, a majority of states have passed statutes permitting wiretapping and bugging. However, some rarely make use of the law, and cost can provide one reason. The average cost of an electronic surveillance or wiretap is about $35,000, and less than 20 percent actually produce incriminating evidence. There have been cases in which the cost exceeded $2 million.

Debate over the Issue

The President's Commission on Law Enforcement and Administration of Justice stated (1968: 468):

> The great majority of law enforcement officials believe that the evidence necessary to bring criminals to bear consistently on the higher echelons of organized crime will not be obtained without the aid of electronic surveillance techniques. They maintain these techniques are indispensable to develop adequate strategic intelligence concerning organized crime, to set up specific investigations, to develop witnesses, to corroborate their testimony, and to serve as substitutes for them—each a necessary step in the evidence-gathering process in organized crime investigations and prosecutions.

The Task Force on Organized Crime stated (1976: 148):

> Because of their organization and methods of operation, organized crime activities require sophisticated means of evidence gathering. Often witnesses will not come forward; and members of some organizations are bound either by an oath of silence or threats of violence. Often the use of informants is of limited value, and many organizations are difficult, if not impossible, for undercover agents to penetrate to the point where they can obtain useful evidence.
>
> One way to break through these conspiratorial safeguards is to enact a State statute permitting non-consensual wiretap and microphonic surveillance. States should recognize the conflicting needs of effective law enforcement and individual rights and provide for adequate protection of such rights by statute consistent with the problem of organized crime within their own jurisdictions.

The task force noted the report of the National Wiretap Commission (1976), which revealed that wiretapping has been particularly effective in gambling, fencing, and drug investigations.

Herbert J. Stern, a United States attorney in New Jersey, logged an enviable record in successfully prosecuting organized-crime figures and corrupt public officials: in less than four years he convicted eight mayors, two secretaries of state, two state treasurers, two county leaders, a congressman, and more than sixty other public officials. Stern reports: "My office has never applied for a wiretap. None of the cases that we've discussed involved any wiretapping." He adds, however, that "where it is indispensable, is in the gambling operations. Unless you just want to be satisfied with picking up street runners, the lesser likes who are just collecting, who tend to be poor and insignificant in terms of criminal activity, while letting the higher-ups go free, you have to use eavesdropping" (Hoffman 1973: 238).

Ramsey Clark, former United States attorney general, has been a constant critic of electronic surveillance and wiretapping. He has argued that in cities where wiretapping has been used extensively, if not promiscuously (e.g., New York), organized crime is still flourishing. He states that wiretapping is slow, costly, and ineffective (1970: 288) and reports that the FBI used electronic surveillance against organized crime from the late 1950s until July 1965. "Hundreds of man-years of agent time were wasted. As many as twenty bugs were used in a single city. So far as is known not one conviction resulted from any of the bugs" (1970: 290). Clark's real fear, however, has been the potential for abuse, and he has cited several cases, including the bugging of Martin Luther King, Jr., by the FBI. Clark has argued (1970: 287):

> Privacy is the basis of individuality. To be alone and be let alone, to be with chosen company, to say what you think, or don't think, but to say what you will, is to be yourself.
>
> Few conversations would be what they are if the speakers thought others were listening. Silly, secret, thoughtless and thoughtful statements would all be af-

fected. . . . To penetrate the last refuge of the individual, the precious little privacy that remains, the basis of individual dignity, can have meaning to the quality of our lives that we cannot foresee.

Herman Schwartz, representing the American Civil Liberties Union, adds (1968: 161):

To permit law enforcement authorities to wiretap, even under limited circumstances, would seriously impair this privacy so necessary to a free society. Awareness by the public of the power to wiretap is alone sufficient to reduce drastically the sense of security and privacy so vital to a democratic society. The mere thought that someone may be eavesdropping on a conversation with one's wife or lawyer or business associate will discourage full and open discourse.

On the other hand, the effectiveness of bugs and wiretaps for investigating and prosecuting OC cases is highlighted by a number of spectacular cases such as PENDORF, or "penetrating Dorfman," the code name for an investigation of Allen Dorfman. On January 29, 1979, the federal government received a Title III warrant to intercept communications at Dorfman's Amalgamated Insurance Agency Services, Inc. The FBI installed thirteen telephone taps and two listening devices, which they monitored from a phony business office set up for that purpose. Court records indicate the agents intercepted 112,000 telephone conversations, of which 3,602 were pertinent and recorded. As a result, Dorfman, Joey Lombardo (a power in the Chicago Outfit), and Roy L. Williams (president of the Teamsters Union) were convicted of conspiracy to bribe U.S. Senator Howard Cannon of Nevada.

Informants

While law-abiding citizens occasionally provide information about OC, most informants are themselves criminals. The criminal informant (as opposed to the civic-minded-citizen informant) must be active in the criminal "underworld" if he or she is to provide meaningful information. Unfortunately, the investigation and prosecution of OC requires the use of criminal informants, and their use is problematic—in return for cooperation they receive a certain amount of immunity from arrest. This trade-off, "fighting fire with fire," may be subject to abuse: the wider public interest, or the informant, may be sacrificed in favor of an immediate law-enforcement goal.

The criminal informant is usually referred to unofficially by law-enforcement agents as a "stoolie" or "snitch," and officially (in government documents) as a confidential informant (CI). As opposed to the person who becomes a witness for the prosecution, usually in return for leniency, the CI has an ongoing relationship with one or more law-enforcement agents and may never actually testify at a trial. The CI may be motivated by:

1. A desire for revenge.
2. A desire to eliminate competition.
3. Money—a reward provided particularly by federal agencies.
4. A promise of lenient treatment for criminal acts.
5. Any combination of the above.

A person with any of these motivations is hardly one whose veracity can be taken for granted. Journalist Jack Newfield (1979: 12) provides an example; he quotes an FBI agent:

> I once had an informant who told me all sorts of stories. Later on I found out the guy was simultaneously an informant to the New York City Police Department, only I didn't know. What he was telling the police was completely different than what he was telling the bureau. And we were both paying him for his bullshit.

An important alternative to the criminal informant is the use of undercover agents to infiltrate an OC operation. Several enforcement agencies, including the FBI, the Drug Enforcement Administration, and the New Jersey State Police, have used such operatives quite successfully.

---

[1] A basic error that may be committed in regard to the intelligence function by police agencies is to combine it with internal affairs (investigating improprieties committed by police officers). When the investigations of police officers are handled by the intelligence unit, important sources of information—police officers from other units—will tend to "clam up."

[2] For example, see suggestions by Roger Davis (1981) for the use of the social science research technique of *network analysis* as an aid in conspiracy investigations. For further information about this technique, see David Knoke and James Kuklinski (1982).

chapter 18

Organized Crime and Investigative Techniques

Used by permission of AP/Wide World Photos

In this chapter we will examine some of the investigative tools and strategies used to combat OC. Two of these, the investigative grand jury and the grant of immunity, were merely adapted to the problem of dealing with OC, while the strike force and Witness Security Program were developed specifically for that purpose.

The Strike Force

Efforts to investigate and prosecute OC are hampered by a number of problems, not the least of which is the lack of communication, cooperation, and coordination between enforcement agencies. To overcome typical communication failures between agencies at the federal level, in 1961 Attorney General Robert Kennedy set up a system of "area coordinators," federal attorneys who visited the areas assigned to them in order to ensure that information about OC gathered by the various agencies was shared and utilized. From this experience evolved the concept of the strike force (National Association of Attorneys General 1977).

In 1966, the United States Department of Justice established a pilot project in Buffalo, New York, which brought together a group of prosecutors and investigators from various federal agencies. In a period of eighteen months the work of the "Buffalo Project" resulted in the indictment of more than thirty persons involved in OC. The project was made permanent and termed a "strike force." It became the model for similar units formed across the country, each located in a city known to have an OC Family or Families operating.

> Strike forces bring together in one target area personnel from various federal agencies. Each strike force is staffed with between five and ten attorneys who are, in effect, the management control element of the unit. Career prosecutors are chosen for those positions; they may have different areas of expertise, such as tax or anti-trust. Also assigned to the strike force are such other federal, state and local investigative personnel as is considered appropriate in the circumstances. The makeup varies, as does the relationship to state officials. Each member of the strike force remains responsible to his own agency [National Association of Attorneys General 1977: 41].

Strike force investigators are from the FBI; Drug Enforcement Administration; Internal Revenue Service; Bureau of Alcohol, Tobacco and Firearms; Immigration and Naturalization Service; Customs Service; Department of Labor; and the Postal Inspection Service. At times, personnel from the U.S. Marshals Service and the Securities and Exchange Commission are included.

Stewert (1980) notes that the strike-force approach to dealing with OC involves a combination of four characteristics: it is interdisciplinary, insulated, offender centered, and proactive.

The strike-force unit is *interdisciplinary* because it combines investigative and prosecutorial personnel and such specialists as accountants. In addition, the unit draws upon investigators from federal, state, and local agencies.

The strike-force unit is *insulated*—free from local pressures and from the normal bureaucratic and political manifestations that typically inhibit law-enforcement agencies.

While most law-enforcement efforts concentrate on types of offense, the strike-force unit is *offender centered,* targeting the individual OC offender who is typically involved in a wide variety of crimes.

As opposed to most conventional law-enforcement, which is reactive—responding to complaints of criminal activity—the strike force is *proactive*—free to seek out targets to investigate.

The strike force assesses relevant organized-crime intelligence data and targets an OC group for investigation. Appropriate criminal statutes are selected, sources of information identified, and investigative and prosecutive plans formulated. "Investigations employ a variety of sophisticated evidence-gathering techniques including informants, undercover operations, and electronic surveillance, and they extensively examine books and records to trace the flow of illegal funds. The investigations generally last many months or even years before an indictment is returned and the long process of trial, appeal, and sometimes retrial begins" (Blakey 1983: 1109).

The Investigative Grand Jury

The grand jury is a body of approximately fifteen to twenty-four citizens "who have been selected according to law and sworn to hear the evidence against accused persons and determine whether there is sufficient evidence to bring those persons to trial, to investigate criminal activity generally, and to investigate the conduct of public agencies and officials" (*Dictionary of Criminal Justice . . . ,* 1981).

The grand jury is a powerful body that can compel testimony (under a grant of immunity) and issue subpoenas for persons and documents. "Any subpoena issued by a grand jury is presumed to be valid, and when it is properly served it must be obeyed to the full extent of its terms. There is no redress in the courts for persons who have been subpoenaed, nor is a grand jury liable for the subpoenas it issues" (Lewis, Bundy, and Hague 1978: 187). A grand juror cannot be punished or sued for his or her actions as a juror, and the proceedings of the grand jury are secret. Testimony is given under oath and recorded; false testimony is subject to statutes against perjury.

In the *United States* v. *Dionisio* (410 U.S. 1, 93 S.Ct. 764) in 1973 the Supreme Court held: "A grand jury has broad investigative powers to determine whether a crime has been committed and who has committed it. The jurors may act on tips, rumors, evidence offered by the prosecutor, or their own personal knowledge." In 1974, *United States* v. *Calandra* (414 U.S. 338), the Supreme Court ruled that even illegally obtained evidence may be used as a basis for questioning witnesses subpoenaed to appear before a grand jury. Federal grand juries, and those of many states, do not permit subpoenaed witnesses to be accompanied by an attorney. They are, however, free to leave the grand-jury room to consult with counsel at any time.

On the federal level, the Organized Crime Control Act of 1970 requires that an investigative grand jury (called a *special grand jury*) be convened at least every eighteen months in federal judicial districts of more than 1 million persons. It can also be convened at the request of a federal prosecutor, and its life may be extended to thirty-six months.

States vary in their use of the grand jury. Some provide for *investigative* grand juries, which typically collect evidence as part of a larger inquiry into organized criminal activity and/or the corruption of public officials. The grand jury is a *tool* of the prosecutor.

Stewert (1980: 124) states that the investigative grand jury is

> . . . the single most useful tool by which to attack the traditional forms of organized crime. For example, convicted drug pushers, bookmakers, numbers writers and runners, prostitutes, weapons offenders and petty thieves can be summoned before the grand jury, immunized and questioned about the higher-ups in a particular enterprise or activity. If the witness is not already under charges, there is little likelihood that the grant of immunity will jeopardize any prosecution. If the witness testifies truthfully, that witness will be ostracized from the criminal community and thereby neutralized as an organized crime operative. Moreover, the defection of one member of an organization may serve as a catalyst which forces others within the organization to defect and cooperate with the state. Whenever any appreciable number of lower-level offenders are summoned before an investigative grand jury, the higher-ups in the organized crime structure can never be sure of what, if anything, is being said. This alone is sufficient to generate severe tensions within the organized crime structure.

Immunity

The Fifth Amendment to the United States Constitution provides that no person "shall be compelled in any criminal case to be a witness against himself." This is an important protection for the individual, but in practice it can be turned on its ear and used to compel criminals to testify against one another, on pain of fine or imprisonment for those who refuse.

The technique is used in a variety of settings. In the courts of many states and the federal government, the court or the prosecutor may grant immunity to reluctant witnesses. Legislative or administrative bodies involved in investigating criminal activity can also request a grant of immunity. Feature Inset 18.1 shows a congressional request for immunity for three witnesses, a court grant of immunity for one of them, and a court judgment against a recalcitrant witness who refused to testify despite a grant of immunity.

Feature Inset 18.1
Immunity Documents

98th CONGRESS 1ST SESSION

RESOLUTION of the Committee on Governmental Affairs

To immunize from use in prosecution the testimony of Anthony Accardo, Alfred Pilotto, and Ben Schmoutey.

July 25, 1983

Mr. ROTH, from the Committee on Governmental Affairs, submitted the following resolution; which was approved by vote of twelve of the eighteen members of the committee on the twenty-fifth day of July 1983

RESOLUTION

To immunize from use in prosecution the testimony of Anthony Accardo, Alfred Pilotto, and Ben Schmoutey.

Whereas the Permanent Subcommittee on Investigations has been conducting an investigation into organized crime, as well as illegal and improper practices in the field of labor management relations, particularly concerning allegations involving the Hotel Employees and Restaurant Employees International Union, and will be convening a series of hearings to receive testimony on the same;

Whereas the subcommittee may call as witnesses Anthony Accardo, Alfred Pilotto, and Ben Schmoutey, among others, during those hearings;

Whereas the subcommittee anticipates Anthony Accardo, Alfred Pilotto, and Ben Schmoutey may refuse to testify at those hearings on the grounds of self-incrimination; and

Whereas the Organized Crime Control Act of 1970 (18 U.S.C. 6005) provides that by two-thirds vote a committee may seek a court order immunizing testimony from use in prosecutions other than for perjury, giving a false statement or otherwise failing to comply with the court order: Now, therefore, be it

Resolved, That the Committee on Governmental Affairs, pursuant to sections 288b(d) and 288f of title 2, United States Code (Supp. V 1981), directs the Senate Legal Counsel to apply for a court order immunizing from use in prosecution the testimony at hearings by the Permanent Subcommittee on Investigations of Anthony Accardo, Alfred Pilotto, and Ben Schmoutey.

IN THE UNITED STATES DISTRICT COURT
FOR THE DISTRICT OF COLUMBIA

SENATE PERMANENT SUBCOMMITTEE
ON INVESTIGATIONS

United States Senate   Misc. No. 83–0280
Washington, D.C. 20510,

Applicant.

On consideration of the application by the Senate Permanent Subcommittee on Investigations, and the memorandum of points and authorities, and exhibits, in support thereof, the Court finds that the procedural requisites set forth in 18 U.S.C. . 6005 for an order of the Court have been satisfied. Accordingly, it is

ORDERED that Ben Schmoutey may not refuse to appear and testify before the Senate Permanent Subcommittee on Investigations on the basis of his privilege against self-incrimination, and it is

FURTHER ORDERED that no testimony compelled under this Order (or any information directly or indirectly derived from such testimony) may be used against Ben Schmoutey in any criminal case, except a prosecution for perjury, giving a false statement, or otherwise failing to comply with this Order.

United States District Judge

UNITED STATES DISTRICT COURT, SOUTHERN DISTRICT OF FLORIDA

G.J. No. 74-7

United States of America v. *Irving Karl Katzen, a/k/a Harry Katzen*

ORDER

Judgment and Commitment

This cause came on to be heard upon application of the United States to have Irving Karl Katzen, also known as Harry Katzen declared a recalcitrant Grand Jury witness and confined pursuant to 28 United States Code § 1826, and the Court having heard testimony and arguments of counsel, and the defendant having stated to this Court that he will not comply with its Order directing him to answer the questions propounded to him before the Grand Jury for the Southern District of Florida, despite the grant of immunity in that Order duly provided him under 18 United States Code § 6002, the Court finds that the said Irving Karl Katzen has refused and refuses without just cause to comply with this Court's Order directing him to testify and provide information to the Grand Jury, it is therefore,

Ordered and adjudged, that the said Harry Katzen is a recalcitrant Grand Jury witness and in contempt of this Court, and that he be, and hereby is, committed to the custody of the United States Marshal to be confined in jail, there to remain until such time as he is willing to give, and does give, such testimony and provide such information to said Grand Jury, said confinement not to exceed the life of the term of said Grand Jury which was empaneled on May 14, 1974. Confinement not to exceed 18 months.

Done and ordered at Miami, Florida, in the Southern District of Florida, this 3rd day of Sept., 1974.

$\overline{\hspace{2cm}}$ $\overline{\hspace{2cm}}$,

United States District Judge.

Types of Immunity

There are two basic types of immunity (Committee on the Office of Attorney General 1978: 3):

Transactional Immunity. With this type of immunity, a witness who has been compelled to testify about an offense may never be prosecuted for that offense, no matter how much independent evidence may come to light. However, there is one limitation to this blanket protection against prosecution: A witness may not "trigger the automatic immunity as to a second crime [one he is not being questioned about] by volunteering or blurting out information which is not responsive to a question" (Stewert 1980: 232–33). However, "If the witness receives transactional immunity in connection with one crime and is then questioned about a different crime, the immunity will automatically attach to that second crime to the extent that the witness' answers are relevant" (Stewert 1980: 232).

Use Immunity. If a person has use immunity, no testimony compelled to be given and no evidence derived from or obtained because of the compelled testimony may be used if the person should subsequently be prosecuted on independent evidence for the offense. "If there is evidence independent of the immunized testimony that is sufficient to support a prosecution, the witness may be prosecuted on the basis of that independent evidence." Robert Stewert (1980: 233) notes that the prosecutor "faces a very heavy burden in establishing that the evidence is truly from an independent source."

For example, a witness compelled to testify before a grand jury investigating a murder might be compelled to also testify about his involvement in the incident. If that witness had transactional immunity, he could not be prosecuted for any crime, including the murder, about which he was compelled to testify before the grand jury, even though his testimony revealed criminal activity. If the immunity granted was "use" rather than transactional, then the witness could still be prosecuted for any crime revealed in his testimony as long as the evidence used against him was obtained completely independently of the testimony he gave before the grand jury (Committee on the Office of Attorney General 1978: 3).

Penalties

Civil Contempt. A witness who, after being granted immunity, refuses to testify can be subjected to civil contempt proceedings (Stewert 1980: 239):

> The civil contempt proceeding is summary in nature and relatively simple. First the witness is immunized. Upon refusing to answer in the grand jury [or other authorized body] the witness appears before the court. The prosecutor makes an oral application, and the court instructs the witness to testify. The witness then returns to the grand jury room; and, if recalcitrant, is directed to reappear before the court. The prosecutor then makes an oral application for the court to enforce its previous order, which the witness has disobeyed. The prosecutor explains what has occurred before the grand jury, and the foreperson or reporter testifies about those facts. The witness is given an opportunity to be heard; and, thereafter, the court decides whether the witness is in contempt and should be remanded.

"The remand order normally specifies that the witness shall remain confined until either he offers to purge himself of the contempt by agreeing to testify or for the life of the grand jury, whichever is shorter" (1980: 240). The term of a grand jury is usually eighteen months. Legislative committees and administrative bodies, of course, have indefinite terms. In 1970, as a result of his refusal to testify before a New Jersey investigating committee, after being immunized, Jerry Catena (then acting boss of the Genovese Family) was imprisoned for contempt—and he remained there for five years, never testifying.

Criminal Contempt. Another tool for compelling an immunized witness to testify is the use of *criminal contempt*. Stewert (1980: 244–45) notes:

> Procedurally and substantively, a criminal contempt prosecution differs radically from a civil contempt remand. While the latter is summary in nature, the former requires a formal trial. . . . The witness is entitled to the full panoply of due process rights normally available to any criminal defendant.

Being found guilty of criminal contempt can result in substantial sentences of imprisonment, as opposed to the remand for civil contempt (1980: 246):

"The purpose of the remand is coercive [to compel testimony], while the purpose of the criminal contempt sentence is punitive and deterrent." Of course, a witness, whether immunized or not, is subject to the laws against perjury.

Other Consequences. In 1972 the Supreme Court decided the case of *Kastigar* v. *United States* (406 U.S. 441, 92 S.Ct. 1653), which involved several persons who had been subpoenaed to appear before a federal grand jury in California in 1971. The assistant United States attorney, believing that the petitioners (in *Kastigar*) were likely to assert their Fifth Amendment privilege, secured from the federal district court an order directing them to answer all questions and produce evidence before the grand jury under a grant of immunity. The persons involved refused to answer questions, arguing that the "scope of the immunity provided by the statute was not coextensive with the scope of the privilege against self-incrimination, and therefore was not sufficient to supplant the privilege and compel their testimony." The Supreme Court, in upholding the immunity order, quoted from the federal immunity statute:

> . . . the witness may not refuse to comply with the order on the basis of his privilege against self-incrimination; but no testimony or other information compelled under the order (or any information directly or indirectly derived from such testimony or other information) may be used against the witness in any *criminal* case, except a prosecution for perjury, giving a false statement, or otherwise failing to comply with the order [emphasis added].

The Supreme Court concluded that since the statute prohibited the prosecutorial authorities from using the compelled testimony in *any* respect, it therefore ensured that the testimony could not lead to the infliction of criminal penalties on the witness. In a dissenting opinion, Justice Thurgood Marshall pointed out the possibility of using the testimonial information for investigative leads designed to secure evidence against the witness. The court majority agreed that the statute barred such use of the testimony.

Robert Rhodes (1984: 191) points out, however, that *civil* action against a (*criminally*) immunized witness is possible:

> Such a situation has been upheld by the appellate courts. *Patrick* v. *United States*[1] provides an illustration. Patrick's immunized testimony regarding sports gambling before a grand jury revealed undeclared income and led to a jeopardy assessment for wagering taxes amounting to $835,558. Patrick argued he was being punished without due process. The court responded that "the jeopardy assessment is merely a method of enforcing a civil obligation, rather than a form of punishment."

In addition, a grant of immunity does not protect the witness from a loss of social status, employment, and, most important, revenge from those against whom he or she testified.

When to Use Immunity

Rufus King (1963: 651) raises additional issues:

> . . . the immunity bargain is a somewhat unsavory device per se, inaccurate and potentially very unfair; it should be used only sparingly and where it is absolutely required. Immunity grants are always exchanges, a pardon for crimes that would otherwise be punishable, given in return for testimony that could otherwise be withheld. In every case the interrogating authority must enter into a special "deal" with a wrongdoer to buy his testimony at the price of exoneration for something [for which] he would otherwise deserve punishment. . . .
>
> Such bargains are always somewhat blind. Ordinarily the witness will be hostile, so that his examiners cannot be sure in advance exactly what value the withheld testimony will have. And at the same time, especially in broad legislative or administrative inquiries, it is impossible to tell beforehand just what crimes are likely to be exonerated. Conceivably, the witness may have a surprise ready for his questioners at every turn of the proceedings.

Because of the potentially undesirable repercussions, some prosecutors have developed guidelines for consideration when making an immunity decision. The following are from the New Jersey Division of Criminal Justice (quoted in Committee on the Office of Attorney General 1978: 27):

1. Can the information be obtained from any source other than a witness who wants to negotiate immunity?
2. How useful is the information for the purposes of criminal prosecution?
3. What is the likelihood that the witness can successfully be prosecuted?
4. What is the relative significance of the witness as a potential defendant?
5. What is the relative significance of the potential defendant against whom the witness offers to testify? In other words, is the witness requesting immunity more culpable than those against whom she or he is agreeing to testify? Are they in a position to provide evidence against the witness, or superior evidence against others?
6. What is the value of the testimony of the witness to the case (is it the core evidence upon which the prosecution is based)?
7. What impact will immunity have on the credibility of the witness at trial? Are the terms of the immunity agreement so favorable to the witness that the jury will not accept the testimony? Rhodes (1984: 193) notes, however, "that a grant of immunity has a favorable impact on a jury. It makes a defendant's testimony more credible. A prosecutor can point to the witness with a sordid record and say to the jury, 'What reason does Mr. X have to lie? His immunity is assured and if he lies he will be prosecuted for perjury!'"
8. What impact will immunity have on the prosecutor's personal credibility and that of his or her office?

Witness Security Program

Because of the undesirable potential consequences for a witness who testifies against organized crime—either voluntarily or when compelled by immunity—efforts have been made to protect such witnesses from OC retribution. Such efforts are seen by some commentators as "only fair." In addition, they may offer just enough reassurance to coax information from a witness who would like to testify but is terrified by the possible consequences.

The program was instituted by the Organized Crime Control Act of 1970:

> SEC. 501. The Attorney General of the United States is authorized to provide for the security of Government witnesses, potential Government witnesses, and the families of Government witnesses and potential witnesses in legal proceedings against any person alleged to have participated in an organized criminal activity.
>
> SEC. 502. The Attorney General of the United States is authorized to rent, purchase, modify or remodel protected housing facilities and to otherwise offer to provide for the health, safety, and welfare of witnesses and persons intended to be called as Government witnesses, and the families of witnesses and persons intended to be called as Government witnesses in legal proceedings instituted against any person alleged to have participated in an organized criminal activity whenever, in his judgment testimony from, or a willingness to testify by, such a witness would place his life or person, or the life or person of a member of his family or household in jeopardy. Any person availing himself of such an offer by the Attorney General to use such facilities may continue to use such facilities for as long as the Attorney General determines the jeopardy to his life or person continues.

Administration

The program was given over to the United States Marshals Service to administer, with assistance from the Bureau of Prisons. The Permanent Subcommittee on Investigations of the Committee on Governmental Affairs of the United States Senate (hereafter PSI) points out (1981, *Witness Security Program:* 54):

> . . . there was logic to putting witness security in the Marshals Service. Law-enforcement officers wanted the protecting and relocating agency to be in the criminal justice system but to be as far removed as possible from both investigating agents and prosecutors. That way the Government could more readily counter the charge that cooperating witnesses were being paid or otherwise unjustifiably compensated in return for their testimony.

However, the Marshals Service was not prepared for these new responsibilities:

> The Marshals Service had other duties far removed from witness relocation such as Federal court security, the service of subpoenas and other matters related to the support of the judicial system.
>
> The skills required for these duties were not difficult to learn and, as a consequence, the educational requirements for service as a deputy marshal were not demanding.

This has changed. Marshals Service personnel are better trained, and a new position, that of inspector, was created specifically for the Witness Security Program. However, officials had not anticipated the size of this undertaking. They originally expected about two dozen persons to be relocated annually; instead, more than 300 persons are brought into the program each year.

Problems with the Program

There has been a great deal of criticism from within and outside of the program. Critics charge that the Marshals Service shields criminals, not only from would-be assassins, but also from debts and lawsuits; in some cases estranged spouses have been unable to visit their own children. In addition, some protected witnesses have returned to criminal activity. In large part, difficulties with this program are a result of the nature of the "clientele" (Permanent Subcommittee on Investigations 1981, *Witness Security Program:* 53–54):

> Many of the relocated witnesses were either organized crime figures themselves or were in some way associated with organized crime. In relocating these witnesses and their families, the marshals are often dealing with men and women who have never done an honest day's work in their lives.
>
> Many of them were skilled criminals—burglars, embezzlers, arsonists, physical enforcers—accustomed to lucrative financial rewards and a high standard of living. It is the task of the Marshals Service to protect these witnesses, find them homes, documentation and jobs and to advise them on how to go about establishing themselves in their new communities.

The PSI summarizes criticism from within the program (1981: 55):

> . . . Even when prosecutors and agents made no inflated promises, protected witnesses and their families were unhappy with the marshals and with the program. They suddenly found themselves in a strange environment in the hands of men and women who often seemed as overwhelmed as the protected families were by the many challenges of relocation.
>
> Understaffed by as much as 40 percent, the Marshals Service personnel were not only having to protect the relocated families against physical assault. They also had to offer leadership, guidance and assistance in obtaining housing, in finding employment, in actually recreating an existence.
>
> Documentation problems were commonplace. Constrained by a policy that required them to issue only real documentation, the marshals had to rely on other Federal and State agencies for essential papers—social security cards, birth certificates, car registration, passports, school records. The other agencies sometimes did not place a high priority on issuing the new documents. The documentation process became known for its delays.
>
> The marshals had to do things they not only were not trained for but which they didn't like doing. In some ways, they took on the duties of social workers. They had to be babysitters and chauffeurs. They had to listen and seem interested

when their relocated family members told them their troubles. But they couldn't be too interested and concerned for fear that their need for professional objectivity might be compromised.

Once the immediate fear of being murdered subsided, once the relocated families had the time and the presence of mind to take stock of their situation, many of them came to the conclusion they had been used and exploited and that they deserved more subsistence or services or favors from the Government for whom they had testified.

Not surprisingly, they sometimes became angry and resentful. The person they blamed was the marshal assigned to their case. Often they complained to him and his boss and other times they went to their Congressman and Senators or to the news organizations.

If the marshals themselves had been better prepared for their assignment, they might not have made so many mistakes. But often, because their personnel were not trained and because resources were limited, they erred with frequency.

This subcommittee report has listed some of the more typical mistakes that were made. The two most common shortcomings were in the areas of documentation and employment. In addition, witnesses were sometimes exposed to potential physical danger by offhand, thoughtless remarks. Incarcerated protected witnesses were sometimes left unprotected in general population areas of prisons where the threat of retaliatory assault was ever present.

Perhaps the most distressing aspect of the Witness Security Program has been the treatment of noncriminal witnesses who, although a small percentage of those participating, are (morally) entitled to the greatest amount of concern and assistance. The case of Chris and Marie provides an example (Mitchell 1980). The young couple had an infant son; Chris worked as a trainer of racehorses and Marie performed secretarial and bookkeeping functions for an insurance company. Marie left the firm after discovering ties to organized crime and a kickback scheme. Her employer demanded to know what she would do if called before a grand jury; "Tell the truth," she replied. A week later there was a telephone call warning her to "Keep your mouth shut, or else!" The angry couple went to the authorities. In return for her testimony, they were promised federal protection.

The day after her grand-jury testimony, the family was whisked out of their home to a motel. They were temporarily relocated to Albany, New York, and eventually California. They could not tell their parents where they were, nor could Chris take employment as a horse trainer. They were provided with new names, driver's licenses, and Social Security cards. However, they received no help with new employment, and they had to avoid all positions that required a background check. That left only menial jobs. In disgust Chris and Marie left the program.

---

[1] *Patrick v. United States*, 524 F.2d 1109, 1119 (1975). However, Rhodes notes, a prosecutor is prohibited from compelling testimony under a grant of (criminal) immunity simply to

elicit damaging statements for a civil action. The testimony compelled must be relevant to the criminal proceeding. As a result of Patrick's grand jury testimony, which concerned police payoffs, a police lieutenant was indicted. When Patrick refused to testify against the police officer, the latter was acquitted, and Patrick received a four-year sentence for criminal contempt.

chapter 19

Organized Crime:
Policy Issues

Used by permission of the Museum of Modern Art/Film Stills Archive

Public policy with respect to organized crime is the result of interactions between the news media, public opinion, and government, although not necessarily in that order. Government can influence the media by providing "anonymous sources," or by "leaking" information, or by holding public hearings. Investigations by fact-finding bodies, congressional committees, and presidential commissions have provided the grist for news media mills, which in turn have helped to form public opinion about OC. This has resulted in increased allocations for investigative agencies and new laws for dealing with OC. In other words, a symbiotic relationship exists between media representations, including fictional accounts such as *The Godfather*, public reaction, and governmental activity; one (or more) can trigger activity by the other(s). Whether it is the government that influences the media, or vice-versa, with the public playing some type of intervening role, depends on the particular scenario.

Government acted as the independent variable when it provided the disclosures of Joseph Valachi. The media reaction was extensive: newspaper and magazine coverage, televised hearings, a best-selling book,[1] and a motion picture starring Charles Bronson as Valachi. The public was properly primed for further governmental action: the Omnibus Crime Control and Safe Street Acts of 1968 and the Organized Crime Control Act of 1970.

Government Investigations

The importance of organized crime as a national political issue was recognized by Estes Kefauver back in 1950. He headed the first of the major congressional investigations into the phenomenon. It was succeeded by the "McClellan Committee," the Permanent Subcommittee on Investigations (PSI), and the President's Commission on Law Enforcement and Administration of Justice.

The Kefauver Crime Committee

The Special Senate Committee to Investigate Organized Crime in Interstate Commerce had its genesis in Senate Resolution 202, which was submitted on January 5, 1950, by Senator Estes Kefauver, Democrat, Tennessee, who subsequently became chairman of the committee. The resolution was referred to the Committee on the Judiciary, and upon being reported by the chairman of that committee on February 27, 1950, was referred to the Committee on Rules and Administration.

It was reported out of the Rules Committee on March 23, 1950, and on May 3, 1950, was considered and agreed to by the Senate.

A week later, the President of the Senate appointed a committee consisting of the author of the resolution, Senator Kefauver, Senator Herbert R. O'Conor,

Democrat, Maryland; Senator Lester C. Hunt, Democrat, Wyoming; Senator Alexander Wiley, Republican, Wisconsin, and Senator Charles W. Tobey, Republican, New Hampshire.

The function of the committee was to make a full and complete study and investigation to determine whether organized crime utilizes the facilities of interstate commerce or whether it operates otherwise through the avenues of interstate commerce to promote any transactions which violate Federal law or the law of the state in which such transactions might occur.

The committee was also charged with an investigation of the manner and extent of such criminal operations if it found them actually to be taking place and with the identification of the persons, firms, or corporations involved.

A third responsibility which was charged to the committee was the determination as to whether such interstate criminal operations were developing corrupting influences in violation of the federal law or the laws of any state. For purposes of the resolution there was included in the area to be covered the District of Columbia, the respective territories, and all possessions of the United States.

The committee was originally intended by resolution to submit a report to the Senate not later than February 28, 1951, as to its findings with such recommendations as might be deemed advisable. The authority conferred by the resolution was to have terminated on March 31, 1951, but both dates were extended, the date for the report to May 1, 1951, and the date for the committee's expiration to September 1, 1951.

The committee held hearings in pursuance of its charge in 14 cities. They included Washington, D.C.; Tampa, Florida; Miami; New York City; Cleveland, Ohio; St. Louis, Missouri; Kansas City, Missouri; New Orleans; Chicago; Detroit; Philadelphia; Las Vegas; Los Angeles and San Francisco.

In all, it heard testimony from more than 600 witnesses. Many of these were high officials of the federal, state, and city governments in various areas visited by the committee. The record of testimony covers thousands of pages of printed matter. . . . (*Kefauver Crime* Report, 1951: 20–21).

This flurry of activity led the committee to conclude (1951: 2):

There is a sinister criminal organization known as the Mafia operating throughout the country with ties in other nations, in the opinion of the committee. The Mafia is the direct descendant of a criminal organization of the same name originating in the island of Sicily. In this country, the Mafia has also been known as the Black Hand and the Unione Siciliano [sic]. The membership of the Mafia today is not confined to persons of Sicilian origin. The Mafia is a loose-knit organization specializing in the sale and distribution of narcotics, the conduct of various gambling enterprises, prostitution, and other rackets based on extortion and violence. The Mafia is the binder which ties together the two major criminal syndicates [Accardo-Guzik-Fischetti syndicate, whose headquarters are Chicago; and the Costello-Lansky syndicate based in New York] as well as numerous other criminal groups throughout the country. The power of the Mafia is based on a ruthless enforcement of its edicts and its own law of vengeance to which have been credibly attributed literally hundreds of murders throughout the country.

More startling than the committee's conclusions was the extent of public interest in the televised hearings. Theodore Wilson (1975: 353) notes:

> One factor, television, was largely responsible for fixing the public consciousness upon this one investigation. . . . For the first time millions of Americans (some twenty million by one estimate) observed the periodic outbursts of drama and boredom which comprised a congressional hearing as it unfolded. Americans gaped as the denizens of other worlds—bookies, pimps, and gangland enforcers, crime bosses and their slippery lawyers—marched across their television screens. They watched and were impressed by the schoolmasterish Estes Kefauver, the dignified Tennessean who was the committee's first chairman, as he condemned criminals and the system of ineffective law enforcement, graft, and popular apathy which permitted them to thrive.

The highlight of committee activities was the public hearings held in New York City beginning on March 12, 1951, and lasting eight days. At times the hearings drew 86.2 percent of the New York City area television-viewing audience. On March 13, Frank Costello made his first appearance before the committee and, because he objected to the cameras, only his hands were exposed to television viewers. The result was dramatic: Costello's hands were seen twisting and clenching as committee counsel Rudolph Halley fired pointed and accusing questions, many of which Costello refused to answer on the grounds of self-incrimination.

William H. Moore (1974) notes that the Kefauver committee did not actually engage in any extensive investigative undertakings but merely helped to dramatize the views of citizen crime commissions, journalists, and the Federal Bureau of Narcotics. He argues that the committee played a vital role in perpetuating a Mafia-conspiracy interpretation of organized crime in the United States. Wilson (1975: 377) notes that "it is clear that Kefauver and his colleagues, responding to public pressures, were determined from the beginning to find a scapegoat, some type of conspiratorial group with responsibility for much of America's crime." The hearings made Senator Kefauver a national political figure and a contender for the Democratic presidential nomination in 1952. However, the hearings were a source of embarrassment for President Harry Truman (a product of the Kansas City Pendergast machine) and Democratic party officials from urban areas—they denied Kefauver the nomination. (Kefauver, a strong supporter of civil rights, became the Democratic candidate for vice-president in 1956. He died in Washington of a heart attack at age sixty on August 10, 1963.) The Kefauver Committee expired in 1951.

McClellan Committee

In 1956 the Senate Permanent Subcommittee on Investigations (PSI), under its chairman, John L. McClellan of Arkansas, began to look into reports of financial irregularities on the part of officials of the International Brotherhood of Teamsters (IBT). This effort was headed by PSI chief counsel Robert Kennedy. The IBT refused to cooperate, and Senator McClellan (1962: 18) noted:

> The response from the Senate was prompt and decisive. An eight-member bipartisan select committee was established, to be called the Senate Select Committee on Improper Activities in the Labor or Management Field. There were four Democratic members—Senators John F. Kennedy (Mass.), Sam J. Ervin, Jr. (N.C.), Pat McNamara (Mich.), and John L. McClellan (Ark.). There were four Republicans—Senators Joseph McCarthy (Wis.), Irving M. Ives (N.Y.), Karl E. Mundt (S. Dak.), and Barry Goldwater (Ariz.). . . . This Select Committee was launched with a unanimous vote on the afternoon of January 30, 1957.

The Select Committee summoned IBT president Dave Beck, who appeared on March 26, 1957. Beck

> . . . refused to answer any questions about his union or personal finances, taking the Fifth 140 times during the session. By the end of his March 1957 appearance before the committee . . . the ex-newspaper boy turned truckdriver turned top Teamster was ruined. . . . Several months later, in federal district court in Seattle, he was convicted of embezzlement (Moldea 1978: 71).

Beck was replaced by Jimmy Hoffa, whose encounter with the Select Committee and Robert Kennedy was discussed in chapter 14.

The findings of the McClellan Committee resulted in the passage of the 1959 Labor-Management Reporting and Disclosure Act, usually called the Landrum-Griffin Act for its sponsors. The Select Committee expired in 1960, but Senator McClellan remained chairman of the Permanent Subcommittee on Investigations. In 1963 the PSI held televised hearings and introduced the public to its star witness, Joseph Valachi.[2]

Joseph Valachi

In 1962 Joseph Valachi, a convicted drug trafficker and "made-guy" in the Genovese Family, was serving a sentence at the U.S. Penitentiary in Atlanta, Georgia. A fellow inmate accused Valachi of being an informer for the Federal Bureau of Narcotics. His accuser was also a "made-guy," and this made the accusation very serious—life threatening. On June 22, 1963, Valachi was approached by an inmate he thought was Joseph DiPalermo ("Joe Beck"), an enforcer for the Genovese Family. Valachi attacked him with a lead pipe and beat him to death. A little more than one year later, during September and October, 1963, Valachi was in Washington, D.C., appearing before the McClellan Committee.

Valachi was inducted—"made"—into the Maranzano faction during the

Casellammarese War; he had been a *soldato* for more than thirty years. Before a national television audience Valachi told of a secret criminal organization called "La Cosa Nostra," blood oaths, the Castellammarese War, Luciano's murder of Joe Masseria, Salvatore Maranzano and some forty "mustache Petes." He outlined the structure of each Family and explained how they were linked together through a national commission—the "Supreme Court of Organized Crime."

Virgil W. Peterson, a former FBI agent and executive director of the Chicago Crime Commission for twenty-seven years, states (1983: 425):

> Valachi made a remarkable impact on the literature relating to organized crime. In fact, it was Valachi who quite likely coined the name *Cosa Nostra,* using it to denote an Italian criminal organization. During the years following his revelations, the great majority of published books, articles, and news items that have attempted to describe the structure of organized crime in America clearly reveal a heavy reliance on Valachi. Likewise, his disclosures have been accepted without much questioning by many official agencies as well. On some occasions, writers have either misinterpreted portions of Valachi's testimony or attributed to him statements he never made at all.

Peterson notes, however, that "some of Valachi's testimony was extremely vague, confusing, and inconsistent. Not infrequently, it would appear, he either withheld facts that should have been known to him or deliberately lied." In short, Valachi was a low-echelon member of the Genovese Family, a barely literate soldier whose first-hand knowledge was limited to street-level experiences. This did not prevent his disclosures about "La Cosa Nostra" from becoming the core of a chapter on organized crime in a major federal report.

The President's Commission on Law Enforcement and Administration of Justice

In 1964 Lyndon B. Johnson was serving the remainder of the term of John F. Kennedy and seeking election as president; the Republicans nominated Sen. Barry M. Goldwater of Arizona. The Republicans launched what was to become known as a "law-and-order" campaign, attacking the Democratic administration for being soft on crime. Johnson won a landslide victory, but the issue of "crime in the streets" lingered on. In order to blunt criticism (and, Richard Quinney [1974] argues, divert attention away from the Vietnam conflict) Johnson launched his own "war on crime." In a message to the Eighty-ninth Congress[3] the president announced: "I am establishing the President's Commission on Law Enforcement and Administration of Justice. The Commission will be composed of men and women of distinction who share my belief that we need to know far more about the prevention and control of crime." The Commission was headed by Atty. Gen. Nicholas deB. Katzenbach; the Task Force on Organized Crime (there were nine different task forces) was headed by Charles H. Rogovin and included Donald R. Cressey and Ralph Salerno as consultants. Cressey (1969) and Salerno (1969) extended the influence of the president's commission (and Joseph Valachi) by authoring books on organized crime.

In its report to the commission, the Task Force on Organized Crime (1967: 6; emphasis added) states:

> Today the core of organized crime in the United States consists of 24 groups operating as criminal cartels in large cities across the Nation. Their membership is exclusively men of Italian descent, they are in frequent communication with each other, and their smooth functioning is insured by a national body of overseers. To date, only the Federal Bureau of Investigation has been able to document fully the national scope of these groups, and FBI intelligence indicates that *the organization as a whole has changed its name from the Mafia to La Cosa Nostra.*

Hank Messick (1973: 8) argues that the revelations of Valachi relieved the FBI of its neglect of organized crime: "La Cosa Nostra was created as a public image. This simple device of giving the Mafia a new name worked wonders. Hoover was taken off the limb where he had perched so long, and citizens had a new menace to talk about with tales of blood oaths, contracts for murder, secret societies," a picture thirty years out of date. More important, however, were the policy implications.

Budgetary allocations were increased to deal with the "new" menace and in 1967 federal organized-crime strike forces were established in each city with an LCN Family. In 1968 the Omnibus Crime Control and Safe Streets Act was enacted providing law enforcement agencies with legal authority to engage in wiretapping and electronic surveillance. In 1970, Congress passed the Organized Crime Control Act which contains the RICO features discussed in chapter 16. The federal government's preoccupation with LCN has resulted in criticism from local enforcement officials who must contend with non-LCN organized criminal activities. Capt. David A. Dailey, commanding officer of the Organized Crime Division of the Columbus, Ohio, Police Department, told the McClellan Committee

> . . . Cosa Nostra crime families and their associates are major crime problems in some areas. But in Columbus, for example, Cosa Nostra is not a major factor. But we do have an organized crime entity in Columbus which has all of the traits and structural characteristics of a Cosa Nostra gang. The gang is allegedly involved in any number of Federal and interstate violations—arson, narcotics, theft, and fencing, extortion, pornography, weapons infractions, auto theft, fraud, interstate movement of women for prostitution, and gambling. The group has a boss and an underboss and senior members we call sub-bosses but who could just as easily be termed capos. In virtually every regard, this group is a continuing organized criminal gang. But the problem is that none of its members is an Italian-American. Nor do any of its members have ties to Cosa Nostra gang members. Except for a limited interest in the group by the FBI, Federal authorities will not

investigate this organization [Permanent Subcommittees on Investigations 1984, *Profile of Organized Crime: Great Lakes Region:* 95].

John Sopko, counsel to the PSI and a former federal prosecutor in Ohio, said during the same hearing (1984: 75):

> In those cases where we were unable to prove an LCN connection, many of them were turned down by the Justice Department in Washington. . . . In a number of cases we just had to send the agents back out and told them to find us an LCN contact, find us some LCN involvement. If they were able to do it, we then worked the case.

The Media as Models for Organized Crime

While it is obvious that crime and criminals generate a great deal of media attention which can influence the public and public officials, what is the effect of the media on organized crime? Do criminals concern themselves with, and perhaps even act out roles inspired by, television, movies, books, and newspaper and magazine accounts of organized crime?

The notorious ("Crazy") Joey Gallo copied George Raft and later Richard Widmark when he "played" the gangster. Carl Klockars (1974), in his study of a fence, Vincent Swaggi (a pseudonym), notes that Swaggi believed that film characters strongly influence the style if not the techniques of criminals. Criminals also read, and they appear to like books about crime. Ianni (1972) reports that one member of the Lupollo family began to refer to the family patriarch as the "Godfather" soon after Mario Puzo's book was published. Rubinstein and Reuter (1978a) report that all their informants had read *The Valachi Papers* or seen *The Godfather*. This writer was with an OC figure when he pointed to Gay Talese's (1971) book *Honor Thy Father* in the writer's library and began discussing its central character, Joseph Bonanno. He also stated that he never heard the term *Cosa Nostra* until it was popularized by Valachi—after which low-level OC figures began using it. Renée Buse (1965: 206) reports that when ("Big") John Ormento, a *caporegime* in the Genovese Family, was arrested for violating narcotics laws, federal agents found in his Lido Beach, New York, home a copy of Frederic Sondern's (1959) *Brotherhood of Evil:* "It had obviously been read carefully, as dog-eared pages and underlined passages marked the text which dealt with Ormento." On March 21, 1980, Angelo Bruno, the 69-year old patriarch of the Bruno crime Family was killed by a shotgun blast as he sat in front of his unpretentious row home in south Philadelphia. Philip ("Chicken Man") Testa, Family underboss, succeeded Bruno. On March 15, 1981, the 57-year old Testa was killed by a bomb blast that exploded at his south Philadelphia home. Peter Lupsha states that when law enforcement officers entered Testa's house after the bombing they found two videos, *Godfather I* and *Godfather II* next to the VCR. On the side of Testa's favorite chair was a copy of Demaris' book (1981) on

Jimmy Fratianno, *The Last Mafioso,* in which he had been making marginal notes and comments (personal correspondence).

Testifying before the PSI, Robert Delaney, an undercover detective for the New Jersey State Police, reported (1981, *Waterfront Corruption:* 372):

> The movies, "Godfather I" and "Godfather II," have had an impact on these crime families. Some of the members and associates would inquire of me, had I seen the movie? I said, yes. They would reply that they'd seen it three and four times. One young man said he'd seen it 10 times.
>
> At dinner one night at a restaurant, Patrick Kelly and I were with Joseph Doto, who is the son of Joseph Adonis, and known as Joey Adonis, Jr. Joey Adonis, Jr. gave the waiter a pocketful of quarters and told him to play the juke box continuously and to play the same song, the theme music from the "Godfather." All through dinner, we listened to the same song, over and over.
>
> Senator NUNN. In other words, you are saying sometimes they go to the movie to see how they themselves are supposed to behave, is that right?
>
> Mr. DELANEY. That is true. They had a lot of things taught to them through the movie. They try to live up to it. The movie was telling them how.

That criminal organization can reflect media influence is highlighted by Ianni (1974: 95). He reports that "Bro Squires," a pseudonym for a prominent black narcotics dealer in Newark, New Jersey, decided upon a paramilitary organization: "He got the idea from the movie The Battle for Algiers." Ianni states that the Squires organization was patterned after the movie—"and it worked."

Responding to Organized Crime: Policy Implications

Responding in a rational manner to organized crime requires a sense of proportion, if not an appreciation of American history. Organized crime in America can be conceived of as one stage along a continuum dating back to the earliest days of our history. Our colonial forebearers exhibited many of the activities currently associated with organized crime: bribery, usury, and monopoly, not to mention the seizure of land by force, indentured servitude, and slavery. Early American adventurers cheated and killed native Americans, and chartered pirates—privateers—plundered the high seas. During the War of 1812, and later during the Civil War, profiteers accumulated fortunes while others suffered and died. The range wars in the West, the frauds, bribery, violence, and monopolistic practices of the "robber barons"—all are part of the context in which we must understand modern forms of organized criminality.

Organized crime has provided an opportunity for certain groups to move into the wider legitimate society on a level that would otherwise not be available. There are, of course, ethical and moral objections to "blasting" or "thieving" into the middle or upper strata, but this has been a feature of our history from the earliest days. We must also note that very few management-level members of OC have been able to escape either assassination or significant prison terms. Indeed, one can be impressed with law-enforcement efforts against OC, constrained as they are by the requirements of a democratic system that provides a great deal of legal protection to even its criminal citizens.

There are three basic (but not mutually exclusive) responses to organized crime:

1. Expanding the authority of law enforcement.
2. Increasing law-enforcement resources.
3. Decreasing criminal opportunity (decriminalization).

Expanding Law-Enforcement Authority

The first response is inexpensive—at least with respect to scarce tax dollars. It involves the enactment of statutes that would make it easier to investigate, prosecute, and punish persons involved in organized criminal activity. For example, legislation could be enacted that would make it easy for law-enforcement agencies to use wiretapping and electronic surveillance. We could also give the FBI and DEA complete access to state and federal income-tax returns.

While this response may be financially inexpensive, there are potential costs. Herbert Packer (1968) notes that criminal justice can be conceived of as a continuum ranging from *crime control* to *due process*. Crime control requires law-enforcement efficiency, while due process presents law enforcement with an "obstacle course." Crime control stresses ease of investigation and prosecution; due process stresses limits on the ability of government to investigate and convict. In other words, our ability to respond to OC is limited by our concern for privacy and freedom.

Increasing Law-Enforcement Resources

The second response is financially expensive—it requires an increase in budgetary allocations for law enforcement. Richard Neely (1982: 28) points out that this will also mean an increase in the surveillance of persons not involved in OC:

> One example should illustrate the point. Cheating on federal and state income taxes is pervasive in all classes of society; except among the compulsively honest, cheating usually occurs in direct proportion to opportunity. Why, then, do we not expand the Internal Revenue Service and its state counterparts? Every new revenue agent pays his salary and overhead at least eight times. The answer is that we do not really want Rhadamanthine enforcement of the tax laws. . . .

. . . Most people probably feel as I do about forgiving their neighbor's tax trespasses in return for minimal harassment by Uncle Sam. . . .

Decriminalization

The third response, reducing profit-making criminal opportunity, was an argument frequently advanced by those favoring the legalization of gambling: "It will take away profits from organized crime." Of course, it has done no such thing. The legal lottery, for example, has not hurt illegal numbers operators; it has merely caused more people to gamble. In Chicago, the illegal numbers game thrives despite the success of the Illinois State Lottery; the illegal operators provide better odds and do not report winners to tax officials. The daily lottery provides illegal operators with a free layoff service so that they can always balance out their bets. Of course the real reason for the rush to all forms of legalized gambling is revenue—an "easy" way for elected officials to raise money without raising taxes. This led to aggressive advertising campaigns to encourage people to gamble. Whatever else may be said about organized crime, its operatives do not advertise their services on radio and television.

There is an alternative to the American—"Las Vegas"—model of legalized gambling. The "British Model" is based on a view of gambling as a social problem; legal gambling is tolerated, not to secure revenue, but because the alternative appears even more socially harmful. The promotion of gambling through advertisement and entertainment is not permitted (Skolnick 1978). England also provides a model for moving the drug problem out of criminal justice, thus reducing criminal opportunity. Under government supervision, narcotic drugs are dispensed to registered addicts.

Latent Functions

Any strategy for responding to OC may have negative, unintended consequences. Providing drugs to registered addicts would reduce illegal profits and make the remaining black market unattractive to OC. However, the impact of making illegal substances readily available, both to current abusers and to potential abusers, is not known. It could conceivably increase the drug-abusing population, much as legalized gambling has increased the number of persons who gamble regularly.

A successful law-enforcement effort against heroin will reduce available supply without affecting demand. The result: an increase in the retail price of heroin and an increase in criminal activity by heroin addicts. Or, a rise in the price of heroin may cause more persons to become involved in drug trafficking (either heroin or a variety of substitutes). On the other hand, reducing the level of law enforcement will increase the available supply of drugs, increase competition, and lower both prices and profits.

While drug trafficking has had only a limited economic impact in the United States, most notably in south Florida, cocaine and marijuana trafficking has had a dramatic impact in countries of Latin America. Profits from drug trafficking have allowed criminals in several countries to corrupt and distort the governmental process. On the other hand, trafficking in heroin has provided financial support for anticommunist irregulars operating in Southeast Asia and Afghanistan.

Reducing opportunity can have serious consequences. As noted in part 3, Prohibition helped convert "street thugs" into "crime czars." Without Prohibition these persons and their multiplicitous followers would probably have remained criminals of a more conventional, but often more dangerous, type. In some communities that lack adequate legitimate economic opportunity, OC may be a major employer. A crackdown on illegal gambling under such circumstances can have serious, unintended consequences, as otherwise unemployable persons seek new sources of income. There is no reason to believe that by merely reducing the opportunity for involvement in OC we will reduce criminality. The reduction of opportunity, if it is to be meaningful in terms of making society safer, must include changes that will substantially widen legitimate opportunity for those who will otherwise *innovate*. For some it is already too late. Ghetto youngsters in many urban areas have already tasted *la dolce vita*—their role models and way of life have already been established. What reasonable alternative can we offer youngsters who have been earning hundreds of dollars a day for distributing drugs?

Justine Dintino and Frederick Martens (1980: 66) review the unintended consequences of "random law enforcement," that which is not part of a well-defined plan for dealing with OC:

> . . . as risks are increased through law enforcement, the more rational, professional criminal entrepreneurs will profit from the mistakes of their relatively amateur, "irrational" colleagues. Said differently, the individual criminal entrepreneur who is unable to minimize competitive factors and risks associated with the increase in enforcement would more than likely be driven out of business or be eliminated by either competitors or the police (or both). In effect, this would expand domain for the more professional criminal entrepreneur and possibly strengthen criminal organization.

Charles R. Thom, police commissioner of Suffolk County, New York, highlights such a situation (Task Force on Organized Crime, 1967: 30n):

> It is somewhat startling to learn that the syndicates are particularly happy with the consolidation of the nine police departments into the Suffolk County Police Department, as they feel that protection is easier to arrange through one agency than through many. The intensive campaign against gamblers initiated by this department . . . had the astounding side effect of solving the recruitment problem

of the syndicate, as our drive successfully stampeded the independents into the arms of the syndicate for protection, and the syndicate can now pick and choose which operators they wish to admit.

Dintino and Martens (1980) point out that improperly focused law enforcement can result in an illicit market being effectively organized by an OC group.

Jonathan Rubinstein and Peter Reuter (1977: 102) found that in New York City *reduced* police activity with respect to the numbers apparently dealt a damaging blow to OC:

> The dominance of Italian-American operators at least until the time of the Knapp Commission [investigating police corruption] is . . . quite striking. While they were never exclusive operators of the racket, and several large Numbers operations in the Bronx and Brooklyn are operated by members of other ethnic groups, it is not an exaggeration to say that the Numbers was an Italian-run racket until quite recently.

By 1977, however, the number of independent operations was increasing, and the men running them black and Hispanic. Rubinstein and Reuter speculate on the reason for the changes (1977: 146–47):

> . . . it is clear that corrupt policemen were important agents in the operations of Numbers banks prior to 1970 and are relatively unimportant now. Without implying that corrupt police discriminate in the acceptance of bribes, we might assume a strong preference on their part to take money from established operators who can offer credible promises to keep the peace. Also, these established operators had the necessary connections to make arrangements with corrupt agents in the other criminal justice agencies which were necessary to assure their dominance. Certainly the police would have incentives to cooperate with the existing Numbers operators in disciplining their controllers who might be tempted to leave the bank. The elimination of routine, embedded corruption in the police, combined with a reduction in street-level enforcement seems sufficient to explain emerging autonomy of black and Hispanic racket operators.

Conclusion

Organized crime evolved out of moralistic laws that created opportunity for certain innovative actors. As circumstances changed, so did available opportunity, and organized crime proved quite dynamic. Beginning as essentially a provider of "goods and services," it entered racketeering and legitimate business, adapting to changing laws and social and economic conditions. Policy for responding to OC must be based on an appreciation of history, an understanding of the "side effects" of proposed policy changes, and the realization that organized crime has proven to be indeed a dynamic phenomenon.

---

[1] In his (1968) book Peter Maas provides an author's note that is quite revealing: "The *Valachi Papers* could not have in fact been written without the help and encouragement of a

number of concerned individuals, particularly in the Department of Justice and the Federal Bureau of Investigation."

[2] Peter Maas (1968: 40) states that Senator McClellan visited Valachi privately at the District of Columbia jail just before the hearings began: "According to Valachi, he requested he skip any mention of Hot Springs, in McClellan's home state . . . ," which was notorious for its wide-open gambling operations.

[3] "Crime, Its Prevalence and Measures of Prevention." Message from the President of the United States. House of Representatives, 89th Congress, March 8, 1965, Document no. 103.

References

Abadinsky, Howard
    1983   *The Criminal Elite: Professional and Organized Crime.* Westport, Conn.: Greenwood.
    1981   *The Mafia in America: An Oral History.* New York: Praeger.

Adams, Nathan M.
    1977   "America's Newest Crime Syndicate—The Mexican Mafia." *Reader's Digest* (November): 97–102.

Albini, Joseph L.
    1971   *The American Mafia: Genesis of a Legend.* New York: Appleton-Century-Crofts.

Alexander, Herbert E., and Gerald E. Caiden
    1985   *The Politics and Economics of Organized Crime.* Lexington, Mass.: D. C. Heath.

Allsop, Kenneth
    1968   *The Bootleggers: The Story of Prohibition.* New Rochelle, N.Y.: Arlington House.

Allum, P. A.
    1973   *Politics and Society in Post-War Naples.* Cambridge: Cambridge University Press.

Anderson, Annelise Graebner
    1979   *The Business of Organized Crime: A Cosa Nostra Family.* Stanford, Calif.: Hoover Institution Press.

Anderson, Harry, with Andrew Nagorski and Elaine Shannon
    1984   "An Informer Betrays the Mafia." *Newsweek* (October 15): 56–60.

Anderson, Robert T.
    1965   "From Mafia to Cosa Nostra." *American Journal of Sociology* 71 (November): 302–310.

Andrews, Wayne
    1941   *The Vanderbilt Legend.* New York: Harcourt, Brace.

Aronson, Harvey
    1978   *Deal.* New York: Ballantine Books.
    1973   *The Killing of Joey Gallo.* New York: Putnam's.

Asbury, Herbert
    1942   *Gem of the Prairie: An Informal History of the Chicago Underworld.* Garden City, N.Y.: Knopf.
    1936   *The French Quarter.* New York: Knopf.
    1928   *Gangs of New York.* New York: Knopf.

Aschmann, Homer
    1975   "The Persistent Guajiro." *Natural History* 84 (March): 28–37.

Audett, James Henry

1954   *Rap Sheet: My Life Story*. New York: William Sloane.

Bacherach, Samuel B., and Edward J. Lawler

1976   "The Perception of Power." *Social Forces* 55 (September): 123–34.

Bain, Donald

1978   *War in Illinois*. Englewood Cliffs, N.J.: Prentice-Hall.

Baker, Russell

1977   "Galente Can Have It." *New York Times Magazine* (March 13): 8.

Barboza, Joe, and Hank Messick

1975   *Barboza*. New York: Dell.

Barrett, Lawrence, and John Tompkins

1977   "The Mafia: Big, Bad and Booming." *Time* (May 16): 32–42.

Barzini, Luigi

1977   "Italians in New York: The Way We Were in 1929." *New York* (April 4): 34–38.

1965   *The Italians*. New York: Atheneum.

Beck, Melinda

1985   "Feeding America's Habit." *Newsweek* (February 25:) 22–23.

Beigel, Herbert, and Allan Beigel

1977   *Beneath the Badge: A Story of Police Corruption*. New York: Harper and Row.

Bell, Daniel

1964   *The End of Ideology*. Glencoe, Ill.: The Free Press.

1963   "The Myth of the Cosa Nostra." *The New Leader* 46 (December): 12–15.

Bell, Ernest A., ed.

1909   *War on the White Slave Trade*. Chicago: Thompson.

Bequai, August

1979   *Organized Crime: The Fifth Estate*. Lexington, Mass.: Heath.

Berger, Meyer

1957   "Anastasia Slain in a Hotel Here: Led Murder, Inc." *New York Times* (October 26): 1, 12.

1950   "Gross Won't Name Police Associates." *New York Times* (September 21): 1, 20.

1944   "Lepke's Reign of Crime Lasted Over 12 Murder-Strewn Years." *New York Times* (March 5): 30.

1940   "Gang Patterns: 1940." *New York Times Magazine* (August 4): 5, 15.

1935   "Schultz Reigned on Discreet Lines." *New York Times* (October 25): 17.

Berlet, Chip

1981   "Private Spies." *Chicago Reader* 11 (December 11): 1, 20–27, 32–40.

Berman, Susan

1981   *Easy Street*. New York: Dial Press.

Bishop, Jim

1971   *The Days of Martin Luther King, Jr.* New York: Putnam's.

Bishop, Wayne

1971   "L.E.I.U.: An Early System." *Police Chief* (September): 30.

Blakey, G. Robert

1983   "Organized Crime: Enforcement Strategies." *Encyclopedia of Crime and Justice*. New York: Free Press.

1967   "Organized Crime in the United States." *Current History* 52: 327–33, 364–65.

Blakey, G. Robert, Ronald Goldstock, and Charles H. Rogovin

1978   *Rackets Bureaus: Investigation and Prosecution of Organized Crime.* Washington, D.C.: U.S. Government Printing Office.

Blau, Peter M.

1964   *Exchange and Power in Social Life.* New York: John Wiley.

1956   *Bureaucracy in Modern Society.* New York: Random House.

Bloch, Max, with Ron Kenner

1982   *Max the Butcher.* Secaucas, N.J.: Lyle Stuart.

Block, Alan A.

1979   *East Side—West Side: Organizing Crime in New York, 1930–1950.* Swansea, United Kingdom: Christopher Davis.

1978   "History and the Study of Organized Crime." *Urban Life* 6 (January): 455–74.

1975   "Lepke, Kid Twist and the Combination: Organized Crime in New York City, 1930-1944." Ph.D. dissertation, University of California at Los Angeles.

Block, Alan A. and Frank R. Scarpitti

1985   *Poisoning For Profit: The Mafia and Toxic Waste.* New York: William Morrow

Blok, Anton

1974   *The Mafia of a Sicilian Village, 1860–1960: A Study of Violent Peasant Entrepreneurs.* New York: Harper and Row.

Blum, Howard

1984   "Agents Focus on Detroit Drug Traffic." *New York Times* (February 15): 8.

1977   "New York Gang Reported to Sell Death and Drugs." *New York Times* (December 16): 1, D12.

Blum, Howard, and Leonard Buder

1978   "The War on 138th Street." *New York Times* (six articles appearing on page one from December 18 through December 23).

Blum, Howard, and Jeff Gerth

1978   "The Mob Gambles on Atlantic City." *New York Times Magazine* (February 5): 10–51.

Blum, Richard H.

1984   *Offshore Haven Banks, Trusts, and Companies: The Business of Crime in the Euromarket.* New York: Praeger.

Blumenthal, Ralph

1984   "28 Are Ordered Arrested in U.S. in Mafia Inquiry." *New York Times* (October 2): 1, 17.

1984   "Unknown Arm of Mafia in U.S. Reported Found." *New York Times.* (October 3): 1, 16.

Boissevain, Jeremy

1974   *Friends of Friends: Networks, Manipulators and Coalitions.* Oxford: Basil Blackwell.

Bonanno, Joseph

1983   *A Man of Honor: The Autobiography of Joseph Bonanno.* New York: Simon and Schuster.

Bowman, Jim
    1984   "The Long Hot Summer when Chicago Erupted in Violence." *Chicago Tribune Magazine* (August 29): 7.
    1983a "Beer, Bribery, and Bullets: 'Spike' O'Donnell's Chicago." *Chicago Tribune Magazine* (October 2): 8.
    1983b " 'Greasy Thumb' Guzik: From Brothel to Bookkeeper for Al Capone's Gang." *Chicago Tribune Magazine* (March 8): 10.
Boyd, Kier T.
    1977   *Gambling Technology*. Washington, D.C.: U.S. Government Printing Office.
Brashler, William
    1981   "Two Brothers from Taylor Street." *Chicago* (September): 150–56, 194.
    1977   *The Don: The Life and Death of Sam Giancana*. New York: Harper and Row.
Brecher, Edward M., and the editors of *Consumer Reports*
    1974   *Licit and Illicit Drugs*. Boston: Little, Brown.
Brenner, Marie
    1981   "The Godfather's Child." *New York* (March 2): 18–20.
Bresler, Fenton
    1980   *The Chinese Mafia*. New York: Stein and Day.
Brill, Steven
    1978   *The Teamsters*. New York: Simon and Schuster.
Brinkley, Joel
    1984a "Bolivia in Turmoil at Drug Crackdown." *New York Times* (September 12): 1, 6.
    1984b "In the Drug War, Battles Won and Lost." *New York Times* (September 13): 1, 8.
Broder, Jonathan
    1984   "As a Tradeoff, Soviets Let Afghan Heroin Flow." *Chicago Tribune* (September 2): 12.
Brodt, Bonita
    1981a " 'Royal Family' Are Kings of Killing." *Chicago Tribune* (September 6): 5.
    1981b " 'Royal Family' Boss Gets Death for Killing." *Chicago Tribune* (September 10): 14.
Brown, Michael
    1980   "New Jersey Cleans Up Its Pollution Act." *New York Times Magazine* (November 23): 142–46.
Browne, Arthur
    1985   " 'Family' Heroin Ring Bared." *New York Daily News* (February 22): 3, 19.
Browning, Frank
    1982   "Cocaine Puts Dealers on Freeway to Legitimacy." *Chicago Tribune* (January 5): section 2, 1, 2.
Buenker, John D.
    1973   *Urban Liberalism and Progressive Reform*. New York: Scribner's.
"Bugs Moran Dies in Federal Prison."
    1957   *New York Times* (February 26): 59.

Bullough, Vern L.
    1965   *The History of Prostitution*. New Hyde Park, N.Y.: University Books.
Burnham, David
    1970a   "How Corruption Is Built into the System—and a Few Ideas for What to
             Do about It." *New York* (September 12): 30–37.
    1970b   "Police Corruption Fosters Distrust in the Ranks Here." *New York Times*
             (April 27): 1.
    1970c   "Graft Paid to Police Here Said to Run into Millions." *New York Times*
             (April 25): 1.
Buse, Renée
    1965   *The Deadly Silence*. Garden City, N.Y.: Doubleday.
"By Order of the Mafia."
    1888   *New York Times* (October 22): 8.
Byck, Robert, ed.
    1974   *Cocaine Papers: Sigmund Freud*. New York: Stonehill.
California Board of Corrections
    1978   *Prison Gangs in the Community*. Sacramento.
California Department of Justice
    1978   *Organized Crime and Intelligence Bureau*. Sacramento.
Campane, Jerome O.
    1981a   "Chains, Wheels, and the Single Conspiracy: part 1." *FBI Law Enforce-
             ment Bulletin* (August): 24–31.
    1981b   "Chains, Wheels, and the Single Conspiracy: Conclusion." *FBI Law
             Enforcement Bulletin* (September): 24–31.
Campbell, Rodney
    1977   *The Luciano Project*. New York: McGraw-Hill.
Capeci, Jerry
    1978   "Tieri: The Most Powerful Mafia Chieftain." *New York* (August 21): 22–
            26.
"Capone Dead at 48: Dry Era Gang Chief."
    1947   *New York Times* (January 26): 7.
Caputo, David A.
    1974   *Organized Crime and American Politics*. Morristown, N.J.: General
            Learning Press.
Cartey, Desmond
    1970   "How Black Enterprisers Do Their Thing: An Odyssey through Ghetto
            Capitalism." In *The Participant Observer: Encounters with Social Real-
            ity*, edited by Glenn Jacobs, 19–47. New York: George Braziller.
Carwardine, William H., and Virgil J. Vogel
    1973   *The Pullman Strike*. Chicago: Charles H. Kerr.
Cashman, Sean Dennis
    1981   *Prohibition*. New York: The Free Press.
Chafetz, Henry
    1960   *Play the Devil: A History of Gambling in the United States from 1492
            to 1955*. New York: Clarkson N. Potter.
Chamber of Commerce
    1970   *Marshalling Citizen Power against Crime*. Washington, D.C.: Chamber
            of Commerce.

Chambliss, William
  1975   "On the Paucity of Original Research on Organized Crime: A Footnote
         to Galliher and Cain." *American Sociologist* 10 (August): 36–39.
  1973   *Functional and Conflict Theories of Crime.* New York: MSS Modular
         Publications.
  1972   *Box-Man: A Professional Thief's Journey.* New York: Harper and Row.
Chandler, David Leon
  1975   *Brothers in Blood: The Rise of the Criminal Brotherhoods.* New York:
         Dutton.
Clark, Alfred E.
  1950   "Erickson's Records of Gambling Bare Underworld Links." *New York
         Times* (May 18): 1, 19.
Clark, Ramsey
  1970   *Crime in America.* New York: Simon and Schuster.
Clarke, Donald Henderson
  1929   *In the Reign of Rothstein.* New York: Grosset and Dunlap.
Clarke, Thurston, and John J. Tigue, Jr.
  1975   *Dirty Money: Swiss Banks, the Mafia, Money Laundering and White
         Collar Crime.* New York: Simon and Schuster.
Clinard, Marshall B., Peter C. Yeager, Jeanne Brissette, David Petrashek, and Elizabeth Harries
  1979   *Illegal Corporate Behavior.* Washington, D.C.: U.S. Government Print-
         ing Office.
Cloward, Richard A., and Lloyd E. Ohlin
  1960   *Delinquency and Opportunity.* New York: The Free Press.
Coffey, Thomas M.
  1975   *The Long Thirst: Prohibition in America: 1920–1933.* New York: Norton.
Cohen, Albert K.
  1965   "The Sociology of the Deviant Act: Anomie Theory and Beyond." *Amer-
         ican Sociological Review* 30 (February): 5–14.
Cohen, Mickey
  1975   *Mickey Cohen: In My Own Words.* Englewood Cliffs, N.J.: Prentice-
         Hall.
Cohen, Stanley
  1977   *The Game They Played.* New York: Farrar, Straus and Giroux.
Coleman, J. Walter
  1969   *The Molly McGuire Riots.* New York: Arno. Originally published in
         1936.
Collins, Randall
  1975   *Conflict Sociology.* New York: Academic Press.
Colombo, Furio
  1983   "Meaning of Italy's Vote." *New York Times* (July 13): 21.
Committee on the Office of Attorney General
  1978   *Witness Immunity.* Raleigh, N.C.: National Association of Attorneys
         General (NAAG).
  1977   *State Grand Juries.* Raleigh, N.C.: NAAG.
  1974   *Prosecuting Organized Crime.* Raleigh, N.C.: NAAG.

Conable, Alfred, and Edward Silberfarb
    1967   *Tigers of Tammany: Nine Men Who Ruled New York*. New York: Holt,
            Rinehart and Winston.

Conklin, John E., ed.
    1977   *The Crime Establishment*. Englewood Cliffs, N.J.: Prentice-Hall.

"Conviction of Becker."
    1913   *New York Times* (January 1): 12.

Cook, Fred J.
    1979   "Shaking the Bricks at the FBI." *New York Times Magazine* (March 25):
            31–40.
    1973   *Mafia!* Greenwich, Conn.: Fawcett.
    1972   "Purge of the Greasers." In *Mafia, U.S.A.*, edited by Nicholas Gage,
            89–109. New York: Dell.

Coram, Robert
    1981   "Colombia's Pot Peninsula—a Hot, Deadly, Lawless Land." *Chicago
            Tribune* (May 3): 8.
    1978   "The Colombian Gold Rush of 1978." *Esquire* (September 12): 33–37.

Cornelisen, Ann
    1980   *Strangers and Pilgrims: The Last Italian Migration*. New York: Holt,
            Rinehart and Winston.

Crane, Milton, ed.
    1947   *Sins of New York*. New York: Grossett and Dunlap.

Cressey, Donald R.
    1972   *Criminal Organization: Its Elementary Forms*. New York: Harper and
            Row.
    1969   *Theft of the Nation*. New York: Harper and Row.
    1967a "The Functions and Structure of Criminal Syndicates." In *Task Force
            Report: Organized Crime*, 25–60. Task Force on Organized Crime.
            Washington, D.C.: U.S. Government Printing Office.
    1967b "Methodological Problems in the Study of Organized Crime as a Social
            Problem." *Annals* 374 (November): 101–112.

Crist, Steven
    1982   "Leading Jockeys Cited in Race-Fixing Inquiry." *New York Times* (March
            28): 1, 22.

Cronin, Constance
    1970   *The Sting of Change: Sicilians in Sicily and Australia*. Chicago: Uni-
            versity of Chicago Press.

Crossette, Barbara
    1984   "War in Thailand on Opium Poppy: In One Village It's Not a Pipe
            Dream." *New York Times* (October 18): 2.

Crouse, Russel
    1947   "The Murder of Arnold Rothstein: 1928." In *Sins of New York*, edited
            by Milton Crane, 184–200. New York: Grosset and Dunlap.

Curtis, Charlotte
    1972   "Pal Joey: A Study in Gangster Chic." In *Mafia, U.S.A.*, edited by
            Nicholas Gage, 251–55. New York: Dell.

Dahl, Robert A.
    1968   "Power." *International Encyclopedia of the Social Sciences.* New York: The Free Press.
Daley, Robert
    1978   *Prince of the City.* Boston: Houghton Mifflin.
Davis, Roger H.
    1981   "Social Network Analysis: An Aid in Conspiracy Investigations." *FBI Law Enforcement Bulletin* (December): 11–19.
Defus, R. L.
    1928   "The Gunman Has an Intercity Murder Trade." *New York Times* (July 8): XX 3.
De Franco, Edward J.
    1973   *Anatomy of a Scam: A Case Study of a Planned Bankruptcy by Organized Crime.* Washington, D.C.: U.S. Government Printing Office.
Demaris, Ovid
    1981   *The Last Mafioso: The Treacherous World of Jimmy Fratianno.* New York: Bantam.
    1969   *Captive City.* New York: Lyle Stuart.
Department of Justice
    1975   *Report on the National Conference on Organized Crime.* Washington, D.C.: U.S. Government Printing Office.
Department of Justice and Department of Transportation
    1972   *Cargo Theft and Organized Crime.* Washington, D.C.: U.S. Government Printing Office.
Diapoulos, Peter, and Steven Linakis
    1976   *The Sixth Family.* New York: Dutton.
Dictionary of Criminal Justice Data Terminology
    1981   Washington, D.C.: U.S. Government Printing Office.
DiFonzo, Luigi
    1983   *St. Peter's Banker: Michele Sindona.* New York: Franklin Watts.
Dintino, Justin J., and Frederick T. Martens
    1983   *Police Intelligence Systems and Crime Control.* Springfield, Ill.: Charles C. Thomas.
    1980   "Organized Crime Control in the Eighties." *Police Chief* (August): 66–70.
Dionne, E. J., Jr.
    1984a   "Police Raids in Italy Seize Dozens after a Mafia Chief's Revelations." *New York Times* (October 1): 1, 8.
    1984b   "Informer's Crime Mosaic." *New York Times* (October 4): 1, 18.
    1984c   "The Mafia May Be Wounded, But Nobody's Calling It Dead." *New York Times* (October 7): E 5.
Dobyns, Fletcher
    1932   *The Underworld of American Politics.* New York: Fletcher Dobyns.
Doleschal, Eugene, Anne Newton, and William Hickey
    1981   *A Guide to the Literature on Organized Crime: An Annotated Bibliography Covering the Years 1967–1981.* Hackensack, N.J.: National Council on Crime and Delinquency.

Dolci, Danilo
  1983   *Sicilian Lives*. New York: Pantheon.
Dorman, Michael
  1972   *Payoff: The Role of Organized Crime in American Politics*. New York: David McKay.
Dorsett, Lyle W.
  1968   *The Pendergast Machine*. New York: Oxford University Press.
Drug Enforcement Administration
  1980   "Outlaw Motorcycle Gangs." Washington, D.C.: mimeo.
"Drug Ring Suspect Surrenders after Month in Hiding."
  1984   *Chicago Tribune* (May 10): 3.
Drugs of Abuse
  1979   Reprint from *Drug Enforcement* (magazine of the Drug Enforcement Administration). Washington, D.C.: U.S. Government Printing Office.
Duke, Harry
  1977   *Neutral Territory: The True Story of the Rackets in Atlantic City*. Philadelphia: Dorrance.
Durk, David, and Ira Silverman
  1976   *The Pleasant Avenue Connection*. New York: Harper and Row.
Durkheim, Emile
  1951   *Suicide*. New York: The Free Press.
Edelhertz, Herbert, Ezra Stotland, Marilyn Walsh, and Milton Weinberg
  1977   *The Investigation of White Collar Crime: A Manual for Law Enforcement Agencies*. Washington, D.C.: U.S. Government Printing Office.
Edelman, Bernard
  1980   "Eight Years under Cover." *Police Magazine* (July): 45–49.
Eisenstadt, S. N., and Louis Roniger
  1980   "Patron-Client Relations as a Model of Structuring Social Exchange." *Comparative Studies in Society and History* 2: 42–77.
Engelmann, Larry
  1979   *Intemperence: The Lost War against Liquor*. New York: The Free Press.
Epstein, Edward J.
  1977   *Agency of Fear: Opiates and Political Power in America*. New York: Putnam's.
Feder, Sid, and Joachim Joesten
  1954   *The Luciano Story*. David McKay.
Federal Bureau of Investigation
  1961–1964   *DeCarlo Transcripts*. 4 vols. Newark, N.J.
Feiden, Doug
  1979   "The Great Getaway: The Inside Story of the Lufthansa Robbery." *New York* (June 4): 37–42.
Feinberg, Alexander
  1959   "Genovese Is Given 15 Years in Prison in Narcotics Case." *New York Times* (April 18): 1, 15.
  1950   "A Who's Who of New York's Gambling Inquiry." *New York Times* (October 29): IV 6.
  1944   "Lepke Is Put to Death, Denies Guilt to Last; Makes No Revelation." *New York Times* (March 5): 1, 30.

Ferretti, Fred
   1977   "Mister Untouchable." *New York Times Magazine* (June 5): 15–17, 106–
          109.
Fisher, Sethard
   1975   "Review of the 'Black Mafia.' " *Contemporary Sociology* 4 (May): 83–
          84.
Fitzgerald, F. Scott
   1925   *The Great Gatsby*. New York: Scribner's.
Fong, Mak Lau
   1981   *The Sociology of Secret Societies: A Case Study of Chinese Secret So-
          cieties in Singapore and Peninsular Malaysia*. Oxford: Oxford University
          Press.
Fooner, Michael
   1973   *Interpol: The Inside Story of the International Crime-Fighting Organi-
          zation*. Chicago: Henry Regnery.
   1983   "Interpol." *Encyclopedia of Crime and Justice*. New York: Free Press.
"$4,000,000 Narcotics Seized Here Traced to Rothstein Ring."
   1928   *New York Times* (December 19): 1.
Fowler, Floyd J., Jr., Thomas Mangione, and Frederick E. Pratter
   1978   *Gambling Law Enforcement in Major American Cities: Executive Sum-
          mary*. Washington, D.C.: U.S. Government Printing Office.
"Frank Costello Dies of Coronary at 82; Underworld Leader."
   1972   *New York Times* (February 19): 1, 21.
Franks, Lucinda
   1977   "An Obscure Gangster Is Emerging as the New Mafia Chief in New
          York." *New York Times* (March 17): 1, 34.
Frantz, Douglas, and Chuck Neubauer
   1983   "Teamster Pension Fund Just Fine after Surgery." *Chicago Tribune* (May
          29): 1, 10.
Freeman, Ira Henry
   1957   "Anastasia Rose in Stormy Ranks." *New York Times* (October 26): 12.
Fried, Albert
   1980   *The Rise and Fall of the Jewish Gangster in America*. New York: Holt,
          Rinehart and Winston.
Fried, Joseph P.
   1979   "New Trial to Begin over Drug Charges." *New York Times* (September
          2): 23.
Fuller, Robert H.
   1928   *Jubilee Jim: The Life of Colonel James Fisk, Jr*. New York: Macmillan.
Furstenberg, Mark H.
   1969   "Violence and Organized Crime." Appendix 18 in *Crimes of Violence*,
          vol. 13 (A Staff Report Submitted to the National Commission on the
          Causes and Prevention of Violence). Washington, D.C.: U.S. Govern-
          ment Printing Office.
Gage, Nicholas
   1976   "Five Mafia Families Open Rosters to New Members." *New York Times*
          (March 21): 1, 40.

1975   "Carlo Gambino Dies in His Long Island Home at 74." *New York Times* (October 16): 26.

1974   "Questions Are Raised on Lucky Luciano Book." *New York Times* (December 17): 1, 28.

1971   *The Mafia Is Not an Equal Opportunity Employer.* New York: McGraw-Hill.

Gage, Nicholas, ed.

1972   *Mafia, U.S.A.* New York: Dell.

Galliher, John F., and James A. Cain

1974   "Citation Support for the Mafia Myth in Criminology Textbooks." *American Sociologist* 9 (May): 68–74.

Galliher, John F., and John R. Cross

1983   *Morals Legislation without Morality: The Case of Nevada.* New Brunswick, N.J.: Rutgers University Press.

Gallo, Patrick J.

1981   *Old Bread, New Wine: A Portrait of the Italian-American.* Chicago: Nelson-Hall.

Galvan, Manuel

1982   "Capone's Yacht Sails Calmer Seas Today." *Chicago Tribune* (February 16): Section 2: 1.

Gambino, Richard

1977   *Vendetta.* Garden City, N.Y.: Doubleday.

1974   *Blood of My Blood: The Dilemma of the Italian-Americans.* Garden City, N.Y.: Doubleday.

"Gamblers Hunted in Rothstein Attack."

1928   *New York Times* (November 6): 1.

"Gang Kills Suspect in Alien Smuggling."

1931   *New York Times* (September 11): 1.

"Gang Linked to Union Charged at Trial."

1934   *New York Times* (January 31): 8.

"Gangster Shot in Daylight Attack."

1928   *New York Times* (July 2): 1.

Gardiner, John A.

1970   *The Politics of Corruption: Organized Crime in an American City.* New York: Russell Sage Foundation.

Geiss, Gilbert

1966   "Violence and Organized Crime." *Annals* 364 (March): 86–95.

Gibson, Sonny, and Raparata Mazzola

1981   *Mafia Kingpin.* New York: Grossett and Dunlop.

Goddard, Donald

1980   *All Fall Down.* New York: Times Books.

1978   *Easy Money.* New York: Farrar, Straus and Giroux.

1974   *Joey.* New York: Harper and Row.

Godfrey, E. Drexel, Jr., and Don R. Harris

1971   *Basic Elements of Intelligence.* Washington, D.C.: U.S. Government Printing Office.

Goldstock, Ronald, and Dan T. Coenen

1978   *Extortionate and Usurious Credit Transactions: Background Materials.*
        Ithaca, N.Y.: Cornell Institute on Organized Crime.

Gomez, Linda
1984   "America's 100 Years of Euphoria and Despair." *Life* (May): 57–68.

"Gordon Made by Dry Era."
1933   *New York Times* (December 2): 6.

"Gordon Says He Got up to $300 a Week."
1933   *New York Times* (December 1): 14.

Gosch, Martin, and Richard Hammer
1974   *The Last Testament of Lucky Luciano.* Boston: Little, Brown.

Gosnell, Harold Foote
1968   *Machine Politics: Chicago Model.* New York: Greenwood. Originally
        published in 1937.

Gottfried, Alex
1962   *Boss Cermak of Chicago.* Seattle: University of Washington Press.

Graham, Fred
1977   *The Atlas Program.* Boston: Little, Brown.

Grant, Madison, and Charles S. Davison, eds.
1930   *The Alien in Our Midst: Or Selling Our Birthright for a Mess of Pottage.*
        New York: Galton Publishing Co.

Graziano, Luigi
1975   *A Conceptual Framework for the Study of Clientelism.* Ithaca, N.Y.:
        Western Studies Program of the Center for International Studies, Cornell
        University.

Greenberg, Norman
1980   *The Man with the Steel Guitar: A Portrait of Desperation, and Crime.*
        Hoover, N.H.: University Press of New England.

Greene, Robert W.
1981   *The Sting Man: The Inside Story of Abscam.* New York: Dutton.

Grinspoon, Lester, and James B. Bakalar
1976   *Cocaine: A Drug and Its Social Evolution.* New York: Basic Books.

Grutzner, Charles
1969   "Genovese Dies in Prison at 71; 'Boss of Bosses' of Mafia Here." *New
        York Times* (February 15): 1, 29.

Gusfield, Joseph
1963   *Symbolic Crusade: Status Politics and the American Temperance Move-
        ment.* Urbana, Ill.: University of Illinois Press.

Hagerty, James A.
1933   "Assassin Fires into Roosevelt Party at Miami; President-Elect Uninjured;
        Mayor Cermak and 4 Others Wounded." *New York Times* (February
        16): 1.

Haberman, Clyde
1985   "TV Funeral for Japan's Slain Godfather." *New York Times* (February
        1): 6.

Haller, Mark H.
1971–72 "Organized Crime in Urban Society: Chicago in the Twentieth Century."
        Journal of Social History 5: 210–34.

Hammer, Richard
  1982   *The Vatican Connection.* New York: Holt, Rinehart and Winston.
  1975   *Playboy's Illustrated History of Organized Crime.* Chicago: Playboy
         Press.
Harker. R. Phillip
  1978   "Sports Bookmaking Operations." *FBI Law Enforcement Bulletin* (Sep-
         tember); FBI reprint.
  1977   "Sports Wagering and the 'Line.' " *FBI Law Enforcement Bulletin* (No-
         vember); FBI reprint.
Hawkins, Gordon
  1969   "God and the Mafia." *The Public Interest* 14 (Winter): 24–51.
Herndon, Booton
  1969   *Ford: An Unconventional Biography of the Men and Their Times.* New
         York: Weybright and Talley.
Hess, Henner
  1973   *Mafia and Mafiosi:* The Structure of Power. Lexington, Mass.: D. C.
         Heath.
Hibbert, Christopher
  1966   *Garibaldi and His Enemies.* Boston: Little, Brown.
Hill, Henry, with Douglas S. Looney
  1981   "How I Put the Fix In." *Sports Illustrated* (February 16): 14–21.
Hills, Stuart L.
  1969   "Combatting Organized Crime in America." *Federal Probation* 33
         (March): 23–28.
Hobsbawm, Eric J.
  1976   "Mafia." In *The Crime Society,* edited by Francis A. J. Ianni and Elizabeth
         Reuss-Ianni, 90–98. New York: New American Library.
  1971   *Bandits.* New York: Dell.
  1969   "The American Mafia." *The Listener* 82 (November 20): 685–88.
  1959   *Social Bandits and Primitive Rebels.* Glencoe, Ill.: The Free Press.
Hoffman, Paul
  1983   "Italy Gets Tough with the Mafia." *New York Times Magazine* (November
         13): 164–69.
  1973   *Tiger in the Court.* Chicago: Playboy Press.
Hoffman, Paul, and Ira Pecznick
  1976   *To Drop a Dime.* Putnam's.
Hogan, William T.
  1976   "Sentencing and Supervision of Organized Crime Figures." *Federal Pro-
         bation* 40 (March): 21–24.
Hoge, Warren
  1982   "Bolivia Blooms with Cocaine Kingpin's Cash." *New York Times* (August
         15): 1, 12.
  1980   "Bolivians Find Cocaine Profits Habit-Forming." *New York Times* (June
         26): 2.
Hohimer, Frank
  1975   *The Home Invaders.* Chicago: Chicago Review Press.

Holbrook, Stewert H.
    1953   *The Age of Moguls.* Garden City, N.Y.: Doubleday.
Homans, George C.
    1961   *Social Behavior: Its Elementary Forms.* New York: Harcourt, Brace and
            World.
Homer, Frederic D.
    1974   *Guns and Garlic.* West Lafayette, Ind.: Purdue University Press.
Horne, Louther
    1932   "Capone's Trip to Jail Ends a Long Battle." *New York Times* (May 8):
            IX 1.
Horrock, Nicholas
    1975   "Roselli Describes His Role in a CIA Plot on Castro." *New York Times*
            (June 25): 1.
Ianni, Francis A. J.
    1976   *The Crime Society.* New York: New American Library.
    1974   *The Black Mafia: Ethnic Succession in Organized Crime.* New York:
            Simon and Schuster.
    1972   *A Family Business: Kinship and Social Control in Organized Crime.*
            New York: Russell Sage Foundation.
Inciardi, James A.
    1975   *Careers in Crime.* Chicago: Rand McNally.
Inciardi, James A., Alan A. Block, and Lyle A. Hallowell
    1977   *Historical Approaches to Crime.* Beverly Hills, Calif.: Sage.
International Association of Chiefs of Police Committee on Organized Crime
    1975   *The Police Executive's Organized Crime Enforcement Handbook.* Gaith-
            ersburg, Md.: IACP.
"Interpol"
    1985   *CJ International* (Winter): 1, 9.
Inverarity, James M., Pat Lauderdale, and Barry C. Feld
    1983   *Law and Society: Sociological Perspectives on Criminal Law.* Boston:
            Little, Brown.
Irey, Elmer L., and William T. Slocum
    1948   *The Tax Dodgers.* Garden City, N.Y.: Doubleday.
Iyer, Pico, Jonathan Beaty, Bernard Diederich, and Gavin Scott
    1975   "Fighting the Cocaine Wars." *Time* (February 25): 27–35.
Jacobs, James B.
    1977   *Stateville.* Chicago: University of Chicago Press.
Jeffreys-Jones, Rhodri
    1978   *Violence and Reform in American History.* New York: New Viewpoints.
Jenkins, Philip, and Gary W. Potter
    1985   *The City and the Syndicate: Organizing Crime in Philadelphia.* Lexing-
            ton, Mass.: Ginn Custom Publishing.
    1984   "The Politics and Mythology of Organized Crime: A Philadelphia Case
            Study." Paper presented at the Annual Meeting of the Academy of Crim-
            inal Justice Sciences, Chicago.
Jennings, Dean
    1967   *We Only Kill Each Other.* Englewood Cliffs, N.J.: Prentice-Hall.
"Johnny Torrio, Ex-Public Enemy 1, Dies; Made Al Capone Boss of the Underworld."

1957 *New York Times* (May 8): 32.

Johnson, Earl, Jr.
1963 "Organized Crime: Challenge to the American Legal System." *Criminal Law, Criminology, and Police Science* 54 (March): 1–29.

Johnson, Malcolm
1972 "In Hollywood." In *Mafia, U.S.A.*, edited by Nicholas Gage, 325–38. New York: Dell.

Joselit, Jenna Weissman
1983 *Our Gang: Jewish Crime and the New York Jewish Community, 1900–1940*. Bloomington: Indiana University Press.

Josephson, Matthew
1962 *The Robber Barons*. Harcourt, Brace and World. Originally published in 1934.

Kamm, Henry
1982a "A Modern Mafia Stirs Rage and Fear." *New York Times* (September 12): E 3.
1982b "Pope Begins Visit to Mafia Stronghold." *New York Times* (November 21): 3.
1982c "Gang War in Naples Laid to Jailed Chief." *New York Times* (April 4): 11.

Kaplan, Lawrence J., and Salvatore Matteis
1968 "The Economics of Loansharking." *American Journal of Economics and Sociology* 27 (July): 239–52.

Katcher, Leo
1959 *The Big Bankroll: The Life and Times of Arnold Rothstein*. New York: Harper and Brothers.

Katz, Leonard
1973 *Uncle Frank: The Biography of Frank Costello*. New York: Drake Publishers.

Kefauver Crime Report
1951 New York: Arco Publishing Co.

Kefauver, Estes
1968 *Crime in America*. New York: Greenwood.

Kelly, Robert J.
1978 *Organized Crime: A Study in the Production of Knowledge by Law Enforcement Specialists*. Ann Arbor: University Microfilms.

Kelton, Harold W., Jr., and Charles Unkovic
1971 "Characteristics of Organized Criminal Groups." *Canadian Journal of Corrections* 13 (January): 68–78.

Kennedy, Robert F.
1960 *The Enemy Within*. New York: Popular Library.

Kessel, John
1983 "Mounties Foiled Heroin Dealers." *Toronto Star* (August 24): B 19.

Kidner, John
1976 *Crimaldi: Contract Killer*. Washington, D.C.: Acropolis Books.

Kihss, Peter
1979 "John Dioguardi (Johnny Dio), 64, a Leader in Organized Crime, Dies." *New York Times* (January 16): B 6.

Kilian, Michael, Connie Fletcher, and Richard P. Ciccone.
 1979 *Who Runs Chicago?* New York: St. Martin's Press.
King, Rufus
 1969 *Gambling and Organized Crime.* Washington, D.C.: Public Affairs Press.
 1963 "The Fifth Amendment Privilege and Immunity Legislation." *Notre Dame Lawyer* 38 (September): 641–54.
Kirk, Donald
 1981 "Death of Japan Crime Boss 'Breeds Fear." *Miami Herald* (July 27): 17.
 1976 "Crime, Politics and Finger Chopping." *New York Times Magazine* (December 12): 60–61, 91–97.
Klatt, Wayne
 1983 "The Unlucky Love of King Mike McDonald." *Chicago Reader* (September 23): 8–9, 30–34.
Klockars, Carl B.
 1974 *The Professional Fence.* New York: The Free Press.
Knapp, Whitman, et al.
 1972 *Report of the Commission to Investigate Alleged Police Corruption.* New York: Braziller.
Knoke, David, and James H. Kuklinski
 1982 *Network Analysis.* Beverly Hills, Calif.: Sage.
Kobler, John
 1971 *Capone: The Life and World of Al Capone,* Greenwich, Conn.: Fawcett.
Kogan, Rick, and Toni Ginnetti
 1982a "Skin Flicks Are Reeling in Millions." *Chicago Sun-Times* (August 17): 1, 8.
 1982b "Adult Bookstores: Source of Money for the Mob." *Chicago Sun-Times* (August 16): 1, 14.
Kozial, Ronald, and George Estep
 1983 "Fresh Insight Shed on February 14 Killings." *Chicago Tribune* (February 14): 13.
Krajick, Kevin
 1983 "Should Police Wiretap?" *Police Magazine* (May): 29–32, 36–41.
Kurtis, Bill
 1980 "The Caviar Connection." *New York Times Magazine* (October 26): 132–33, 136–37, 141.
Kwitny, Jonathan
 1979 *Vicious Circles: The Mafia in the Marketplace.* New York: Norton.
Lamour, Catherine, and Michael R. Lamberti
 1974 *The International Connection: Opium from Growers to Pushers.* New York: Pantheon.
Landesco, John
 1968 *Organized Crime in Chicago.* Chicago: University of Chicago Press. Originally published in 1929.
 1933 "Life History of a Member of the Forty-Two Gang." *Journal of Criminal Law, Criminology and Police Science* 24 (March): 964–98.
 1932 *Organized Crime in Chicago.* Chicago: University of Chicago Press. Originally published in 1929.

Langlais, Rudy
    1978   "Inside the Heroin Trade: How a Star Double Agent Ended Up Dead."
            Village Voice (March 13): 13–15.
Lasswell, Harold D., and Jeremiah B. McKenna
    1972   *The Impact of Organized Crime on an Inner-City Community.* New York:
            Policy Sciences Center.
Laytner, Ron
    1980   "The International Sleuths." *West Palm Beach Post* (June 15): D 1, 4.
Lee, Henry
    1963   *How Dry We Were: Prohibition Revisited.* Englewood Cliffs, N.J.: Pren-
            tice-Hall.
Legg, Keith R.
    n.d.   *Patrons, Clients, and Politicians: New Perspectives on Political Clien-
            telism.* Berkeley: Institute of International Studies, University of Cali-
            fornia.
Lens, Sidney
    1974   *The Labor Wars.* Garden City, N.Y.: Doubleday.
    1949   *Left, Right and Center: Conflicting Forces in American Labor.* Hinsdale,
            Ill.: Henry Regnery.
Lernoux, Penny
    1984   "The Seamy Side of Florida Banking." *New York Times* (February 5): F
            1, 8.
Levins, Hoag
    1980   "The Kabul Connection." *Philadelphia* (August): 114–20, 192–96, 198–
            203.
Lewis, Arthur H.
    1964   *Lament for the Molly Maguires.* New York: Harcourt Brace and World.
Lewis, Merlin, Warren Bundy, and James L. Hague
    1978   *An Introduction to the Courts and Judicial Process.* Englewood Cliffs,
            N.J.: Prentice-Hall.
Lewis, Norman
    1964   *The Honored Society.* New York: Putnam's.
Light, Ivan
    1977a   "The Ethnic Vice Industry, 1880–1944." *American Sociological Review*
            42 (June): 464–79.
    1977b   "Numbers Gambling among Blacks: A Financial Institution." *American
            Sociological Review* 42 (December): 892–904.
Lindesmith, Alfred R.
    1941   "Organized Crime." *Annals* 217 (September): 119–27.
Lindsey, Robert
    1985   "Japanese Crime Group Worries U.S." *New York Times* (January 24): 10.
    1984   "New Wilderness Peril: Growers of Marijuana." *New York Times* (Oc-
            tober 23): 8.
Lippmann, Walter
    1962   "The Underworld as Servant." In *Organized Crime in America,* edited
            by Gus Tyler, 58–69. Ann Arbor: University of Michigan Press. Article
            originally published in 1931.

Lloyd, Henry Demarest
1963   *Wealth against Commonwealth.* Edited by Thomas C. Cochran. Englewood Cliffs, N.J.: Prentice-Hall.
Logan, Andy
1970   *Against the Evidence: The Becker-Rosenthal Affair.* New York: McCall
Publishing.
Lombardo, Robert
1979   "Organized Crime and the Concept of Community." Department of So-
ciology, University of Illinois at Chicago Circle. Photocopied.
Loth, David
1938   *Public Plunder: A History of Graft in America.* New York: Carrick and
Evans.
Lubasch, Arnold H.
1984   "11 Indicted by U.S. as the Leadership of a Crime Family." *New York
Times* (October 25): 1, 4.
Lundberg, Ferdinand
1968   *The Rich and the Super-Rich: A Study in the Power of Money Today.*
New York: Lyle Stuart.
Lupsha, Peter A.
1983   "Networks Versus Networking: Analysis of an Organized Crime Group."
In *Career Criminals*, edited by Gordon P. Waldo, 59–87. Beverly Hills,
CA: Sage.
1981   "Individual Choice, Material Culture, and Organized Crime." *Crimi-
nology* 19: 3–24.
Lupsha, Peter A., and Kip Schlegel
1980   "The Political Economy of Drug Trafficking: The Herrera Organization
(Mexico and the United States)." Department of Political Science, Uni-
versity of New Mexico at Albuquerque. Xeroxed paper.
Maas, Peter
1968   *The Valachi Papers.* New York: Putnam's.
MacDougall, Ernest D., ed.
1933   *Crime for Profit: A Symposium on Mercenary Crime.* Boston: Stratford.
Mack, John A.
1973   "The 'Organised' and 'Professional' Labels Criticized." *International
Journal of Criminology and Penology* 1 (May): 103–116.
Maitland, Leslie
1979   "U.S. Air Cargoes Inquiry Is Seeking a Link to Crime." *New York Times*
(May 30): B 1, 2.
Malcolm, Andrew H.
1977   "Police in Osaka Develop a New Anticrime Method: A Drive to 'Shame'
Gangsters from Lawless Ways." *New York Times* (March 17): 8.
Malcolm, Walter D., and John J. Curtin, Jr.
1968   "The New Federal Attack on the Loan Shark Problem." *Law and Con-
temporary Problems* 133: 765–85.
Maltz, Michael D.
1976   "On Defining 'Organized Crime.' " *Crime and Delinquency* 22 (July):
338–46.

1975   "Policy Issues in Organized Crime and White-Collar Crime." In *Crime and Criminal Justice,* edited by John A. Gardiner and Michael Mulkey, 73–94. Lexington, Mass.: D. C. Heath.

Markham, James M.

1983   "Libya Irked at Bonn, Holds Germans." *New York Times* (April 21): 3.

Marshall, Eliot

1978   "State Lottery." *The New Republic* (June 24): 20–21.

Martin, Raymond V.

1963   *Revolt in the Mafia.* New York: Duell, Sloan and Pearce.

McConaughy, John

1931   *From Caine to Capone: Racketeering Down the Ages.* New York: Brentano's.

McClellan, John L.

1962   *Crime without Punishment.* New York: Duell, Sloan and Pearce.

McClory, Robert

1981   "The Jeff Fort Bust: 'Operation Destruction.' " *Chicago Reader* (October 30): 3.

McFadden, Robert D.

1983   "Meyer Lansky Is Dead at 81; Financial Wizard of Organized Crime." *New York Times* (January 16): 21.

McGuiness, Robert L.

1981   "In The Katz Eye: Use of Binoculars and Telescopes." *FBI Law Enforcement Bulletin* (June): 26–31.

McLaughlin, John B.

n.d.   *Sicilian and American Mafia.* Police Training Institute of Illinois.

McPhaul, Jack

1970   *Johnny Torrio: First of the Gang Lords.* New Rochelle, N.Y.: Arlington House.

Merriam, Charles Edward

1929   *Chicago: A More Intimate View of Urban Politics.* New York: Macmillan.

Merton, Robert

1967   *On Theoretical Sociology.* New York: The Free Press.

1964   "Anomie, Anomia, and Social Interaction." In *Anomie and Deviant Behavior,* edited by Marshall B. Clinard, 213–42. New York: Free Press.

1938   "Social Structure and Anomie." *American Sociological Review* 3: 672–82.

Meskil, Paul

1977   "Meet the New Godfather." *New York* (February 28): 28–32.

1973   *Don Carlo: Boss of Bosses.* New York: Popular Library.

Messick, Hank

1979   *Of Grass and Snow: The Secret Criminal Elite.* Englewood Cliffs, N.J.: Prentice-Hall.

1973   *Lansky.* New York: Berkley.

1967   *The Silent Syndicate.* New York: Macmillan.

Michaels, Marguerite

1980   "Where Drug Traffic Is a Way of Life." *Parade* (January 6): 4–5.

Miller, Judith
  1978   "Bankers Gird for More Nasty Questions." *New York Times* (May 27):
          E 4.
Miller, Walter B.
  1958   "Lower Class Culture as a Generating Milieu of Gang Delinquency."
          Journal of Social Issues 14: 5–21.
Mills, James
  1969   *The Prosecutor*. New York: Farrar, Straus and Giroux.
Mitchell, Greg
  1980   "Ordeal of a Prosecution Witness." *New York Times Magazine* (Novem-
          ber 16): 106–120.
Mockridge, Norton, and Robert H. Prall
  1954   *The Big Fix*. New York: Henry Holt.
Moldea, Dan E.
  1978   *The Hoffa Wars*. New York: Charter Books.
Moore, Robin, with Barbara Fuca
  1977   *Mafia Wife*. New York: Macmillan.
Moore, William H.
  1974   *The Kefauver Committee and the Politics of Crime: 1950–1952*. Colum-
          bia: University of Missouri Press.
Moquin, Wayne, and Charles van Doren, eds.
  1976   *The American Way of Crime*. New York: Praeger.
Mori, Cesare
  1933   *The Last Struggle with the Mafia*. London: Putnam.
Murphy, Patrick V., and Thomas Plate
  1977   *Commissioner: A View from the Top of American Law Enforcement*. New
          York: Simon and Schuster.
Musto, David
  1973   *The American Disease: Origins of Narcotic Control*. New Haven, Conn.:
          Yale University Press.
Myers, Gustavus
  1936   *History of Great American Fortunes*. New York: Modern Library.
Myers, Harry L., and Joseph P. Brzostowski
  1981   *Drug Agent's Guide to Forfeiture of Assets*. Washington, D.C.: U.S.
          Government Printing Office.
Nagel, Jack H.
  1968   "Some Questions about the Concept of Power." *Behavioral Science* 13:
          129–37.
Nash, Jay Robert
  1981   *People to See*. New Brunswick, N.J.: New Century.
  1975   *Bloodletters and Badmen: Book 3*. New York: Warner Books.
National Advisory Commission on Civil Disorders
  1968   *Report*. New York: Bantam.
National Advisory Commission on Causes and Prevention of Violence
  1969   *Staff Report: Crimes of Violence*. Washington, D.C.: U.S. Government
          Printing Office.
National Advisory Commission on Criminal Justice Standards and Goals
  1975   *A National Strategy to Reduce Crime*. New York: Avon.

National Association of Attorneys General
  1977   *Organized Crime Control Units*. Raleigh, N.C.: Committee on the Office
         of Attorney General.
National Commission for the Review of Federal and State Laws Relating to Wiretap-
    ping and Electronic Surveillance.
  1976   *Commission Studies*. Washington, D.C.: United States Government
         Printing Office.
Navasky, Victor S.
  1977   *Kennedy Justice*. New York: Atheneum.
Neely, Richard
  1982   "The Politics of Crime." *Atlantic* (August): 27–31.
Nelli, Humbert S.
  1976   *The Business of Crime*. New York: Oxford University Press.
  1969   "Italians and Crime in Chicago: The Formative Years; 1890–1920."
         American Journal of Sociology 74 (January): 373–91.
Newfield, Jack
  1979   "The Myth of Godfather Journalism." *Village Voice* (July 23): 1, 11–
         13.
"New Gang Methods Replace Those of Eastman's Days." *New York Times* (September
    9): section 9, p. 3.
New York State Commission of Investigation
  1978   *A Report on Fencing: The Sale and Distribution of Stolen Property*. New
         York: NYSCI.
  1970   *Racketeer Infiltration into Legitimate Business*. New York: NYSCI.
Nicodemus, Charles, and Art Petaque
  1981   "Mob Jewel Fencing Investigated." *Chicago Sun-Times* (November 29):
         5, 76.
North Carolina Organized Crime Prevention Council
  n.d.   *Organized Crime in North Carolina*. Raleigh: Department of Justice.
Novak, Michael
  1978   *The Guns of Lattimer*. New York: Basic Books
O'Brien, John
  1983   "Gambling Boss Ken Eto Tells of Mob Murder and Intrigue." *Chicago
         Tribune* (May 16): Section 2, 1.
O'Connor, Philip J., and Maurice Possley
  1982   "Thai Envoy Seeking Immunity in Drug Case." *Chicago Sun-Times* (May
         30): 34.
O'Connor, Richard
  1962   *Gould's Millions*. Garden City, N.Y.: Doubleday.
  1958   *Hell's Kitchen*. Philadelphia: Lippincott.
Overly, Don H., and Theodore H. Schell
  1973   *New Effectiveness Measures for Organized Crime Control Efforts*. Wash-
         ington, D.C.: U.S. Government Printing Office.

Packer, Herbert L.
  1968   *The Limits of the Criminal Sanction*. Stanford, Calif.: Stanford University
         Press.

Palsey, Fred D.
1971   *Al Capone: The Biography of a Self-Made Man.* Freeport, N.Y.: Books for Libraries Press. Originally published in 1931.
Pantaleone, Michele
1966   *The Mafia and Politics.* New York: Coward and McCann.
Pearce, Frank
1981   "Organized Crime and Class Politics." In *Crime and Capitalism,* edited by David F. Greenberg, 157–81. Palo Alto, Calif.: Mayfield.
Pennsylvania Crime Commission
1980   *A Decade of Organized Crime: 1980 Report.* Saint Davids, Pa.: PCC.
Permanent Subcommittee on Investigations (of the Committee on Governmental Affairs of the United States Senate)
1984   *Profile of Organized Crime: Great Lakes Region.* Washington, D.C.: U.S. Government Printing Office (USGPO).
1983   *Crime and Secrecy: The Use of Offshore Banks and Companies.* Washington, D.C.: USGPO.
1983   *Organized Crime in Chicago (March 4).* Washington, D.C.: USGPO.
1983   *Profile of Organized Crime: Mid-Atlantic Region (February 15, 23, 24).* Washington, D.C.: USGPO.
1983   *Staff Study of Crime and Secrecy: The Use of Offshore Banks and Companies.* Washington, D.C.: USGPO.
1982   *Hotel Employees and Restaurant Employees International Union: Part 1 (June 22 and 23).* Washington, D.C.: USGPO.
1981   *International Narcotics Trafficking.* Washington, D.C.: USGPO.
1981   *Waterfront Corruption.* Washington, D.C.: USGPO.
1981   *Witness Security Program.* Washington, D.C.: USGPO.
1980a *Organized Crime and the Use of Violence: Part I.* Washington, D.C.: USGPO.
1980b *Organized Crime and the Use of Violence: Part II.* Washington, D.C.: USGPO.
1978   *Organized Crime Activities: South Florida and United States Penitentiary, Atlanta, Georgia (August 1, 2, 3, 9, and 10): part 1.* Washington, D.C.: USGPO.
1971   *Organized Crime and Stolen Securities: part 1.* Washington, D.C.: USGPO.
Petacco, Arrigo
1974   *Joe Petrosino.* New York: Macmillan.
Petacque, Art, and Hugh Hough
1983   " 'Banker' Holds Lansky Secrets." *Chicago Sun-Times* (January 23): 9.
Peterson, Virgil
1983   *The Mob: 200 Years of Organized Crime in New York.* Ottawa, Ill.: Green Hill.
1969   *A Report on Chicago Crime for 1968.* Chicago: Chicago Crime Commission.
1963   "Chicago: Shades of Capone." *Annals* 347 (May): 30–39.
1962   "Career of a Syndicate Boss." *Crime and Delinquency* 8 (October): 339–49.

Pileggi, Nicholas
    1982   "There's No Business Like Drug Business." *New York* (December 13): 38–43.
    1980   "Sindona: A Little Help from His Friends." *New York* (April 7): 55–58.
    1972   "The Godfather's New Recruits." In *Mafia at War,* edited by Thomas Plate, 82–83. New York: New York Magazine Press.
Pitkin, Thomas Monroe, and Francesco Cordasco
    1977   *The Black Hand: A Chapter in Ethnic Crime.* Totawa, N.J.: Littlefield, Adams.
Plate, Thomas, and the editors of *New York Magazine,* eds.
    1972   *The Mafia at War.* New York: New York Magazine Press.
"Police Blotter, The."
    1979   *New York Times* (May 17): B 4.
Post, Henry
    1981   "The Whorehouse Sting." *New York Magazine* (February 2): 31–34.
Prall, Robert H., and Norton Mockridge
    1951   *This Is Costello.* New York: Gold Medal Books.
President's Commission on Law Enforcement and Administration of Justice
    1968   *The Challenge of Crime in a Free Society.* New York: Avon.
"Profaci Dies of Cancer, Led Feuding Brooklyn Mob."
    1962   *New York Times* (June 8): 32.
Quinney, Richard
    1974   *Critique of the Legal Order.* Boston: Little, Brown.
Raab, Selwyn
    1985   "Tapes Show Informer's Role in Fraud Case on Donovan." *New York Times* (March 10): 21.
    1984a "The Drug Pipeline: From Europe to New York." *New York Times* (May 21): 1, 13.
    1984b "U.S. Inquiry Finds Gangsters Hold Grip on Kennedy Cargo." *New York Times* (September 30): 1, 18.
"Racket Chief Slain by Gangster Gunfire."
    1931   *New York Times* (April 16): 1.
Reckless, Walter
    1969   *Vice in Chicago.* Montclair, N.J.: Patterson Smith.
Reece, Jack
    1973   "Fascism, the Mafia, and the Emergence of Sicilian Separatism." *Journal of Modern History* 45 (June): 261–76.
Rehfeld, Barry
    1984   "The Crass Menagerie." *New York Magazine* (October 15): 50–53.
Reid, Ed
    1970   *The Grim Reapers.* New York: Bantam.
Reid, Ed, and Ovid Demaris
    1964   *The Green Felt Jungle.* New York: Cardinal Paperbacks.
Reif, Rita
    1984   "Gould Jewels to Be Sold at Auction." *New York Times* (Janaury 3): 21.
Reisman, W. Michael
    1979   *Folded Lies: Bribery, Crusades, and Reforms.* New York: Free Press.

Repetto, Thomas A.
  1978   *The Blue Parade.* New York: Free Press.
Reuter, Peter
  1983   *Disorganized Crime.* Cambridge: MIT Press.
Reuter, Peter, Jonathan Rubinstein, and Simon Wynn
  1983   *Racketeering in Legitimate Industries: Two Case Studies. Executive Summary.* Washington, D.C.: U.S. Government Printing Office.
Rhodes, Robert P.
  1984   *Organized Crime: Crime Control vs. Civil Liberties.* New York: Random House.
Richardson, James F.
  1975   "The Early Years of the New York Police Department." In *Police in America,* edited by Jerome Skolnick and Thomas C. Gray, 15–23. Boston: Little, Brown.
Riding, Alan
  1984   "Shaken Colombia Acts at Last on Drugs." *New York Times* (September 11): 1, 6.
Riordon, William L.
  1963   *Plunkitt of Tammany Hall.* New York: Dutton.
Robbins, William
  1984   "Trial Offers a Glimpse Inside of the Mafia." *New York Times* (October 29): 15.
Roberts, Sam
  1984   "A Profile of the New American Mafia: Old Bosses and New Competition." *New York Times* (October 4): 1, 18.
Roebuck, Julian, and Wolfgang Frese
  1976   *The Rendezvous: A Case Study of an After Hours Club.* New York: Free Press.
Rome, Florence
  1975   *The Tattooed Men.* New York: Delacorte.
Romoli, Kathleen
  1941   *Colombia.* Garden City, N.Y.: Doubleday, Doran.
Rosen, Charles
  1978   *Scandals of '51: How the Gamblers Almost Killed College Basketball.* New York: Holt, Rinehart and Winston.
Ross, Irwin
  1980   "How Lawless Are the Big Companies?" *Fortune* (December 1): 57–58, 62–64.
Rottenberg, Dan
  1983   "Book Review of 'The Wall Street Journal: The Story of Dow Jones and the Nation's Business Newspaper.'" *Chicago Magazine* (January): 90–91.
Royko, Mike
  1971   *Boss: Richard J. Daley of Chicago.* New York: Dutton.
Rubinstein, Jonathan
  1973   *City Police.* New York: Farrar, Straus and Giroux.
Rubinstein, Jonathan, and Peter Reuter
  1978a   "Fact, Fancy, and Organized Crime." *The Public Interest* (Fall): 45–67.

1978b   *Bookmaking in New York.* New York: Policy Sciences Center. (Preliminary, unpublished draft).

1977   *Numbers: The Routine Racket.* New York: Policy Sciences Center. (Preliminary, unpublished draft).

Salerno, Ralph, and John S. Tompkins
1969   *The Crime Confederation.* Garden City, N.Y.: Doubleday.

Sann, Paul
1971   *Kill the Dutchman: The Story of Dutch Schultz.* New York: Popular Library.

Schelling, Thomas C.
1971   "What Is the Business of Organized Crime?" *American Scholar* 40 (Autumn): 643–52.

Schmetzer, Uli
1982   "Naples Mafia—Slaughter with a Vengeance." *Chicago Tribune* (March 7): Section 3, 1.

Schmidt, William E.
1984   "New Era, New Problems for South's Sheriffs." *New York Times* (September 10): 1, 15.

Schnepper, Jeff A.
1978   *Inside the IRS.* New York: Stein and Day.

Schorr, Mark
1979   "The .22 Caliber Killings." *New York* (May 7): 43–46.

1978   "Gunfight in the Cocaine Corral." *New York* (September 25): 48–57.

"Schultz Aide Slain; 7th in Five Months."
1931   *New York Times* (June 22): 2.

"Schultz Product of the Dry Law Era."
1933   *New York Times* (January 22): 23.

"Schultz Succumbs to Bullet Wounds without Naming Slayers."
1935   *New York Times* (October 25): 1.

Schumach, Murray
1977   "30 Indicted in Queens Heroin Crackdown." *New York Times* (April 15): 1, 37.

Schur, Edwin M.
1969   *Our Criminal Society.* Englewood Cliffs, N.J.: Prentice-Hall.

1965   *Crimes without Victims.* Englewood Cliffs, N.J.: Prentice-Hall.

Schwartz, Herman
1968   "Wiretapping Problem Today." In *Criminological Controversies,* edited by Richard D. Knudten, 156–68. New York: Appleton-Century-Crofts.

Sciascia, Leonard
1963   *Mafia Vendetta.* New York: Knopf.

Scott, James
1972   "The Erosion of Patron-Client Bonds and Social Change in Rural Southeast Asia." *Journal of Southeast Asian Studies* 32 (November): 5–38.

Seedman, Albert A.
1974   *Chief!* New York: Arthur Fields.

Seidl, John M.
1968   "Upon the Hip—A Study of the Criminal Loanshark Industry." Ph.D dissertation, Harvard University.

Seidman, Harold
  1938   *Labor Czars. A History of Labor Racketeering.* New York: Liveright.
Seigel, Max H.
  1977   "14, Including Alleged Charter Member of Purple Gang, Charged in Heroin Conspiracy." *New York Times* (December 20): 27.
Serao, Ernesto
  1911a   "The Truth about the Camorra." *Outlook* 98 (July 28): 717–26.
  1911b   "The Truth about the Camorra: Part II." *Outlook* 98 (August 5): 778–87.
Servadio, Gaia
  1976   *Mafioso: A History of the Mafia from Its Origins to the Present Day.* Briarcliff Manor, N.Y.: Stein and Day.
  1974   *Angelo La Barbera: The Profile of a Mafia Boss.* London: Quartet Books.
Shaw, Clifford, and Henry D. McKay
  1972   *Juvenile Delinquency and Urban Areas.* Chicago: University of Chicago Press. Originally published in 1942.
Shaw, David
  1984   *Press Watch.* New York: Macmillan.
Sheridan, Walter
  1972   *The Fall and Rise of Jimmy Hoffa.* New York: Saturday Review Press.
Sherman, Lawrence W.
  1978   *Scandal and Reform: Controlling Police Corruption.* Berkeley; University of California Press.
  1974   *Police Corruption: A Sociological Perspective.* Garden City, N.Y.: Doubleday.
Siciliano, Vincent
  1970   *Unless They Kill Me First.* New York: Hawthorn Books.
"Siegel, Gangster, Is Slain on Coast."
  1947   *New York Times* (June 22): 1.
Silberman, Charles E.
  1978   *Criminal Violence, Criminal Justice.* New York: Random House.
Simons, Marlise
  1984a   "Peruvian Rebels Halt U.S. Drive against Cocaine." *New York Times* (August 13): 1, 6.
  1984b   "Revolt in Bolivia Embarrasses U.S." *New York Times* (July 17): 1, 5.
Simpson, Anthony E.
  1977   *The Literature of Police Corruption.* New York: John Jay Press.
Simpson, John R.
  1984   "INTERPOL—Dedicated to Cooperation." *Police Chief* (June): 31–34.
Sinclair, Andrew
  1962   *The Era of Excess: A Social History of the Prohibition Movement.* Boston: Little, Brown.
Skolnick, Jerome H.
  1978   *House of Cards: Legalization and Control of Casino Gambling.* Boston: Little, Brown.
Smith, Alson J.
  1962   "The Early Chicago Story." In *Organized Crime in America,* edited by Gus Tyler, 138–46. Ann Arbor: University of Michigan Press.

Smith, Dwight C., Jr.
    1982   "Paragons, Pariahs, and Pirates: A Spectrum-Based Theory of Enter-
            prise." *Crime and Delinquency* 26 (July): 358–86.
    1978   "Organized Crime and Entrepreneurship." *International Journal of Cri-
            minology and Penology* 6: 161–77.
    1976   "Mafia: The Prototypical Alien Conspiracy." *Annals* 423 (January): 75–
            88.
    1975   *The Mafia Mystique*. New York: Basic Books.
Smith, Dwight C., Jr., and Ralph Salerno
    1970   "The Use of Strategies in Organized Crime Control." *Journal of Criminal
            Law, Criminology and Police Science* 61: 101–111.
Smith, Richard Austin
    1961a   "The Incredible Electrical Conspiracy." *Fortune* (May): 161–64, 210,
            212, 217–18, 221–24.
    1961b   "The Incredible Electrical Conspiracy." *Fortune* (April): 1932–37, 170,
            175–76, 179–80.
Smith, Richard Norton
    1982   *Thomas E. Dewey and His Times*. New York: Simon and Schuster.
Smith, Sherwin D.
    1963   "35 Years Ago Arnold Rothstein Was Mysteriously Murdered and Left
            a Racket Empire Up for Grabs." *New York Times Magazine* (October
            27): 96.
"Son Gains Control of Mob, FBI Says: Bureau Asserts Patriarca is New England
Mafia Chief."
    1984   *New York Times* (October 28): 31.
Sondern, Frederic, Jr.
    1959   *Brotherhood of Evil: The Mafia*. New York: Farrar, Straus and Cudahy.
Special Committee to Investigate Organized Crime in Interstate Commerce
    1951   *Kefauver Crime Report*. New York: Arno.
Spergel, Irving
    1964   *Racketville, Slumtown, Haulberg*. Chicago: University of Chicago Press.
Spiering, Frank
    1976   *The Man Who Got Capone*. Indianapolis: Bobbs-Merrill.
Stevens, William K.
    1984   "Organized Crime a Growth Industry in India." *New York Times* (October
            14): 4.
Stewert, Robert C.
    1980   *Identification and Investigation of Organized Criminal Activity*. Houston:
            National College of District Attorneys.
Stoler, Peter
    1984   "The Sicilian Connection." *Time* (October 15): 42–51.
    1942   *A Presentment Concerning the Enforcement by the Police Department
            of the City of New York of the Laws against Gambling*. New York: Arno
            Press (reprint, 1974).
Sutherland, Edwin H.
    1973   *Edwin H. Sutherland: On Analyzing Crime*. Edited by Karl Schuessler.
            Chicago: University of Chicago Press.
    1972   *The Professional Thief*. Chicago: University of Chicago Press. (Originally
            published in 1937).

Suttles, Gerald D.
  1968   *The Social Order of the Slum.* Chicago: University of Chicago Press.
Swanberg, W. A.
  1959   *Jim Fisk: The Career of an Improbable Rascal.* New York: Scribner's.
Takahashi, Sadahiko and Carl B. Becker
  1985   "Organized Crime in Japan." Osaka, Japan: Kin'ki University.
Talese, Gay
  1971   *Honor Thy Father.* New York: World Publishing.
  1965   *The Overreachers.* New York: Harper and Row.
Task Force on Organized Crime
  1976   *Organized Crime.* Washington, D.C.: U.S. Government Printing Office.
  1967   *Task Force Report: Organized Crime.* Washington, D.C.: U.S. Government Printing Office.
Taylor, Ian, Paul Walton, and Jock Young
  1973   *The New Criminology.* New York: Harper and Row.
Teresa, Vincent, with Thomas C. Renner
  1973   *My Life in the Mafia.* Greenwich, Conn.: Fawcett.
Thomas, Jo
  1984   "Islands' Bank Secrecy Is Lifted for U.S." *New York Times* (July 27): 3.
Thomas, Ralph C.
  1977   "Organized Crime in the Construction Industry." *Crime and Delinquency* 23: 304–11.
Thompson, Craig, and Allan Raymond
  1940   *Gang Rule in New York.* New York: Dial.
Thrasher, Frederic Milton
  1968   *The Gang: A Study of 1,313 Gangs in Chicago.* Chicago: University of Chicago Press. (Abridged version). Originally published in 1927.
Toby, Jackson
  1958   "Hoodlum or Business Men; An American Dilemma." In *The Jews: Social Patterns of an American Group,* edited by Marshall Sklare, 542–50. Glencoe, Ill.: Free Press.
Touhy, Roger
  1959   *The Stolen Years.* Cleveland: Pennington.
Train, Arthur
  1922   *Courts and Criminals.* New York: Scribner's.
  1912   "Imported Crime: The Story of the Camorra in America." *McClure's Magazine* (May): 83–94.
Treaster, Joseph B.
  1984   "Jamaica, Close U.S. Ally, Does Little to Halt Drugs." *New York Times* (September 10): 1, 8.
Tuite, James
  1978   "Would Benefits of Legalized Betting on Sports Outweigh the Drawbacks?" *New York Times* (December 19): B 21.
Turkus, Burton, and Sid Feder
  1951   *Murder, Inc.: The Story of the Syndicate.* New York: Farrar, Straus and Young.

Turner, Wallace
    1984a "Hawaii Criminal's Pledge to Talk Seen as Door to Underworld." *New York Times* (July 24): 7.
    1984b "U.S. and Nevada Agents Crack Down on Casinos." *New York Times* (January 28): 1, 7.

"21 People Indicted on L.I. as Carting Plot Is Charged."
    1984 *New York Times* (September 14): 20.

"2 Convicted of Gambling Charges."
    1983 *Chicago Tribune* (January 19): Section 2, 3.

"$2,000,000 Lottery Unmolested Here."
    1935 *New York Times* (March 4): 1.

"2 Women Wounded as Gang Opens Fire in Upper Broadway."
    1933 *New York Times* (May 25): 1.

Tyler, Gus, ed.
    1962 *Organized Crime in America.* Ann Arbor: University of Michigan Press.

Tyler, Gus
    1975 "Book Review of 'The Black Mafia.' " *Crime and Delinquency* 21 (April): 175–80.

"Unger Indicted in Drug Conspiracy."
    1928 *New York Times* (December 11): 1.

United States General Accounting Office
    1981 *Stronger Federal Effort Needed in Fight Against Organized Crime.* Washington, D.C.: U.S. Government Printing Office.

United States Senate Subcommittee on Administrative Practice and Procedure
    1978 *Hearings on Oversight of the Witness Protection Program.* Washington, D.C.: U.S. Government Printing Office.

"Usury Racket Stirred Gang War."
    1935 *New York Times* (October 25): 17.

Van Dyke, Craig, and Robert Byck.
    1982 "Cocaine." *Scientific American* 246 (March): 128–34, 139–41.

Villano, Anthony
    1978 *Brick Agent.* New York: Ballantine.

Vold, George
    1979 *Theoretical Criminology.* 2d edition prepared by Thomas J. Bernard. New York: Oxford University Press.

Volsky, George
    1979 "Indictment in Miami Depicts Rise and Fall of Narcotics-Smuggling Gang." *New York Times* (May 6): 26.

Wall, Joseph Frazier
    1970 *Andrew Carnegie.* New York: Oxford University Press.

Wallace, Anise
    1983 "Morgan's Bold Plan for the Teamsters." *New York Times* (December 4): C 3.

Wallace, Irving David, David Wallechinsky, and Amy Wallace
    1983 "The Palisades Massacres." *Parade* (January 23): 18.

Wallance, Gregory
    1982 *Papa's Game.* New York: Ballantine.

Walsh, Marilyn E.
  1977   *The Fence*. Westport, Conn.: Greenwood.
"Waxey Gordon Dies in Alcatraz at 63."
  1952   *New York Times* (June 25): 1.
"Waxey Gordon Guilty; Gets 10 Years. Is Fined $80,000 for Tax Evasion."
  1933   *New York Times* (December 2): 1.
Weber, Max
  1968   *Economy and Society*. Edited by Guenther Roth and Claus Wiltich. New
          York: Bedminster Press.
  1958   *Protestant Ethic and the Spirit of Capitalism*. New York: Scribner's.
Wendt, Lloyd, and Herman Kogan
  1943   *Lords of the Levee*. Indianapolis: Bobbs-Merrill.
Werner, M. R.
  1928   *Tammany Hall*. Garden City, N.Y. Doubleday, Doran.
Wessel, Milton R.
  1963   "The Conspiracy Charge as a Weapon against Organized. Crime." *Notre
          Dame Lawyer* 38 (September): 689-99.
Wethern, George, with Vincent Colnett
  1978   *A Wayward Angel*. New York: Marek Publishers.
Whitaker, Mark, with Elaine Shannon and Ron Moreau
  1985   "Colombia's King of Coke." *Newsweek* (February 25): 19-22.
White, Frank Marshall
  1908   "The Bands of Criminals of New York's East Side." *New York Times*
          (November 8): V 9.
"Who Took the Stone of Alphonse Capone?"
  1981   *Chicago Tribune Magazine* (September 6): 6.
Whyte, William Foote
  1961   *Street Corner Society*. Chicago: University of Chicago Press.
Wiederich, Bob
  1984   "Mexican Heroin Makes a Comeback." *Chicago Tribune* (April 2): Sec-
          tion 2, 1, 4.
Williams, T. Harry
  1969   *Huey Long*. New York: Bantam.
Wilson, James Q.
  1978   *The Investigators*. New York: Basic Books.
Wilson, Theodore
  1975   "The Kefauver Committee, 1950." In *Congress Investigates: 1792–1974*,
          edited by Arthur M. Schlessinger, Jr., and Robert Burns. New York:
          Chelsea House.
Winick, Charles, and Paul M. Kinsie
  1971   *The Lively Commerce*. Chicago: Quadrangle.
Withers, Kay
  1982   "Sicilian Bishops Attack the Mafia," *Chicago Tribune* (October 19): 5.
Woetzel, Robert K.
  1963   "An Overview of Organized Crime: Mores versus Morality." *Annals* 347
          (May): 1–11.

Wolf, Eric R.
    1966   "Kinship, Friendship, and Patron-Client Relations in Complex Societies."
           In *The Social Anthropology of Complex Societies,* edited by Michael
           Banton, 1–22. London: Tavistock Publications.

"Woman, 2 Men, Slain as Gang Raids Home in Coll Feud."
    1932   *New York Times* (February 2): 1.

Wright, Michael
    1979   "Phenix City, Ala., Leaves Ashes of Sin in the Past." *New York Times*
           (June 18): 14.

Wrong, Dennis
    1968   "Some Problems in Defining Social Power." *American Journal of So-*
           ciology 73 (May): 673–81.

X, Malcolm
    1973   *The Autobiography of Malcolm X.* New York: Ballantine.

Yeager, Matthew G.
    1973   "The Gangster as White Collar Criminal: Organized Crime and Stolen
           Securities." *Issues in Criminology* 8 (Spring): 49–73.

Zilg, Gerard Colby
    1974   *DuPont: Behind the Nylon Curtain.* Englewood Cliffs, N.J.: Prentice-
           Hall.

Name Index

Abadinsky, Howard, 21, 22, 23, 169, 238
Albini, Joseph L., 136, 168
Allsop, Kenneth, 134, 136, 140, 141, 142, 143, 145, 147
Allum, P. A., 65
Anderson, Annelise Graebner, 239
Andrews, Harvey, 45
Asbury, Herbert, 88, 95, 96
Aschmann, Hommer, 162
Audett, James Henry, 89

Bacherach, Samuel B., 7n
Barzini, Luigi, 55, 56, 57
Becker, Carl, 165
Beigel, Allan, 268
Beigel, Herbert, 268
Bell, Daniel, 74
Bequai, August, 134
Berger, Meyer, 100, 105, 117, 118, 126
Berlet, Chip, 286
Bishop, Jim, 151n
Blakely, G. Robert, 298
Blau, Peter M. 16
Bloch, Max, 242n
Block, Alan A., 79, 82, 105, 106, 238
Blok, Anton, 58
Blum, Howard, 201
Boissevain, Jeremy, 15, 16
Bonnano, Joseph, 112, 117, 119, 120, 122, 123, 124
Bowman, Jim, 141, 151n
Boyd, Kier T., 176, 192n
Brashler, William, 124, 149, 150
Brecher, Edward M., 197
Bresler, Fenton, 195, 196, 199
Brill, Steven, 231, 232, 234
Broder, Jonathan, 199
Brodt, Bonita, 158

Brody, Jane, 206
Browne, Arthur, 157
Browning, Frank, 210
Brzostowski, Joseph P., 274
Bundy, Warren, 298
Buse, Renee, 317
Byck, Robert, 204, 206

Cain, James A., 79
Campane, Jerome O., 273, 276
Campbell, Rodney, 114
Capeci, Jerry, 80, 82
Cartey, Desmond, 188
Chafetz, Henry, 181, 183
Chambliss, William, 91
Chandler, David Leon, 109
Clark, Ramsey, 293
Cloward, Richard A., 73, 74
Coenen, Dan T., 190, 272
Coffey, Thomas M., 91, 137
Cohen, Mickey, 109
Cohen, Stanley, 189
Collins, Randall, 14, 15, 110
Colombo, Furio, 62
Conable, Alfred, 95, 97, 99
Cook, Fred J., 250
Coram, Robert, 162
Cordesco, Francesco, 109
Cressey, Donald R., 3, 12, 17, 20, 82

Dahl, Robert A., 7n
Davis, Roger, 295
De Franco, Edward J., 221
Demaris, Ovid, 149, 240, 317
Dintino, Justine J., 247, 321, 322
Dionne, E. J., Jr., 78n
Dobyns, Fletcher, 134, 143, 147

Dorsett, Lyle W., 89
Durk, David, 77, 202, 250

Englemann, Larry, 85
Estep, George, 145, 151n

Ferretti, Fred, 157
Fooner, Michael, 288
Franks, Lucinda, 80
Frantz, Douglas, 234, 235
Freeman, Ira Henry, 117

Gage, Nicholas, 14, 77
Gallo, Patrick J., 108-9
Galvan, Manuel, 145
Gambino, Richard, 55, 63, 65, 66, 111, 151n
Gibson, Sonny, 82
Ginnetti, Toni, 224
Goddard, Donald, 72, 155, 160, 230
Godfrey, E. Drexel, 283, 284
Goldstock, Ronald, 190, 272
Gomez, Linda, 204
Gosch, Martin, 81
Gosnell, Harold Foote, 87, 134, 147
Gottfried, Alex, 134
Grant, Madison, 87
Greenberg, Norman, 188

Haberman, Clyde, 164, 165
Hague, James L., 298
Hammer, Richard, 62, 81, 102, 103, 225n
Harker, R. Phillip, 176
Harris, Don R., 283, 284
Hegarty, Edward D., 220
Hess, Henner, 16, 58
Hibbert, Christopher, 63
Hill, Henry, 189
Hobsbawm, Eric J., 57, 58, 63, 66, 111
Hoffman, Paul, 61, 293
Hogan, William T., 3
Holbrook, Stewart H., 52
Homans, George C., 16
Horne, Louther, 146, 147
Horrock, Nicholas, 150
Hough, Hugh, 127n

Ianni, Francis A. J., 14, 17, 22, 63, 65, 74, 75, 76, 77, 109, 111, 158, 318
Inciardi, James A., 56, 111
Inverarity, James M., 195

Jenkins, Phillip, 154
Jennings, Dean, 106, 107
Johannesen, Robert W., 274
Johnson, Earl, Jr., 255
Johnson, Malcolm, 148
Joselit, Jenna Weissman, 98, 102, 124
Josephson, Matthew, 46, 48, 50, 52

Kamm, Henry, 62, 66
Katcher, Leo, 88, 97, 98, 99, 100, 127n
Katz, Leonard, 116
Kefauver, Estes, 148
Kihss, Peter, 243n
Kilian, Michael, 228
King, Rufus, 91, 305
Kinsie, Paul M., 223
Kirk, Donald, 165
Klatt, Wayne, 130
Klockars, Carl B., 317
Knoke, David, 295n
Kobler, John, 92, 133, 135, 137, 140, 141, 142, 143, 144, 145, 146, 147
Kogan, Herman, 130, 131, 137
Kogan, Rick, 224
Kozial, Ronald, 145, 151n
Krajick, Kevin, 290
Kuklinski, James H., 295n
Kwitny, Jonathan, 238

Landesco, John, 131, 132, 136, 137, 140, 141, 142, 145, 223
Langlais, Rudy, 157
Lasswell, Harold D., 184
Lauderdale, Pat, 195
Lawler, Edward J., 7n
Lee, Henry, 96
Lens, Sidney, 227, 242n
Lewis, Merlin, 298
Lewis, Norman, 56, 58, 60
Lippman, Walter, 168, 237
Lloyd, Henry Demarest, 53
Logan, Andy, 89, 96, 97, 98
Lupsha, Peter A., 76, 77, 160, 317

Maas, Peter, 127n, 191, 322n, 323n
McConaughy, John, 63
McClellan, John L., 235, 314
MacDougall, Ernest D., 170
McFadden, Robert D., 106, 108
McGuiness, Robert L., 289, 290
McKenna, Jeremiah B., 184
McPhaul, Jack, 135, 136, 144, 145
Maltz, Michael D., 4, 239
Marshall, Eliot, 181
Martens, Frederick T., 247, 321, 322
Martin, Raymond, 19, 121
Merriam, Charles Edward, 133
Merton, Robert, 69, 73
Meskil, Paul, 14, 77, 80, 118, 119
Messick, Hank, 92, 106, 107, 155, 156, 193n, 316
Michaels, Marguerite, 162
Mitchell, Greg, 308
Mockridge, Norton, 252
Moldea, Dan E., 231, 232, 314
Moore, William H., 313
Mori, Cesare, 67n
Murphy, Patrick V., 249
Musto, David, 211
Myers, Gustave, 44, 48, 49, 51, 52
Myers, Harry L., 274

Nagel, Jack H., 7n
Nash, Jay Robert, 133, 152n
Navasky, Victor S., 235, 236
Neely, Richard, 319
Nelli, Humbert S., 91, 92, 111, 113, 130, 135, 147, 148, 229
Neubauer, Chuck, 234, 235
Newfield, Jack, 295
Nicodemus, Charles, 221

O'Connor, Philip J., 214
O'Connor, Richard, 46, 101
Ohlin, Lloyd E., 73, 74

Packer, Herbert L., 90, 167, 249, 319
Pantaleone, Michele, 61
Petacco, Arrigo, 110
Petacque, Art, 127n, 221
Peterson, Virgil, 130, 149, 150, 315
Pileggi, Nicholas, 157, 242
Pitkin, Thomas Monroe, 109

Post, Henry, 223
Potter, Gary, 154
Prall, Robert H., 252
Puzzo, Mario, 317

Quinney, Richard, 14, 315

Raab, Selwyn, 201, 265
Reece, Jack, 59
Rehfeld, Barry, 172
Reid, Ed, 149
Reif, Rita, 48
Repetto, Thomas A., 88
Reuter, Peter, 81, 154, 155, 168, 173, 181, 190, 191, 237, 271, 317, 322
Rhodes, Robert P., 304, 308n
Richardson, James F., 249
Ristic, Henry, 243
Rome, Florence, 164
Romoli, Kathleen, 161
Rosen, Charles, 181
Rottenberg, Dan, 80
Royko, Mike, 134, 140
Rubinstein, Jonathan, 81, 168, 173, 181, 190, 192, 271, 317, 322

Salerno, Ralph, 11, 17, 117, 122, 124
Sann, Paul, 100, 103
Scarpitti, Frank R., 238
Schelling, Thomas C., 168, 169
Schlegel, Kip, 160
Schmidt, William E., 251
Schnepper, Jeff A., 102
Schorr, Mark, 77
Schur, Edwin M., 197, 249
Schwartz, Herman, 294
Sciascia, Leonard, 59
Seedman, Albert A., 169
Seidman, Harold, 144, 228
Serao, Ernesto, 64, 65
Servadio, Gaia, 57, 58, 59, 61
Shaw, Clifford, 71, 72, 73
Shaw, David, 81
Sherman, Lawrence W., 249
Siciliano, Vincent, 188
Silberfarb, Edward, 95, 97, 99
Simons, Marlise, 206
Simpson, Anthony E., 251

Simpson, John R., 288
Sinclair, Andrew, 52, 90, 91, 100
Skolnick, Jerome H., 320
Smith, Alson J., 132
Smith, Dwight C., Jr., 14, 80
Smith, Richard Austin, 236
Smith, Richard Norton, 103, 104, 114
Smith, Sherwin, 100
Sondern, Frederic Jr., 124, 317
Spiering, Frank, 146, 151n
Stewert, Robert C., 284, 297, 299, 303
Sutherland, Edwin H., 73
Suttles, Gerald D., 72
Swanberg, W. A., 46, 47, 48

Takahashi, Sadahiko, 165
Talese, Gay, 14, 115, 122
Taylor, Ian, 70
Teresa, Vincent, 21, 170, 189
Thomas, Jo, 242
Thrasher, Frederic Milton, 73
Toby, Jackson, 75, 76
Train, Arthur, 109
Turkus, Burton, 92, 104, 105, 106,
    107, 127
Turner, Wallace, 190
Tyler, Gus, 85

Unger, Sanford, 250

Van Dyke, Craig, 204, 206
Vold, George, 168
Volsky, George, 212

Wall, Joseph Frazier, 52
Wallace, Amy, 80
Wallace, Anise, 234
Wallace, Irving, 80
Wallechinsky, David, 80
Walsh, Marilyn E., 220
Weber, Max, 53
Wendt, Lloyd, 130, 131, 137
Werner, M. R., 87
Wethern, George, 25
Whitaker, Mark, 162
White, Frank Marshall, 96
Wiederich, Bob, 201
Williams, Harry T., 115
Wilson, James Q., 250, 265, 313
Winick, Charles, 223
Withers, Kay, 62
Woetzel, Robert K., 17
Wolf, Eric R., 16
Wright, Michael, 193n
Wrong, Dennis, 7n

Subject Index

Abbandando, Frank, 125
Abbatemarco, Frank, 121
Accardo, Anthony, 148, 149, 150
Addams, Jane, 78n
Adonis, Joe, 88, 252, 252n, 318
Adonis, Joe, Jr., 318
Aiello brothers, 144, 145
Aiuppa, Joseph, 229
Alderisio, Felix, 149
Alderman's War (1916), 138-39
Amato, Baldasarre, 78n
American Museum of Natural History, 87
Amphetamines. *See* Drugs, synthetic
Anastasia, Albert, 99, 116, 117-18, 124, 127, 231
Anastasio, Anthony, 117
Anderson, Thomas C., 88-89
Angiulo, Jerry, 240, 241
Anomie, 69-70, 71, 73, 76
Apalachin (N.Y.) crime "convention," 124-25
Associates, organized crime, 17, 19-20, 39
Astor, John Jacob, 44
Atlantic City, N.J., 229
Aurelio, Thomas A., 115

Bandidos. *See* Motorcycle gangs
Bankruptcy fraud. *See* Scam
Bank Secrecy Act, 240, 243n
Barbara, Joseph, 124
Barbiturates. *See* Drugs, synthetic
Barnes, ("Nicky") Leroy, 157-58
Battaglia, Sam, 149
Beck, Dave, 231, 314
Becker, Charles, 97
Bender, Tony, 116, 232
Bennett, Harry, 52

Berman, Otto, 104
Betillo, David, 113
Bioff, Willie, 148, 149
Black Guerillas, 165
Black Hand, 109, 110, 135, 150n
Black Tuna Gang, 211-12
Blacks and organized crime. *See* Organized crime, blacks and
Bonanno crime family, 78n, 123-25, 201
Bonanno, Joseph, 14, 112, 122, 123-25, 128n
Bonanno, Joseph, Jr., 127n
Bonanno, Salvatore ("Bill"), 14, 125, 127n
Bonney, William H., 52
Bonventre, Cesare, 78n
Bookmaking, 131, 172-81
Boss, *(capo)* of crime family, 9, 11, 17, 20, 21-22, 23
Boston, Bank of, 240-41
Bowdach, Gary, 188-89
Bradley, William V., 230
Brando, Marlon, 25
Bridges, Harry, 242n
Browne, George, 148
Bruno, Angelo, 317
Bruno crime family, 23
Buchalter, Louis ("Lepke"), 74, 99, 104-6, 127, 148, 237
"Bugging." *See* Electronic surveillance
Bureaucratic organization, 9, 12, 14, 15, 25, 26, 66, 98
Buscetta, Tommaso, 62
Business Racketeering, 236-39
"Bust out." *See* Scam
Byrne, Jane, 150, 159, 166n

Caifano, Marshal, 149

Calabria, 56. *See also Onerate Societa*
Camorra, 62-66; *Nuova Camorra,* 65-66
Campagna, Louis, 148
Campezio, Antony, 148
Capo. See Boss
Capone, Al, 4, 72, 92, 93, 95, 102, 132, 136-47, 151n
Capone, Frank, 140
Capone, Louis, 106, 127
Capone, Matt, 147
Capone, Ralph, 147
Caporegime, 11, 12, 17, 20, 21
Carnegie, Andrew, 51, 52
Carnegie Institution, 87
Carrozzo, Michael, 135
Casino gambling, 188-89
Castellammarese War, 112-113, 117, 118, 119, 120, 315
Castellano, Paul, 239, 243n
Castro, Fidel, 150, 160
Catena, Gerardo, 238
Central Intelligence Agency, 150, 160, 199
Cermak, Anton, 133-34, 150n
Chicago, University of, 51, 71
Chiesa, Dalla, 61-62
Christian Democratic Party, 60, 61, 62
Cicero, Ill., 139-40, 151n
Cirillo, Louis, 156
Cleveland, Grover, 51
Cleveland syndicate, 93, 107
Cocaine, 160, 204-10
Cohen, Mickey, 107
Coll, Vincent ("Mad Dog"), 90, 100, 101
Colombians. *See* Organized crime, Colombians and
Colombo (Profaci) crime family, 12-23, 224
Colombo, Joseph, 14, 122
Colosimo, James, 134-35, 136-37
"Commission" of organized crime bosses, 11, 20, 122, 125
Communists and the Mafia, 60, 61, 62
Consigliere, 11, 17
Conspiracy, 268, 273-76
Consumer Credit Protection Act, 272-73
Corallo, Anthony, 120, 127n, 233, 235, 243n
Corruption, 46, 49, 88, 133, 147, 249-52. *See also* Police corruption

Cosa Nostra, 12, 23
Costello, Frank, 88, 92, 99, 112, 114-16, 118, 124, 313
Coughlin, John, 130, 135
Croker, Richard, 97
Crosswell, Edgar, 124
Cuba, syndicate gambling in, 108
Cubans. *See* Organized crime, Cubans and
Cuccia, Ciccio, 59
Cultural transmission, 71-73
Curley, James M., 88
Currency and Foreign Transactions Reporting Act of 1970. *See* Bank Secrecy Act
Cutola, Raffaele, 65, 66

Dalitz, Moe, 93, 190, 192n
D'Andrea, Anthony, 138-39
Davidoff, Harry, 233
Davis, "Dixie," 100
De Cavalcante, Sam, 229, 239, 242n
Delaney, Robert, 318
de Mange, George Jean, 101
De Sapio, Carmine, 127n
Dever, William E., 133, 139
Devery, William, 97
Dewey, Thomas E., 102, 104, 105, 106, 113, 114
Diamond, "Legs," (John T. Nolan), 90, 99
Differential association, 70-71, 73, 74
Differential opportunity, 73-74
DiGregorio, Gasper, 125
Dilia v. United States, 291
Dioguardi, John, 233, 235, 239, 243n
Dorfman, Allen, 233-35, 294
Dorfman, Paul, 233-34
Dragna, Jack, 107
Dragna crime family, 107, 224
Drew, Daniel, 45, 46-47
Drew University, 46
Drucci, Vincent, 137, 143
Drug Enforcement Administration, 80, 157, 195, 265
Druggan, Terry, 137
Drugs, synthetic, 212-14
Drug trafficking (*see also* names of individual drugs), 33, 39, 77, 99, 103; Mafia involvement in, 62; penalties for, 263, 264
DuPont family, 52

Dwyer, Bill, 99, 100, 115

Eastman, Monk, 95, 96, 97, 99
Egan's Rats, 102, 145
Electronic surveillance, 14, 288-94
El Rukns, 158-59, 166n
Erie Ring, 45-46
Eto, Ken, 169, 170n

Farrell, Frank, 96
Fay, Larry, 99
Federal Bureau of Alcohol, Tobacco
    and Firearms, 4, 248
Federal Bureau of Investigation, 4, 20,
    81, 135, 146, 150, 157, 237-38,
    250, 286
Federal Bureau of Narcotics, 80, 197,
    250. See also Drug Enforcement
    Administration
Fein, Benjamin, 228
Fencing of stolen goods, 220
Ferro, Vito Cascio, 109
Ficcorata, Anthony, 220-21
First Ward, 72, 130, 135
Fischetti, Charley, 140, 147
Fischetti, Rocco, 147
Fisk, Jim, Jr., 45, 47, 51
Fitzsimmons, Frank, 236
Five Points Gang, 95, 96, 97, 113, 135,
    136
Flagler, Henry, 50
Florida, drug trafficking in. See Orga-
    nized crime, Cubans in; Colom-
    bians in
Ford, Henry, 52
Fort, Jeff, 158-59, 165n
Forty-two Gang, 17, 149
Fratianno, Jimmy, 19, 240, 318
Freedman, Monroe, 235
Freud, Sigmund, 204

Gagliano, Gaetano, 119
Galente, Carmine, 77, 78n, 80, 81
Gallo, Albert, 121
Gallo, Joey, 72, 121-22, 123
Gallo, Larry, 121, 122
Gallo brothers organization, 121
Gambino, Carlo, 14, 21, 118-19, 122,
    123, 238, 239

Gambino, Joseph (brother of Carlo),
    118
Gambino, Joseph (cousin of Carlo), 238
Gambino, Paul, 118, 238
Gambino (Mineo) crime family, 20, 22,
    117-19, 191, 201, 231, 239
Gangs, 72, 73, 85, 95-96, 131
Garibaldi, Giuseppe, 63
Garrison, C.K., 45
Genna brothers, 138, 141, 142
Genovese, Vito, 112, 116, 117
Genovese (Luciano) crime family, 17,
    20, 21, 23, 113-17, 220, 231, 232,
    238, 314
Giancana, Sam, 17, 149-50
Gibson, Sonny, 82
Gigante, Vincent, 116
Gioe, Charlie, 148
Gioielli, Joseph, 121
Giuliano, Salvatore, 60-61, 67
Gleason, Thomas ("Teddy"), 230
Goldstein, Martin, 126
Goldwater, Barry, 143-49, 315
Gordon, Waxie, 99, 101-3
Gould, Jay, 45, 47-48, 51
Gould Foundation, 48
Grand jury, 298-99
Grant, Ulysses S., 48
Greenberg, Max, 102
Gross, Harry, 252
Gugliemini, Salvatore, 238
Guzik, Jake, 92, 136, 137, 146, 147,
    151n
Guzik, Sam, 147

Hague, Frank, 88
Hallucinogens. See Drugs, synthetic
Harriman, Averell, 52
Harrimman, Edward H., 52
Harrison, Carter, Jr., 132, 135
Harrison Act, 197, 204
Hells Angels. See Motorcycle gangs
Hennessey, David, 151n
Heroin, 155, 157, 159, 195-203
Herrera crime family, 159, 201
Higgins, Vannie, 99
Hill, James Jerome, 52
Hines, James J., 99
Hobbs Act, 268, 289, 291
Hoff, Max, 92
Hoffa, James, 231-36, 316
Hogan, Frank, 114

Holman, Currier J., 239
Hoover, Herbert, 146
Hoover, J. Edgar, 105, 146, 250, 287.
    See also Federal Bureau of Investigation
Hopkins, Mark, 50
Hotel Employees and Restaurant Employees International Union, 228, 229
Hughes, Charles Evans, 88
Hull House, 78n
Humphreys, Murray, 147
Huntington, Collis, 50

Immunity, 150, 299-305
Informants, 249-50, 260, 265, 294
Insull, Samuel, 147, 152n
Intelligence, 283-87, 295n
Internal Revenue Service, 146, 149, 248, 254-62
International Alliance of Theatrical Stage Employees, 148
International Brotherhood of Teamsters, 228, 231-36
International Ladies Garment Worker's Union, 228
International Longshoremen's Association, 96, 117, 228, 238
Interpol, 287-88
Irey, Elmer Lincoln, 102, 146
Irish and organized crime. *See* Organized crime, Irish and
Italian-American Civil Rights League, 122-23
Italian-American organized crime. *See* Organized crime, Italians and
Italian immigration, 55, 75, 110
Italy, 55. *See also* Cammora; Mafia; Sicily

Jackson, Jesse, 159
James, Jesse, 4
Japanese. *See* Organized crime, Japanese and
Jews. *See* Organized crime, Jews and
Johannesen, Robert W., Jr., 274, 281n
Johnson, Enoch ("Nucky"), 88, 92
Johnson, Jerome, 123
Johnson, Lyndon, 315
Johnson County War, 52

Jones, Eddie, 149, 150
Jordon Marsh & Company, 47

Kansas City, Mo., organized crime in, 89
Kastel, Phil, 115
Kastigar v. *United States,* 304
Katz v. *United States,* 289-90
Kefauver Committee, 115, 127n, 148, 311-13
Kelly, Edward J., 88
Kelly, Paul, 96, 97, 135, 229
Kenna, Michael, 130-31, 135
Kennedy, John F., 235, 243n
Kennedy, Robert, 235-36, 243n, 297, 314
Kerner Commission, 76
King, Martin Luther, Jr., 151n, 290
Kinship in organized crime, 14
Kleinman, Morris, 192n
Kropier, Martin, 104

Laborers International Union of North America, 228-29
Labor racketeering, 99, 100, 105, 144, 227-36, 238-39, 242n, 243n
La Guardia, Fiorello, 88, 103, 115
Lansky, Jake, 106, 112
Lansky, Meyer, 81, 82, 92, 102, 106-8, 113, 114, 160
Lanza, Joseph, 114
LaRocca, Anthony, 39
LaRocca, John, 39
Las Vegas, 107, 189-90
"Laundering" money, 163, 240-42, 251
Law Enforcement Intelligence Unit, 285-86
Lazar, Sam, 92
Lazia, John, 89
Lewis, Joe E., 151
Licata, Nicholas, 14
Lincoln County War, 52
Livorsi, Frank, 112
Loansharking, 190-92, 193n, 272-73
Lombardo, Joe, 234, 235
Long, Huey, 88, 115
Lotteries, legal, 181, 183, 320. Lotteries, illegal. *See* Numbers
Lucas, Charles, 156-57

Lucchese, Thomas, 14, 118, 119-20, 122
Lucchese crime family, 233
Luciano, Salvatore ("Lucky"), 81-82, 92, 95, 99, 104, 106, 107, 112, 113-14, 116, 117, 148

McClellan Committee, 231, 235, 243n, 313-14
McDonald, Mike, 130-31
McErlane, Frank, 92, 137, 141
McGuire, Phyllis, 150
McGurn, Jack, 145, 151n
McSwiggin, William H., 142
Madden, Ownie, 99, 101
Mafia, 15, 56-62, 66; attacked by Pope John, 62; Communists and, 60, 61, 62; drug trafficking and, 62, 201; in United States, 109-11, Nuovo Mafia, 61-62; in United States, 109-11
Magaddino, Stefano, 14, 122, 124, 125
Magliocco, Joseph, 122
Maione brothers, 125
Mangano, Vincent, 117, 118
Mann Act, 135, 223
Maranzano, Salvatore, 82, 112, 113, 117, 118, 120, 124, 151n, 314
Marcantonio, Vito, 88
Marcus, James, 127n, 243n
Marijuana, 160, 210-12
Marijuana Tax Act, 211
Marinelli, Albert C., 99
Marron, Vernon, 39
Masseria, Joe, 99, 107, 112, 113, 117, 118, 124
Matthews, Frank, 155-56, 276
Mayfield Gang, 92
Meli crime family, 232
Mellon, Andrew, 90-91, 146
Merlo, Mike, 141
Mexicans. See Organized crime, Mexicans and
Middle Atlantic-Great Lakes Organized Crime Law Enforcement Network, 286-87
Mineo, Al, 117
Mitchell, John, 122
Moran, George ("Bugs"), 132, 142, 144, 145
Morello, Giuseppe, 109

Morgan, Charles, 45
Morgan, J. Pierpont, 51-52
Mori, Cesare, 59, 67
Morton, Samuel ("Nails"), 137
Motorcycle gangs, 3, 23
Murder, Inc., 126-27
Murphy, Charles, 97
Mussolini, Benito, 58, 59-60, 65, 112, 114, 116, 123

Naples, 56, 62, 63. See also Camorra
Narcotics. See names of individual narcotics
National Association of Manufacturers, 87
National Cigarette Service, 21
Ness, Elliot, 146
Networks in organized crime. See Patron-client networks
Net worth case, 255-59
Newport, Ky., 188, 192-93n
Nitti, Frank, 92, 147, 148, 149
Nixon, Richard, 236
Noe, Joe, 89
Nuestra Familia, 165n
Numbers, 100, 149-50, 155, 156, 181-87

O'Banion, Dion, 137, 141-42
O'Donnell, Bernard, 137, 142
O'Donnell, Edward ("Spike"), 137, 140, 141
O'Donnell, Myles, 137, 140, 142
O'Donnell, Steve, 137, 140
O'Donnell, Thomas, 137, 140
O'Donnell, Walter, 137, 140
O'Donnell, William ("Klondike"), 137, 139, 142
O'Hare, Edward J., 146, 151n
Olmstead v. *United States,* 289
Omerta, 56, 57, 161
Onorate Societa, 66
Organized crime *(see also* Drug trafficking; "Laundering" money; Motorcycle gangs): Arabs and, 201; arbitration in, 20, 168-69, 170n, 237; blacks and, 74, 75, 154, 155-59; business of, 167-70; Colombians and, 75, 160-64, 207, 251; Cubans and, 75, 160; ethnic

succession in, 74-78; franchising, 154, 155; groups, 9; Hispanic, 76, 154, 159-64 (*see also* individual nationalities); Irish and, 74, 76, 89, 95, 154; Italians and, 42, 67, 75, 76, 89, 108-28, 154, 155; Japanese and, 77, 164-65; Jews and, 74, 75, 76, 89, 98-108, 154; as a legitimate business, 239-40; membership in, 6, 12, 17-21, 26, 74; Mexicans and, 75; political machines and, 76-77, 85-89, 95-99, 130-31; politics and, 159, 162, 165, 199, 206; Puerto Ricans and, 75, 158; rules in, 12, 21, 22-23, 35-38; Sicilian immigrants and, 77
Organized Crime Control Act of 1979, 3, 299, 311. See also RICO
Orgen, Jacob, 99, 105
Outlaws. See Motorcycle gangs

Pagans. See Motorcycle gangs
Panico, Savatore, 223
Pappalardo, Cardinal Salvatore, 62
Partito, 16, 66
Patriarca, Raymond, 21, 170, 240
Patrimonial organization, 14-15, 22
Patron-client networks, 14-17, 57, 66
Pendergast, James, 89
Pendergast, Tom, 88, 89
Pen register, 292
Peraino, Anthony, 224
Persico, Carmine, 121, 169
Petrosino, Joseph, 110
Phenix City, Ala., 188, 193n
Pilotta, Alfred, 228
"Pineapple Primary," 143
"Pizza Connection," 78n
Plate, Tony, 191
Plunkitt, George Washington, 86
Police corruption, 96, 97, 188, 249, 252, 268
Political machines. See Organized crime, political machines and
Pools, sports, 187-88
Pornography, 224-25
Powers, John, 138-39
President's Commission on Law Enforcement and Administration of Justice, 315-17

President's Commission on Organized Crime, 157
Profaci, Joseph, 14, 120-22
Profaci, Rosalie, 14
Prohibition, 42, 44, 60, 89-92, 93n, 102, 132, 136-37
Prohibition Bureau, 90, 96
Prostitution, 33, 39, 135, 222-24
Protestant ethic, 53
Provenzano, Anthony, 232, 236
Provenzano, Nunzio, 232, 233
Provenzano, Salvatore ("Sammy"), 232, 233
Puerto Ricans. See Organized crime, Puerto Ricans and
Pullman, John, 127n
Purple Gang: Detroit, 92, 144, 145; New York, 77-78

Quaaludes, 160, 166n, 213

Racketeer Influenced and Corrupt Organizations Statute. See RICO
Raft, George, 72
Ragen, James, 138
Ragen's Colts, 138, 151n
Rao, Joe, 101
Regional Information Sharing Systems, 286-87
Reina, Gaetano, 119
Reles, Abe, 126-27
Ricca, Paul (De Lucia), 148, 149, 150
RICO, 269-72, 275
Rispetto, 17, 21, 22, 67n, 161, 170n
Rivas, Carlos Enrique Lehdr, 162
Robber barons, 41
Rockefeller, John D., 50-51
Rockefeller, Nelson, 52, 122
Rockefeller Foundation, 51
Rockefeller University, 51
Roe, Terry, 150
Roemer, William Jr., 150n
Roosevelt, Franklin D., 88
Roosevelt, Theodore, 97
Roselli, John, 150
Rosen, Nig, 99, 154
Rosenthal, Herman, 97
Rothkopf, Lou, 93, 107, 192n
Rothstein, Arnold, 74, 98-100, 102
Royal Family, 158

Runyon, Damon, 98
Russell Sage Foundation, 49, 190
Russo, Anthony, 239
Ryan, Thomas P., 230

Sacco, Vanni, 60
Sage, Russell, 48-49
Saietta, Ignazio, 109
Saint Valentine's Day Massacre, 145
Saltis, Joe, 92, 137, 141, 142
Scalise, Frank, 117, 127n
Scam, 221-22
Schenck, Joseph, 148
Schultz, Dutch, 89-90, 92, 99, 100-104
Schwartz, Charles, 92
Sciacca, Paul, 125
Scotto, Anthony, 231
Securities theft, 216-20
Shapiro, Jacob ("Gurrah"), 74, 99, 104, 105, 237
Shapiro brothers, 126
Sheldon Gang, 143
Sheridan, Walter, 236
Sicily, 15, 55, 57, 59, 60, 75. *See also* Mafia
Siegel, Benjamin ("Bugsy"), 72, 82, 92, 106-8, 112, 113, 189-90
Silverman v. *United States,* 289
Sinatra, Frank, 150
Sindona, Michele, 62
Small, Len, 137
Smith, Alfred E., 96
Solano, Vincent, 228
Soldati (soldiers). *See* Membership
Solomon, Charles ("King"), 99
South Improvement Company, 50
Special Committee to Investigate Organized Crime in Interstate Commerce. *See* Kefauver Committee
Spilotro, Anthony, 234
Standard Oil, 50-51
Stanford, Leland, 49-50
Stanford University, 50
Starr, Ellen Gates, 78n
Steinman, Moe, 238-39
Stracci, Joseph, 112
Strauss, Phil, 126, 127
Strike force, 297-98
Strollo, Anthony. *See* Bender, Tony
Stromberg, Harry. *See* Rosen, Nig
Sullivan, Timothy, 97, 99

Tammany Hall, 86, 87, 95-98, 99
Taylor Street, 72, 149
Teamsters Union. *See* International Brotherhood of Teamsters
Tennes, Mont, 131-32
Terranova, Ciro, 112
Testa, Phil, 317
Thompson, William Hale, 132-33, 143
Tieri, Frank, 80
Toco, William, 14
Torrio, Johnny, 92, 99, 135, 136, 137, 139, 140, 142, 145
Trans-America Wire Service, 107
Truman, Harry, 148
Tucker, Sam, 93, 192n
Turkus, Burton, 106, 127. *See also* author index

Underboss of a crime family, 9, 11, 17
Unione Siciliana, 111, 135, 138, 141, 145
United States Steel, 52
United States v. *Behrman,* 197
United States v. *Calandra,* 299
United States v. *Dionisio,* 298-99
United States v. *Sullivan,* 146, 254
Usury, 49, 190, 193n. *See also* Loansharking

Valachi, Joseph, 118, 191, 311, 314-15, 316
Van Buren, Martin, 95
Vanderbilt, Cornelius, 44-45, 48, 50
Vatican, 62, 225n
Vizzini, Cologero (Don Carlo), 60, 61
Volstead Act, 90, 102

Waterfront Commission, 230
Weinberg, Bo, 90, 104
Weinberg, George, 90
Weiss, Hymie, 137, 142
Weiss, Mendy, 104, 105, 106
White slavery. *See* Prostitution; Mann Act
Whyos Gang, 95, 96
Williams, Alexander ("Clubber"), 96-97
Williams, Edward Bennett, 115-16
Williams, Roy, 235

Wilson, Frank, 146
Wire-service, 131-32, 181, 189
Wiretapping. *See* Electronic surveillance
Witness Security Program, 305-9
Workman, Charles, 104

Yale, Frankie, 99, 135, 136, 144, 252n

Yamaguchi. *See* Organized crime, Japanese and
Yerkes, Charles Tyson, Jr., 147, 152n

Zerilli, Joseph, 14
Zwillman, Abner ("Longie"), 102, 148, 154